James Champlin Fernald

The economics of prohibition

James Champlin Fernald

The economics of prohibition

ISBN/EAN: 9783743304550

Manufactured in Europe, USA, Canada, Australia, Japa

Cover: Foto ©ninafisch / pixelio.de

Manufactured and distributed by brebook publishing software (www.brebook.com)

James Champlin Fernald

The economics of prohibition

PREFACE.

The author has long believed that a new system of Political Economy is urgently needed. The old system has well been called "The Dismal Science." It is the stamping-ground of selfishness, every man to get as much and give as little as possible, and by systematized heartlessness to work out an industrial millennium. The statement of the case is its refutation. Human brotherhood must have a place in any science which deals with humanity.

It is refreshing to see the modern Economics becoming more human and more republican, giving large place to the principles of co-operation. By so doing it is also becoming more Christian. Its highest triumph must be to incarnate in terms of material science those sublime utterances of the Son of Man: "One is your Father, which is in heaven," and "All ye are brethren." That other thought, too, must be brought into any perfect system, "He that is greatest, let him be your servant:" —all power the servitor of all weakness—power sweeter, nobler, and more generous—weakness happier, purer, and more secure.

As part of this great problem of co-operation or brotherhood, the question, "What shall we do with the liquor traffic?" comes promptly to the front. From this point of view it soon ceases to be a question. The brother cannot destroy the brother. It is not republican to debauch the citizen. It is not co-operative to degrade the fellow-laborer.

The relation of the liquor traffic to Economics is one which the masters of the science have scarcely begun to touch. The case is much like that of a generation ago. When slavery was rocking the continent and soon to deluge it in blood, Political Economy was too busy to discuss a theme like that. But when, in 1858, Eli Thayer declared, "Why, sir, we can buy a negro-power in a steam-engine for $10, and feed and clothe that power one year for $5. Are we the men to pay $1,000 for a negro slave, and $150 a year to feed and clothe him?" then the problem was nearing its solution. It is worthy of remark that the recent emancipation of slaves in Brazil has been made wholly on economic grounds.

So, we believe, it will be with Prohibition. When all men come to see that there is no money in the liquor traffic, except for the trafficker, and for him only by loss to every one else, a final end will be put to this system of organized robbery.

The author does not hope, spite of most careful endeavor, to have avoided all errors. The subject is vast. Cause and effect interlace. At some points it is impossible to get beyond conjecture. But he has taken great pains to secure all attainable facts, and to give nothing which is not fully substantiated.

This book is written for "the plain people," who are the bone and sinew and the hope of the land. Hence a conversational has been preferred to a formal style, seeking to put the results of scholarship into common speech. For the same reason round numbers have been used in preference to complete ones. For instance, to almost every one $50,000,000 conveys a more intelligible idea than $49,106,590. It is also easier to remember. Hence, for the purposes of a popular treatise it is really more accurate, as it is certainly pleasanter reading.

The author gratefully acknowledges his obligations to Dr. Hargreaves, the pioneer in this line of study, whose "Wasted Resources" and "Worse than Wasted" have been frequently quoted. Much material has been taken from *The Voice*, not because of any political bias, but because on many points no such complete and painstaking collection of facts was to be found elsewhere.

The book is sent out with the earnest hope that it may be found useful in building up a single department of the Economics of the Future, which shall seek through the laws of earthly relationships to bring all humanity nearer in happiness and virtue to the one God, Maker of heaven and earth. May it also help toward the speedy removal of the chief fronting evil of our civilization, before the hearts that are aching shall break, and the feet that are tempted shall fall; till the saloon's dread shadow shall nevermore darken the love-light of home, nor dim the brightness of childhood's morning!

CONTENTS.

PREFACE, ... i

CHAPTER I.
THE ECONOMIC ARGUMENT.

President White and Commercialism—The Presidential Election of 1888—"The Tariff a Friend of the Liquor Trade"—Renewal of the Battle of 1840—Prohibition Will Do More than Tariff for the Wool Interest—The Tribute Annually Levied on New York City by the Saloons—How Prohibition Will Benefit Every Honest Industry, ... 9

CHAPTER II.
PAYING THE PIPER.

Cost of Liquor to the Consumers in 1889—Annual Increase—Indirect Expense Equals Direct—Estimates of Crime, Pauperism, Sickness, Insanity, etc.—Lost Time of Liquor-Makers—Cost of Splendid Saloons—Drink Waste, Two Thousand Millions, ... 17

CHAPTER III.
DOES HIGH LICENSE PAY?

It Cannot Possibly Repay the Loss—National and State Receipts from the Liquor Traffic—Liquor Receipts and Expenses in Philadelphia under the Brooks Law—In Ohio under the Dow Law—In Omaha with $1,000 License—Loss of Police Efficiency — Depreciation of Property — Sidewalks and Saloons, ... 32

CHAPTER IV.

HIGH LICENSE AS A MONOPOLY.

"Taxing it to Death"—Reducing the Number of Saloons—A Simple Question of Arithmetic—The Grocery Problem—The Sugar Trust—A Convention of Dentists—Mr. Onahan's Figures for Chicago—Internal Revenue Reports Show More Liquor Sold by Fewer Saloons—The Whiskey Trust Reducing the Number of Distilleries—Effect on the Power of the Saloon in Politics—A Tax upon the Poor, ... 46

CHAPTER V.

HIGH LICENSE AS RESTRICTION.

License-Paying Saloon-Keepers to Enforce the Laws against Illicit Selling — Increased Arrests for Drunkenness in Chicago—Testimony of the Chicago *Daily News*—How it "Abolishes the Dives" in Chicago—In St. Louis—Testimony of the St. Louis *Republic*—Fearful Condition of Omaha—Testimony of Omaha *Daily Bee*—Police Reports—Official Statement of the Nebraska Non-Partisan Amendment League—Table of High-License and Low-License Cities—High License in St. Paul—Philadelphia under the "Brooks Law"—Pittsburgh's 700 "Speak-Easies"—Why More Drunkenness in Fewer Saloons, ... 60

CHAPTER VI.

HIGH LICENSE AND THE CONSUMER.

The Consumer Pays the Entire Bill—Wealth-Producing Qualities Destroyed—The Workmen of Sheffield, England—What the *National Labor Tribune* says—The Consumer as the Consumee—Charles Lamb's Pathetic Words—What Oliver Ames & Son Found—Mr. Micawber's Wisdom—$200,000 for a Glass of Beer—English Workingmen and Saloons—Saloons and the Haymarket Massacre—In the Cronin Trial—The Piper to Raise his Price, ... 83

CHAPTER VII.

THE HARVEST OF DEATH.

The Duke of Alvah and the "Bloody Council"—The Graves of a Host—The Cash Value of a Man—Statistics of Mimico Industrial School on the Cost of Feeding Boys—Price of a Negro Slave—A Man Estimated as Capital on the Basis of What he Can Earn—The Saloon Does not Pay its Own Funeral Expenses—Whiskey and the Inquisition—Have You a Boy to Spare? 95

CHAPTER VIII.

A STEP TOWARD PROHIBITION.

An Unrighteous Method is Sure to Prove Unwise—The Fewer Saloons Have Greatly Increased Power—Harder to Close the Saloons when the People Have Become Used to Spending the Money—The Higher the License for the Saloon the Lower the Public Sentiment for Prohibition—"Free Rum" and the Texas Steer—Opinions of Nebraska Clergymen—James G. Blaine on the Tendency of Liquor Revenues—A Step that Has Never Stepped—The Old-Time License in Maine, Michigan, Iowa, and Kansas—Distillers Atherton and Iler on "The True Policy for the Trade," . . . 100

CHAPTER IX.

LOCAL OPTION.

Advocated as Peculiarly American—The Principle of "Home Rule"—Allowing Prohibition Wherever Enforcement is Possible—Obtainable Sooner than State or National Prohibition—Claimed to be Eminently Successful in Practice—Objected that no Community Can Have the Right to Legalize a Wrong—Local Option in Cincinnati—The American Idea not Piecemeal but Aggregate Liberty—Squatter Sovereignty—Douglass and Lincoln—Surrenders the Centres of Power—Always in Politics—Professor Scomp and Mr. Johnson on Results in Georgia—Local Option for the Tariff and the Cholera, ... 123

CHAPTER X.

SUPPLY CREATES DEMAND.

The Law of Luxuries and Vices—Dr. Felix L. Oswald on the Natural Aversion for Alcohol among all Living Things—Man not Excepted—Creating an Appetite—Experience of a Cincinnati Merchant—How the Dealer "Works up a Trade"—Why the Liquor Men Agitate for Repeal of Prohibition—Illicit Sales May Supply an Existing Demand—But not Create a New One—The Slander of "Wanting Whatever is Prohibited"—Testimony of "Nasby"—Rev. Edward Ellis—The Brooklyn *Eagle*—The National Liquor Traffic One Vast Organized Temptation, ... 137

CHAPTER XI.

THE TRUE RESTRICTION.

Difficulty of Restriction—The Steady Ratio of Income and Intemperance—Prohibition as a Restriction—The Saloons of Council Bluffs—The Clerk's Drink in Kansas—The Young Farmer and the Closed Saloon—The Cities in a State of Siege—Law as an Educator—The Druggist at the Telephone—Words of Judge Pitman—No Stocks of Liquor Waiting—No Saloon Rent Going on to Prevent Sunday-Closing—Then "Local Option" Can Punish the Seller in the Next Town—"Boot-Leggers" Fight Shy of Minors — "The Grandest Place to Bring up Boys," 148

CHAPTER XII.

WHO WILL ENFORCE THE LAW?

Enforcement of Laws by "The Citizen, Male or Female"—The Private Individual as Detective and Patrolman—Interference is Trespass—What Executive Officers Are For—Usurping Legislative Functions—American Kings—Repeal as a Method of Enforcement—General Grant on Enforcement—Enforcement by Representatives—Repeal the Non-Enforcing

Officers—The Watchman in the Mill—" Enforcing the Laws We Have"—The Lending Umbrella—The Stronger the Law the Easier to Enforce it—How Kansas Disposes of Non-Enforcing Officers, ... 160

CHAPTER XIII.

MAINE.

" Nasby's" Experience with the " Maine Law"—The Other Side—The New York *World* on Non-Enforcement in Lewiston—"A Political Pull"—Stealthy Approach toward Re-Submission—Put on the Stripes—Testimony of Governor Dingley—Governor Perham—Senator Frye—Judge Davis—Republican Convention of 1882—Internal Revenue Receipts Decreased in Maine while Increasing in the Nation—Not a Distillery or Brewery in the State—The Savings Banks Full, ... 171

CHAPTER XIV.

KANSAS.

Testimony of Probate Judges—" Drunkenness Reduced Ninety per cent."—" The Police Force Reduced"—" Growing in Favor Every Year"—Testimony of County Treasurers—Governor Martin's Address—Maynard's " Truth about Kansas"—" Joints" and How to Get into Them—How Leavenworth is " Ruined"—Chief Justice Horton's Testimony—" The Drunkard's Paradise"—One Hundred and Fifty-three Business Men Testify—The Manufacture of Steel Cells Ruined—The Demand for Barrels " Fallen off Terribly" — No Wife-Beating Now — Scarcity of Tramps—Views of Governor Humphrey—Report of the Farmers' Loan and Trust Company—The *Western Baptist* on Topeka —Full of Churches and Not One Saloon—Families Who Once Suffered through the Father's Intemperance now " Dwelling in a Cosey Home of Their Own," . . . 181

CHAPTER XV.

IOWA.

Prohibitory Amendment Carried by Thirty Thousand—Thrown Out by Supreme Court—Prohibitory Law Passed—Always Liable to Repeal—Effects of the Law—Letter from Governor Larrabee—Enforced in Eighty-five Counties—Evaded in Fifteen, Chiefly River Counties—Great Decrease of Crime—"Has Not Injured any Business Except the Saloon Business"—Opposing Judges Converted to the Law by Observing its Effects—Testimony of Fifty-eight Prosecuting Attorneys—Great Decrease of Drunkenness—Often Seventy-five to Ninety per cent.—Former Revenue from Saloons More than Made Good by Increased Prosperity—Merchants Now Receive the Money that Formerly Went to Saloons—The Truth about the Rebel Cities—Burlington, Dubuque, and Davenport—Testimony of Judges of the District Courts—Governor Larrabee's Farewell Message—Governor Boies's "Statistics of Ifs"—How a Lawyer Got Liquor in Iowa—Governor Boies's Idea of "Complete Want of Legal Restraint"—The State Debt Wiped Out, ... 232

CHAPTER XVI.

RHODE ISLAND.

How the Amendment was Adopted—Immediate Decrease of Arrests in Providence—Drunkenness Decreased One-half; All Crimes, One-third—Why the Law was Hated—Mr. Walter B. Frost Tells of Bank Clearings Increased $32,000,000—Savings Bank Deposits Increased $6,000,000—Rise in Value of Real Estate—Enforcement Shrewdly Relaxed—Repeal by Surprise and Corruption—Non-Enforcement of License—More Drunken Men in One Week than in Three Years of Prohibition—A Quarter of a Million Dollars Goes into the Saloons of Newport that Should Go to the Grocer and Butcher and other Respectable Dealers, . . . 266

CHAPTER XVII.

ATLANTA.

Low License Till 1886—Prohibition One Year and a Half—
Mayor Hillyer's Testimony—Decrease of Arrests and Increase of Trade—"The Attitude of the Newspapers throughout the Union is Greatly to be Deprecated"—Editorial of the *Constitution*—Property Increased $2,000,000—Taxes Not Increased—Former Saloons Occupied by Tradesmen—More Goods Bought—Easier to Collect Bills—More Children in Schools and Sunday-Schools, and Better Dressed—Henry W. Grady's Great Speech—One Distress Warrant under Prohibition to Twenty under License—No More Garnisheeing—Crime Decreased More than One-half—The Hand of the National Rum Power—"Yellowstone Kit"—Prohibition Goes out and High License Comes in—Interviews with Business Men in Atlanta *Commonwealth* Six Months Later—Poor Sales and Bad Collections—Women Waiting on the Corners Saturday Night—Arrests Jump from 6000 to 10,000—Table of Replies from Forty-seven Business Men—Bad Debts Increased—One Saloon Keeper Sells More to Workingmen—"They Do Not Ask for Credit, but Pay as They Go"—Low License, Prohibition, and High License Tested on the Same Ground — Prohibition Immeasurably the Best, ... 276

CHAPTER XVIII.

THE NEW LANDS.

Starting Well—The Dakotas Reversing the Liquor Victories of the East—Fifty Thousand Men Pouring into Oklahoma in Twenty-four Hours—Without Homes, Without Law, Without a Magistrate—Without Crime Because Without Whiskey—Attempt of the Liquor Men in Congress to Put the New Territory under "the Laws of Nebraska"—Speech of Major Pickler against it—Amendment Defeated—White Men Still to be Treated as Well as Indians, ... 315

CHAPTER XIX.

THE LABORING MEN.

Average Cost of a Workingman's Drink—If he Drinks Six Days, he Will Drink Seven—How $1,000 is Spent—Swallowing a Square Rod of Land at Every Drink—Where One Workingman's $10,000 Went—The Cost of a Saloon Celebration of Washington's Birthday—Socialists and Saloons—Spending the Surplus—The Child's Hoop—The School-Girl's Hat—Helpless in a Strike—The Slaves of the Saloon—Powderly and Arthur, ...

CHAPTER XX.

THE BEST CUSTOMERS.

A Limit to the Food One Man Can Eat and the Clothes One Man Can Put on—Silk Underwear vs. Red Flannel—Sober Workingmen Will Outbuy the Saloon-Keeper Thirty to One—The Saloon Destroys the Buying Power of the People, .

CHAPTER XXI.

THE TRADESMEN.

Trade the Life of Civilization—The Money Saved from the Drink Bill will Circulate through all Channels of Trade—Spent in Drink it Will Not—Per cent. for Labor in the Liquor Business Compared with Other Industries—Liquors vs. Dry Goods—One Bartender Can Take in as Much Money as a Storeful of Drygoods Clerks in the Same Time—No Other Business Can Compete with the Liquor Trade and Live—Other Branches of Business Trust—The Saloon Sells for Cash—The Bad Debts Are Left for Grocer and Boarding-House Keeper—Put Two Thousand Millions into Useful Industries and See What Effect it Will Have on Trade—What Prohibition Did for One Local Option Town,

CHAPTER XXII.

THE FARMERS.

The Desolate Farm—The Accomplished Hostler—Signing the Farm Away—" It Hurts his Judgment"—Cost of a Bushel of Corn—How the Liquor Traffic Robs the Farmer—It Destroys his Market—" The Cider Racket"—Judge Agnew on Cider—Amount of Alcohol in Cider and in Beer—Danger of Salicylic Acid—Feed and Clothe the Drunkard, and the Farmer Will Get the Money, ... 358

CHAPTER XXIII.

THE HOME.

The Saloon Makes the Man a Stranger to his Home—What he Spends on the Saloon he Cannot Spend on the Home—Woman's Responsibility—Poor Feeding Tends to Hard Drinking—Woman's Wonderful Patience—The Wife-Beater on Shipboard—Women Drinking at Put-in-Bay—The Beer-Garden's Darkened Stalls—Wine Sauces and Jellies—The Bad Manners of " Good Society," 378

CHAPTER XXIV.

THE NURSERY.

The Sure Inheritance of Alcoholism—Pre-natal Drunkenness—Beer for Nursing Mothers—Cows Fed on Beer Mash—The Increased Quantity of Milk an Addition of Alcohol and Water—The Danger Greater with Wet Nurse than with Mother—The Doctor and the Young Mother—Giving the Baby Actual Drams—How to Avoid it, ... 388

CHAPTER XXV.

POLITICS.

One of the Greatest Factors in Every Life—The Saloon Now Has Absolute Mastery of Our Politics—Testimony of the

Chicago *Times*—Morality the Chief Factor in Politics as in the Rise and Decline of Nations—Church and State—Government Enforcing the Seventh Commandment in Utah—Lincoln against Douglass on the Moral Wrong of Slavery—D. R. Locke Explains "The Infernal Part which the Liquor Traffic Plays in Politics," 397

CHAPTER XXVI.

THE PRESS.

The Daily Paper Forming all a Man's Thought—The Eminent Lawyer—Simple News not to be Found in a Partisan Paper—Slander as a Profession—Why the Prohibitionist Reads Both Sides—General Palmer on the Purchasable Press—How Individual Citizens May Block that Game—Dakota Prohibition Victories and the New York Press—Temperance Literature as a Power, ... 408

CHAPTER XXVII.

THE CHURCH.

The Christian Church an Economic Institution—Economics of Moses—Of Christ—Of Pentecost—Of Paul and James—Of the Judgment Day—James Russell Lowell's "Parable"—Is the Church Doing Anything against Intemperance that is Comparable to the Magnitude of the Curse?—Young Men in Dayton Saloons—Church Not to Do Something, but to Do Everything—Shall the Church Spare Wrong as Soon as it Goes into Politics—When Christ Confronted an Evil Traffic, 418

CHAPTER XXVIII.

CITIES AND IMMIGRANTS.

One fourth of Our People in Cities—The Thinkers and Leaders Have Given Them up—Their Evils Admitted to Have "Come to Stay"—Power of Roughs Vastly Greater in City than in Country—The Saloon Drains the Country—Anarchizes the City—The State Must Rule the City—The Vicious Classes Must Submit—The Better Classes Must be Helped—Immigration Must be Sifted—No Sieve Like Prohibition—No Foreign Provinces, Dialects, or Feuds Wanted in America—But from All Nations One People, . . . 431

CHAPTER XXIX.

THE DEVIL'S FOREIGN MISSION.

Fifty Million People in the Congo Basin to be Clothed—Statement of Rev. James Johnson—No More Cloth Wanted by Natives—Drink the Article in Demand—Statement of Mr. W. P. Tisdel—Of Mr. Hornaday—An English Trading Company Which Trades without Dealing in Liquor—The Destruction of the Natives as an Economic Question—Old Idea of Cortez and Pizarro—Better Method among the Colonists of the Northern States and Canada—Killing the Goose that Lays the Golden Eggs—Course Taken by Rome—By the Saracens—Rev. Dr. Sims—Natives Seldom Sober Enough for Service Sunday Morning—Ship with Two Missionaries on Deck and One Hundred Thousand Gallons of Rum in the Hold—Gin Out-Travels the Missionary—Stanley With Rum and Without—Riches of the Upper Congo—Destroying All Trades but One—A Native Pastor Finds the Curse of Drink Worse than that of Slavery—What the United States Can Do, ... 441

CHAPTER XXX.

THE GATES OF PARADISE.

The Riches of Oklahoma—The Profit of Our Export Trade—What Our Liquor Money Would Buy—Flour by the Million Barrels—Twenty Million Pounds of Buckwheat Cakes—$150,000,000 Worth of Beef, Mutton, Pork, and Veal—Sugar and Spices, Coffee and Tea, Milk and Butter—All Going into the Homes of the Hungry—Boots, Shoes, and Rubbers—Blankets and Carpets—Cassimeres, Doeskins,

Diagonals, and Suitings—Three Hundred Thousand Worsted Shawls—Thirty Million Yards of Dress Goods—The Poor Can Go to Church—$45,000,000 Worth of Furniture—$50,000,000 for Anthracite and Bituminous Coal—Will Give the Miners Work—Will Double the Pastors' Salaries and Missionary Contributions—Will Help Literature and Education—A Boom in Real Estate—Women Will Have Some Chance to "Make Home Beautiful"—All Who Work and All Who Trade Will Share in the Prosperity—The Two Thousand Million Revenue of Righteousness, . . . 454

CHAPTER XXXI.

THE "ORIGINAL PACKAGE" DECISION.

Abraham Lincoln on Supreme Court Decisions—The Right of Opposition—The Demand for Reversal—Effects of the Decision in Kansas—Brewers and Box Makers in Kansas City, Mo., Rushed with Business—The New Border Ruffian Invasion—Topeka Drunk *vs.* Topeka Sober—Effects in Iowa—New Statistics of the Benefit of Prohibition—Prosperity of Kansas and Nebraska Compared—Liquor Revenue in Maine—United States District Attorney Ady's Claim—All Prohibitory Laws "Dead Matter" Now—The Wilson Law Will Not Bring Them to Life—The Police Power of the States Destroyed—Congress has None to Take Its Place—Forcing Sales Within the States—"Like Any Other Commodity"—Slaves Under the Dred Scott Decision—Supreme Judge Elliott of Indiana at National Bar Association—This Decision Ignores Moral Considerations—Decision of "Kansas Cases" in 1887 to the Contrary—The Outlook, . . . 476

STATISTICAL TABLES.

Consumption of Intoxicants in 1889, ... 18
Cost of Liquor to Consumers in 1889, ... 18
Increased Consumption of Liquors in 1889, ... 18–19
Inmates of Cleveland Workhouse Confessedly Intemperate, . 22
Indirect Cost of the Liquor Traffic, ... 30
Cost of Ohio State Institutions for Crime, Pauperism, Insanity,
    etc., and Returns from the Dow Law, ... 37
Ohio County Infirmaries, ... 38
Chicago Saloons under Low and High License (Mr. Onahan), . 48
Increased Consumption of Liquor in the United States in 1888,
    with Decrease of Liquor Dealers, ... 51
Same in 1889, ... 51
Arrests in Omaha for 1888, ... 63
Proportion of Arrests for Drunkenness and Disorderly Conduct
    in Fourteen High License and Fifteen Low License Cities, . 67
Commitments to County Prison, etc., in Philadelphia in 1887
    and 1888, ... 75
Arrests in Pittsburgh, Allegheny, Scranton, Wilkesbarre, Lancaster, and Reading, in 1887 and 1888, ... 76–78
Cost of Feeding Boys at Mimico Industrial School, . . 100
Nebraska Clergymen on High License, ... 112–116
Probate Judges of Ninety-Seven Counties of Kansas on Effects
    of Prohibition, ... 184–193
County Treasurers of Kansas on Effects of Prohibition, . 206–213
Prosecuting Attorneys of Fifty-eight Counties of Iowa on
    Decrease of Crime, ... 240–247
District Judges of Iowa on Benefits of Prohibition, . 252–255
Business Men of Atlanta on Trade under Prohibition and High
    License, ... 300–307
How an income of $1000 would be expended in Massachusetts in
    1883, ... 321
Expenditures of 100 Workingmen vs. one Saloon-keeper, 342–343
How the Liquor Traffic Robs the Farmer, ... 365–368
Division of $800,000,000 among Other Industries (Dr. Hargreaves), ... 456
Division of $900,000,000 among Other Industries (Mr. Calvin
    E. Keach), ... 457

CHAPTER I.

THE ECONOMIC ARGUMENT.

"I will undertake to give bond for the fulfilment of a contract that if the city of Philadelphia will stop selling liquor, and give me as much as was expended for liquor last year to run the city next year, I will pay all the city expenses, no one shall pay taxes, and there shall be no insurance on property, and a good suit of clothes shall be given to every poor man, woman, and child, and a barrel of flour to every needy and worthy person, and then I shall make a half million dollars by the operation."—*P. T. Barnum.*

PRESIDENT WHITE, of Cornell University, some years ago declared "Commercialism" the prevailing vice of the American people, using this striking illustration: "If, for instance, it should be made to appear that the spread of Mohammedanism would be of great commercial advantage to one of our great cities—if it would lead to the building of railroads and the opening of new channels of profitable trade —enough money could easily be raised to build a mosque equal to the Taj Mahal."

We have recently been passing through a battle of "Commercialism." The victorious party has conquered on a simple question of trade. If the result had been reversed, and the Democratic Party had conquered instead of the Republican, they would have conquered likewise on a question of trade—a somewhat different view of the tariff question. It would have been a victory of "Commercialism" still. By both Democrats and Republicans, all other questions of social morality and good government have been dropped out of sight for the tariff. Speakers of national reputation have addressed great audiences by the hour, and from first to last discussed absolutely nothing but tariff. Metropolitan dailies have filled their columns with arguments for or against a protective tariff. Anarchism, and the reckless immigration that feeds it, the spreading leprosy of Mormonism—these have had a paragraph in some corner. Temperance has received an occasional pat on the shoulder or an occasional kick, according to the temper of the publication. But the pat or the kick has been quite incidental, and without turning from the line of march of the tariff agitation. Wherever you have seen a group of men in excited talk you could tell, while out of hearing, that the tariff was the theme.

So, with firing of guns and ringing of bells, with sound of trumpet and the cheers of millions, we have come to the exact economic position which we reached forty-eight years ago! The half century intervening has been one of the most momentous in the history of the world. Our Union preserved through four years of war; slavery abolished from our own and at last from all civilized nations; the French Empire overthrown; Italy made a nation; the temporal power of the Pope abolished; German unity made victorious; the Irish Question shaking the British Empire; the Congo discovered and the great heart of the Dark Continent opened to civilization; and the United States of America have made a countermarch upon antiquity, and got just where they were in 1840!

Whatever influences moved President Cleveland to

precipitate this discussion in the first place, unquestionably the liquor traffic has been one main agent in keeping it at the front. The New York *Bar* said, on December 30th, 1887: "The tariff is, therefore, a friend of the [liquor] trade, and all should lend themselves to stirring it up. While politicians have their hands full with the tariff, they will be very sure to let everything else slide, and Prohibition, which has lately been making so much noise, will evaporate." With its usual Satanic sagacity, the liquor traffic saw its opportunity:

> "Like the bat of Indian brakes,
> Her pinions fan the wound she makes,
> And soothing thus the dreamer's pain,
> She drinks the life-blood from the vein."

The traffic has kept the great wings of its hundred and fifty thousand saloons fanning the tariff, and, under cover of that agitation, has gone on sucking the nation's life-blood and making its grip more immovable and deadly. So successfully has this been done that thousands of good men, temperance men, Christian men, have forgotten in the storm of tariff discussion that there was any temperance question before the nation. They have waived out of sight the waste of treasure, the corruption of youth and destruction of manhood through intemperance, and virtually decided that, if they could have the tariff as they wanted it, the liquor traffic might do what it pleased. Even Prohibitionists have fallen into the snare, and in groceries and offices and street-cars and homes have talked "Tariff," forgetting their own mightier issue. Thousands of them have even "gone and voted" one of the old party tickets, because of the feeling that this tariff question *must* be settled, whatever became of Prohibition.

But, as our shrewd Josh Billings said, "There's no use argyin' agin' success." The thing has worked well for one set of managers. The Republicans have found a Presidency in the tariff, and the Democrats have come near enough to try it again. The event has proved that the most successful thing for any party is to touch the pocket nerve of the American people. What are Prohibitionists to do about it? Why, touch the pocket nerve for Prohibition! If we can convince the American people *that liquor selling does not pay*, we have made our case. We shall be on ground that will command the Presidency of the future. The nation cannot be kept forever fighting the battle of 1840. Prohibitionists must array the Commercialism of America on the side of Prohibition. We must show the people that, even on that ground, we have all the argument, and hold the key to the national prosperity.

During the recent campaign a Prohibitionist was arguing with a Republican wool-buyer. The wool-buyer urged with utmost confidence the necessity of a high tariff for the wool interest. The Prohibitionist was trying to show that, perhaps, it did not matter so very much. The writer asked the Republican debater this question: "Suppose we could put woollen dresses, and jackets, and stockings, and underwear on all the drunkards' wives and children, and woollen blankets on all their beds, wouldn't that create a greater boom in the wool interest than any tariff that could be levied?" "Why, of course it would!" was the instant reply, "if you could only get all the people to think so." The business of Prohibitionists must be to "get all the people to think so."

One great influence that shook down slavery was that

in the Border States, where slave labor and free labor could be seen side by side, the belief had come widely to prevail that slavery was unprofitable. West Virginia, East Tennessee, Kentucky, and Missouri contained enough Anti-Slavery men to make those sections untenable ground for the Southern Confederacy. If we can cause a similar persuasion to prevail regarding the liquor traffic, we can shake its hold, even upon the great centers of its power. For instance, we are told that three-fourths of the 8,000 saloons in New York City are kept by foreigners. The saloons of the United States average a yearly income of $7,000 each.* At this rate, the foreigners' three-fourths of New York's saloons take in more than $40,000,000 every year. It ought not to be a very hard matter to convince the level-headed merchants of the Metropolis that it does not pay to let 6,000 foreigners levy an annual tribute of $40,000,000 upon the city. They will see it quickly enough, if they can be got to think about it. As yet, very little has been done to lead them to consider the temperance question upon the commercial side. They have looked upon it as "a moral issue," which "practical men" were too busy to attend to.

In the late campaign we were not adequately prepared to contest this side of the question. We have been arguing the matter for so many years on moral and humanitarian considerations that we could not change front quickly enough to meet the new demand. The rush of the battle went by us, and left us on higher but deserted ground. If we had had the artillery of the Economic Argument well in hand, we might have gone down upon

---

* 150,000 saloons taking $1,100,000,000 gives $7,333 each. This would be, however, a very small estimate for New York City.

the commercial level where the other parties met, and fought the most tremendous battle we have ever waged. We could have forced the tariff-debaters to answer us. We could have convinced thoughtful men of the old parties how much more important Prohibition is than Tariff, *commercially*, and so have rolled up a mightier vote. We must be prepared to do that next time.

The liquor men boast of having sent "tons" of their literature into West Virginia. We must send thousands of tons of ours throughout the land, to show the people what splendid prosperity awaits every branch of trade the moment they will stop the $1,000,000,000 outlay for intoxicants. Our debaters should be full to the brim with economic facts, and crowd them upon the thought of the nation.

On this line we can turn the flank of the liquor traffic, and make hostile parties change their front of battle. We can take all the sneering out of the mouths of the enemy, when we make it plain to the thought of the common people that the prosperity of every man, woman, and child in the nation is touched disastrously by the drink traffic.

The temperance battle of the near future must be fought on the commercial and economic ground. Our strongest thinkers, our ablest writers, must force the fighting on this issue, till we make the people see that it is worth while to push every other commercial question into the background long enough to stop this intolerable drain upon the national prosperity. We have all the argument, and can command the situation. It is for us to convince everybody who has anything to sell, North or South, East or West, that there is the most glorious advance in store for his business the moment we can stop the outlay for whiskey and beer. Tell the lumbermen of Michigan how many thousands of drinking farmers will shingle their houses and barns, or build new ones, as soon as they "quit their meanness," and how many thousands of houses will be built in all our suburbs for the workingmen when none of them drink away the money that might pay the rent or buy the cottage. Show the shoe manufacturers of Massachusetts what it means to take all the bare feet of drunkards' children off the ground. Let the iron men of Pennsylvania know that new stoves will be at once needed in a hundred thousand homes when the saloon-keeper ceases to get the money. Tell the miners they will have work all winter through, getting coal enough to put into those stoves. Tell the cotton-planters of the South that there will be about 10,-000,000 new calico dresses and aprons wanted as soon as the 2,000,000 tipplers cease to tipple, and go home with some spare change. Let the ranchmen of Dakota and New Mexico, and Armour's men in Chicago, know that there's going to be beef on thousands of tables where now are a few cold potatoes, as soon as we can carry Prohibition. Tell the wool-growers of Ohio that everybody in this country is going to be wrapped in woollen and sleep under blankets when the blizzards blow and the thermometer ranges about zero, and men no longer heat up with liquid fire in order to exterminate their families with atmospheric cold. Tell the grocer he can sell for cash and say good-by to bad debts when the dimes no longer go into the saloon-till. Tell the farmer there is going to be an unheard-of demand for flour and meal and butter and cheese and eggs as soon as the bloated beer-holders cease fostering that industry, and begin filling out the hollow cheeks of wives and children with wholesome food. Show the High License man how much more it is worth in cash to abolish the crime and pauperism which the saloon produces than to share the profits with the criminal and pauper maker. Tell our colleges that the temptation of our young men will henceforth be education instead of intoxication. Tell the author, editor, and publisher that good books and papers are going to be owned and read in a hundred homes, where now a single greasy copy of the *Police Gazette* is thumbed in one saloon. And tell the church that tens of thousands will crowd to her doors as soon as they can come clad so as not to be stared at ; and as, in deliverance from hunger and cold, blows and curses, from the desolate days and nights of fearful watching which the legalized dram-shop inflicts on the innocent, they shall be lifted out from despair, and grasp some tangible evidence that a beneficent Providence indeed rules in the affairs of men, and that for them the Son of God is manifested, that He might destroy the works of the devil.

There's not an honest industry nor a good cause in all our broad domain but will find immediate advance and prosperity in the wiping out of the liquor traffic.

CHAPTER II.

PAYING THE PIPER.

"After fifteen years on the bench I believe four-fifths of all crimes committed are the result, directly or indirectly, of the use of intoxicating liquors. Much of it is due to beer. Three or four glasses of beer cause a stupor, which is conducive to the condition in which a crime can be committed. Nearly all homicide and felonious assault and battery cases are the result of drinking. It follows that three-fourths of the expense to the State for the prosecution of criminals is attributed to the same cause. It also fills the insane asylums, and causes untold misery in thousands of families. What family has escaped? Scarce a family in the State but has lost one of its members or a near relative. If you had seen what I have seen, read the thousands of letters I have read, you would know why I stand here to night and plead for Prohibition."—*Judge White, in Address at Pittsburg, May 28th,* 1889.

"The Chicago *Morning News* estimates that more than 4,000 saloons were open in that city last Sunday, and that $75,000 must have been spent for wine, spirits, and beer during that one day."—*Southern Baptist Herald.*

This nation has been wonderfully stirred of late over something that has rarely troubled governments—a surplus of revenue. Suppose that had been a deficiency. Suppose an administration in four years of power had run our finances $120,000,000 behindhand. That administration would have gone down as Vulcan fell when Jupiter hurled him from Olympus. There would not have been contest enough to make the election interesting. What shall we say, then, of a deficiency almost ten times as great in one year? For we have passed the Eleven Hundred Million Notch in our expenditure for intoxicants.

From the preliminary report of the Commissioner of Internal Revenue of the United States for the year 1889, we obtain the following statistics:

WITHDRAWALS FOR CONSUMPTION IN 1889.

Fermented liquors.. .... 25,119,853 barrels
Distilled spirits.......... .... 77,164,640 gallons

What did these cost the consumer? We give the figures according to Dr. Hargreaves's estimates, which have stood unchallenged for many years. To the distilled spirits which leave the warehouse containing fifty per cent. of alcohol, we must add one-fifth for reduction to forty per cent., the ordinary retail strength, making the amount at retail 92,597,568 gallons. This at $6 per gallon, gives the following:

Cost to consumers....................	$555,585,408
Fermented liquors at $20 per barrel,	
Cost to consumers	502,397,060
Add	
Imported liquors	15,986,800
California wines.......................	34,000,000
Total...............................	$1,107,969,268

which the intoxicating liquors consumed in the United States in the year from July 1st, 1888, to June 30th, 1889, cost the consumers.

The increase over the year ending June 30th, 1888, was:

Increase of distilled spirits.......... 5,599,154 gallons
Increase of fermented liquors....... 439,634 barrels

It is noticeable that the table is provided with a column for "Decrease," but *that is utterly blank;* there is not a figure in it. Reducing the barrels of beer to gallons, at 31 gallons to the barrel, gives

Fermented liquors	13,628,654 gallons
Distilled spirits	5,599,154 "
Total	19,227,808 gallons

increase of distilled and fermented liquors in 1889 over 1888. Increased cost to the people, $49,106,590.

The people of the United States are spending for intoxicants more than $1,100,000,000, and increasing the expenditure at the rate of about $50,000,000 a year. What nation can long endure such a drain? How can we help having poverty and distress?

The immensity of the outlay can be seen by considering the further fact that the total imports of the United States in 1888 were but $723,879,813, and the customs duties collected on the same were only $219,091,173.

This $1,100,000,000, then, is the cost to the drinkers of the nation. From this we should deduct, according to Mr. E. J. Wheeler,* $124,000,000 as the total receipts from all forms of tax and license paid by the liquor traffic to the nation and the States. This would bring the actual cash loss to the nation a little below $1,000,000,000. But the selling price of both beer and whiskey is estimated so low in the above table that we may claim the benefit of the margin, and safely hold the entire loss to be not less than $1,000,000,000. With the rate of increase given above of $49,000,000 a year, the only trouble is that the expense will be apt to run

---

* "Prohibition, the Principle, the Policy, and the Party," p. 73.

beyond the estimate by the time this book gets fairly before the public. It will soon far outrun that amount. A thousand million dollars in a single year, and this going on steadily year after year ! It would have bankrupted the Roman Empire, when her nobles dined luxuriously on peacocks' brains. It would have bankrupted Spain, when the wealth of the New World was pouring in and her knights shod their steeds with silver. If any foreign power were to demand such a tribute, we would turn this whole country into an armed camp, and put a musket into the hand of every fourteen-year-old boy sooner than pay it. But we patiently hand it over to our 150,000 liquor barons, and only beg them to have a little mercy, and give us a rest for part of Sunday, and from midnight to daylight on other days. Even that we can't get, but we submit. Oh, patient America ! Where are the memories of Concord and Bunker Hill and Gettysburg ?

Still, this estimate only touches the outer edge of the deficit. Every man who drinks loses from labor a steadily increasing amount of time. It is probable that, from first to last, he loses an amount of time equal to the cost of his drinks. If this estimate were to be allowed, it would just double the $1,000,000,000. But it would probably be challenged, and be thought weakest where it is strongest. Men would be cited who drink hard and work hard to the day of their death. But they die in the midst of their strength, and the loss is of all the years they might have lived. If the hard drinker lives much beyond thirty, infirmities, sicknesses, and incapacity increase rapidly upon him, with their inevitable loss of working time and power. For the man who goes on "sprees," there will be days of lost labor from a few hours' debauch. By the most moderate computation, which, I believe, has not been challenged, there is lost the labor of 700,000 drunkards, amounting to $175,000,-000, and enough of the labor of 2,000,000 tipplers to make about $225,000,000—a total of $400,000,000 every year.

Then, behind every idle drinker waits a procession of men, every one of whom has to stop because that man's work is not done. The drunken shipmaster does not make the port in time. The drunken drayman does not haul up the goods promptly. The drunken porter is not on hand in time to get them in, and every clerk and accountant in the establishment is hindered accordingly. The mill starts late because the engineer was on a spree last night. The painter cannot paint your buggy because the drunken blacksmith has not finished the iron work. The slaters cannot go upon your roof because the drunken carpenter did not get the wood-work done. All over the land are sober men waiting with idle hands for drunken men to bring up their work ahead of them. At a very moderate estimate, we may count this indirect loss by sober men equal to one-tenth the direct loss of labor by drinking men—$40,000,000 every year.

But drinking men often become paupers, or pauperize those dependent upon them. Here estimates become difficult. Mr. Fred H. Wines, in the compendium of the Tenth Census (1880), says: "It is almost, if not quite, impossible to obtain the statistics of pauperism."

That, however, does not invalidate what we have, but only shows us that our ascertained facts will be sure to fall short of the real facts. Sixty-seven thousand inmates of almshouses were reported to the Census Office in 1880. Their support, by the average of many institutions, may be put at $100 each per year, making a total of $6,700,000. The amount of out-door relief given can be only distantly approximated. In the State of New York, where the cost of maintaining paupers in county poor-houses is $678,037.76, the out-door relief given in the same counties is $498,866.10, or about two-thirds. Supposing this ratio to exist throughout the country, that would give $4,466,666 for out-door relief. This is far below the true amount, for it makes no account of private charity as exercised by churches, lodges, and individuals, which would mount up to millions more. It does not count the support of the army of tramps, commonly estimated at 3,000,000 persons, when they are not in infirmaries or work-houses. Yet they live, and they earn but a very small fraction of their own living. Whether by begging or stealing, their support comes out of the community. There are many districts where a ceaseless procession of them levy a regular tribute upon the farmers, who dare not refuse for fear of vengeance to their crops, buildings, or families. We give up in despair the attempt to compute these extras, merely mentioning them to prevent any one charging our sum total as excessive. So far from that, vast items are necessarily left out. It is worth noting here that almost without exception the tramp is a drinker.

The report of the work-house at Cleveland, O., gives these remarkable statistics:

Habit of Life.	Males.	Females.	Total.
Confessed themselves intemperate	1,906	319	2,225
Claimed to be temperate	140	16	156
Total	2,046	335	2,381

Out of 2,381 inmates 2,225 confessed themselves intemperate. Only 156 "claimed to be temperate," and the officials evidently take small stock in that "claimed." True, it may be said that the work-house is to some extent a penal institution. It is on the border-land between pauperism and crime, but its inmates are just the material of which tramps are made, and its figures are a pretty good barometer for the whole class. If ever the cost of the tramps and vagrants can be ascertained, it may be set down almost solid to the charge of intemperance. The criminal statistics of Prohibition Iowa for 1887 report just *one* vagrant. In omitting a guess at unreported pauperism, we are making a large concession to the safe side.

Adding the $4,466,666 of estimated out-door relief to the $6,700,000 infirmary expenses, we have $11,166,666 for National pauperism. Dr. Hargreaves ascribes nine-tenths of this to intemperance. We are willing to put it at three-fourths. It hardly can be less than that. For, where pauperism is ascribed in official reports to insanity, idiocy, and disease, these very things are largely the results of intemperance in the subjects, or inherited from intemperate parents. Many of the crippling injuries are received because either the sufferer was drunk or somebody else was; and of the helpless classes, a very large number would not be thrown on public charity except that intemperance has made their natural protectors unable to support them. Three-fourths, then, of the total $11,166,666 would be a little over $8,000,-000, which we may take as a thoroughly safe estimate of the pauperism due to intemperance.

Drinkers often become criminals. Here, too, adequate statistics are exceedingly difficult to obtain. Mr. Wines says, in his pamphlet on "Crime, the Convict and the Prison": "The problem involves many elements, some of which are very obscure." He takes the number of inmates of prisons and reformatories, as given in the census of 1880 at 70,000, and remarks: "Assuming that the charge for keeping up the prisons, including buildings and repairs, is not less than $200 a year for each prisoner, this item of expense will amount to nearly or quite $15,000,000 annually." He adds an estimate of the cost of arrest and trial, and says: "These three items, taken together, constitute the enormous sum of $50,000,000 annually raised by taxation to defend the community against the ravages of crime."

Some question might be raised about institutions where the labor of prisoners is utilized, so that they are self-supporting. These are chiefly penitentiaries, where the prisoners are of adult age and sentenced for long terms. In jails and juvenile reformatories and work-houses this would not be the case. Even if we were to allow a deduction for this, it would probably be more than compensated by the fact which Mr. Wines states, that his estimate does not include the cost of the private detective force, the sums paid by the accused to their attorneys, nor the losses to individuals resulting from successful fraud or depredations. So we may allow Mr. Wines's $50,000,000 to stand as a reasonable estimate of the national outlay for crime. Of this, many estimate nine-tenths, and the lowest estimate I have seen is three-fourths, as due to intemperance.

How just this is will appear from a few citations. Of 8,588 arrests in Cleveland for the year 1887, 4,720, or more than one-half, were credited to "*Intoxication,*" pure and simple. Adding the offences usually due to intemperance, the amount runs up toward eighty-eight per cent. There would, of course, be room for difference of opinion here. Not all the cases of "assault," etc., are due to intemperance. But, on the other hand, there are many offences resulting from the use of liquor, of which the criminal record gives no sign. The clerk becomes a drinker, then a gambler, robs his employer, and is arrested for "theft" or "embezzlement," with no hint of the intemperance, without which he would never have become a criminal. The late D. R. Locke (Nasby) states that numbers of boys are taught to steal in the beer saloons where they have been induced to run up a beer bill, and are put in communication with pawnbrokers who will receive anything they bring without asking any questions. Arrests from this cause would be credited to "petty larceny." On the scaffold, it has become so common as scarcely to excite remark for the condemned man to say, "But for whiskey I should never have been here." A large proportion of our murders are committed directly in saloons, or on going from them. Yet all these cases appear on the record as "murder," and only individual inquiry can learn that liquor had anything to do with them. It is stated in a recent number of the *National Baptist*, that "out of 45,000 criminals arrested in Philadelphia in a single year, 40,000 were arrested for offences immediately connected with liquor." This is eighty-eight per cent. On the whole we are much more in danger of understating than of overstating the case. Taking this, then, as a reasonable estimate, three-fourths of $50,000,000 would be $37,500,000, which liquor-crime costs the nation.

But this is not all. Mr. Wines says : "It is startling to know that, of 50,000,000 inhabitants (in 1880), over 400,000 are either insane, idiots, or deaf mutes, or are inmates of prisons, reformatories, or poor-houses. If to these we add the out-door poor and the inmates of private charitable institutions, the amount will swell to nearly or quite 500,000, or one per cent. of the population." At that rate the number would now be about 600,000. But we will keep to the records of 1880, and consider only the 400,000 who were inmates of charitable institutions. Of that number the 70,000 who were prisoners and the 67,000 who were paupers have been already considered. Those deducted would leave 263,000 "defective persons." Assuming the average cost of their maintenance to be $200 (and in many of these institutions it runs up to nearly $300 per capita, as skilled teachers and physicians must be employed at great expense), the cost of maintaining these "defective persons" would exceed $52,000,000. If we estimate one-third of these disabilities to be due to intemperance, actual or inherited, we shall have $17,000,000 annual loss to the nation from the insanity, blindness, deafness, and other disabilities which intemperance produces. The relation of insanity to intemperance is a point deserving careful study. State and National Boards are now greatly exercised over the rapid and undeniable increase of insanity. It is worthy of inquiry whether a ratio does not exist between that and the increased consumption of liquor within the last twenty years. We see plainly that liquor will make a person insane for a little while. It would seem reasonable to suppose that enough of it might make him so permanently.

Drink produces sickness. A careful computation gives about 150,000 persons simultaneously sick in the United States, as the result of using intoxicants, at a cost of more than $50,000,000. This does not include the number who are sick, because some one else uses it—the women and children starved, chilled, beaten, heartbroken, crowded into filthy, malarial alleys and cellars, for whom simple Prohibition would have the effect of the best kind of fresh-air fund all the year round. The sickness which is thus the indirect result of intemperance is at least equal to that which directly results. It is probably far greater, but we will put it down at another $50,000,000—in all, $100,000,000.

But there are those who will object, "You are not counting the receipts from this industry. The liquor business gives employment to 500,000 men, including all who work about brewery, distillery, and saloon." But from the standpoint of political economy these men produce nothing. No addition to the national wealth comes from their labor. They must be counted and reasoned about simply as non-producers. What is the reasoning in such cases?

When Victor Emmanuel became King of Italy he found a host of monks who simply did nothing. He confiscated their estates and sent them off, because Italy could not afford to support them in idleness. But if all our liquor men would turn monks, we could build them splendid monasteries and pension them for the rest of their lives for a small fraction of what they cost us while they make and sell liquor. We pity the European nations with their great standing armies. Where is the harm? Those soldiers are kept busy. They work hard at their endless drill. They corrupt nobody. They harm nobody. The answer is, it doesn't matter how hard they work so long as nothing comes out of their working. Other men earn the money to feed and clothe them, and get nothing in return. The standing armies of all Europe are estimated at 28,000,000, including the reserves, and their cost at $600,000,000 annually. The United States could assume the support of that tremendous armament, *pay the entire military bill of all Europe* out of our cash outlay for liquor, and still have $400,000,000 to spare if the liquor outlay was stopped. Can we afford to let it go on? It would be a yet truer comparison to liken these liquor employés to an invading army of 500,000 men. If they were to turn their attention to burglary, and each steal $2,000 per year, and one out of every ten kill his man every year—which would be unusually prosperous and unusually murderous burglary—still they would not be as destructive as now. For this leaves out all the indirect cost, and we cannot count less than 60,000 deaths from intemperance every year, many carrying the estimate to 100,000.

Hence, so far from counting the support of these liquor employés as a deduction from the total drink cost, it is an added item—the support of 500,000 non-producers. Their work in any productive industry, at a reasonable average for all grades of skill employed, would be $300,000,000. They would add at least that much to the national wealth, which is now a dead loss, and must be carried to the debit side.

What fortunes the leaders in this business wring out of the toiling masses, a few examples will show. A Chicago reporter took occasion to look up a few of the palatial drinking-places of that city. The first, which seemed rich and fine enough, cost $15,000. "But, in quest of still finer saloons, the reporter went into one a few steps away, and was fairly dazzled by the glitter of mirrors, polished brass, and stained-glass screens, with gaslights placed behind to show off their beauties. 'This cost $44,000,' said the proprietor, 'and if you don't believe it, I can show you the bills. This is no contract job either. I said to the man who fixed it up, "Go ahead and send in your bills."' This establishment is fitted up with imported English oak and mahogany wood. A wide fireplace is built in one corner of Minton tile and polished brass. Wherever a window can be put, a fanciful design in stained glass is placed, and a half dozen fine oil paintings decorate the walls. Across the street is another place that cost $24,000. It is fitted with marble. The bar mirrors cost $2,000, and the screen in front of the entrance, composed of massive carved walnut, with a mirror and clock, cost $1,400. A short tour about the principal streets showed that there were a dozen other places where the thirsty pedestrian can satisfy his appetite for alcoholic beverages in saloons costing from $20,000 to $30,000 to fit up." As if this were not enough, New York has one saloon, and Indianapolis has now another, where silver dollars are actually used to pave the floor. Of the new one we are told: "The floor is laid with the most expensive tiling, and 160 silver dollars just from the mint are inlaid." With all the poverty and distress in the land, our workingmen are actually tramping silver dollars under foot as they go to get their drinks. Is it any wonder there should be hard times? What can the best tariff legislation do to put this locked-up money in circulation?

Where the money comes from may be seen by an incident related by Mrs. Foote, of the Ohio Woman's Christian Temperance Union, in a recent address. She said: "I went into the home of a man who works in the Cleveland rolling-mills, in the intolerable heat of a great furnace, and earns $3 a day. It was a wretched home, with uncarpeted floor and broken windows, a rickety table and a few damaged chairs for furniture. I went into the pantry to get something for the sick child I had come to see, and there was a little sugar lying on a small square of brown paper, a little tea on another, a bit of butter on one of the wooden plates given at the grocery stores. There was not a dish in that pantry except a little handful of cracked plates and cups to set their miserable table. The bedroom was wretched past description. All along that street were other homes to all appearance just like that one." When there are Minton tiles in the saloon there's no crockery in the workingman's pantry. It doesn't matter how many dollars he earns, if they go to pave the saloon floor.

Adding these various items, we have for the United States the following bill:

Lost labor of drunkards and tipplers	$400,000,000
Lost labor of sober men	40,000,000
Pauperism	8,000,000
Crime	37,500,000
Insanity and disability	17,000,000
Sickness	100,000,000
Lost labor of liquor-makers	300,000,000
Total	$902,500,000

It is to be observed that these estimates are almost all based on the census of 1880. At that time the direct cost of intoxicants, as estimated by Dr. Hargreaves, was but $733,816,495 for the year. With the increase in the consumption of liquor from $734,000,000 to $1,100,000,000, it is certain that these indirect losses must have advanced in equal proportion. That would make these items amount to not less than the direct cost now, or another $1,100,000,000.

We will call it, to be absolutely on the safe side $1,000,000,000, or just the net cost of the liquor after deducting receipts from tax and license. This makes a grand total of $2,000,000,000 annual loss to the nation from the liquor traffic.

We came out of our Civil War with a debt of $2,800,-000,000, and we thought that was terrible. Our only consolation was that it had saved the Union and set free the slaves. Now, in a time of profound peace, we are sacrificing every eighteen months more than the entire debt of the Civil War in maintaining the liquor traffic, to reduce our freeborn men to a slavery more hopeless than that of Southern plantations.

CHAPTER III.

DOES HIGH LICENSE PAY?

"Four new distilleries will be opened in Moore County in a few weeks. This will boom the State."—*The Memphis Avalanche.*

"WE BOOM.—While the towns about us have been bragging of their progress, we have kept quiet and got in our work without kicking up any cloud of dust. Brag is all right in its way, but we don't propose to come out with a double-leaded, scare-head article every time a citizen hangs a new front gate. Booms are good enough in their way, but there must be merit behind them. With no disposition to claim this as the only growing town in Arizona, and with no desire to kill the growth of rival towns, we humbly call attention to the fact that since January 1st, fourteen new saloons, three poker-rooms, and four retail tobacco-stores have been opened in the place, and at the present moment eighteen men are engaged in building a jail capable of accommodating thirty prisoners. We have done all this without any brag or bluster, and we propose to keep right on in the same quiet fashion, leaving the outside world to judge for itself as to where it shall seek new homes and invest its capital."—*The Arizona Kicker.*

THE latest statistics carry the direct cost of intoxicants to $1,000,000,000 annually for the United States. As the indirect cost has at least equalled the direct in time past, it is probable that it does now, though we have no statistics on crime, pauperism, etc., later than 1880. This is certainly a bad showing. But can we not make up for it by a High License on the drink traffic?

Well, there is one thing very certain to start with—*we cannot make it* ALL *up*. We cannot get back the $1,000,000,000 cash expenditure by any license we can put upon the trade, because that would be to require distillers, brewers, and saloon-keepers to do business for nothing, and give in the materials used to boot. This is not only too great a stretch of benevolence to expect from the liquor men, but a financial impossibility. We shall have to let them make some money out of us, if we let them do business at all. But all they make out of us will be dead loss to us, because what we buy of them does us no earthly good. Then whatever money we spend for liquor drags after it, dollar for dollar, and million for million, lost time, lost labor, crime, pauperism, insanity, doubling the liquor expenditure right along. High License, which cannot repay the direct outlay for liquor cannot touch the indirect.

If any community could ascertain just what its saloon-keepers are making, it could better afford to lay a direct tax upon the people of that whole amount and pay it to the saloon-keepers year after year without getting anything in return, than it could afford to spend the same money at their bars and drink their liquor. For then the community would *save the whole indirect cost.*

You would say of any workman who goes on a Saturday spree, it would be better for him to go down to the river and throw in all he would spend in the saloon and go home sober, for then he would be fit for something Monday morning. He would be sure not to get into the lock-up, and tolerably safe against smashing his furniture, stabbing his wife, or beating out the brains of his little children. The same is true of a community, only more surely true, for while one drinking man may chance to avoid crime, out of a thousand men a certain number will commit crime while under the influence of liquor as surely as the sun will rise. By paying for the liquor and *not* drinking it we could save all that, and it would be cheaper. It would pay any father better—not to speak of the mother—to buy green apples at the highest market price and throw them into the swill-pail than to let his boy eat them for nothing. For then he would save the wakeful nights and the doctor's bill.

It would pay the nation to buy the entire liquor product at retail prices and dump it into the two seas rather than to buy it at the same price and swallow it. Poured into the ocean, that would be the end of the expense. Poured into the people's stomachs, that is only the beginning, for the millions for lost time, lost labor, sickness, insanity, pauperism, and crime have still to be paid.

Take, now, the revenue of $98,000,000* which the general Government collects from the liquor traffic. That is very nearly $1 in $10 of the people's outlay. There is evidently no profit in that. For it is "we, the people," who are the Government, and "we, the people," who are spending the money. It is "we" who expend the $1,000,000,000, and it is the same "we" who get back the $98,000,000. That cannot pay. The whole nation can no more afford to do business at an outlay of $10 for $1 received than any individual can afford to do business at the same rate. It is no answer to say that we are rich enough, and make enough in other ways to bear the loss for a good while to come. If Wanamaker were to find that one of the departments of his great store was costing him $10 for every $1 received, that department would be promptly closed out. It would not satisfy him that the other departments were bringing in enough to save him from immediate bankruptcy. Such a drain

---

* This amount was $92,630,384.89 in 1888, but increased to $98,036,041.59 in 1889.

would be stopped by any business man of sense. Why should it not be stopped by the whole people if they have sense? It is not good financiering to get $98,000,-000 by a direct expenditure of $1,000,000,000, and the indirect loss of another $1,000,000,000.

The only real answer to this is, that the money would be spent anyway, and the Government may as well get what it can out of it. We have no very great respect for this argument. We cannot see how it differs from the saloon-keeper's "If I don't sell somebody else will, and I may as well have the money." But we are not writing for a set of politicians, *but for the people.* The *people* who spend this $1,000,000,000 for liquor can stop spending it, and by so doing stop the loss of the other $1,000,000,000. They would then give up the $98,-000,000 revenue. But would that not be the best investment a nation ever made—to give up $98,000,000 in order to save $2,000,000,000?

The argument that stopping the tax would not stop the consumption of liquor does not apply here, for our plan is to stop the consumption and so, of course, stop the tax. Let the people vote that intoxicants shall not be manufactured or sold for beverage. Then the people could richly afford to resign the present tax on their manufacture and use. True, a certain illicit production and sale might continue for some time, but the immediate saving, even from a partial enforcement of the law, would outnumber by hundreds of millions the tax that would be given up. It does not pay the nation to keep the traffic for the tax.

Does High License pay the States?

The Internal Revenue Report for 1889 gives 171,669 retail dealers in both distilled and malt liquors. There were 27,700 druggists in the United States in 1880, and of course a larger number now. Each of these would be classed as a "Retail Liquor Dealer" in the Internal Revenue Report. If we deduct these, we have less than 150,000 saloon-keepers. If we were to impose upon them a license of $1,000 each in every State, as is done in the cities of Nebraska, all the States together would collect from the liquor traffic less than $150,000,000. All the States together would spend $2,000,000,000. Manifestly that could not pay.

But almost all that are called High License States charge a less rate than that, about $500—as in Illinois and Pennsylvania—being thought very good. This cannot pay them, since double the amount could not pay, if made national and distributed evenly through all the States. The loss would be distributed as evenly and as far.

Let us take the case of Pennsylvania, where the famed Brooks Law exists, with its $500 license. The Pittsburg *Times* gives the total collections from saloon licenses in the State for 1888 as $1,837,869. *The Voice* computes the indirect loss on the basis of Dr. Hargreaves's estimates at $76,000,000, or $40 loss for $1 received. But if we take the entire loss direct and indirect at the increased rate since Dr. Hargreaves's book was written, Pennsylvania's loss on the basis of population would be now $160,000,000, and her receipts for license under the Brooks Law would be $1 in $88 of the total cost of the drink traffic.

To take the case of Philadelphia alone, its collections under the Brooks Law were $673,500. But as long ago as 1870, its criminal and charitable expenses resulting from intemperance were estimated by Prison Agent

William J. Mullen as $2,500,000. In view of the increase of population, it will be a very moderate estimate to add one-fourth to Mr. Mullen's figures, making upward of $3,000,000 charitable and criminal expenses now due to intemperance, for which the saloon kindly pays about $1 in $5.

What, then, becomes of the claim that "High License reduces taxation?"

Ohio has a "tax," so called, of $250 on every saloon, under what is known as the Dow Law. At every election time, farmers and tradesmen are solemnly told, "The Dow Law reduces your taxes." With many persons this single idea overrides all questions of humanity or morality. If "it reduces my taxes," it is vain for the minister to talk of moral wrong, or for the reformer to grow eloquent over human suffering. The hearts of their hearers are buttoned up as tight as their pocket-books with the thought, "it reduces my taxes." Well, it doesn't. So you can afford to be moral and human beings after all.

The account stands thus:

State Benevolent Institutions for Insane, Idiotic, etc., not including Soldiers' and Sailors' Orphans' Home.............$969,256	
Charge one-third of this to intemperance (which is far too little)...................	$323,085
State Penal and Reformatory Institutions, not including County Infirmaries.....$759,498	
Allow nine-tenths of this for intemperance..	613,550
Total due to intemperance............	$936,635
State proportion of Dow Law Tax, one-fifth of $2,225,000.............................	$445,000.

That is, the Dow Tax pays less than one-half of the State expenses due to intemperance.

The expenses by counties show the same.

For County Infirmaries (which in such a State as Ohio may be set down solid to intemperance, the exceptions not making an appreciable difference)....... $685,765
Out-door relief, 78 counties reporting....... 380,432

Total................................. $1,066,197.
Dow Tax for same..................... 284,253.
A little more than one-fourth.

The municipal taxes are more difficult to chase down. Take, as a specimen, the city of Cleveland, which may be fairly called the brightest, fairest, and best-governed of the large cities of Ohio :

Police expenses for 1887 were............... $257,501
Amount of Dow Tax credited in Police Account. 130,765.

More than eighty per cent. of the offences for which arrests were made were such as are commonly due to intemperance—more than one-half reported simply as " Intoxication." Eighty per cent. of $257,501 is $206,000.

That is, the liquor traffic causes $200,000 of police expenses, and pays $130,000 toward meeting them. We believe the ratio would not be better if followed through the pauper and criminal expenses of all our cities. The Dow Law appropriates $150 for each saloon toward the taxes of the municipality where the saloon is located. But any one who has seen much of intemperance will be sure that $150 will not nearly pay for the crime and pauperism caused by one saloon year after year. That is the whole case. The saloon does not pay expenses. The Dow Law which does not reduce taxation in State and county does not in the city.

Omaha, Nebraska, may be called the champion High License city. Of the economic effect of the system there, *The Voice* of May 30th, 1889, publishes the following particulars:

"Two hundred and sixty thousand dollars is, in round numbers, the amount of revenue that the city of Omaha, Neb., draws annually from her High License saloons. Each saloon pays $1,000 per year, and at the beginning of 1889 there were about 260 licensed saloons in operation. That is an enormous liquor revenue for a city of only 110,000 population."

* * * * * *

During the present year, according to the Omaha *World*, the total tax levy is 48 mills on the dollar; while in the city of Des Moines, in the Prohibition State of Iowa, according to the Iowa *State Register* for May 11th, the total levy is only 22¼ mills on the dollar. "And it is to be remembered," adds the *Register*, "that the property valuation for taxation purposes in Des Moines is less than forty per cent. of its real valuation, while in Omaha this valuation is placed at a high figure in order that the city may make as good a business showing as possible."

Even this striking comparison does not tell the whole story. The people of the $1,000 High License city of Omaha groan under constantly increasing burdens of taxes. This statement is not made upon authority hostile to Omaha or her liquor system, but upon the testimony of one of her leading daily newspapers, the Omaha *World*.

In a recent issue of the *World*, bitter complaints were made about the taxes. That journal said, among other things:

"*Property owners and tax-payers of Omaha must look with some concern upon the tax figures of this year.* Aside from the special taxes for public improvements, property owners will be expected to pay $974,000 for regular city taxes by July 1st. This is an increase of nearly a quarter of a million of dollars over last year. For the past four years the volume of regular city taxes collected from property owners has been as follows:

"For 1886, $475,000; for 1887, $625,000; for 1888, $739,000; for 1889, $994,000.

"The burden of city taxes has therefore increased thirty per cent. over last year. Is it not about time to call a halt? . . .

"The levy is three mills heavier than last year, the valuation is several millions greater, and the amount which will be collected is a quarter of a million greater than in 1888. Is it not about time for tax-payers to protest?"

The Iowa *State Register*, commenting upon this cry of distress, says:

"It will be hard on the 'exiles' who left Iowa hoping to find a place of prosperity and personal liberty in the Nebraska metropolis."

"It will be hard" also upon the High License advocates everywhere. Omaha has tried High License for a longer period than any other American city, having charged every saloon $1,000 per year for nearly eight years. If the liquor revenue argument is worth anything, if an immense rum revenue reduces taxes in a city, the fact ought to appear in Omaha, with her annual income of $260,000 from the saloons. But the burden of taxes has increased steadily in that city, the increase having been thirty per cent. in the last year. The rate of taxation is higher than ever before, and is more than twice the tax-rate prevailing in Prohibition Des Moines, although in Des Moines property is valued for taxation purposes at only forty per cent. of its real value.

The Omaha newspaper from which we have quoted does not state the reasons for the increasing taxation. But there can hardly be a doubt that the crime-producing High License saloons are largely responsible for it. In a city where the work of the saloon is so destructive that there is one arrest for every ten of the population, it is not to be expected that taxes will be low.

In the matter of police expenses, there is a heavy item, which cannot be put into dollars and cents—viz. : *It reduces the efficiency of the police.* By natural necessity, it is a great part of their business to watch saloons. Crimes are always liable to occur there. Criminals are sure to resort there. The average policeman, obliged to hover around the saloon in heat and cold, in storm and sleeplessness, is almost sure to seek alcohol's quick relief. It is for the saloon-keeper's interest to be on good terms with him, and make it pleasant for him to " step in and get a drink." The result is thus given in the Cleveland *Press :*

" The efficiency of the police force is becoming seriously impaired by the persistent use of intoxicating liquors by a goodly number of the patrolmen. All the men do not drink ; probably not over twenty per cent are habitual guzzlers : but of these are several officers who are, when sober, good and reliable policemen. They are never actually drunk while on duty, but keep just so full all the time. Their breaths are laden with whiskey fumes so dense that even a strong man cannot stand and talk to them without turning away. . . . This drinking habit is slowly growing, and unless a stop is put to it, there will be as many drunkards in the policemen's chairs in the police court as there are on the prisoners' bench. It was only a few days ago that an officer was so full of liquor in the police court that he went to sleep, and it was only by the efforts of his brother patrolmen that he was straightened up to testify."

In this condition of things it must require a greater number of men for the same amount of protection.

Now observe, *it is the licensed saloon* that does this. Make the saloon an outlaw, make the liquor-seller a criminal, *ipso facto*, and the policeman will not have to be on good terms with him as now. He will not have to guard and take care of his place as now. Put only temperate men on your force, and the only connection they will have with the "boot-leggers" will be to "run them in"—like any other criminals. It is the *authorized* saloon that makes the policeman's case so hard. He must be near it. If a row occurs, or a man is killed in a saloon on his beat, the question will be, "Where were you? You knew such things were likely to happen there. Why were you not on hand?" He must keep his eyes, ears, and thoughts on the drinking-places, and himself within easy reach of them. Yet he cannot close them up nor stop their selling. He will often have to watch for criminals there, and must keep on good terms with the proprietor. It is idle to say our license does not give protection. It must, for taxation involves protection; and it gives it. I have seen a saloon-keeper push to his door a poor fellow who was just tipsy enough to be exasperating, and beckon two policemen. When they tried every way to avoid interference, he said, "I want you to arrest him," and—with manifest disgust and reluctance—the officers laid hold on the poor fellow, who then began kicking, biting, and rolling on the ground, and so was dragged away, while the man who had sold him the liquor stood in his doorway coolly watching the scene. Prohibition would have made such a thing impossible. Then if the liquor-seller had contrived to make his man drunk, he would have been amazingly shy of calling on the police to take care of him. He would have been studying the most private and secret way to avoid an interview with any member of the force, and would rather have seen anything than a uniform. It is the taxed or licensed traffic that enables the saloon-keeper to be on good terms with the police, and compels the policeman to be a satellite of the saloon.

But even as regards taxation, the expense of the saloon is more than a matter of police. Rev. Dr. Peddie, in a recent address, said: "I know a minister who had to sell his home at $4,000 below its fair valuation because a saloon was started next door to his. No den of drink can be started without spreading depreciation in the price of houses and honest business places all around it."

Now the assessment is going to be lower on that priced-down property, and somebody must pay a higher rate in order to make up. Reducing the value of property has the same effect as increasing taxes, and is a far greater hardship. The saloon building may rent for more than it would for any other purpose, but all the surrounding property is injured. Very few owners of real estate want to have a saloon opened in the immediate neighborhood of their property, however willing they might be to have it somewhere else.

In one of our cities a fine residence on a beautiful street was advertised for rent at a very low rate. It seemed a most tempting offer till we reached the corner, and looked across the pretty lawn. On the adjoining lot, fronting on the street below, a brewery reared its tall chimneys, poisoning the atmosphere above, while the human beings that haunted it poisoned the atmosphere below. It only needed to look in each other's eyes, and we walked on without opening the gate.

A professional man owned a building on a busy street, renting the lower part for a store, and occupying the upper rooms. In the building next adjoining was a saloon, so placed that its door was almost under his windows, and till after midnight his family would be kept awake by the talk, at once loud and low, that went on around that door. He has even had stones thrown through his windows to the imminent danger of the occupants. Why did he live there? Because if he left the rooms he could not rent them to any other respectable family with that saloon adjoining. The owners of those two pieces of property could have well afforded to have their taxes doubled immediately, if they could have got rid of that brewery and that saloon.

Whatever reduces the volume and profit of honest trade has the same effect.

For instance, here is a village with no saloons, and badly needing new sidewalks. Some man reasons: "Now if we would let in three saloons here, at the Dow Law rate, we could take in $450 a year. That would build our sidewalks nicely, and not increase our taxes." But those saloons are going to take from your people from $2,500 to $5,000 apiece. The tax-paying power of some of your people is going to be reduced by that amount, say $10,000 for your three saloons. That money will be taken from all the retail business of the town, and by the interlacings of business will make everybody in the village in some way poorer—except the saloon-keepers. So, while your taxes may not be raised, *your money to pay them with is lessened*, which comes to the same thing. Here, for instance, is a dry-goods merchant who would have to pay $25 of that $450, if it was added to the tax levy. He will save that. But he will sell $500 less goods, because his customers spend their money for whiskey. How much has he saved? He could better have afforded to build those sidewalks out of his own pocket, and made them a present to the village, than to have saved the tax by letting in the saloons.

Professor Ely tells us that in a republic "taxation is

simply one form of co-operation." So considered, the idea of raising taxes from the saloon is this: Here are a hundred business men desiring some public improvement. A liquor-dealer comes in and says: "Come down to my place, gentlemen, and drink all you can, and I will contribute to this improvement one-tenth of what you spend at my bar, which will probably pay the entire expense." This is hailed, strange to say, as a very generous proposition, and as a way of really getting the improvement for nothing, till one quiet man observes: "I don't care to drink the liquor. Would there be any objection to my contributing directly toward the improvement one-tenth of what it would cost to make me drunk and saving the other nine-tenths?" Then suddenly it dawns upon the others that they might all do the same, and that it would actually be cheaper to subscribe the cost of the improvement outright than to pay ten times as much by way of the saloon in order to get the one-tenth contributed. Besides which it occurs to them that the result of the liquor-drinking will be headaches and unfitness for business the next day, the spoiling of a good many hats and suits of clothes, with perhaps drunken quarrels and who shall say what besides?

Behold the nation! Whatever we want to raise in taxes it is immeasurably better to raise by some direct assessment than to pay from ten to fifty times as much through the saloon in order to get it with its long train of poverty, ruin, and crime. For while the saloon increases taxes with one hand, it cuts down the value of property and the volume of honest business with the other—a combination that no license can pay for.

CHAPTER IV.

HIGH LICENSE AS A MONOPOLY.

"The assertion of the free-trade Democrats that the tax on whiskey should be continued, because in conformity to moral considerations whiskey ought to be taxed, is a piece of cheap and contemptible demagogy. The tax upon whiskey conserves no moral principle, and serves no moral end. It does not restrict or regulate the traffic in the slightest degree. The traffic is as free with as it would be without the tax. . . . The proof of this, if any were needed, is found in the opposition of the principal manufacturers and dealers in whiskey to the abolition of the tax. . . . The issue is merely an economic one. If the tax is needed to meet the obligations of the Government, and enable it to carry out a wise and liberal policy of defence and improvements, then let the tax remain."—*Cleveland Leader.*

"We have had High License in Illinois five years, and while it is a success as a revenue measure, it is an undisguised failure as a temperance measure. It in no way checks the consumption of intoxicating liquors as a beverage, nor does it in the least degree lessen the evils and crimes from such use. Call High License what it is, an easy way to raise a revenue from vice, but let there be an end of indorsing it as a temperance or reform measure."—*Chicago Daily News.*

THERE was a time when good men thought that High License might be made to stop the liquor traffic, and talked grandly of "taxing it to death." It is observable that no one now talks of "taxing it to death." High License has silently receded from its early claim. The utmost claim of High License now, is that

"IT REDUCES THE NUMBER OF SALOONS."

There is nothing more amusing than the simplicity with which this claim is advanced and swallowed by estimable men. It seems to be viewed as a simple question of arithmetic, thus:

If 100 saloons sell $500,000 worth of liquor in one year, 50 saloons will sell one-half of $500,000, which is $250,000.

Then the advocates of High License rub their hands and smile, and say, "We have stopped the sale of $250,000 worth of intoxicating liquors. What a grand temperance work is this!"

Then they proceed to the next example—viz. :

"If 100 saloons make 30 drunkards and 300 cases of intoxication every year, then 50 saloons will make 15 drunkards and 150 cases of intoxication in one year."

This solution makes them happier still. They have saved 15 men from becoming confirmed drunkards, and prevented 150 cases of intoxication. What a noble work!

They do not think to inquire whether the work has really been done. They don't *need* to know the facts. *Their theory shows that it must be so.*

Well, suppose we experiment a little with the theory. Here is a city with 100 groceries; if we can reduce them to 50, the grocers will sell only one-half as many goods as before, and the people will only eat one-half as much.

But a live grocer will say, "I'll give you $1,000 to be one of the 50, if you'll shut the other places by law and keep them shut. *These people are going to eat just as much as before*, and I can make more than twice the money by selling double the amount of goods over one counter."

This is no longer matter of conjecture. The science of monopoly has, within the last few years, made rapid strides. It has become the study of every business to reduce the number of establishments, while increasing the product and the profit. A familiar example of this is the Sugar Trust. A great syndicate bought up all the sugar refineries in the country, and at once closed a large part of them expressly to make more money—not with the least idea of reducing, permanently, the consumption of sugar. By the fewer establishments the Trust can at once reduce the cost of production and increase the price to the consumer, thus making money at both ends.

Suppose a Convention of Dentists, desiring to preserve the teeth of the nation, were to hold a jubilee over this, assuming that the consumption of sugar was reduced in proportion to the reduction in the number of refineries! That would be a joke worthy of Mark Twain. But it is gravely perpetrated in the interests of "temperance," great newspapers solemnly congratulating their readers on the reduction or even the non-increase of the number of saloons as so much in the interests of "temperance." The following extract from a letter of Mr. Onahan, of Chicago, has been going the rounds of the papers:

"The substantial and incontrovertible fact is that High License has arrested the multiplication of saloons in Chicago—that whereas in 1882-83, under a license of $52 per year, we had 3,919 licensed saloons, in 1887-88 we have substantially no more, while the population has increased from 500,000 to 900,000. So that it is not unreasonable to assume we would have 6,000 or more saloons except for the intervention of High License."

Supposing all this to be exactly as claimed, what does it prove? Does it show that the consumption of liquor or the production of drunkenness has been in any way reduced? Not necessarily. Both these may have been increased, and all the facts given by Mr. Onahan remain true. For, THIS IS JUST WHAT HAS HAPPENED TO ALL

THE MANUFACTURES OF THE UNITED STATES. The Census Report of 1880, Vol. II., page 926, remarks:

> "The fact that in the face of a *large increase* in the number of hands employed in manufactures, of *the material consumed*, and of the value of the products, the number of establishments *shows hardly an appreciable gain* from 1870 to 1880, notwithstanding an increase of thirty per cent. in population, is *amply accounted for by the well-known tendency to concentration of labor and capital in large shops and factories.*"

Here we have all the elements of the Onahan letter, a heavy increase of population, and scarcely a perceptible increase in the number of establishments. We ought, then, according to the High License theory, to conclude that the people have used less of all manufactured goods in proportion to their number than ten years before. But the hard facts of the Census show that they used very much more. The smaller number of establishments used more materials, employed more hands, and produced more goods. Why may not the same number of saloons, then, in Chicago have sold more liquor and made more drunkards than ever before?

It is a question of fact. But we cannot get the facts considered. Over and over we call for the facts regarding the consumption of liquor, and the High License men will steadily revolve around the one point of the number of saloons. We cannot get them to touch the question of the consumption of liquor. But this is the key of the situation—the one thing of consequence. If the liquor is consumed, the intemperance will follow. We do not care very greatly how many saloons there are, if the same amount of liquor is consumed. If just as much liquor would be drunk in one great public caravansary as in all the saloons of a city, we should not consider it any gain for temperance to reduce all the separate establishments to that one place of wholesale debauchery. We call the battle to this one point,

THE CONSUMPTION OF INTOXICANTS,

And we affirm :

1. That no advocate of High License—as far as we have been able to learn—has ever attempted to show that High License reduces the consumption of intoxicants. This is strong *prima facie* evidence that the thing cannot be done. It is a point that the friends of High License would be eager to make if they could.

2. By the law of monopoly, the reduction in the number of saloons, or their non-increase, *would lead us to expect larger sales and greater consumption* of liquor ; for that has been the rule with every other business in the nation.

3. The evidence shows that with the reduction or non-increase of the number of saloons, the consumption of liquor and consequent intemperance *have steadily and heavily increased.*

We turn first to the Internal Revenue Report for 1888. There we find (p. 30) that the number of retail dealers in all kinds of liquors has decreased from 196,792 in 1887 to 176,748 in 1888. This many would consider a most gratifying showing. As the number of States and cities that have employed High License during that time has been greater than ever before, we are willing to credit High License with a considerable share of this decrease, though we think much of it has been due to other causes. At any rate we have a decrease of liquor-dealers of 20,044. Twenty thousand less retail liquor-dealers in one year ! The High License men would claim that as a wonderful gain for temperance.

We claim that it does not indicate necessarily *any* gain for temperance, and that those 20,000 fewer men may have sold a great deal more liquor. We turn to page VI. of the same report, and there is the proof that they have. The report gives:

>Consumption of distilled spirits *increased* over that of 1887.................... 4,185,095 galls.
>Or from 67,380,391 galls. in 1887, to 71,565,486 galls. in 1888. (This includes fruit brandy.)
>*Increase* in *consumption* of fermented liquors was 1,558,693 bbls. at 31 galls. per bbl...........................48,319,483 galls.
>
>TOTAL INCREASE, all kinds of liquors..52,504,578 galls.

That is to say, 20,000 *fewer* liquor-dealers sold 52,000,000 gallons *more liquor* in a single year; just 1,000,000 gallons a week more. The Internal Revenue Report for 1889 shows that the same double process is still going on. The number of retail dealers in all kinds of liquors has *decreased* to 171,669, a decrease of 5,079. The consumption of all kinds of liquor has *increased* by 19,226,697 gallons. That is to say, 5,000 *fewer dealers* sold almost 20,000,000 gallons *more liquor* in 1889 than in 1888. After that do not be surprised if we are inclined to snap our fingers at the statement that High License reduces the number of saloons. That does not touch the question. Tell us about the consumption of liquor.

Or take the single State of Pennsylvania. What are the facts there? During the best days of the Brooks Law no proof was ever offered that it reduced the consumption of intoxicants. The New York *Herald* published some statements seemingly very strong to the contrary. The recent Brewers' Congress at Buffalo, N. Y., received the following report from its Vigilance Committee, under the head of Pennsylvania:

"The result of the High License law, passed in the preceding year, has been to reduce the number of drinking-places by about one-half, and to completely ruin a great number of smaller brewers, whose production was confined to the retail demand at their own bars. *Concerning the effects of the law upon the consumption of intoxicating drinks, there are so many contradictory reports in circulation that it is difficult to arrive at a correct conclusion. From the revenue returns it appears that the sale of beer-stamps has increased, but whether increased exportation to adjoining States or increased home consumption accounts for this, we cannot say.*"

The sale of beer-stamps is practically always for consumption. That has increased in Pennsylvania. But it is possible the increase may not have been for use in Pennsylvania. In other words, all the Brewers' Association *is sure of* is the reduction of the number of establishments. It *does not know* that the consumption of liquor has diminished, and *the indications are* from the Internal Revenue Returns *that it has increased*. So even the experience of Pennsylvania, under the unhindered dominion of the lauded Brooks Law, does not touch the one vital question—the consumption of intoxicants.

Everything seems to confirm the statement of the *Christian Union*, when appealed to by a correspondent for statistics to show that High License had decreased the consumption of liquor relatively to population. The *Christian Union*, a vigorous advocate of High License, answered February 23d, 1887:

"The friends of High License are not able to furnish any statistics upon this point."

They give nothing but decrease in the number of dealers, and to this our reply stands good that, as shown by the official reports of the Internal Revenue Bureau for the whole United States, 20,000 Fewer Dealers sold 52,000,000 More Gallons of Liquor in the year 1888 than were sold in 1887; with similar results in 1889.

But we are prepared to show that the liquor men themselves are at work to do this very thing of reducing the number of establishments *in the interests of their trade.* A "Whiskey Trust" has been formed, called the Western Distillers' Association, for the express purpose of reducing the number of distilleries. The President, J. B. Greenhut, of Peoria, in his address before the annual meeting of the association in Peoria, stated that the stock of the St. Paul distillery had been offered them, and had been positively declined. He also said:

"Our policy should be to run upon prices low enough, and for as long a time as necessary to overcome those outside concerns that have been or are now attempting to take advantage of our position.

*   *   *   *   *   *

"Outside competitors must be made to understand that we are in dead earnest in this matter, that they can hope for no profits in the business, and only see ruination and losses as recompense for their parasitic ventures. After we have succeeded by such means in convincing our opponents that there is no possible chance for them to prey on us, or induce us to take them into our fold, we shall then be able to proceed unmolested in the pursuit of our legitimate business."

Can that be a good restrictive measure which is part of the policy of the liquor men themselves in the interest of their business?

A recently-published interview with a leading brewer predicts that when the English syndicate shall have secured control of all the breweries, they will control the distilleries, and will then move for a uniform saloon license of from $3,000 to $4,000 throughout all the States, by this means crushing out all independent saloon-keeping, and bringing the entire business into the hands of the great "Trust," which will then proceed to plant just so many saloons, and just at such points as will give the greatest profit. While we cannot say how authoritative this prediction is, it deserves to be considered and an outlook kept along that line, for it seems to be perfectly feasible and business-like, and in the very line to which the monopolist tendency of other business is working.

It should be remembered that the strongest of all monopolies is a monopoly made by law. An independent monopoly has either to buy competitors out, or "freeze them out" at vast expense. But a Government monopoly has simply to sit down and see the Government shut up all competing concerns. In a town the writer knows are two livery stables, where there is just a good business for one. One man has been in the business there for twenty years. The other establishment has incessantly changed hands. The first man says, "I don't know but I shall have to break up every man in town before I can make the business pay." But now, put on a good, stiff Livery License, and you would help him out. Now, it is of no use for him to buy out the other establishment, for a new man immediately steps in to be bought out. But make the license such that two establishments could not possibly afford to pay it, let him be the first man to pay, and the law would keep other men out. "You can't let a horse or carriage in this town till you pay a $1,000 license," would settle the case for all adventurers when one strong business man was already in the field. That is just what we propose to do for the liquor-sellers, and call it "restriction!"

This is just the way it works in Nebraska. "There," a friend assures us, "in the smaller towns, the $1,000 saloonist is the great man of the town." He pays more toward the taxes than any other one man. He is consulted in regard to all public improvements. He controls the floating vote, holding it all in his single hand. The State has saved him from competition. Often he controls the politics of the town.

This brings us to another claim often made in favor of High License, that

"IT REDUCES THE POWER OF THE SALOON IN POLITICS."

What is the answer? Is the political power of any other business reduced by making it a monopoly—concentrating it in fewer hands? Have the Pennsylvania Railroad Company and the Standard Oil Company less power than the small corporations they have superseded? John D. Rockefeller's little finger is thicker than the loins of all the small operators his company has absorbed. *The greatest danger from the liquor traffic in our politics is its condensation.* A cricket ball is made of compressed feathers. Any man who has had it hit him in full career on the cricket ground will wish he could have had a pailful of loose feathers thrown at him instead. Boil the liquor traffic down by High License till you get it all into the hands of the men of most capital, best business talent and most staying power, and all with a single policy, and they will be such a power in our politics as the East India Company once was in the politics of England.

This last point may seem to be a little aside from the

main purpose of this chapter, but it has this connection. When the Saloon Syndicate is perfected and gains its final grip upon our politics, *it will not let the business interests of the traffic be hurt by any legislation that can be devised.* It will not allow anything that will effectually lessen the consumption of liquor. We are not swerving from the economic question. For the great importance of the consumption of liquors from an economic point of view is, that *if the liquors are consumed the people will pay for them* the money which might be spent for better things and help worthier business; and the consumption of the liquors will draw after it all the attendant train of drunkenness, poverty, and crime. Since the High License Monopoly has no power to Lessen the Consumption of Intoxicants, it is impotent to deliver the nation from the thousand million dollars of direct expenditure for liquor and the other thousand millions of indirect injury and loss.

One practical effect of this, as of most other monopolies, is

A TAX UPON THE POOR.

It is a characteristic of indirect taxes that they are distributed not according to what a man owns or earns, but according to what he consumes.

Suppose, for instance, there were a heavy tax on quinine in a manufacturing district. There is one capitalist, and there are thousands of workingmen. However malarious the district may be, the capitalist and his family can only consume the amount of quinine which the human system will bear—the dose, we will say, for six or eight people. That will be all they will contribute to that tax—a very trifling sum, scarce worthy of footing up on the State Auditor's books. But those thousands of workingmen and their families will use it in quantities that are reckoned by thousands of dollars, and the amount they will contribute to the tax will be very heavy. Or, to put it in shorter statement, the capitalist, owning his millions, will pay no more tax than any poor workman in his employ who owns nothing. That is the charm of indirect taxes to the well-to-do classes. They get the tax mostly out of the poor.

In fact, in such a case, the capitalist might not pay even one man's share. He might live on a fine hill out of the reach of the malaria, while his thousands of workmen had to live in low, swampy lands that were full of it. He and his family would use no quinine and pay no tax, while the poor laborers would use it in quantities, and pay thousands of dollars. Of course that would be popular with the capitalist, unless he was troubled with a human heart.

It is the same with liquor. The capitalist, even if he gets " as drunk as a lord," can drink only what it takes to make one man drunk. The drunken workingman will drink just as much, and so contribute as much to the revenue. To be sure the rich man may drink more expensive liquors. But in that case they will very likely be imported, and if he drinks them at home, he will pay not a cent of your " high license," but only the tariff charge at the port of entry.

Or the rich man may " treat" more freely. But that is doubtful. Many a poor fellow who goes into a saloon Saturday night with twenty or thirty dollars of wages in his pocket, which are all his earthly possessions, and comes out without a cent, has spent more than his employer would have done, even if he should be a drinking man. But, on the other hand, the employer may be perfectly temperate, and so contribute not one cent to the license, which he sees descending with its whole weight upon the miserable poor. It is the workingmen and the poor who pay most of the nation's Thousand Million Drink Bill. It is the workingmen and the poor who chiefly sustain our long array of saloons, which Dr. Hargreaves computes * " would form a city having more dwellings than there are in Philadelphia and Pittsburg combined, and as many dwellings remain as would make another city as large as Sacramento, Cal." If by some crusade we could induce all our workingmen and all the poor to stop drinking, High License would very suddenly cease to be popular with the wealthy classes.

But why do the workingmen endure it? Because they do not see that they *are* taxed. It is this which has made indirect taxes a favorite expedient with all oppressive governments, because as is said, " the people do not feel them." By which it is meant, not that the people do not feel the privation and poverty the tax may cause, but they do not feel it *as tax*. They do not know when they pay the tax, and they attribute their misery to everything except the right cause.

Hence they will pay patiently in indirect taxation, a sum which would drive them to downright rebellion if it were assessed directly. High License is only the tyrant's scheme for fleecing the people without their knowing it. But our people have a remedy against the tyranny which no other people ever had so completely. The people are the rulers, and they can stop the drink tax and the

---

* " Worse than Wasted," p. 48.

drink expenditure, whenever they say the word. If they can only once be made to see that this whole scheme is to raise a revenue out of the poor, for the "relief" of the capitalists, we believe they will stop it very suddenly.

CHAPTER V.

HIGH LICENSE AS RESTRICTION.

"In November, 1867, Massachusetts repealed her prohibitory law substituting license, its friends in all parties combining for the achievement. The chaplain of her State prison in his annual report, 1868, stated : ' The prison has never been so full. If the tide of intemperance, greatly swollen by the present wretched license law, is suffered to rush on unchecked, a fearful increase of crime will result. The State must soon enlarge the prison or build another.' The chief constable of the State asserts, annual report, 1869 : ' This law has opened about 2,500 bars and over 1,000 other drinking-places, where liquors are sold presumably not by the glass.' Governor Claflin, of Massachusetts, informed her Legislature in 1869 : ' The increase of drunkenness and crime the last six months, compared with the same time in 1867, is very decisive as to the operation of the license law. The State prison, jails, and houses of correction are being rapidly filled. Enlarged accommodations will soon be required if commitments increase as they have since the law went into force.' "—*Tract No. 2 of the Ohio Woman's Christian Temperance Union.*

"The patrons of 4,000 Philadelphia saloons will swear off to-day—from drinking at their old resorts. The majority of them will continue to drink somewhere, however."—*Philadelphia Times.*

"The High License Law of Nebraska is the grandest law for the liquor traffic there is."—*Peter E. Iler, President of the Willow Springs Distilling Company, Omaha, Neb.*

There are those who will admit that High License does not decrease the consumption of liquor, who will yet claim that it is a valuable restriction. "It abolishes the dives," they say. They maintain that the saloon-keeper who has paid his high license will at once become a detective to see that no other man sells without a license; that the traffic will be in the hands of "a better class of men," who will be more likely to observe regulations about selling to inebriates, minors, etc.; that the fewer saloons can be more easily watched by the police, and crime, disorder, and drunkenness, in part, at least, prevented.

Does the performance justify the promise? Is High License useful as a Restriction?

For answer we turn again to Chicago, and quote again the extract from the letter of Mr. Onahan:

"The substantial and incontrovertible fact is that High License has arrested the multiplication of saloons in Chicago—that whereas in 1882-83, under a license of $52 per year, we had 3,919 licensed saloons, in 1887-88 we have substantially no more, while the population has increased from 500,000 to 900,000. So that it is not unreasonable to assume we would have 6,000 or more saloons, except for the intervention of High License."

Very well. We will accept Mr. Onahan's statement, that the number of saloons has not appreciably increased (only five per cent) in five years. But the *consumption of beer has increased* from 872,000 barrels in 1882 to 1,674,000 barrels in 1887. The same number of saloons sell 800,000 more barrels of beer. How much more of distilled liquors we are not informed. Probably the increase would be proportionate. Where, then, is the gain for temperance?

The consumption of liquor has increased. How can it but be that intemperance should increase likewise? Statistics show that it has. The arrests for drunkenness and disorderly conduct have increased from 18,000 in 1882 to upward of 27,000 in 1887, or fifty-three per cent. Now we can appreciate the statement of the Chicago *Daily News*, independent in politics, and the most successful daily paper financially in the West, in its issue of April 9th, 1888 :

" We have had High License in Illinois five years, and, while it is a success as a revenue measure, it is an undisguised failure as a temperance measure. It in no way checks the consumption of intoxicating liquors as a beverage, nor does it in the least degree lessen the evils or crime from such use. . . . The dives and dens, the barrel houses and thieves' resorts are as bad and as frequent in this city to-day, after five years of High License, as they ever were. Call High License what it is, an easy way to raise a revenue from vice, but let there be an end of indorsing it as a temperance or reform measure."

The above extract disposes of another point in the claim of High License as a Restriction, the claim that

"IT ABOLISHES THE DIVES."

That sentence is worth singling out by itself—viz. :

" . . . The dives and dens, the barrel houses and thieves' resorts are as bad and as frequent in this city to-day, after five years of High License, as they ever were."

But Chicago may be an exception. Well, St. Louis has had for some years a $550 license. Of its effect, the following account is given in the St. Louis *Republic*, the leading Democratic daily in that city, in its issue of November 11th, 1888 :

" These dives (the lowest) are so numerous in the city, their organization is so compact, their *clientèle* so extensive, that as long as present conditions remain they will control the city completely. . . . Our present license law was intended to break their power, but as far as it applies to St. Louis it has rather served to increase it."

But the license may not be high enough. Well, they

have a $1,000 license in Omaha. How does that work ? The Omaha *Daily Bee*, a Republican paper and the most active champion of the High License system in Nebraska, said editorially, December 10th, 1888 :

"No one can deny that the license system as now existing in our city has been a source of corruption and irregularity. It has had a demoralizing effect upon members of the City Council and the City Clerk. It has exacted political support from the low dives and bummers; it has compelled the orderly liquor-dealers to support with money and influence the very worst element of the city, and has used the liquor men to do the dirty work at primaries and elections. The reason for this is easy to find. The License Board is made up of the Mayor, President of the City Council, and City Clerk, each holding an elective office. The temptations to abuse the position as a member of the License Board are manifold. There are opportunities to make corrupt bargains. In return for pecuniary or political support a member of the Board can grant license to disreputable individuals or wink at violations of the license law. The average member of the License Board plays for political power, for re-election, and he keeps his eye to the main chance to gain the solid support of the liquor men."

The police reports of Omaha for 1888 give the following :

The total number of arrests for the year was 11,910. The following is an analysis of the causes of arrest :

"Vagrants, 3,162 ; drunk, 2,450 ; prostitutes, 2,442 ; fight, 1,076 ; keepers of houses of ill-fame, 423 ; assaults of all kinds, 119 ; disorderly persons, 182 ; disturbing the peace, 115 ; inmates of houses of prostitution, 73 ; assignation houses, 24 ; selling liquors on Sunday, 9 ; selling liquors after midnight, 8 ; selling liquors to minors, 7 ; selling liquors without license, 33 ; selling liquors on election day, 2 ; obstructing view to saloon, 4 ; all other offences, 1,781."

The record shows that 2,962, or about one-fourth of all the arrests, are of prostitutes, keepers of houses of ill-fame and assignation, and inmates of houses of prostitution. This large number is explained by the peculiar system of licensing prostitution that prevails in Omaha.

Aside from the so-called "arrests" for prostitution, the total number of arrests in Omaha last year was 8,948; and of this number 6,968, or just about four-fifths, were for the offences of drunkenness, vagrancy, fighting, assault, disorderly conduct, disturbing the peace, and violating the liquor laws—offences, with scarcely an exception, growing out of the saloons. A very large percentage of the remaining one-fifth of the arrests was undoubtedly due to liquor-selling. This is the proud record made in Omaha, where no man can lawfully sell a drop of any kind of liquor over the bar without paying $1,000 for a license.*

---

* The *Voice Extra* for January, 1889, from which the above facts are taken, gives the following explanation of this matter, which, so far as we are able to learn, no one has attempted to disprove:

THE PRICE OF CRIME.

Each prostitute and keeper of a house of ill-fame or assignation is required to come to the police court at the first of each month and pay her monthly fine and costs. The fine for a prostitute is $3, with $3 costs; for a "landlady," $7, with $3 costs; for a keeper of a house of assignation, $25, with $3 costs. They simply go to the police-court bar, pay the price fixed for their right to do business, and depart to continue their sinful lives with the assurance that they have bought immunity from the city. And this farcical procedure is called "arresting" prostitutes. It is repeated each month, and at the end of the year the monthly totals are aggregated, and the grand total is set down in the police returns. This is how Omaha came to make 2,962 "arrests" of the sort last year. The uninitiated person, looking at the police returns, would suppose that Omaha's authorities are rigorously virtuous individuals engaged in a great crusade to stamp out vice. The truth is, they have set up a system making prostitution a legalized business, to be conducted like liquor selling under certain regulations, chief of which is the payment to the city of a share of the profits.

PROSTITUTION MONEY FOR EDUCATION.

The entire revenue from prostitution, for the year 1888, is as follows: License fees, or "fines," as they are politely called, $10,330.

The following letter appeared in the Chicago *Standard* (the leading Baptist paper of the Northwest), August 8th, 1889:

"Restrict, does it? On all wet days, when our army of pavers and shovellers cannot work, the saloons are crowded with customers from morning till late into the night. Say, kind reader, can you imagine what forebodings afflict the patient, sorrowing wife whose life is made miserable by the carousals of a drunken husband? Mr. Slocum, the author of the Nebraska High License Law, is dead now, *but he lived long enough to repent of his work,* and was often heard to say that it was *the saddest mistake of his life, and he would never cease to deplore it.* Instead of this law being a promotive of temperance, it has proved itself to be an efficient auxiliary to drunkenness and debauchery.

* * * * * * * *

"'High License' is a fraud.

"S. M. BENEDICT."

LINCOLN, NEB., July 17th, 1889.

We quote further from an address to the people of Nebraska from the State Non-partisan Prohibitory Amendment League:

"*To the People of Nebraska:*

* * * * * * * *

HIGH LICENSE,

has wholly failed to remedy the evils of the liquor traffic. If it has reduced the number of saloons, it has proportionally increased the

---

Costs, $8,178. Total, $18,508. The fines go to the School Fund and the costs to the General Incidental Fund; so that the largest part of the blood money from prostitution is used to educate Omaha's children!

This shows the demoralizing tendency of High License liquor laws. Omaha takes $1,000 each from her saloons and has found it so easy to raise a big revenue from vice that the principle is extended to the social evil.

destructive power of those doing business, by reducing competition and increasing their patronage. Enabled to do so by reason of the monopoly given to them, and urged by the necessity of meeting the payment of large license fees, the saloon men have practised every device to make more attractive their places of business and to increase the number and incite the thirst of drinkers, thus luring to poverty, shame, and crime many young men for whom the cheap groggery has no attractions. By the testimony of the brewers and distillers themselves, High License has not checked the use of intoxicating liquors in Nebraska, while crime, pauperism, insanity, and waste and misery produced by the drink habit, have kept pace with the growth of the population."

Such is the record of High License in its home—in the State of Nebraska, which has tried it longest, and at the highest figures.

We add the following table taken from *The Voice* of January 24th, 1889, whose statements, at the expiration of now more than a year, have never been disproved:

A STARTLING COMPARISON.

THE PROPORTION OF ARRESTS FOR DRUNKENNESS AND DISORDERLY CONDUCT GREATER EVEN IN HIGH-LICENSE THAN IN LOW-LICENSE CITIES.

The following table compares 14 High-License with 15 Low-License cities. In the High-License cities the license fee ranges between $500 and $1,000; in the Low-License cities, between $25 and $200. The figures are for 1887. The table shows:

First. That 14 High-License cities whose license fee averages $710 have a saloon to every 267 persons, and an arrest for drunkenness and disorderly conduct to every 38 persons, which arrests are 57.2 per cent. of the total arrests.

Second. That 15 Low-License cities whose license fee averages $116 have a saloon to every 170 persons, and an arrest for drunkenness and disorderly conduct to every 37 persons, which arrests are 55.6 per cent. of the total arrests. Estimates of population, except as otherwise stated, are from the report of Dunn's Mercantile Agency for 1888:

City. (Facts furnished The Voice direct by the Mayors and Chiefs of Police.)	Population.	License Fee of Ordinary Saloon.	No. Saloons.	No. Population to one Saloon.	Total No. Arrests.	No. Arrests for Drunkenness and Disorderly Conduct.	No. Population to one Arrest for Drunkenness and Disorderly Conduct.	Per Cent. of Arrests for Drunkenness and Disorderly Conduct to Total Arrests.
Omaha	‡100,000	$1,000	246	406	6,125	2,154	46	35
Galesburg	13,500	1,000	17	795	733	643	21	88
*Minneapolis	‡175,000	1,000	240	729	5,876	3,404	51	58
Joliet	20,000	1,000	49	408	1,150	705	28	61
Rockford	22,000	1,000	25	440	401	305	72	76
Kansas City	‡175,000	800	483	362	7,020	3,866	45	49
Bloomington	22,000	600	53	415	877	457	48	52
St. Louis	500,000	550	†1,750	285	17,939	10,441	48	58
Detroit	‡180,000	500	1,100	163	9,400	6,160	29	65
Quincy	34,500	500	110	313	808	449	76	55
Peoria	33,000	500	140	235	1,983	794	41	40
Muskegon	25,000	500	75	333	413	§413	60	§100
Saginaw City	20,000	500	69	290	554	237	84	43
Chicago	900,000	500	8,044	229	46,505	27,632	33	59
New York	‡1,500,000	200	8,016	187	81,176	45,241	33	55
Cleveland	200,000	200	1,500	133	8,568	4,957	40	57
Milwaukee	‡190,000	200	1,098	173	4,401	3,135	61	71
Cincinnati	300,000	200	2,300	130	11,925	5,959	50	49
Columbus	80,000	200	425	188	4,831	2,369	33	49
Poughkeepsie	20,207	125	123	164	489	219	92	44
Wilmington	‡58,000	100	160	362	2,203	1,397	42	61
Brooklyn	‡757,755	100	3,356	226	28,567	14,030	54	49
Binghamton	22,361	90	86	260	1,112	735	30	66
San Francisco	‡305,000	84	2,857	107	20,385	9,368	32	46
Paterson	51,031	75	650	78	2,718	1,690	30	62
Jersey City	‡165,000	50	1,105	149	6,168	1,993	83	32
Yonkers	20,000	50	92	217	1,268	934	21	73
Baltimore	430,000	50	2,500	192	27,200	19,815	24	73
Cohoes	21,480	25	204	105	667	408	52	61
Summary.		Average License.						
14 High-License cities.	2,220,000	$701	8,301	267	100,683	57,660	38	57.2
15 Low-license cities.	4,170,774	116	24,472	170	201,758	112,259	37	55.6

* Partial Prohibition, saloons being confined to a particular district.

† Estimated from half-yearly report.

‡ Estimates furnished the *World Almanac* by the Mayors.

§ In reply to an inquiry as to the reliability of these figures, the following despatch was received :

MUSKEGON, MICH., January 18, 1889.

THE VOICE, 18 & 20 ASTOR PLACE, NEW YORK : Whole number of arrests in 1887, 413 ; of which 361 for drunks and 52 for disorderly conduct and other causes.

JOHN KUPPENHEIMER, *Secretary Board of Police and Health.*

These facts are developed:

1. The license fee is more than six times larger in the High-License than in the Low-License cities.
2. The difference between the *number* of arrests for drunkenness and disorderly conduct is very insignificant.
3. The *proportion* of arrests for drunkenness and disorderly conduct to the total arrests is greater in the High-License than in the Low-License cities.

Changing the place does not change the fact. The following letter was published in *The Voice*, April 18th, 1889. We would call special attention to its very clear and striking financial estimates as well as its testimony to facts:

HIGH LICENSE IN ST. PAUL.

HOW IT INCREASES THE PROFITS OF THE SALOONS, BUT FAILS TO DIMINISH DRINKING.

EDITOR THE VOICE: At first view of High License it is generally accepted that the additional tax is an additional burden on the liquor business. Is this correct? Let us see.

The expense of running any business is to that extent a tax upon the business, and must be deducted from the profits of the trade or business. Now under the low $100 license St. Paul had 700 saloons. When the license was raised to $1,000, the number of saloons was reduced fifty per cent. to 350 in 1888. One-half the saloons dropped out, and the expense of running them ceased to be a tax upon the business.

Now the average expense of running a saloon under the old $100 fee and supporting the saloon-keeper's family, I think no one in this city would place under $1,500 annually. Now, under the $1,000 High License 350 saloons have ceased to draw their support from the profits of the trade. Three hundred and fifty saloons at $1,500 expense each is $525,000—the amount of burden which the liquor traffic in St. Paul was at one stroke relieved of by High License. The additional tax of High License on each remaining saloon was, however, $900, amounting on 350 saloons to $315,000. Now deduct this additional burden of $315,000 from the $525,000 of expense saved to the trade by the stopping of 350 saloons, and the gain to the liquor traffic in St. Paul by the operation of High License is

$210,000, or $600 to each and every remaining saloon in the city! No wonder the saloon-keepers of St. Paul are satisfied with High License.

The same general results of additional profits to the saloon-keepers would be obtained should the license fee be raised still higher, for no one in St. Paul claims that High License has in any way decreased the quantity of liquor consumed.

If High License reduced the amount of liquor sold or drunk, there would be some compensation in it to society, but evidence is accumulating from all High License States, and especially from the large cities, what we know to be the case in St. Paul and Minneapolis, that crime and all immorality were never so rife as now. As to the restrictive sections of the High License law, they are not at all regarded nor enforced in a single instance, as was said by the Rev. S. G. Smith, the champion of High License in this city, in his late speech before the Legislative Assembly.

But the thought I wish to emphasize is, that the more you curtail the number of saloons, the more you increase the profits of the trade in any locality, for the amount of business done not only continues the same, but is steadily on the increase, proving that nothing but Prohibition can at all reach the case as a remedy.

A. D. DAVISON.

ST. PAUL, MINN.

The following statements about the High License cities of St. Louis, Kansas City, and St. Joseph, are from the St. Louis *Republic* for May 2d, 1889:

In St. Louis the license business is all transacted by the Collector. He is bound by the law to observe certain very strict rules. But the lawless saloons, by means of their political influence, compel him to evade them all.

Under the Missouri law, every would-be saloon-keeper must present to the Collector a petition signed by a majority of the assessed tax-paying citizens of the block. The Collector, instead of investigating the signatures to a petition, simply takes the sworn statement of the applicant and then passes out the license. "If somebody discovers afterward," says the *Republic*, "that half of the names on the petition are also on the gravestones in Bellefontaine Cemetery, that is a small matter; the license has been issued and the city has the money."

The *Republic* gives additional information about the failure of this restrictive petition revision, as follows:

"Every effort but one which has been made in three years past to prevent saloons, by preventing a legal petition, has failed. *It is not at all improbable that half of the saloons open in this city to-day are licensed on insufficient petitions.* Saloons are frequently opened and run for several weeks, and, in some instances, for several months, with neither petition nor license. A saloon-keeper is usually given the same liberty in the matter of the payment of his license that is given a merchant in the payment of merchants' tax, notwithstanding the fact that the High License of $550 is supposed to be a regulatory tax, imposed to prevent the multiplicity of saloons as much as to raise a revenue from them."

The following striking description of the methods of the brewers' monopoly of St. Louis is given by the *Republic*:

"It is known by those who have taken the trouble to investigate the subject that more than one-half of the saloons of the city are opened and operated by the breweries, and used as agencies for thrusting on the market the beer they manufacture, thus creating a demand, instead of merely supplying a natural demand, for intoxicants. Every new neighborhood is promptly supplied with a beer saloon. If some enterprising citizen erects a big factory to employ a large number of mechanics and workmen, the brewer has a beer saloon open at the side door or just across the street before the manufacturer has finished his building or engaged his employés. The Hamilton-Brown Shoe Company have just finished one of the largest shoe factories in the West. The machinery is not yet in working order, but a brewer has already opened a saloon on Lucus Place, next to the magnificent building, where every employé can stop and get a glass of beer, or procure a bucketful at the dinner hour. Of course this is very annoying to the gentlemen who have freely invested their money in a great industrial enterprise, for they must feel quickly the demoralizing effect of the drinking thus superinduced; but they have no remedy. The saloon is there. They could only complain. The brewer has the 'pull,' and the saloon is hard to put down.

"These saloons are first fitted up in elegant style by the brewers, then some fellow who, in all probability, couldn't pay a month's rent or secure a petition or a bond, is put in charge as 'proprietor.' The brewery then sends an agent around the block to get a few names on a petition. (The saloon has been opened and stocked with liquors already, but as it is nobody's business nobody minds that). The petition is filed with the Collector, and accompanied by an affidavit that it is all right. The Collector takes it without question, and Mr. Brewer or his agent pays six months' license for the 'proprietor.' The aforesaid lucky 'proprietor' is then a full-fledged saloon-keeper, and it does not take long for him to blossom out as a ward politician with 'influence.' But the brewer holds an iron-clad mortgage on the saloon and everything in it. While the saloonist is living off the profits made on the wines and liquors he sells, the brewer is paying off his own account on the proceeds of beer sales. It is safe to say that half of the saloons in the city have been opened in that way. About two-thirds of all the bonds of saloon-keepers are signed by the brewers. It is in this way that they maintain an almost absolute control over the saloon interests and can dominate this powerful political agency as they please."

The license fee in St. Louis is $550. Other cities of Missouri have even higher license rates, notably Kansas City ($850) and St. Joseph ($750). The *Republic* declares the same demoralizing tendencies prevail there, and that the liquor interests are absolute masters of the situation in both Kansas City and St. Joseph. It says:

"What affects this city of half a million people affects largely the whole State ; but the evil is not to be appreciated as far as the State is concerned, without taking into calculation *the cities of St. Joseph and Kansas City also, where exactly the same methods are employed and the same plans are productive of increased intemperance, too many saloons and beer bossism in politics.* One very convincing proof of the dangerous power of this saloon system is seen in the fact that the Representatives of these three cities in the Legislature are (with two or three notable exceptions) all arrayed aginst the only measure which strikes at the evil and proposes to put it under control. In fact, the strong opposition to all temperance and reform laws comes from the same source."

But we are assured that High License has done good in Pennsylvania. It reduced the number of saloons in Philadelphia 4,000 in a single year. It has reduced them to about 1,200 for the whole city for the year 1889. It has reduced the number of arrests for drunkenness and disorder. It has reduced the number of saloons in Pittsburgh to 93 for the same year.

This is the claim. But it is a very suspicious one. Why should High License work so differently in Pennsylvania from what it does everywhere else? Is it in some way connected with the character and disposition of William Penn? Let us sift the matter a little. The doctors have a distinction on which they lay great stress, between *post hoc* and *propter hoc*—that is, whether one thing simply follows another or is caused by it. A good lady stated that her digestion had reached such a point, that, as she said, "I can't even eat bread. Why, this afternoon I crawled out into the kitchen and ate a piece of bread and a raw onion, and that bread has been distressing me ever since."

There was apparently a certain lack of discrimination in her case. So in regard to the Brooks Law. It does provide for a High License (not very high) of $500. Therefore every good result is due to that High License. This has been the argument obstinately persisted in and sent far and wide over the country for the past two years. But what are the facts? The Brooks Law has a bondsman clause making it necessary for two owners of real estate in the immediate neighborhood to be bondsmen for the saloon-keeper in $2,000, that he will sell strictly according to law—*i.e.*, not to inebriates, not to minors, not on Sunday, etc. This provision would go a good way toward stopping the offences for which arrests are made, AND THIS PROVISION WOULD BE EXACTLY AS GOOD AND EFFECTIVE IF THE SALOON-KEEPER DID NOT PAY ONE CENT OF LICENSE. Then the judges to whom the licensing power is given are invested with a large discretion. They are men of high character, and have used that power of refusal to the utmost. It is chiefly this discretionary power which has reduced the number of licenses. In Philadelphia last spring 3,212 applications for licenses were filed, being 2,000 more than were granted the preceding year. Undoubtedly these applicants all stood ready to pay the $500, and but for the discretionary power of the judges, Philadelphia would now have the 3,000 saloons, instead of the 1,200 which they actually licensed. In Pittsburgh, the rejected applicants say with amusing unanimity, "It was not the $500, but Judge White."

But they will not be troubled in that way much longer. Eleven days after the defeat of the Prohibitory Amendment the Supreme Court virtually abolished the discretionary power of the judges, so that it is now obligatory upon them to issue licenses to many applicants whom they would have once refused.* Now a great cry is rising from Pennsylvania because of this decision. But why ? *They still have High License.* We have been told all this time that it was High License that was keeping down the number of saloons. Let it go on keeping them down! A citizen of Germantown is quoted as saying, "Up to this time we have had but one saloon on this side of the

---

* 310 licenses have been granted in Pittsburgh for 1890. The number in Philadelphia is not known at the time this book goes to press.

ward, but under this decision next year we shall have them by the score." But they still have the High License. It is just as high as ever. The Supreme Court decision has not touched the license. Let us, then, have a fair and honest confession at last that *it has not been the High License that was doing the work*, which has been so persistently attributed to it. The good has been done chiefly by that discretionary power of the judges which this decision practically annuls, and *not* by the High License, which still continues in force, though all Pennsylvania now admits it cannot do the work.

From whatever cause, the number of arrests for drunkenness and crime are now rapidly increasing in the cities of Pennsylvania. Whether arrests were avoided before the vote on the Prohibitory Amendment, or whether the saloon-keepers have become more reckless since its defeat, these are the facts (we quote from the *Political Prohibitionist* of 1889):

" It is not, however, the effect of the Brooks Law in decreasing the number of saloons that is to be taken as the test of the temperance value of the measure. To ascertain whether it operated to promote temperance, the police records of the various cities must be studied. Let us first examine the records in the only two counties where there was a very large reduction in the number of saloons—Philadelphia and Allegheny counties—the first including the city of Philadelphia, and the second including the cities of Pittsburgh and Allegheny.

PHILADELPHIA, PITTSBURGH, AND ALLEGHENY.

" The Brooks Law took effect in Philadelphia June 1st, 1888. The following comparative figures are furnished by Joshua L. Baily : *

---

* Mr. Baily was very prominently connected with the efforts to secure the restrictions of the Brooks Law. He has carefully watched its workings in Philadelphia. He said in *The Voice* for January 31st, 1889 :

" That there has been a diminution in drunkenness or in the consumption of liquors at all in proportion to the decrease in the num-

Commitments to County Prison in corresponding months of 1887 and 1888 :

	1887.	1888.	Decrease in 1888.
June	2,737	1,563	1,174
July	2,728	1,645	1,083
August	2,736	1,817	919
September	2,755	1,904	851
October	2,598	1,526	1,072
Total	13,554	8,455	5,099

Commitments to House of Correction in corresponding months of 1887 and 1888 :

	1887.	1888	Decrease in 1888.
June	490	320	170
July	502	281	221
August	590	495	95
September	540	380	160
October	631	437	194
Total	2,663	1,823	840

The number of Sunday commitments to the Philadelphia County Prison, as officially reported on the following Monday mornings, were :

June 1, 1887, to Nov. 1, 1887.................. 679
June 1, 1888, to Nov. 1, 1888.................. 194

Decrease under the restraining act............ 485

ber of saloons no one would have the temerity to claim. Indeed, there is an absence of proof that there has been any diminution whatever in the consumption of liquors, while it is conceded on all sides that the parties holding the licenses, with perhaps a very few exceptions, are doing a greatly-increased business, many of them having doubled and some of them increased their sales many fold. They are enjoying a monopoly, and there are many of them who would rather pay a largely increased license fee than have that monopoly infringed. The efforts to have the present law repealed or essentially modified do not come from this class, but come mostly from those who have been shut out of the business and who desire to regain the licenses of which they have been deprived. . . . I have thus endeavored to show the character and purposes of the restraining act of 1887, and its results, as far as I have been able to ascertain them. I think it must be apparent that whatever good has come from the law is to be attributed to its restraining—shall I not say prohibitory ?—features, and that there is no ground whatever for the claim that some have set up, that these good results have been reached through High License."

The commitments of women were:

June 1, 1887, to Nov. 1, 1887..................... 74
June 1, 1888, to Nov. 1, 1888..................... 21

Decrease 53

"Apparently a large decrease of crime was effected in the city of Philadelphia. But was it really the Brooks Law that wrought the change, and are the Philadelphia figures to be accepted as modifying the unfavorable testimony from other High License cities? If so, similar and even greater changes for the better ought to have been accomplished in Pittsburgh and Allegheny, for the restrictions of the Brooks Law were applied more rigidly there than in Philadelphia.

"But the official figures for Pittsburgh, furnished by the authorities of that city, show as follows:

Year.	License fee.	No. of saloons.	Total arrests.	Arrests for drunkenness.
1887	$100–300*	1,500†	8,565	1,914
1888	500	244	10,443	2,123
Incr. in '88	400–200	1,256†decr.	1,878	199

And the figures for Allegheny also show an actual increase in the total number of arrests as well as in the arrests for drunkenness and disorderly conduct. These figures are furnished by Henry Huntshager, Mayor's Clerk:

Year.	License fee.	No. of saloons.	Total arrests.	Arrests for drunkenness.	Arrests for disorderly conduct.
1883	$100–300‡	...	1,992	723	841
1884	100–300‡	...	2,945	780	1,042
1885	100–300‡	...	2,868	794	1,114
1886	100–300‡	...	2,575	790	1,030
1887	100–300‡	363	3,081	918	1,321
Average for above five years:					
	$100–300‡	...	2,692	801	1,069
1888	500	78	3,042	894	1,192
Incr. in '88	400–200	285 decr.	350	93	123

"During the year following the great reduction in the number of saloons in Pittsburgh and Allegheny, the Pittsburgh newspapers frequently spoke of the great increase of unlawful selling and of the failure of the law to diminish drunkenness. The Pittsburgh *Commercial Gazette* said, December 13th, 1888:

---

* $100 for beer only; $300 for strong liquors.   † Approximate.
‡ $100 for beer saloons; $300 for strong liquors.

"'The magnitude of the illegal liquor traffic is really astonishing. There is scarcely an alley or a side street in any of the wards of the lower part of the city, as well as on the South Side, that does not contain from one to twenty groggeries, where beer and whiskey are sold in defiance of the law. To publish a complete list of these "saloons" would require several columns of an ordinary-sized newspaper. A legalized seller when asked yesterday if he was aware of the violations going on, said : "Yes, certainly I am, but what am I going to do about it? I paid the county $500 to protect my business, but yet I see men selling all around me without license. *I can't inform on them because such a course would injure my trade.* The people who sympathize with the lawbreakers would not patronize me if I made a fuss over the unjustness of my having to pay for what others are doing without paying.'"

The same paper said, April 8th, 1889 :

"'If the drunkenness yesterday [Sunday] can be taken as a standard, more drunkenness is visible to the church-goer, as well as others, on Sunday than in the days of low license and free whiskey, and this in the face of the fact that the police are vigilant and determined to crush out the "speak-easies." There were a good many drunken men on the streets of Allegheny last night. They staggered along in pairs, and people wondered how they got their whiskey on Sunday.'

RESULTS IN OTHER CITIES.*

"In all the other cities of Pennsylvania that have been heard from intemperance and crime have increased under the Brooks Law.

"*Scranton.*—B. R. Wade, Chief of Police of Scranton, reports for his city as follows :

Year.		Total arrests.	No. of arrests for drunkenness.	Disorderly conduct.
1883	Low License.	864	720	22
1884	"	938	795	24
1885	"	1,400	537	139
1886	"	1,465	1,090	86
1887	"	1,266†	999†	71†
1888	High License.	1,860	1,396	111

"A glance shows that the increase of arrests in Scranton under High License has been frightful. Before the Brooks Law went into effect the license fee in that city was only $60 for hotels and $20 for restaurants. Then in 1888 a uniform fee of $300 was charged—five times as much as the highest former rate. But the arrests in the High License year of 1888, as compared with the last full year of Low

---

* For further information see *The Voice* for May 30th, 1889.
† Nine months only.

License (1886), show the following percentages of increase: Total arrests, twenty-seven per cent.; arrests for drunkenness, twenty-eight per cent.; arrests for disorderly conduct, thirty-nine per cent.

"*Wilkesbarre.*—The Wilkesbarre *Record* gives the following comparative figures of arrests in that city for two Low License years and two High License years, each year ending on the 31st of March:

	Low License.		High License.	
	1886.	1887.	1888.	1889.
Total arrests	1,846	1,711	2,072	1,844
" " (males)	1,688	1,560	1,876	1,690
" " (females)	157	151	196	854
Drunk	624	660	1,084	766
Disorderly	580	446	429	400
Assault	212	189	239	234

"*Lancaster.*—The Chief of Police of this city recently sent a letter to the Philadelphia *Press* (printed in that paper February 24th, 1889), in which he said:

"'Crime is seemingly on the increase as our population increases. Drunkenness and petty larceny are prevalent offences. Prostitution is on the increase. Drunkenness among women is on the increase. We find by experience that we have much trouble with young men and girls under or about arriving at age, who are intoxicated and disorderly on our streets, through receiving intoxicating drinks, not from licensed saloons, but in hell-holes known here as "beer clubs," or in houses where beer is delivered in quantities. Many of these young people are frequently of very respectable parents. We have time and again asked young girls, when having them under arrest, the cause of their condition, and invariably the answer has been "drink."'

"*Reading.*—Chief of Police Mahlon Shaaber, in *The Voice* for April 18th, 1889, gave the following statistics:"

Year.	Total arrests.	No. of arrests for drunkenness.	Disorderly conduct.
1883 Low License.	1,141	257	226
1884 "	1,088	374	228
1885 "	1,145	378	135
1886 "	1,194	575	83
1887 "	1,107	399	100
1888 High License.	1,346	358	120

The latest information on the subject comes from the Agent of the Law and Order League, under date of January 5th, 1890, as follows:

PITTSBURGH'S 700 "SPEAK-EASIES."
THE AGENT OF THE LAW AND ORDER LEAGUE ON THE WORKINGS OF THE BROOKS LAW.

There are just 92 licensed saloons in Pittsburgh paying the $500 fee under the Brooks High License Law, but it is not an easy matter to give the exact number of "speak-easies" or unlicensed saloons in operation, for the reason that the business of these is conducted with such caution and secrecy that it is almost impossible to gain entrance to them unless introduced by some of their regular patrons or through detectives cunning in ascertaining their raps and passwords or obtaining keys when they are distributed to customers.

As the Agent of the Law and Order League, and as a licensed detective empowered to employ detectives, I have prosecuted about 150 proprietors of "speak-easies" since May 1st, 1888, for selling on Sunday, a fine of $50 and costs being imposed under the Act of 1855, which, providentially, was not repealed by the Brooks High License Law. Many of these quit the business. Others continued selling, and were prosecuted under the Brooks Act, but the composition of our grand juries is such that nearly all the bills were ignored and the costs imposed upon me. One or two, however, languish in the workhouse as a result of these prosecutions.

But to return to the subject. The police authorities of the city, through Inspector McAleese, claim that they have a list of over 700 "speak easies" with the locations and testimony to convict, but, dog-in-the-manger like, they will neither prosecute themselves nor furnish the information to any one who will. These "speak-easies" flourish under the guise of "boarding," "rooms to let," grocery stores, and in cellars, garrets, and stables, and run very secretly.

We are in a most deplorable state. Our county detective announces annually or oftener that he is just getting ready to wipe out the "speak easies," but we never hear of any results. Our police are the creatures of a ring whose political power is perpetuated by the liquor element, and, as a consequence, when it does strike a blow at the unlicensed liquor-dealer it is generally directed against a man who has no political pull or a poor woman. One word from the Chief of the Department of Public Safety would exterminate the "speak-easy," but the ring, whose creature he is, says to him, "Thus far shalt thou go, but no farther."

From the Brooks Law or any other license law, high or low, good Lord, deliver us.

A. WISHART, *Agent Law and Order League.*

With this showing of the results of the Brooks Law, the star example of the benefits of High License, we are content to rest our case; and we protest that nowhere on the face of the earth has High License yet been shown to have value as a restriction in reducing the evils of intemperance.

Many thoughtful people still have one ground of incredulity regarding such statements, even when the evidence is perfectly clear. "How is it possible?" they exclaim. "We can see how the fewer saloons may, perhaps, sell as much liquor. But how can they sell more? Above all, how is it conceivable that they should produce *more* drunkenness?"

Well, we think we can explain even that. Let us take the dry-goods business for an illustration. Now, in any city reduce the number of establishments one half —not by decay of trade, but by sharp legal enactment. Those that remain will at once double their business. They will not nearly double their expenses. They will have a splendid margin of profit. They will have the power of concentrated capital. They will begin to introduce more elegant goods in greater variety. The lady who goes in to make some simple purchase finds herself in the midst of an animated scene. All around her are goods whose very sight is a temptation. Among the crowd are friends admiring and buying. The increased variety, the better assortment, are attractive. The probability is that, if she has the money, she will buy far more than she thought of doing. A country pastor walked with the writer through a great metropolitan dry-goods store. On coming out, he said: "I don't know how it is, but my wife and I came here one morning and spent about $15, and when we got home we made up our minds that if we had gone to our little home store we should have spent less money, and while we might not have bought such elegant things, we should have got more nearly what we wanted. The abundance and elegance here are bewildering."

So it is in the High License saloon. The closing of many throws the whole trade into the number that remain. As shown in the St. Paul letter before quoted, the increased expense, including the license, bears no proportion to the increased trade. All observers agree that the saloons soon begin to "put on a great deal of style." They introduce plate-glass, carving and gilding, oil paintings and bevelled mirrors and skilled musicians. In the evening they are all ablaze with light. The man not caring very much for a drink, who would pass by the poor, plain saloon, or, if he went in, simply take a drink and pass on, is attracted by all this glare and glitter. In that crowd he is pretty sure to find friends. He steps in for just one drink. There is merry talk and cheer all around him. It is pleasant to stay. First one acquaintance asks him to drink, then another. He is introduced to new acquaintances, and must drink with them. After drinking with one it is a slight and an affront not to drink with another. After being "treated," it is stingy not to "treat." The man who went in for one drink takes a dozen and comes out drunk. Perhaps as the stimulant mounts to his brain he quarrels with some one. In a great, drinking crowd there is always likely to be some man "fighting drunk." Then there is "disorderly conduct," and, perhaps, a murder. In a word, the more attractive the saloons are made, the worse they are. Thousands of men—and, what is worse, thousands of boys—who would pass the "doggeries" with utter scorn will be drawn into the gilded saloon, and where the crowd is thickest, temptations to intoxication are thickest, too. Thus it is easy to see why the arrests for drunkenness and disorderly conduct should be more numerous in High License than in Low License cities, as the official reports show that they are. As regards reducing the evils of intemperance, High License does not restrict.

CHAPTER VI.

HIGH LICENSE AND THE CONSUMER.

" The tax on spirits oppresses no one. IT IS PAID ONLY BY THE CONSUMER."—*James G. Blaine, Letter to the Philadelphia Press, November 22d, 1882.*

" Who pays the license? OF COURSE THE CONSUMER! For the big and rich marble palace tavern-keeper, it [High License] is a sort of additional revenue. He can easily charge five cents more for whiskey. That gives him for every one hundred drinks sold $5, while his daily license at the rate of $500 is but $1.66, and of $1,000 but $3.32. Of course no whiskey-drinker will object to pay five cents more for a drink under High License. That explains why not a few of the tavern-keepers favor High License."—*Washington Sentinel (Brewers' Organ), March 3d, 1888.*

THAT the consumer does pay the entire liquor tax or license, as the above quotations show, appears further from the frequent argument that to repeal the United States tax would be " to flood the country with cheap whiskey"—that is to say, it is the tax which keeps it from being cheap now. The producer having to pay a tax, gets it out of the consumer by raising the price of the product. It is the same with the State assessments. All the liquor-seller pays or has to pay is what he gets from those who buy of him.

Mike Mulligan, newly landed, starts a saloon on $50 borrowed from his cousin who has been here a little longer. Soon he repays the loan, then buys the building, then a corner lot, builds him a house, and has money to lend. Where has it all come from? Out of the pockets of the poor fellows who have drunk at his bar; out of the mouths and the very life of their wives and children. Every cent the State can wring from him comes from the same source. When it collects its High License revenue, then, the State is gathering in the food which the drunkard's wife and children should eat, the shoes which should cover their bare and bleeding feet, the fuel which should warm their chilly rooms, the bedding which should cover them in the bitter nights. Some have argued that this is cruel. But there is another consideration. It is unprofitable.

IT DESTROYS THE WEALTH-PRODUCING QUALITIES

of a people. The very thing that makes slave labor unprofitable is that the slave has no motive. His coarse clothing and daily hoe-cake are all he will get anyway. Passing through Baltimore early in the war, the writer saw a negro sawing wood with such imperceptible motions that the Yankee boy burst out, "Why, I never saw a man work so slowly in all my life. I don't see how he can." My father answered, "That man is a slave. It's of no use for him to work any faster; he would make nothing if he did." Hence the paralysis of slavery.

Hence, too, the paralysis of drink. All the inspiration a man's home might be to him it ceases to be, and becomes an oppression and a reproach when he has made it wretched. There is little to rouse the patriot in the old heroic stanza if you make it read,

> Strike for your tenement rooms without fires!
> Strike for the wife that in rags retires,
> Strike for the babe that starving expires,
> Saloons and a License Land!

When many families have reached this point, opportunities of work are offered in vain. A correspondent of the New York *Tribune*, of May 16th, 1883, writing from Sheffield, England, where, he says, beer is easier to get than water, writes as follows :

HOW THE WORKMEN LIVE.

Said Dr. Webster, who has been United States Consul at Sheffield for twelve years :

" People earning their pounds a week are actually contented to live year after year, perhaps, without a bedstead, and in just such homes as you have described."

" How do you account for this ?" I inquired.

" The workmen here," he replied, " do not have the same ambition that our artisans at home have. They have no desire to rise. If they can get enough to keep them in bacon, bread, and *beer* they are content. They indulge in betting and *drinking*. For instance, the grinders are a well-paid class of men, and just now the hollow-grinding branch of that business is having a boom. They could easily earn £3 a week. But they won't work. Saint Monday must be kept, and Saturday very little work is done, and the result is, as a large manufacturer told me the other day, that the employers are obliged to send thousands of dozens of razors to Germany in blank to be ground, while Sheffield men are *drinking*, dog-fighting, and betting. They seem to have but little care for the future. Many of them contribute to a burial society and a sick fund, and they know that if the worst comes to the worst the workhouse stands ready to receive them."

Such is a people from whom all motive, except the desire for intoxicants, has perished.

For this state of things increasing wages bring no relief. Of the working people of England, Mrs. Mary Bayly writes : *

" The five years which preceded 1877 were a time of unusual prosperity in the way of earning money ; work was comparatively plentiful and wages high. During those years *the increase in the consumption of intoxicating drink was enormous;* the home consumption of

---

* Gustafson, " Foundation of Death," p. 252.

cotton goods *went down* eight per cent. Those who watched the homes of the poor during those dreadful years state that their moral condition then fell to a lower point than had ever been known before. There were happy exceptions not a few; but to the vast majority the large sums earned brought rather a diminution than an increase of all that is worthy the name of prosperity."

How bitter to wives and children must have been those increased earnings with no increase of comfort, but only increased degradation of the bread-winner instead!

The *National Labor Tribune* says:

"The injurious effects of intemperance on industry are found by investigation to be extinction of disposition for practising any useful art or industrious occupation. Such, indeed, will be found to be the universal tendency of this vice. Those who indulge in strong drink have little inclination or even capacity for improvement. Selfishness and apathy predominate in the character of the drunkard, and feelings of amendment, however frequently they may arise, are quickly dissipated in the love of sensual gratification."

In this traffic the consumer should be called the consumee. It is the man that is consumed, and not the liquor. Alcohol burns the red corpuscles from the blood, the grip from the muscles, the iron steadiness from the nerves; and, with a certain Satanic selection, paralyzes and dries up the highest and finest nerve-centers of the brain till love, hope, ambition, energy, enterprise fade. Above all, the majestic will power dies, and such gleams of good as remain are powerless for want of that controlling energy to put them into action and hold them to the mark. No man accomplishes anything great without an intense determination that lasts through day and night, through months and years. But intemperance is the death of determination. This was, perhaps, never more forcibly expressed than in the words of the brilliant and gifted Charles Lamb:

"The waters have gone over me; but out of the black depths could I be heard, I would cry out to all those who have but set a foot in the perilous flood. Could the youth to whom the flavor of his first wine is delicious as the opening scenes of life, or the entering upon some newly-discovered paradise, look into my desolation, and be made to understand what a dreary thing it is when a man shall feel himself going down a precipice with open eyes and a passive will; to see his destruction and have no power to stop it, yet feel it all the way emanating from himself; to see all godliness emptied out of him, and yet not be able to forget a time when it was otherwise; to bear about him the piteous spectacle of his own ruin; could he see my fevered eye—feverish with last night's drinking and feverish for to-night's repetition of the folly; could he but feel the body of death out of which I cry—hourly with feebler outcry—to be delivered; it were enough to make him dash the sparkling beverage to the earth in all the pride of its mantling temptation."

No, do not think we are going to be pathetic! We simply want to make the point that intemperance strikes at the root of wealth-production. To this we have important industrial testimony. After Massachusetts, in 1867, repealed her prohibitory law and substituted license, Oliver Ames & Son, of North Easton, testified: "We have over 400 men in our works here. We find the present license law has a very bad effect upon them. Comparing our products in May and June, 1868, with our manufactures for the same months of 1867, we find we produced eight per cent. more goods with 315 men that year than with 400 men in the same months of 1868. We attribute this falling off entirely to the repeal of the prohibitory law and the present greatly increased use of intoxicating liquors."

Intemperance also destroys the spirit and habit of self-denial—the spring of wealth. It is an old story that it is not so much what a man earns as what he saves that makes him rich or poor. Even Mr. Micawber understood the philosophy which he could never practise.

"'My other piece of advice,' said Mr. Micawber, 'Copperfield, you know. Annual income twenty pounds, annual expenditure nineteen, nineteen six; result, happiness. Annual income twenty pounds, annual expenditure twenty pounds ought and six; result, misery. The blossom is blighted, the leaf is withered, the god of day goes down upon the dreary scene, and—and, in short, you are forever floored. As I am!'

"To make his example the more impressive, Mr. Micawber drank a glass of punch with an air of great enjoyment and satisfaction, and whistled the College Hornpipe."

It is worth noticing that Dickens, who was by no means a temperance man, but painted men as he saw them, always represents Mr. Micawber in the crises of his experience, when his financial affairs were at some desperate pass, with a bottle sticking out of his pocket or brewing a delicious punch on—somebody's—table.

Saving requires self-denial, and intemperance is the death of self-denial, and renders the intemperate man at length incapable of practising it in any form or for the shortest possible time. He would give his life or his soul for a drink. Of this *The London Tid-Bits* gives the following striking illustration:

A COSTLY "BEER."

A GLASS FOR AN IDEA WHICH HAS PAID $200,000 SO FAR.

Two hundred thousand dollars may seem a large sum for a small article, but it was virtually paid by a man of great resources who had an ingenious expedient for saving the horseflesh of the world. About ten years ago a veterinary surgeon, who was with the army at Bombay, found that the excessive heat of that country caused the tops of the horses' necks to sweat freely, and thereby produce sores under the leather collar. All the expedients that he could suggest were of no avail to remedy this state of things. One-fourth of the horses used for draught purposes were laid up by what is called "sore neck."

This "vet." in his younger days had studied chemistry, and he found that sulphate of zinc was the best and almost only cure for horses' "sore necks," but the difficulty in applying this preparation lay in the fact that the horses had to rest during the time of its application, otherwise the collar would rub it off, and there was no chance for the horse's recovery. A thought struck him that to make a zinc pad and fit it under the collar would, at any rate, prove an ameliorative, and maybe cure. The man, though ingenious in his way, was much given to drink, and was looked upon by the officers of the army as a "ne'er-do-weel" with bright ideas. While this was simmering in his mind and before he had put it into an actual test he happened to be in a drinking bar.

His finances at this time were at the lowest ebb, for his future was mortgaged for all it was worth, and the publican refused to trust him with any more drinks. An American drummer happened to be representing a large leather house, and knew a good deal of the difficulty with which the American farmers of the Southwest had to contend. The two men got into conversation, and, as a natural result, the veterinary surgeon spoke of the idea that was uppermost in his mind, and said that he thought he knew of a remedy for that most troublesome complaint from which all horses in hot countries suffered. The American was perfectly convinced that he was talking to a man of good ideas though bad principles, and asked what he would take for the idea.

"I am awfully hard up and can get no more drink on trust, so I will give you the idea for a glass of beer."

"Done!" said the other.

The American at once saw there was probably millions in this, and he conceived the notion that the matter oozing from the sores on horses' necks would corrode the pad and produce sulphate of zinc—thus the disease would provide its own remedy. He also saw that zinc, being a non-conductor of heat, would keep the parts cool. The more he thought of it the more he liked it, and although his business should have kept him in Bombay some months longer, he in a few days took the first steamship to Liverpool and then to Boston. Arriving in Boston, he threw up his appointment with the house and started the manufacturing of zinc pads, after obtaining a patent for the idea, and he is now worth $200,000. These zinc pads are used in every country on earth, and are the greatest blessing the farmer enjoys.

The story bears the appearance of truth, and all who

have seen much of drinking men have known those of whom it might easily have been true.

The following forcible words of Dr. Thomas Guthrie, of Scotland, are taken from his Memoirs, Vol. I., pp. 378-879.

"Seven years of my ministry were spent in one of the lowest localities of Edinburgh; and it almost broke my heart, day by day, to see, as I wandered from house to house, and from room to room, misery, wretchedness, and crime; the detestable vice of drunkenness, the cause of all, meeting me at every turn and marring all my efforts. Nothing ever struck me more, in visiting those wretched localities, than to find that more than half of these families were in the church-yard. The murder of innocent infants in this city by drunkenness 'out-Herods Herod.' I believe we will in vain plant churches and schools, though they be thick as trees in the forest, until this evil is stopped."

Let any one say what (that is worthy of the name of civilization) may be expected of a man with a drunken wife, or a child with a drunken mother. It must be remembered that a good wife is also a wealth-producer, and most truly so when she gives her whole time to the care of home, husband, and children. Mrs. Bayly, in the same letter previously referred to, says:

"I have persuaded very many women to give up all paid labor and to devote themselves entirely to their families. I can recall no instance where this change was not advantageous, even pecuniarily, for the waste and destruction caused by neglected children are indescribable. Where the wife has to earn money the children are usually in rags. Just a few indispensable articles of clothing are purchased ready-made at a slop-shop, at a price so low one wonders how anything can have been paid for making up. The mother at home can encourage honest trade by buying decent material which she makes up herself. But how is all this possible while thousands and thousands of pounds are swept into the publicans' tills every Saturday and Sunday night?"

In his papers on "How the Poor Live," published

during the summer of 1883 in the *Pictorial World*, Mr. George R. Sims says :

" The gin palaces flourish in the slums, and fortunes are made out of men and women who seldom know where to-morrow's meal is coming from. . . . A copper or two, often obtained by pawning the last rag that covers the shivering children on the bare floor at home, will buy enough vitriol madness to send a woman home so besotted that the wretchedness, the anguish, the degradation that await her there have lost their grip."

When Macaulay's "historian from New Zealand shall take his stand on a broken arch of London Bridge to sketch the ruins of St. Paul," what a story he will have to tell of the cause of the ruin ! How future centuries will wonder at the tolerated barbarities of the nineteenth !

Rich and poor alike should consider that the destruction of the wealth-producing qualities which we have shown to be due to intemperance is, from an economic standpoint,

THE DEADLIEST INJURY THAT CAN BE DONE TO A PEOPLE.

It is a deadlier injury than even the actual slaughter of the people. The first Napoleon drained France of men, till in his late campaigns he had to implore his War Department, " Send me no more boys."

But they were all they had to send. Yet if the destruction once stops—if the war is ever over—the men are soon replaced. Ten years makes every boy of ten a man. It is the standing wonder of political economists how soon a land recovers from desolating war, if only an industrious, enterprising people are left. Look at our own South after the Civil War. Look at France after the Franco-German War, not only desolated by conquest, but compelled to pay an indemnity of a thousand millions for the privilege of being desolated. Yet in a brief term of years the indemnity was paid, and France under republican institutions on the way to a better prosperity than she had known without war under the empire. But if the wealth-producing qualities are once destroyed, vain is the perfection of climate, vain the fertility of the soil. Some of the fairiest lands on earth lie desolate under Turkish misrule. Egypt, once the granary of the world, is now tramped by the miserable Fellaheen, barely owning a waist-cloth and a rice-kettle. False methods of revenue more than all else have done it. The Sultan and the Khedive have kept up their rude magnificence by the desolation of their people, till they can no longer do that, but have had to mortgage their kingdoms to the bankers of Europe. No nation can live by eating out its own vitals, for the time will come when it will need what it has been eating, and there is no provision in the universe for supplying vitals to order. When they are once consumed, a nation, like an individual, must take the consequences.

In the case of intoxicants, we have also to face this further danger that

THE CONSUMER WILL BECOME A DESTROYER.

The *National Temperance Advocate* says:

" The recent formidable mobs of the unemployed in London have an ominous significance. The drink waste in Great Britain is enormous, and nothing is more natural under such circumstances than that there should be great poverty and suffering. A recent report shows that the poor guardians of London have 91,000 paupers on the parish rolls compared with 71,000 for the corresponding month last year. This shows that the London 'prisoners of poverty' are increasing at a rapid rate. Beer and bad trade are closely linked together. Abolish the one and the other would quickly improve. It is impossible for the people of any country to waste their substance as largely as in Great Britain for strong drink and not have legitimate industries greatly paralyzed thereby."

In our neglected slums are generated the pestilence, the pauper, and the criminal—worst of all the pauper and criminal by hereditary descent, born to the inheritance, and not to be lifted out—a savage race begotten in the very heart of civilization, forever a drain upon the resources of the industrious and the good, a standing menace to the perpetuity of nations and of civilization, a peril to every life and every home. The Anarchists of Chicago met in saloons to prepare for the fatal Haymarket massacre. They meet in saloons now, planning to avenge their comrades who met the penalty of the law. The saloon constantly comes to the front in the Cronin murder trial of the same city. The *Standard* says:

"The saloons of Chicago were a conspicuous figure in the Cronin trial. In the history of this detestable crime it played an important part, as in all other like cases. It is there that murder is planned, and thither murderers resort when the deed is done, to drown in drink any slight pain of conscience they may feel. But this inevitable stain upon our civilization has revealed itself in a new way. A poor washerwoman had a story to tell of overhearing the last words of the murdered physician, his cry to God and Jesus, as he fell under the blows which met him as he entered the fatal door. The attempt to discredit her testimony brought to light some of her own sorrowful history. We quote from the published record:

"'Q.—You were asked by the lawyer for the defence if you had trouble with your husband. Will you tell the jury what the trouble was? [Objected to, overruled, and exception taken.] A.—My husband had lots of money in his pocket about April 1st. I went to Ertel and said to him: 'Don't give my husband any more drink here.' He got mad and took his revolver and drove me out. I ran out in the street. After that he sold my husband drink and kept him there four days and five nights and took $470 out of his pocket. That was the cause of my suit.

"'Q.—Counsel asked you whether you had not been kept out of your house on two occasions. State why? A.—My husband was mad because I sued the saloon-keeper, and he put a new lock on the door and locked me out of the house.'

"The suit which this outrageously abused woman brought against Ertel was tried before a Chicago judge, who fined him $20—the lightest punishment the law would allow! What is to be done with such an evil as this, save to wipe it out altogether?"

Remember, the saloon license in Chicago is $500.

Let us be sure that if this thing goes on the piper is going to raise his price. We are training in our saloons an army of ragged, debauched, conscienceless victims, dead to every worthy ambition and tender emotion, unfit to be citizens of a republic, impossible long to control by the ordinary restraints of law. If this work goes on it means in the near future a standing army. When virtue and intelligence are gone the bayonet must come in. Security must be had from somewhere. A standing army, vast in proportion to the size of our territory and the populousness of our cities, will be an enormous drain of revenue beyond any statistics which can now be arrayed. Its heaviest cost cannot be given in cash. It will mean the downfall of our liberty in a military despotism. A nation of drunkards will need a Napoleon, and sober men will have to submit to him as the only refuge from the worse tyranny of imbruted mobs.

CHAPTER VII.

THE HARVEST OF DEATH.

"I will make a man more precious than fine gold; even a man than the golden wedge of Ophir."—*Isa.* 13 : 12.

"For among my people are found wicked men: they lay wait, as he that setteth snares; they set a trap, they catch men."—*Jer.* 5 : 26.

"Thou land devourest up men, and hast bereaved thy nations."—*Ezek.* 36 : 13.

"The great London fever of 1789 took scarcely anybody but drunkards and tipplers. Dr. Cartwright, of New Orleans, says the yellow-fever in 1866 took 5,000 drinking men before it touched a sober man. In the United Kingdom of England, Ireland, and Scotland, one visit of cholera swept away over 10,000 persons—not half a dozen teetotalers in that number. In the city of Montreal 360 teetotalers had the cholera, and but one of them died, while 1,500 drinking men died of the disease."—*New Era.*

"All who sell liquors in the common way, to any that will buy, are poisoners-general. They murder His Majesty's subjects by wholesale; neither does their eye pity nor spare. They drive them to hell like sheep. And what is their gain? Is it not the blood of these men? Who, then, would envy their large estates and sumptuous palaces? A curse is in the midst of them. The curse of God is in their gardens, their groves – a fire that burns to the nethermost hell. Blood, blood is there! The foundation, the floors, the walls, the roof, are stained with blood."—*John Wesley,* 1760.

WHEN the Duke of Alvah went to the Netherlands, he thought he had hit upon the most brilliant scheme of revenue ever invented. Words could not express his delight and triumph at its facility. His only wonder was that no one had thought of it before. It was "popular," too—with his retainers and his royal master. The King had screwed out all the money he dared by direct taxation, yet had been always cramped for funds, in debt to his soldiers and his servants, and with a grumbling people to boot. Alvah relieved him instantly of all this perplexity and gave him more money than he ever had before. He kept his troops fat and well fed, with gold rings and jewels for the common soldiers to gamble over in the guard-room. He did not increase the taxes, and —within his administration—nobody grumbled. His method of raising a revenue was sublime in its simplicity and directness. It was simply to cut off the head of anybody who had anything, and then take all he had. Taxes of ten or fifteen per cent. became contemptible beside this ample scheme. It is said that the President of the "Bloody Council," which conducted the details of the business, suffered from terrible nightmares, in which he imagined blood to be dripping from the walls and furniture. But the Duke was superior to any such sensitiveness, and went on his popular and prosperous way.

There was found, however, to be one great difficulty with this invention. Killing the producers stops production, and where production puts nothing in, not even tyranny can get anything out. The number of rich men is limited, and when they are decapitated for public expenses the supply may run out. As this fact began to appear the scheme declined in popularity.

The shrewder Yankee, in the nineteenth century, has hit upon an ampler scheme. He will not execute the rich men—except incidentally. More money can be made out of the wholesale slaughter of the middle classes and the poor. There are plenty of them. The supply will not soon run out.

To maintain that revenue requires the slaughter of 60,000 men every year. But the revenue is said to be "the easiest of all revenues to collect." The man who is killed never objects, because he never believes he is going to be killed. The system is superior to electricity in this respect, because the awful chair, with its straps and wires, plainly speaks to the condemned of coming doom. But the saloon gives no warning that disturbs its victim. He talks loudly of his "personal liberty," while the deadly coils are fastened around him. The man who kills him does not object, because he makes so much in the process that he can easily furnish the moderate revenue the Government demands. General Charles H. Grosvenor, of Ohio, as reported in the New York *Tribune* of 1883, said of the Scott Law :

"It is simply a tax law which permits anybody to engage in the sale of liquors and beer who can pay the tax. . . . It repeals the statute of 1854 (which forbade selling to be drank on the premises), and thereby affords protection to the liquor-seller. While it is unpopular with the brewers of beer for obvious reasons, it is popular with the dealers generally, for it gives them a quasi-respectability. What will be the effect of this law? There will probably be 12,000 payments under it, and $2,500,000 is a low estimate of the money that will flow into the local treasuries of Ohio from this source. This money will come to the relief of the overburdened tax-payers of the State as the quails filled up the camp of the children of Israel. The liquor-dealers are abundantly able to pay it, and those who do will *make more money* than heretofore, for from four to five thousand dealers will be compelled to shut up their shops. . . . The source of revenue is inexhaustible and perennial."

The reference to the quails is strikingly appropriate, as any one may see by reading the account,* which concludes as follows :

---

* Num. 11 : 31–35.

"And while the flesh was yet between their teeth, ere it was chewed, the wrath of the Lord was kindled against the people, and the Lord smote the people with a very great plague.

"And He called the name of that place Kibroth Hattaavah, because there they buried the people that lusted."

Yes, this revenue ends in the graves of a host.

But all the shocking barbarities of the old Spaniard's tyranny are avoided. There is no Star-Chamber trial, no dreadful scaffold, no gleaming axe, no severed heads, no dripping blood.

The killing is not done abruptly in an instant, but humanely lengthened out through a long term of years. Fathers and mothers, wives and children, become gradually used to the sorrow and degradation, and when the victim finally dies there is, for the most part, no sudden shock. To be sure, he may be shot or stabbed in a saloon, or hanged for shooting or stabbing some one else there. He may meet a fatal fall on the way home, or freeze to death in some neglected alley. But even these things relatives have learned to anticipate in many a dreary day and wakeful night; and they only happen to a small fraction of the 60,000—though, of course, no one can tell exactly who these will be. But for the most part the decline is gradual, unless attacks of delirium tremens intervene to give it a sensational character, of course very trying to the feelings of friends, but not susceptible of economic valuation. On these points Gough and other princes of the platform have exhausted eloquence, till American business men have hardened themselves into profound insensibility. "The easiest of all revenues to collect" is a sufficient answer. We must view these things philosophically. Even moralists and ministers tell us it is quite incompetent to plead the moral guilt of murder in a question of legislation. This may be urged from the pulpit—the saloon-keeper does not go to church; or in the religious press—while the saloon-keeper reads the *Police Gazette*. But when we come to the only practical way in which the public sentiment of a community can touch the liquor-seller—legislation—then moral considerations are quite out of place. If we attempt to argue that to take the mother's boy, the light of her eyes and the impulse of her every heart-beat, and just at the threshold of dawning manhood, when all her tender care from babyhood might have happy and rich return, entice him into a den and lay him drunk on her door-step, and to carry this on through years till she sits broken-hearted by the grave, where she can scarcely weep for very bitterness of sorrow—if we attempt to argue that this should be stopped because it is wicked, learned theologians stop us short, and tell us that is union of Church and State! These great men ought to know, but it is very hard for plain people to understand. They insist, however, that law can deal only with the injury to society.

Well, we are prepared to take the matter up on the hard, cold, economic basis, and we ask, Have you ever considered

THE CASH VALUE OF A MAN?

The baby a year old, in an average American family of moderate means, represents an investment of not less than $50, which may easily run up to a hundred. If we consider the mother's time worth anything, it will run beyond that amount. For if she were engaged in some remunerative employment, she would have to pay from $2 to $7 a week to hire done what she does for her child. Her necessary loss of time from her work for its sake might be a much heavier expense. Yes, the baby boy a year old must be valued at $50. For each of the next four years he must average as much—$250 for the first five years. For the next ten, expenses increase. There are the summer and winter suits larger every year—and how they do wear out! How the shoes are stubbed through! There is the flannel underclothing, and there are the overcoats that won't stretch as he grows, even if they would hold together. Then the food to keep that stature rising and that machinery in motion—well, boarding-house keepers, who ought to know, would as soon board a man as a hearty twelve-year-old boy at the same table. We know a table where the man of the family is flanked by two sturdy boys, and outflanked in the eating at every meal.

A recent number of the Philadelphia *Record* gives the following very interesting statistics of the actual first cost of the food of a healthy boy:

"Dr. McKinnon, the Superintendent of the Mimico Industrial School in Canada, has furnished the Toronto *Mail* with an interesting statement on the subject. There are 108 boys in the school, who are kept in good bodily health, and whose subsistence is bought in a wholesale way that would somewhat cheapen the cost as compared with ordinary household expenditure. The boys have all they wish to eat, and the Superintendent's accounts, not being complicated by expenses for sustenance for other persons, furnish valuable data not otherwise readily obtainable. The following statement shows the average weekly expenditure per boy:

	Cents.
Flour	18
Oatmeal and other meal	½
Barley and beans	½
Rice, sago, etc	8 1/10
Coffee, cocoa and tea	2 3/10
Sugar and syrups	7 7/10
Salt, pepper and other condiments	½
Fresh fruits	1
Fruits preserved and dried	½

Fresh meat and fish............................	17 3/10
Meat and fish cured............................	1 6/10
Butter and cheese...............................	8 6/10
Other provisions................................	3 7/10
Vegetables..	24
Milk...	14
Total...	$1.07 3/10

"The cost of food, as above given, does not include the expense of preparing it, or incidental expenditure for superintendence, etc. But the average disbursement is astonishingly small. So far as subsistence goes, to raise a boy is not much more costly than to a raise a pig. If a healthy boy can be properly fed for $56 a year, there is less discouragement in the task of increasing the male population of the country than pessimist observers are wont to insist upon."

It is to be observed that the allowance for fresh meat is very small—less than a pound of beefsteak a week at New York prices. The allowance for milk is less than two quarts a week at the same rates. Even at country prices, these items would be very small for many families. Families, of course, must buy at retail prices. Also the expense of preparing, etc., will raise the price somewhat. At this rate, $75 a year would be a very moderate allowance for the food of a boy *not* "in an industrial school." Clothing, bedding, and breakage have all to be added.

On the one side, however, we must remember the host of little fellows who are not well fed, whose food falls short of even that moderate allowance, and whose clothing tells a sad story of cheapness. On the other, we must consider the host who are fed at fully double the rates given in Dr. McKinnon's table, and clothed proportionately well. Then for these latter there are the school-books, the skates and the base-balls, the jack-knives and the bracket-saws, the gift books and the juvenile papers—all which help to make the boy worth growing up—intellectual, ingenious, good, and home loving. We may average the whole at $100 a year—surely a very moderate estimate—making $1,000 for those ten years, and the boy worth $1,250 at fifteen. Beyond that, the limits are wide, from the young man supporting himself, to the student at an expensive college spending thousands a year. It must be remembered, however, that it costs the man's expenses to raise him, even if in these latter years he earns all he costs and more. His parents and society may receive then more than the cost, but all that value has gone into him, and must be counted in his worth at maturity. We cannot average it at less than $200 a year from fifteen to twenty-one. Few persons would care to take a boy of fifteen, to do for him as they ought till he should be twenty-one, for so little as $200 a year. That makes, then, $1,200 for those six years, or $2,450 as the cost of a man at twenty-one. Of course, many are reared at far less expense. It is generally, however, with the loss of many real advantages. On the other hand, many have expended upon them vastly more in families that are counted among the wealthy. It would seem very moderate and reasonable to put the average cost of an American young man of twenty-one at $2,000.

But the cost of a thing does not always indicate its value. It might cost a vast sum to throw new soldiers into a starving garrison, and they would be worse than worthless when they arrived. However this argument might apply in China, it has no place in America, with its ample field for all worthy manhood. We may get some idea of the value of a man from the selling price at the South thirty years ago. A good, steady, industrious, able-bodied man would then sell for $1,500. He would be a man who had no school training, and none of the deftness and power which come from inherited education. On the basis of his value as an investment—his wealth-producing power—our American young man must be valued much higher than on the basis of his cost. If he lives and has his health, he can earn from $300 a year up to sums which seem fabulous, for the next forty years. Let us take the case only of wage-workers at from $300 to $1,200 a year. Three hundred dollars a year is the interest on $5,000 at six per cent, and the man who can steadily earn $1 a day for 300 working days each year is worth $5,000. The man who can earn $600 a year is worth $10,000, and the man who can earn $1,200 a year is worth $20,000.

So long as there is a field for wealth-producing power, the destruction of a man is the destruction of wealth. The 60,000 men annually destroyed by the liquor traffic are worth at cost, at $2,000 each, $120,000,000. Supposing them sober, industrious, and intelligent, as but for the drink traffic they might have been, and they would be equal in productive power to an investment of $300,000,000 at the very least. Considering the intelligence and achieving power of educated Americans and considering how many men of the finest advantages and most splendid abilities from the professions and mercantile life go to swell the dreadful death-roll of drunkenness, it does not seem too much to estimate their average possible earnings at $600 a year, and the total wage-earning power of the men annually destroyed at $36,000,000, making their value as capital $600,000,000. If every saloon in the United States paid a $1,000 license, that would yield $150,000,000. Adding the entire Internal Revenue Tax paid to the United States Government, we should have $248,000,000. This is far in excess of anything collected in our day or likely to be for a generation to come. But even at that generous allowance, the saloon would not pay its own funeral expenses.

Alvah boasted that he had executed 18,000 men in the Netherlands in six years, or 3,000 a year. The liquor traffic, with its 60,000 a year, outdoes Alvah twenty to one, and we have no one to do what even the cold-blooded Philip II. ultimately did—recall the butcher and stop the slaughter. We talk of the cruelty of the Inquisition, and rejoice that the world is at length free from its baleful shadow. But Llorente, the historian of the Inquisition, estimates the victims burned alive at its altars in the three hundred years from Torquemada to the beginning of the present century at only 31,912. Thirty thousand in three hundred years, and we call that cruel! But it was only 300 men a year, while our Whiskey Inquisition burns alive nearly twice as many in one year as the Inquisition did in three hundred years, and we consider it a valuable source of revenue, "the easiest of all revenues to collect." We talk of "regulation and taxation," and we wonder the old popes supposed they could "regulate" the Inquisition. We do not know that they ever thought of taxing it. How appalling are the atrocities of former generations!

"Woe unto you, Scribes and Pharisees, hypocrites, for ye build the tombs of the prophets and garnish the sepulchres of the righteous, and say, If we had been in the days of our fathers, we would not have been partakers with them in the blood of the prophets."

In view of such facts the *Christian Index* asks:

HAVE YOU A BOY TO SPARE?

The saloon must have boys, or it must shut up shop. Can't you furnish it one? It is a great factory, and unless it can get 2,000,000 boys from each generation for raw material, some of these factories must close out and its operatives must be thrown on a cold world, and the public revenue will dwindle. "Wanted—2,000,000 boys," is the notice. One family out of every five must contribute a boy to keep up the supply. Will you help? Which of your boys will it be? The minotaur of Crete had to have a trireme full of fair maidens each year; but the minotaur of America demands a city full of boys each year. Are you a father? Have you given your share to keep up the supply for this great public institution that is helping to pay your taxes and kindly electing public officials for you? Have you contributed a boy? If not, some other family has had to give more than its share. Are you selfish, voting to keep the saloon open to grind up boys, and then doing nothing to keep up the supply?

In view of such facts, Dr. J. G. Holland wrote, accepting a death rate much higher than we have given:

"The property of the liquor interest, covering every department of it, depends entirely on the maintenance of this army. It cannot live without it. It never did live without it. So long as the liquor interest maintains its present prosperous condition, it will cost America's sacrifice of one hundred thousand men every year. The effect is inseparable from the cause. The cost to the country of the liquor traffic is a sum so stupendous that any figures we should dare to give would convict us of trifling. The amount of life absolutely destroyed, the amount of industry sacrificed, the amount of bread transformed into poison, the shame, the unavailing sorrow, the crime, the poverty, the pauperism, the brutality, the wild waste of vital and financial resources, make an aggregate so vast—so incalculably vast, that the only wonder is that the American people do not rise as one man and declare that this great curse shall exist no longer. The truth is, that there is no question before the American people to-day that begins to match in importance the temperance question. The question of American slavery was never anything but a baby by the side of this; and we prophesy that within ten years, if not within five, the whole country will be awake to it."

CHAPTER VIII.

A STEP TOWARD PROHIBITION.

"And why not, (as we be slanderously reported, and as some affirm that we say,) Let us do evil, that good may come? whose damnation is just."—*Rom.* 3 : 8.

"As matters now stand, it is absolutely necessary for the entire trade to organize and get to work. Wake up, especially those who are always known as very generously permitting others to do the work. This time *it is business;* so, each and every one lay aside any petty trade jealousies you may have : *the enemy is strong, and to vanquish him requires good work, strong work, and work together, with your battle-cry,* 'High License against Prohibition.' Some dealers may not realize this condition of affairs in the trade, but all will very soon find out that, though the trade cannot now defeat Prohibition, High License can, as it will receive the support of a large majority of the press throughout the State, and the almost unanimous support of all fair-minded, sensible, and practical men."—*Bonfort's Wine and Spirit Circular, January 25th,* 1889.

THERE are many temperance men who say, "I do not believe in license as a finality, or a desirable thing in itself. But I believe if we can keep raising the license higher and higher, making the saloons fewer and fewer, we can at length sweep away altogether the few that remain. In short, I favor High License as a step toward Prohibition."

To this plan there are several serious objections :

1. If license is wrong, it will prove unwise. Never in all history did good men make anything by "doing evil that good might come." The universe is not constructed on that principle. We do not ask any one to

take this on sight. We cannot stop to prove it. It will bear thinking over, and will prove itself.

2. This plan does not correctly gauge the facts. It is based on the false assumption *that the saloons which remain will each be of the same grade and power as the saloons you started with.* Facts show—as stated in previous chapters—that the saloons which remain when High License has done its utmost will have at least as much capital, consumption of liquor, and political influence as the whole number had in the beginning, only concentrated in fewer hands. Which will be the easiest to conquer? Would it be more difficult to stamp out in Louisiana, for instance, 500 little, petty lotteries, or the great Louisiana State Lottery, with its capital of millions, its prizes of fortunes, farms, and gold watches, and with generals and eminent politicians on its official board?

3. This plan proceeds upon a false estimate of human nature. Are people more ready to break up a damaging business run by irresponsible individuals, or to sacrifice *their own* money, which they have become accustomed to receiving and spending? Take a single town where there is one saloon run by one man who pays no license and no tax. The manufacturer loses two days on an average in the week from many of his workmen,* because they drink at that saloon. He says, "It's a heavy tax to me and makes no return to anybody." The grocer looks over his list of "bad debts" which he cannot collect, because his customers have spent all their money in the saloon. He says, "It's a heavy loss to

---

* The Oliver Ames Company, in Massachusetts, after Prohibition had been repealed and High License substituted, reported eight per cent. less work done by 400 men than by 315 in the same months of the previous year.

me and no good to anybody." All sober men who see their sons and their neighbors tempted and endangered say, "What is this business doing for the community, that we should let one man work all this havoc for his own private profit?"

The policeman who every little while has to stop a fight or arrest a drunken desperado, at the risk of his own life and limb, says, "If they'd let me lock up that old rumseller I could stop all this nonsense." It will not be hard to bring all the respectable men of this community to say, "Let's shut that place up."

But now put on the saloon a $1,000 license. Let the people get used to spending it, and the whole case is changed.

If the manufacturer complains, they say, "If we shut that man's place up, are you willing to pay his $1,000 a year to the tax fund?" "Well, no." To the grocer, "Are you?" "Hardly." If the policeman grumbles, the answer is, "Where are you going to get your pay if you stop that man's license? Why, *your whole salary is paid out of his money*." Saintly women pray and plead, temperance orators thunder, and the silent answer of the majority is, "If we let these people have their way, they'll take $1,000 out of revenues of this town. Then we should all have our taxes increased to make it up. Better let well enough alone."

If the money is used—as in some States—for the school fund, the superintendent of schools is told, "If we close that saloon we shall have to cut down your salary," and unless he is a rare man he is silenced. Even the minister is unconsciously influenced by the same argument. He does not reason so, but he talks with solid business men who do, and has a feeling that they know more than he does about "practical matters." They say to him, "We would be as glad as you to close that saloon, but public sentiment is not ready for it. It would be a useless agitation and very likely divide your church in the attempt to do an impossibility. We are doing the best we can in burdening the saloon and making it pay for some part of the damage it does." But it is that very $1,000 license *which has made that public sentiment.*

If we could have the issue between a liquor traffic paying not one cent of public revenue on the one side, and on the other side prohibition of the whole business that brings such woe and curse, Prohibition would come with a rush.

"Ah, yes!" is the taunting answer, "you want free rum." Well, we once saw a mad Texas steer holding possession of a market-place. Men, women, and children were crowded into stores, the furious animal charging up to the very doors. Horses and carriages were parked in lots, whose gates had been hastily opened before them and shut behind them. A man came up very bravely with a flint-lock musket within easy range of the animal and fired. There was a little puff of smoke. The gun had "flashed in the pan." The gun looked big enough in all conscience, but the steer looked bigger than before and far more wicked. Another man came up with a Sharp's rifle, and called to the other, "Get out of the way with your pop-gun." What did he want that man out of the way for? Ah, he wanted the steer free, didn't he? Yes, free just long enough to be killed: He couldn't shoot him while the flint-lock man stood between. The flint-lock man was very accommodating, and got over a fence. The Sharp's rifle was levelled one instant; there was a sudden "crack"; the great head and horns went crashing to the ground, and men, women, and children were safe. Yes, we want rum free just long enough to kill it. Good high license friends, get out of the way with your pop-guns! We can't shoot through you. Leave us face to face with our unlicensed liquor traffic, and Prohibition will bring it down.

4. Religious and political papers, and the liquor organs themselves, agree that the American people will not endure free rum, and if the liquor men will not accept High License, they will infallibly be given over to Prohibition.

The Journal and Messenger, of Cincinnati, says:

"It is well known that the brewers and distillers of the country are not in favor of High License. They simply say, better for us to pay a High License than to submit to Prohibition. They are choosing the least of two evils, feeling sure they must submit to one or the other."

The *Freie Presse*, a German liquor organ of Chicago, in its issue of April 29th, 1889, says:

"The Chicago *Tribune* has advocated, with the determination and zeal which mark it, the cause of Local Option and High License since Iowa and Kansas went Prohibition. To some German Republicans who took exception to this, Mr. Medill explained *that the only way in which the adoption of Prohibition laws in all the Northwestern States*, with the possible exception of Wisconsin, *could be hindered* was to leave it to localities to decide whether there would be 'license' or 'no license.' Local Option and High License were the *only barriers* against the Prohibition craze, and the good results of High License would soon lessen the number of those States which had come out against the granting of licenses. How accurately Mr. Medill calculated the effect of High License on Anglo-Americans the vote by which the Prohibition amendment was defeated in Massachusetts shows. It was the great argument of the friends of personal liberty there that Prohibition would stop the sale of liquor, while the license taxes would bring in a heavy income to the community that impose them. That took with the voters, and Prohibition was beaten by an immense vote. We believe now that it is owing to the far-sighted-ness of Mr. Medill and the energetic position of the *Tribune* that Illinois has escaped paper Prohibition, and the city treasury of Chicago has received about $2,000,000 a year from the saloons. This is sometimes severe on the saloon-keepers, BUT IT IS INSURANCE AGAINST PROHIBITION."

In the recent Amendment contest in Pennsylvania the liquor-dealers of Philadelphia wore High License badges on election-day, marshalled their voters and won the election behind that symbol. In Massachusetts, the Boston papers gave as one reason for the defeat of the Amendment a "general desire to give the new High License Law a fair trial." The *Herald*, two days before the election, came out with an elaborate article for High License against Prohibition, with these striking headlines:

HIGH LICENSE.

IT WILL GIVE $900,000 A YEAR TO BOSTON. BUT THE AMENDMENT WILL LOSE IT ALL.

Of the defeated Amendment in Michigan, Miss Frances E. Willard, who worked for the Amendment through the stormy campaign, said: "Its epitaph might be, Died of High License." Wherever there is danger of Prohibition, the politicians who favor the liquor interest hasten to pass or promise High License Laws, as they did in the States above referred to.

On this point we are able to give a remarkable series of statements by clergymen of Nebraska, which has had a license of $1,000 since 1881. These statements were given in answer to questions sent out by Rev. G. M. Prentice.*

In the condensation of the replies in the following tables, we give only the questions and answers (3 and 4 of the series) bearing on this single point.

* A 47-page pamphlet containing the full replies from which these tables have been made may be had by addressing Rev. Benjamin J. Ripley, Windsor, N. Y. The price is ten cents.

NAMES OF CLERGYMEN.	Post Office.	Official Position or Number of Years' Residence in the State.	3. Does High License make Prohibition More Easily Attainable? If not, why not?	4. How do Liquor Men Look upon High License?	Further Remarks as to High License and its Effects.
Methodist Episcopal.					
*S. H. Henderson	Stockville.	Judge, Frontier County.	No, most emphatically.	Favor it; know it is High License prevents Prohibition in Nebraska.	But for High License Law we would have Prohibition.
D. C. Winship	Oakdale.	Sec. N. Neb. M. E. Conf.	No!!	As their only salvation from Prohibition.	High License makes liquor traffic many supporters.
W. G. Vessels	Broken Bow.	Sec. W. Neb. M. E. Conf.	No; its greatest impediment.	All liquor-dealers able to pay urge High License.	Not had it in this city one saloon had it not been for license fees and tax paid by them.
C. A. Lewis	Sterling.	Sec. Neb. M. E. Conf.	No.	With favor.	Peter Iler, great distiller, Omaha, recommends High License as bar to Prohibition.
C. H. Dayhoff	Vacoma.	For Presiding Elder, T. C. Clendening.	Does not; makes far more difficult.	With much favor; endorse it to a man.	Recent Omaha paper says hundreds of dives there pay no license.
W. G. Miller	Lincoln.	P. Eld. Lincoln Dist.	Questionable.	With favor compared with Prohibition.	Tends to elevate respectability of saloon and drink habit.
J. B. Maxfield	Omaha.	P. Eld. Omaha Dist.	No; a thousand times no!	Liquor men here all favor it.	High License most formidable obstruction in path of temperance.
G. A. Smith	Nebraska City.	P. Eld. Neb. City Dist.	Think not.	Feel it their only hope in this State.	The money bait is powerful.
A. C. Calkins	York.	P. Eld. York Dist.	No; license is hush money.	As in no way of hurt to their trade.	A whiskey scheme to defer Prohibition.
J. W. Shank	Central City.	P. Eld. Gd. Island Dist.	Does not; preventsaptation for it.	Rejoice in it, as protection from Prohibition.	Money obtained quiets public conscience.
W. R. Jones	Hastings.	P. Eld. Hastings Dist.	Not a bit; makes it harder.	All favor $1,000 as their only hope.	Strongest agency of the devil to perpetuate rum traffic.

A STEP TOWARD PROHIBITION.

Name	Place	Years	Worst foe of Prohibition?	They all want it *high*.		Remarks
C. A. Mastin	Minden	6 years at least.	No; worst foe of Prohibition.			Devised to forestall submission; has effectually accomplished it.
C. A. Hale	Arcadia	6 years at least.				
E. J. Randall	Clay Center	28 years.	Think not; public conscience quieted.	Liquor men its fast friends.		Greatly augments liquor evil by giving "respectability."
*C. N. Dawson	Omaha	2 years.	Positively no; reverse.	Fight and spend money to retain it.		
†H. S. Hilton	Central City	2½ years.		Favor it.		
H. A. Barton	Neligh	2 years.	Makes it decidedly harder to get.	Earnestly and enthusiastically favor it.		It compromises Prohibition.
‡R. G. Adams	Fairmount	10 years.	Certainly does not. Makes it harder to get.	Without any alarm. Satisfied.		Liquor men desperately oppose Prohibition.
J. W. Stewart	Beatrice	P. Eld. Neb. Conf. 1885-87.	No, because of revenue.	All favor it.		Makes saloons more attractive.
P. C. Johnson	Osceola	P. Eld. W. Neb. Conf., 1883-87.	Most emphatically, no, sir.	Endorse it heartily.		Makes it difficult and dangerous to propose Prohibition.
Wesley K. Beans	York	P. Eld. York Dist., 1887.	No.	They chuckle over it with ghoulish glee.		Advocated by most bitter, persistent and uncompromising foes of Prohibition.
J. R. Priest	Bremer	6 years at least.	No, emphatically, no!! Chief obstacle to Prohibition.	It suits them.		Would have had Prohibition long ago but for High License.
*F. M. Easterbrook	Elgar	21 years.	No! reverse is true.	Saloon men want it.		Many wink at it because it will save them tax.
C. F. Heywood	Lyons	30 years.	No; its greatest barrier.	With favor.		Many go to gilded High License palaces who would not to low dives.
†Charles W. Savidge	Grand Island	6 years.	No; sworn enemy of Prohibition.	Look on it as their ideal.		If not for High License, people would rally for Prohibition. Work of death and ruin going on with greater rapidity than before.
‡P. S. Mather	Indianola	6 years at least.	No.			
George S. Davis	Lincoln	Ed. Neb. *Methodist.*	No, in almost every way.	Stand by it as barrier to Prohibition.		A gigantic, infamous system of bribery.
‡J. T. Roberts	Greenwood	5 years.	No; sedative to temperance conscience.	As the bulwark of liquor traffic.		All anti-Prohibitionists unite with liquor men in glorifying it.

* Formerly Presiding Elder Beatrice District Nebraska M. E. Conference.
† Serves a parish giving a support of between $1,000 and $2,000.

NAMES OF CLERGYMEN.	Post Office.	Official Position or Number of Years' Residence in the State.	3. Does High License make Prohibition More Easily Attainable? If not, why not?	4. How do Liquor Men Look upon High License?	Further Remarks as to High License and its Effects.
Methodist Episcopal (cont'd).					
George H. Wehn...	Rising City.	Financial Agent M. E. College.	Think not.	Favorably.	
A. R. Wightman...	Lincoln.	Sec. Faculty Neb. Wesleyan Univ.	Bar to Prohibition.	Favor it generally.	Divides temperance men.
D. Marquett...	Schuyler.	Pres. Neb. Central College.	Makes it more difficult.	Well satisfied.	Failure both as temperance and revenue measure.
C. F. Creighton...	Lincoln.	Chancellor Neb. Wesleyan Univ.	Makes it all but out of the question.	All liquor men approve it.	Postpones issue between Prohibition and rum.
J. B. Leedom. ...	Central City.	P. Eld. Norfolk Dist.	Does not.	As fortifying their business.	
Congregational.					
D. B. Perry...	Crete.	Pres. Doane College.	High License a bribe to tax-payers.	Favor it as against Prohibition.	Makes many citizens tolerant of saloons.
Amos Dresser...	Dover	Mod'r Gen. Ass., Neb, 1871–77.	No! blunts public conscience.	Cherished by liquor league.	Makes saloon a terrible power and political menace.
J. E. Brereton	Ashland.	Nearly 3 years.	A thousand times no!	They encourage it.	Acts as public bribe and sears conscience.
*John L. Maile	Omaha.	Supt. Neb. Am. Home Miss. Society.	Greatest hindrance to Prohibition possibly devised.		
John Aakin...	Kearney.	4 years.	No.	Prefer it to Prohibition.	
George Hindley...	Weeping Water.	P'n. Weeping Water Acad.	Believe it does.	Like it better than Prohibition.	
Lewis Gregory...	Lincoln.	Mod. Gen. Ass.,1876, '78, '82.	Cannot say.	Cannot say.	Party managers responsible for delay in Prohibition.
Isaac E. Heaton...	Fremont.	Ex-Mod'r & Cl'k Gen. Asso.	But for it we should have Prohibition.	Have learned to like it.	Liquor men prefer High License than risk Prohibition.

A STEP TOWARD PROHIBITION. 115

Name	Location	Position				
A. A. Cressman	Wahoo.	Sec. Wahoo Board of Education.	Strongly favor it	Makes tenfold more difficult.		No check to drunkenness, crime; no advance; step backward.
C. S. Harrison	Franklin.	17 years.	They love it.	A great hindrance.		A wall of rock between liquor men and Prohibition.
Allen Clark	Nebraska City.	3½ years.	A unit in support of it	Less easily attainable.		Temperance people regard it worse than no law.
H. A. French	Lincoln.	Ed. Neb. Cong. News.	With great favor.	No, because of revenue.		Liquor oligarchy anxious to keep it to prevent Prohibition.
M. L. Holt, Baptist.	Omaha.	5 years Pres. Gates Col.	They *like* it.	Tends to destroy Prohibition sentiment.		Every saloon man would vote for it to-day; a step backward.
C. E. Bentley	Surprise.	Pres. State S. S. Conf., 1888.	Know Prohibition more difficult under High than Low License.	Strongest wall, highest bar against Prohibition.		One of its blighting curses is its demoralization of women.
A. W. Snider	Columbus.	Clk. Loup & Elkhorn Asso.	Favor it.	No; delays it.		Gives saloon business standing and respectability.
†L. W. Terry	Grand Island.	5 years.	Very favorably.	No; ten per cent more difficult.		I was High License man but confess law failure *in every particular.*
H. C. Woods	Lincoln.	Supt. Missions, Kan., Neb., Col., S. Dak., Wyo., and N. Mex.	With approval.	Practicable demonstration that Prohibition only will rid of saloons.		Immense revenue appeals irresistibly to pockets of people.
L. B. Stifson	York.	18 years; ed. York *Star.*	Well satisfied.	No; a solid rock in its way.		A law to defeat submission.
‡A. W. Lamar	Omaha.	2 years.	Favorably.	No; harder to get it.		As a "step toward Prohibition" it is hopeless. High License is our incubus; we hate it.
B. Bedell	Sterling.	Mod'r Nemaha Ass.	It is their helper.	Makes harder to get Prohibition.		
§O. A. Williams	Lincoln.	8 years.	Satisfied.	No.		
Z. C. Rush	Albion.	Mod'r Loup & Elkhorn Ass.	Favor it to a man.	More difficult to obtain.		Whiskeymen fight Prohibition to better advantage under it.
L. T. Fisher	Geneva.	Mod'r York Ass.	Do not fight it bitterly, fear people will demand Prohibition.	Think not.		

* Referred to Editor *Rising Tide* for answer. ‡ Parish support over $3,000.
† Serves parish giving support between $1,000 and $2,000. § Serves parish giving support between $2,000 and $3,000.

NAMES OF CLERGYMEN.	Post Office.	Official Position or Number of Years' Residence in the State.	3. Does High License make Prohibition More Easily Attainable? If not, why not?	4. How do Liquor Men Look upon High License?	Further Remarks as to High License and its Effects.
Baptist (cont'd).					
E. A. Russell	Ord.	Gen. S. S. Miss. & Fin. Sec. Am. Bap. Pub. Soc. 32 years.	Yes.	Larger ones favor it.	We are suffering from an influx of saloon men.
F. T. Cassell, M.D.	Hastings.		Makes Prohibition far more difficult.	No complaints.	Our greatest obstacle in the way of Prohibition.
A. W. Clark	Omaha.	Sec. State Conf., 1887.	Makes Prohibition more difficult.	Enthusiastic in its favor.	Often asserted but for High License we would have Prohibition.
Presbyterian					
John N. Mills	Beatrice.	Referred to Judge E. M. Hill, 17 years in State.	No; more in the way than anything else.	Suits them to a dot.	If not for revenue we would soon be rid of traffic.
J. H. Reynard	Central City.	10 years.	No; stifles conscience of voters.	With great favor.	A fraud, a delusion and a snare to temperance cause.
Thomas L. Sexton	Seward.	6 years; Synod'cal Miss., 1887.	Do not see how it can.	Always vote for it.	
Frederick Johnson	Elsinore, Cal.	Mod'r Neb. Synod, 1887.	No; makes more difficult.	With great favor.	Brings into business a shrewd class who become leaders in politics.
James M. Kerr	Kearney.	Referred to J. W. Dryden, Att'y-at-law; 13 years.	No; revenue perpetuates license system.	Well satisfied.	
W. F. Ringland	Hastings.	Pres. Hastings College.	Makes more difficult to secure.	Uniformly favor it.	The most dangerous position in which traffic can be lodged.
Christian.					
W. P. Aylesworth	Fairfield.	Pres. Fairfield College.	Not directly, I think.	Prefer it to Prohibition.	Many conservative temperance people rest on High License.

Name	City	Position	Years	Does it stand in way of it	Without exception favor it	Comments
R. C. Barrow	Tecumseh.	State Evangelist.	20 years.	Does not; stands in way of it.	Men leaning to Prohibition tolerate curse for price it pays.	
Charles B. Newman.	Lincoln.		6 mos.; "Near here in Missouri all my life."	No; much harder.	Favor it in the main.	Intrenches liquor traffic in financial greed of people.
J. Z. Briscoe, Esq...	Lincoln.	Pres. State Christian Conf. and Miss. Soc.		Still to be solved.	With favor from business point of view.	Men now vote for High License who would otherwise work for Prohibition.
William Sumpter	Unadilla.	Sec. Neb. Ch. Miss. Soc.				More dangerous than low license; attracts respectable citizens and young men by making saloons attractive.
Evangelical Lutheran.						
J. S. Detweiler	Omaha.	Sec. Gen. Synod. 1883-86.	Does not.	They rather favor.		
Lloyd Knight and George H. Schnur.	Yutan.	Schnur, Pres. Neb. Synod.		Yes.		
A. B. Shrader	Grand Island.	Sec. Neb. Synod.		No; because of revenue.	They endorse it.	Saloon men all favor license, oppose Prohibition.
Conrad Heber	Omaha.	Travelling Sec. Neb. Synod.		No.	Perfectly satisfied.	Saloon men know it postpones Prohibition.
Reformed Presby.						
H. P. McCherkin	Wahoo.		5 years.	Stands directly in way of Prohibition.	All favor it.	Saloon men endorse law as great defence against Prohibition.
Officers of Temperance Organizations.						
L. R. Palmer	Hastings.	Grand Chief Templar Neb. I.O.G.T.		No; it is the great bar to Prohibition.	All in favor of it.	A $250 saloon is a "doggery;" people prohibit it quicker than a $1,000 one.
Charles Watts	Omaha.	Grand Sec. I.O.G.T.		Neb. No.	Unanimously favor it.	Total failure as temperance or reform measure.
Mrs. M. A. Hitchcock	Fremont	Pres. Neb. W.C.T.U. (Over 200 unions.)		No; it retards the work.	They like it now very much.	High License makes Prohibition almost impossible.
Mrs. Z. A. Wilson	Lincoln.	Cor. Sec. Neb. W.C.T.U.		Barrier to Prohibition in many ways.	Well satisfied.	
Mrs. C. M. Woodward	Seward.	V. Pres. & Organizer Neb. W.C.T.U.		A bar to Prohibition.	They support it.	A bribe and anodyne to the mind and conscience.

In his famous letter of November 22d, 1883, in favor of distributing the United States Internal Revenue Tax among the several States on the basis of their population, Secretary of State James G. Blaine said:

"On the basis of the Census of 1880, it would pay about $1.75 per capita to all the people. *The tendency would be to increase rather than diminish* as time wore on.

* * * * * * * *

"It makes the tax on spirituous and malt liquors *a permanent revenue* to all the States, enabling them thereby *definitely to readjust and reduce their own taxation.*"

When taxes have been "definitely readjusted and reduced" on the basis of a certain source of revenue, do people become more or less ready to destroy that source of revenue?

The answer is to be found in the experience of Illinois after the enactment of the Harper Law, fixing the liquor license at $500. In the Legislature the next year a proposal was made to reduce the fee to $250. The answer was: "Gentlemen, if you do that, you will derange the finances of a thousand cities and towns." And it was not done.

To all this evidence against the claim of High License to be a step toward Prohibition, we add the utter absence of any proof that it has ever had that effect. When and where has it ever stepped in that direction?

The license fee in Maine, previous to the adoption of Prohibition, was $1, for the use of the licensing board.* Iowa had no State license, but towns and cities gave licenses as they pleased, often at merely nominal fees—$50 to $100. In Michigan the license fee fixed by the Revised Statutes of 1846, ch. 41, was "not less than $5, nor more than $20." It was from this that Michigan

---
* Revised Statutes, 1847, ch. 36, sec. 4.

passed to Prohibition in 1850 to 1855. In Kansas, according to the old "Dram Shop Act," the license was from $100 to $500 at the discretion of the licensing board. It is said rarely to have exceeded $200 to $300, and could not be called a High License. The step from High License to Prohibition is "the missing link" which no man can supply. The plea that High License is a step toward Prohibition is an absolutely baseless assumption without one single fact in its favor. It is an *à priori* theory never realized in the actual world in one instance that any man can put his finger on. If we want the revenue from High License, let us say so. If not, let us not be deluded with the argument that it is a step toward Prohibition when exactly the opposite has been found to be the fact wherever it has been tried.

President Atherton of the National Liquor Dealers' Protective Association takes quite a different view of the matter. He is the official head of the foremost organization of distillers, wholesale liquor-dealers and other liquor men (as distinguished from the brewers) in the country. He has been President of the National Protective Association ever since it was started in 1886.

He has written the following letter, which may be found in the "Prohibition Leaflet," entitled "The Fight for Life or Death in Nebraska" (italics and capitals being supplied by the editor):

Brands of Fine
Kentucky Whiskies
"Atherton,"
"Mayfield,"
"Clifton,"
"Windsor."

THE J. M. ATHERTON COMPANY,
LOUISVILLE, KY., March 2, 1889.

"*E. A. Fox, Esq., Eaton Rapids, Mich.*

"DEAR SIR: Your letter has been on my desk for

some time without reply, because of my absence most of the time from the city. *The two most effective weapons with which to fight Prohibition are High License and Local Option.* The difficulty is that the remedy is almost as bad as the disease. High License is a vague, indefinite term, and is variously construed in different localities. I think $500 entirely too high, and a very unjust tax upon the liquor trade. Two hundred and fifty dollars is as much tax as the ordinary retail liquor-dealer can afford to pay and sell anything like old whiskey or pure liquors, however cheaply he may buy them. *The true policy for the trade to pursue is to advocate as high a license as they can in justice to themselves afford to pay, because the money thus raised tends to relieve all owners of property from taxation and keeps the treasuries of the towns and cities pretty well filled.* THIS CATCHES THE ORDINARY TAX-PAYER, *who cares less for the sentimental opposition to our business than he does for taxes on his own property.* The point is to prevent the gross imposition in the way of excessive and exorbitant taxation, under the name of High License. Local Option is local Prohibition, but *the experience is that there is always enough license counties mixed in with the No-License counties to practically supply the latter with all the liquor they need.*

"I think Local Option is less objectionable in its practical operations than the extreme High License. *Sooner or later the trade may be able to defeat the Local Option feature*, BUT UNTIL PROHIBITION IS DESTROYED, OR ITS POLITICAL EFFORTS BROKEN, I REPEAT THAT OUR BEST WEAPONS TO FIGHT IT WITH ARE HIGH LICENSE AND LOCAL OPTION BY TOWNSHIPS. *If Lo-*

cal Option can be defeated without encouraging Prohibition, it should be done. These are my views in a general way. Of course each locality and State has its peculiarities, and must modify its views to such existing conditions, but I think the suggestions I have herein given you are sound.

"You will please pardon me for the neglect or discourtesy in delaying this reply, but my absence from the city most of the time is the reason. Would be glad to give you any information or give any suggestions at any time. With kind regards,

"Yours truly,

"J. M. ATHERTON."

HOW ILER & CO. VIEW IT.

There is a most desperate contest in Nebraska during the present year on the question of Prohibition. It is a straight issue between Prohibition and High License, and the liquor men are preparing to fight with all their resources for High License. A very interesting statement from the liquor standpoint, showing how the rum people regard High License, was made by Iler & Co., of Omaha, the leading distillers of Nebraska, in *Bonfort's Wine and Spirit Circular* for October 25th, 1889. It is as follows:

"The issue to be voted on is an alternative, either Prohibition or High License. It is impossible for any one to foretell the outcome of this election, and, of course, *we are all in hopes to win for High License*, and thought that the outcome of the elections in the East would assist us materially; but we are afraid that the Prohibition victory in the Dakotas has about offset that. That Prohibition should be defeated next year in Nebraska is not only of great importance for the welfare of the State, but also of the country at large. *If we can carry High License*, it will be the commencement of an era of great prosperity for this State. With Prohibition on the east, south, and north of us, a liberal license policy will draw vast amounts of capital to this State. There are already a number of Prohibition orators, male and female, stumping the State, while the anti-Prohibition Party seems to be dormant. Early and most energetic action cannot be urged too much. The winter season is the best time to circulate anti-Prohibition literature, direct as well as through papers, among the voters. In winter the farmers have time to read, while next summer, or shortly before the election, they will be too busy. There is no doubt but that good, sound arguments, demonstrating the fallacies of Prohibition, if properly circulated, will give us a majority against Prohibition. We are somewhat afraid that the Eastern States, now being safe, will render us no assistance."

With such evidence, as the lawyers say, "We rest."

CHAPTER IX.

LOCAL OPTION.

" For none of us liveth to himself, and no man dieth to himself."
—*Rom.* 14 : 7.

" The State is the normal unit of sovereignty, and it is opposed to sound theories of government to transfer to local fractions the decision of a question of such general and far-reaching importance. . . . Legislation of this kind breaks the educational force of law. What can be voted up or down by the people of a village or a county —what is right in one district and wrong in another—loses all moral significance."—*Judge Robert C. Pitman.*

"Besides, the reformation of a town, or even of a State, is but the emptying of its waters from the bed of a river, to be instantly replaced by the waters from above ; or like the creation of a vacuum in the atmosphere, which is instantly filled by the pressure of the circumjacent air. The remedy, whatever it may be, must be universal - operating permanently at all times and in all places. Short of this, everything which can be done will be but the application of temporary expedients."—*Dr. Lyman Beecher's* " *Six Sermons on Intemperance,*" preached in the year 1825.

OF all the remedies for intemperance short of absolute Prohibition, none has been more highly praised than this. None has received the support of a greater number of good men. It is urged in its behalf :

1. That this system is peculiarly American, allowing each community to manage its own affairs in its own way.

2. That it allows Prohibition to be enacted wherever it can be enforced ; that where the local sentiment in favor of drink is strong enough to defeat a local ordinance

against it, that sentiment would be strong enough to prevent the execution of a State or National law if that were enacted.

3. That Local Prohibition can be obtained where State or National Prohibition could not be; or at any rate, very much sooner; that a Local Option Law can be passed in States where a State Prohibitory Law would be defeated, and by it a large part of the State, including all the rural districts, can be put under immediate Prohibition.

4. That facts sustain its claims; that in several States it has been highly successful, notably in Georgia, where by Local Option many whole counties and numerous towns and villages are under complete Prohibition.

This is certainly an attractive showing. But there are objections to the system both on the ground of Theory and of Fact.

(A) To the Theory of Local Option it is to be objected:

1. *That it is wrong to give any community the right to legalize a wrong;* and that the business which makes madmen, idiots, murderers, and paupers, and blasts the returns of honest industry and the happiness of home, and does a host of citizens to death, is morally and politically wrong. No community can make the wrong right by a majority vote, and the State has no right to allow any community to legalize such a wrong within its borders. For it must be remembered that Local Option *means the option to permit* as well as the option to prohibit. By a weak—and somewhat cowardly—fear of the word Prohibition, it has become common to speak of a Prohibitory town like Alliance, O., for instance, as "a Local Option town." But all towns in Ohio are Local

Option towns. Cincinnati has as much Local Option as Alliance. *An option is a choice*, and there never was a choice with but one thing to choose from, except poor Hobson's "That or nothing." Cincinnati takes the option of permitting the sale, Alliance the option of prohibiting it. That is all. The Municipal Council of Cincinnati have the option of prohibiting the liquor traffic all through Cincinnati to-morrow if they choose. Their idea of Local Option is to have it continue, and that is precisely what the law means to allow them to do, if they please. In a word, Local Option authorizes each locality to choose whether it will destroy its citizens or not. The State has no right to authorize such a choice.

2. That it is un-American and un-republican. The American idea of liberty is distinctively *not* of piecemeal, but of aggregate liberty. "That these colonies are, and of right ought to be, free and independent STATES." The towns were never independent. No town on American soil ever had authority to legalize anything contrary to the general welfare—till Local Option laws came in at this late day. That is not American but Italian independence. In Italy, a few centuries ago, any town might go to war with any other—Milan with Venice, Florence with Pisa. It was so in ancient Greece, where Athens waged long and destructive wars with Sparta, and Thebes with both, and every city could make its own treaties with all others, declare war and conclude peace at its pleasure. It was a system of weakness and ultimate ruin, bringing both Greece and Italy under the spoiler's yoke. Our fathers never proposed any such policy of disintegration. That system would have made it of no consequence to Virginia that Great Britain closed the port of Boston : of no conse-

quence to Massachusetts that Tarleton ravaged South Carolina; and of no consequence to either that the British attacked New Orleans. Even before the adoption of the Constitution our fathers recognized that the country was one, and died for that idea on many a hard-fought field from Maine to Georgia. The very first object of the Constitution was, as stated in its preamble, "to form *a more perfect union;*" and this ideal, cemented by the struggle of the Civil War, has been growing upon the people ever since. The very fighting point in that struggle was the assumed right of any State to act for itself without reference to the wish or the welfare of all the States. That claim went down in blood. Now, what we refused to the gallant South we propose to grant to each little municipality, and call it "American." In the thunder of a hundred battle-fields the American people have proclaimed that this idea is not American.

The principle of Local Option is simply the Douglas doctrine of "Popular Sovereignty," or, as it was sometimes called, "Squatter Sovereignty," applied to a new issue.

Stephen A. Douglas, in 1854, said:

"If Kansas wants a slave-State constitution, she has a right to it: if she wants a free-State constitution, she has a right to it. It is none of my business which way the slave clause is decided."

Abraham Lincoln replied:

"He (Douglas) contends that whatever community wants slaves has a right to have them. *So they have if it is not a wrong. But if it is a wrong, he cannot say people have a right to do a wrong.*"

We stand with Abraham Lincoln. We declare that system not American which makes the same act lawful in one town and criminal in another five miles away, so that a travelling man would need a colored map of the State spotted like a leopard to tell him in which towns liquor-selling is a protected right and in which it is a punishable crime.

(*B*) The Fact:

1. Local Option is inadequate protection. The rapid transit of our age is against it. That is not very effective Prohibition which a railroad train will carry a man out of in half an hour.

The mother in a Local Option town does not know but her boy will be made a drunkard within twenty miles of her home, the whole power of law upholding the tempter in the process. The wife does not know but her husband will come home drunk from the next town and beat her to death, as the result of a purchase which is as lawful in that neighboring town as the purchase of groceries. Such things continually happen.

Rev. Wayland Johnson, of Dalton, Ga., assures us there is a " large and, in Georgia, constantly increasing number of intelligent and respectable people who are Prohibitionists at heart, but who doubt the practicability of the present Prohibition measures. The last are cool-headed, thoughtful men who believe in Prohibition absolute and uncompromising, but are thoroughly sick of the Local Option farce that stretches a restriction rope around one county while a deluge of bottles, jugs, and kegs flows in from the next. That this sort of traffic is inconsiderable and working very little injury, is the common notion among those who have a pleasant faculty of seeing only what they desire to see. But that such is not the fact is evident to any one who is not hopelessly blind to the clearest daylight occurrences in every community. That the number of besotted young men and heart-wrung mothers is increasing instead of diminishing in this Local Option State is the surprised exclamation of all good people who do not weigh evidences in the balance of their hopes." Such a law cannot be permanently successful. A protective law should be as wide as the danger and the need.

2. Local Option surrenders to the liquor traffic the centers of population and power. This is our answer to argument (2) in its favor.

It allows the liquor traffic to maintain legalized strongholds in the midst of our civilization. All the towns of a county may be under Prohibition except the county-seat. But the men of the county must go there for almost every transaction involving law, and often for other business. While the liquor traffic is legalized there, intemperance will invade the surrounding towns. The village boy rarely spends his life in the village where he was born. Still more rarely does the farmer's boy remain on the farm. The prizes of wealth and ambition are in the cities; and Local Option gives up those very places to the enemy.

The young man who goes into business there is every day throwing off provincial ideas as narrow and petty and "behind the times." All around him are the legalized saloons, recognized places of business with as good a standing before the law as his own, and patronized by men in the highest station. The very idea of Prohibition is scouted as foolish and fanatical. He is adapting himself to city life. Why should he not adapt himself to this phase of it? Why should he not discard Prohibition as something petty and provincial?

Here, as in other cases, it will be observed, that it is the *legalized* saloon that does this. The clandestine sale in spite of a State Prohibitory Law would not have the same effect, for it would be an outlawed, criminal thing which his honest principles would brace him against as against other crimes. This was precisely the case with the Bangor editor of whom "Nasby" tells, who said: "Up to twenty-one I never saw it, and after that I did not want it." When he went to Bangor *he was still on Prohibition ground*. Liquor enough is sold there, they say, but it is sold clandestinely. In order to get it he would have had to engage in a law-breaking transaction, and buy in a saloon that might any time be raided, and himself summoned as a witness before a criminal court. There is no charm in that kind of thing for a decent young man who has not formed an appetite for liquor.

Then, too, the outnumbered temperance people in the cities have a right to the re-enforcement of the temperance voters in the rural districts. John B. Finch, in an address delivered in Tremont Temple, Boston, in 1883, declared:

"The people in the cities where the evil element controls, are entitled to protection by the State. Is it a truly brave man and leader who would say to the drunkard's wife and child in Cincinnati, 'I regret that you live in the city, but as you do, I see no help for you, for the saloon-keepers control the city, and I am in favor of Local Option'? It is treason to God and humanity to advocate the policy of the State turning the helpless in the great cities over into the hands of the drunkard-makers by Local Option. Ohio is a State. Every home in it is entitled to State protection."

Local Option gives up the temperance men—and women —of the cities to be governed by the slums.

3. Local Option keeps the question constantly in politics. It is always to be decided over again at every election—a struggle that tends to weary temperance people out, and in which, by the trickery of politics, they

are always liable to be conquered by surprise. It gives the rum power the advantage of "eternal hope."

On this and other practical points we are able to call two witnesses from Georgia, the banner State of Local Option—Rev. Wayland Johnson, of Dalton * (already quoted), and Professor H. A. Scomp,† of Emory College, Oxford. It is fair to suppose that they know what they are writing about.

Professor Scomp says:

"Another objection to Local Option is that it is too temporary and too local. Under the Georgia general law a county may, upon petition of one-tenth of its voters, determine the question every two years. As the law allows of license for one year, nothing is more common than for the saloonist to renew his license upon some pretext after an election has been ordered and before the result has been announced. Then if Prohibition wins, the dramseller falls back upon his 'vested-rights' and plies his trade for about one-half of the whole period during which Prohibition is to operate. It is very easy for the liquorites to keep up the agitation for the second year, and so the matter is never settled. Local Option is the creature of cliques and political rings. A county has been carried for Prohibition but by a bare majority. The liquor men constantly look forward to the opportunity for resuming their business. Often the rumseller moves his saloon just a few miles, barely beyond the county limits, and brings a wagon into requisition, which delivers the liquor, of course bought at the saloon (?), to the thirsty customers. The law is too temporary to deprive the saloonist of the confident expectation of an early return to his former place, and so he remains an active factor in opposing it, and all the more *as his money is still invested in the traffic.* Thus Local Option nurtures a viper in its own bosom.

* * * * * * * *

"Local Option is constantly in politics. Georgia furnishes innumerable examples of this—*e.g.*, of the 111 members of the House who voted for the Local Option Bill in 1885, only about twenty were re-

---

* "The Weaknesses of Local Option," in *The Voice* of March 22d, 1888.

† "Local Option in Georgia," in *The Voice* of February 9th, 1888.

turned to the same branch of the next' Legislature. The champions of Prohibition are steadily relegated to the shades of private life by the political bosses, who find that such men are not available by reason of their temperance records. Why? The liquor power is against them. Local Option *permits the liquor power to remain organized* in its interests in the State, and it is always ready to seize upon the first opportunity to restore itself. Such opportunities are continually offered in the political ring-work around the court-houses."

Mr. Johnson says :

" There is not a county in the State where the question is settled within even a fair degree of probability. The condition of Atlanta is the condition of every county where Prohibition has had a practical test. It is settled in one way to-day and in another way to-morrow."

4. It disintegrates the temperance forces. This is our answer to argument (3) in its favor.

By Local Option partial Prohibition may be sooner obtained, with all its disadvantages, but the complete triumph which might be won is rendered impossible. It is snatching a limited and transient advantage to lose a wide and permanent one. It is to limit every temperance man's view to his own county or town. When he can say, " We have no saloons in our town or county," if his friend replies, " We are cursed with them still," his answer is likely to be, " You must vote them out as we did. If you don't, we can't help it." It is to substitute for the Christian precept, " Bear ye one another's burdens" that very different text, " The Devil take the hindmost"—and he does. It gives politicians unequalled power to "shut up" temperance men. " Have you voted out your saloons?" " Yes." " Then what are you fussing about? Let other places do the same if they want to. If not, it's none of your business." Or if the answer is, " No," the politician replies. " Well. if you can't get them out of your one town or county, how do you think you could out of the whole State?"

On this point Professor Scomp says:

"Local Option is the weakest of bonds for uniting the people of a State to secure legislative action. Time and again has the query been propounded to us: 'If four-fifths of Georgia is under Prohibition, why do you not sweep the State?' Kind friends, a great writer has said: 'Collect the thunder into a single peal, and it will rend the heavens; divide it into a thousand parts, and each becomes but a plaything for a child.' So of Local Option. In 1884–85 the demand for a general law against liquor was accumulating, heaping up, so to speak, ready to overleap all bounds, and tear in pieces all opposition. The Macon *Telegraph*, a vigorous anti-Prohibition paper, urged the Legislature to accede to the popular demand for a Local Option Law, otherwise the Democratic Party was likely to be rent asunder.

"The law was carried, yet to-day the temperance cause in the State would doubtless be stronger and far more efficient had the law been defeated. Then the State was a unit and working for a common end and in hearty co-operation. Since May, 1885, no *State* Temperance Convention has assembled and no *State* work has been inaugurated. The thunder peal has died away in low mutterings, ever and anon, from a county here or there over the State.

"Had the Legislature of 1885 refused the law, the next Legislature would have been a most pronounced temperance body, and measures more stringent than the Local Option Law would have been adopted. But the combined strength necessary for State work was divided. To each county was served out a mess of Local Option pottage, the smallest possible ration which could still or silence the hungry cry for legal Prohibition. Temperance was turned away to the counties, and ceased knocking at the doors of the Statute-making Power. Thus with more of temperance sentiment than could be found in almost any other State, Georgia was left with the weakest bond of all among her temperance workers, and to-day it is one of the hardest of States to organize for effective work in the temperance cause.

"Local Option has left Georgia without a temperance organization, and with no plan of concerted State action. The forces which ought to be united for the reduction of certain liquor strongholds lack a head and a common objective aim.

"Local Option is of all forms of temperance legislation the least able to resist those temporary revulsions which come in the course of every great moral or popular movement. Such ebbings of the tide leave the option ship stranded high and dry—stern seaward. At such times of low sentiment the vigilant enemy is always ready; the abolition of the law is but short work and the labor of years is overthrown. Such is the ultimate fate of all such temporary measures. Adopted as an experiment, the law continues to be regarded as on trial and a change is always anticipated. Hercules grew weary of a battle perpetually renewed, and the hydra would eventually have conquered had the contest continued one of simple endurance. So temperance men, not having the money and selfish incentives of their foes, at last tire out and give over the conflict, usually with the promise of High License, ample restrictions, regulations, etc., which promises liquordom never yet has redeemed.

"The wisest Local Option temperance men *expected to use the measure as a stepping-stone to general Prohibition.* 'Let us work on, redeeming county after county, until not more than a dozen liquor strongholds be left, then with one grand *coup d'état* we will sweep the State.' Such was the popular delusion. On the other hand, the rum power sagaciously conjectured that Local Option might be used as a breakwater against the temperance tide about to flood the State. To gain time and *scatter their opponent's forces* was their shrewd policy. Local Option might stave off the final doom; so it became the law of the land. A halt was called, and temperance enthusiasm was allowed to expend itself in crushing the hydra's heads in the counties, only to find the task perpetually renewed. The Prohibition line was broken, and rum still had its hand upon the legislating power.

* * * * * * * *

"No, no. Local Option was never a permanent temperance law; no country ever yet stopped and stayed there. Forward or backward must be the course, and alas! the bugles always sound retreat. Best go beyond and not indulge in this fatal lotus-eating, but ground Prohibition in the Constitution of the supreme, fundamental law of the land."

All Americans are our fellow-countrymen. All men are those for whom Christ died. This thought is the vital breath of all missions to the heathen and of all Christian philanthropy at home; as that grand, early missionary said, "I am debtor both to the Greeks and to the barbarians, both to the wise and to the unwise." This spirit of Christ's out-reaching Gospel must be applied to our national curse. Wherever it spreads its wings of darkness the legions of temperance reform must crowd in, to conquer the evil for those who suffer most from it, and have least power to defend themselves. By all that we know of the blessings of Prohibition in any one locality, we are bound to reach out to places yet unredeemed. The temperance men of the country are debtors to the boys of the city, to the weeping mothers and desolate wives and worse than orphaned children, to spread over them the ægis of uniform law with the ballots—and, if need be, the bullets—of State and Nation behind it. In such a day as this let no man retreat across the imaginary line of a municipality and witness the slaughter of his countrymen far and wide around, with the surly question of the first murderer, "Am I my brother's keeper?"

Why have we never tried Local Option for our Tariff? The seaports where public sentiment was sufficient might collect duties, and if goods came in free at other ports, it would be because public sentiment was not strong enough to prevent, and we could not help it. Ah, no! we will not leave the protection of cotton and woollen goods to Local Option. For that we invoke the strong arm of the Nation. It is only for the protection of our sons, of home, humanity, and character, that we will divide the country up into helpless fragments that cannot combine together.

It is especially bad strategy to effect this disintegration and disorganization of the temperance forces at a time when the liquor traffic is organizing and consolidating as never before. It is to fight by detachments against a concentrated army. It is to apply a local remedy for a national curse. It is absolutely sure without further experiment that Local Option can never relieve our country from the terrible economic loss of life and treasure produced by the liquor traffic.

One question then remains: What practical action should Prohibitionists take in regard to Local Option? We can best answer by an illustration:

Suppose that when cholera threatens our shores our Government should commit all quarantine regulations to Local Option. We should argue and protest against such a law as unwise, un-American, inadequate, and even inhuman. We should do our utmost in every honorable way to get the people to see its folly, and the Government to replace it by an adequate national law which would defend the people against the national curse. But in our own town we would do our utmost to make local quarantine accomplish all there was in it. We would appeal to the council, stir up the board of health, arouse the citizens, clean the streets, cellars, and sewers, police the roads, and strive by our local precautions to make the devastation as light as possible. We would do the same in all other towns we could reach—yet all the while maintaining our protest against the legislation that gave us up to fight by counties and municipalities a nation-sweeping pestilence. The atmosphere is national; the winds that blow are continental. The elemental laws rolling in the pestilence on the wings of the wind would soon teach us that no man liveth and no man dieth to himself. A great cry would go up for a system of protection wide as the land. None of us may sit selfishly down in our little plot of ground and placidly see the young men of neighboring towns and cities going to destruction. If we do, God will require it of us, and the plague we thought we had fenced off shall somehow find our sons and brothers in the march of His avenging Providence.

The reason Local Option cannot be made successful is, that God does not intend that it shall be. He never meant any company of men to sit down in safe seclusion and see their fellows drift by to destruction. "He hath made of one blood all nations of men to dwell on all the face of the earth." Let those who are shut up to Local Option wring from it all the good they can, yet never resting in it, but reaching out beyond their own narrow boundaries in the spirit of a broader patriotism and a truer humanity.

CHAPTER X.

SUPPLY CREATES DEMAND.

"Again, I find that the constitutions treated are like the movable feasts, never twice alike. If I can produce the precise tint of flushing to-day, in a man, by six ounces of sherry or three ounces of the finest whiskey—the Encore whiskey, for example, which is said to be the purest—*I am told in a week or two that the quantity has lost its effect, and that I must change the drink or give a little more.* Then I shake in my shoes, lest by yielding I should encourage my patient to rely on the drink, to increase it and become a tippler."—*A Physician's Letter to Dr. B. W. Richardson.*

"But when the enormous profits of brewing came to be known, when men hungering for money saw there was a net profit of from $1 to $2 on every barrel sold, capital and business capacity were put into it, and the style of conducting the business was changed entirely.

"When you went into the business you did not wait for a demand for your stuff, but you set about *creating* a demand. And you went about your work cleverly. You established beer shops where there had never been a call for them, and you proceeded with an ingenuity that was devilish and a persistency that was infernal to *make* customers for your product. You laid traps for the people. You took houses and rooms everywhere, and put into them men fitted by nature for the business, and made it to their profit to entice men and boys into your places to be taught to drink beer. The number whose stomachs were already trained to the liquid were altogether too few for your purpose, and you began a regular systematic recruiting of the ranks of drunkards, which you have faithfully followed ever since, your success in this nefarious trade increasing with the money you make by it."—*The Toledo Blade—Reply to Letter of an Indignant Brewer.*

THE usual law of economics is, that demand creates supply. Let there be a great influx into any region of a population who must be fed, and there will be more farm labor invested and transportation facilities created to supply the demand for food.

But with luxuries the case is often different, and the supply creates the demand.

One carpet or piano introduced into a backwoods settlement will create a demand unfelt before. The sagacious Romans understood this, and hence held their conquests so long. The barbarians were terrible because their only trade was war. It was their only pastime, too. The Roman commanders encouraged merchants to follow in the track of their armies, and to introduce the luxuries and refinements of civilization, till there arose a demand for them which would make the conquered people averse to war and even glad of the Roman authority, which made possible among them the arts of peace.

But this is especially the law of vices. One gambling hall or one well-advertised lottery introduced into the most moral town will soon develop a passion for gambling among numbers of men who would otherwise have gone through life without thinking of such a thing as possible. The opening of a house of prostitution in the most quiet district is a signal to all decent families to arise and be gone. It is not merely the fear of the disorder that will come in. It is that all who have families to care for know that the vicious element will create a rapidly-increasing demand for vicious indulgence.

This is most emphatically true of intoxicating drink. It appeals to no natural demand of a healthy human orgianization.

Dr. Felix L. Oswald writes:

"Dogs, cows, horses, sheep, and even hogs shrink from the taste of rum as they would shrink from the bitter waters of the Dead Sea.

After days of burning thirst, a caged wolf will still turn with loathing from a pailful of lager beer ; and the beasts of the wilderness would prefer the most insipid ditch-water to the best flavored wine. The oft-repeated fable that the Abyssinian baboons can be captured by the simple plan of exposing pots full of intoxicating drinks, seemed to imply an exception from that general rule, till the naturalist Brehm ascertained the fact that the taste of the noxious liquor has to be disguised by a large admixture of syrup, and that, instead of being attracted by the fumes of the brandy, the victims of that stratagem are in fact stupefied by brandy-drugged syrup or honey, as they might be killed with sugar-coated strychnine pills. The trapper who kills wolves by scattering their haunts with pieces of poisoned meat might as well suppose that the dupes of his trick had been attracted by the scent of the poison. To animals in a state of nature the undisguised taste of alcohol in all its forms is invariably repulsive.

"Has man alone lost that protective instinct of his fellow-creatures ? The truth is, that no other protective instinct of our fellow-creatures is more fully shared by man than the instinctive aversion to the noxious products of fermentation. To the palate of an unseduced child lager beer is as unattractive as cesspool water, brandy as nauseous as turpentine, pure alcohol as shockingly repulsive as sulphate of quinine. In other words, nature has not waited for the advent of Greek dictionaries and abstruse lectures on analytical chemistry, but, in a language as intelligible to children and savages as to scholars and sages, has ever denounced alcohol as a foe to health and life. That warning reaches every class of creatures, down to the animalculæ of the duck-pond, the tiny inhabitants of a water-drop which, under the lens of a microscope, can be seen wriggling with animated specks of all possible forms, every one of which will instantly dart to the opposite corner of its little sea if its fluid should at any point be polluted with a spray of alcohol. The same warning comes even to the child of the confirmed drunkard, for no fact in human physiology has been demonstrated by more abundant proofs than the truth that no human being was ever *born* with a passion for alcoholic beverages. That passion may be acquired in some cases more easily than in others, but its first development is always due to the influence of evil associations, never to the promptings of an innate appetite ; and a strict investigation of alleged exceptions would only confirm the correctness of Dr. Zimmerman's remark, that ' the effects of education are too often mistaken for hereditary tendencies.'

it might, indeed, be questioned if the taste of *any* other poison is more universally abhorred by all unperverted children of nature than the taste of alcoholic fluids."

Yet alcohol has the power of creating in any human constitution an artificial demand as mysterious as it is undeniable and deplorable. The following incident has gone the rounds of the papers, and no one seems to have thought of denying it:

A Cincinnati merchant was advised by his physician to take a tablespoonful of brandy in a glass of water every day after dinner. In a short time he said to his wife, "You are not giving me the full amount these last few days. It does not have the same effect." A week or two passed without remark, when he again complained: "Wife, you have been reducing the amount of the brandy again. I can feel the difference." The wife answered, "My dear, since you spoke of it before, I have been giving you two tablespoonfuls every day." The merchant leaned back in his chair with sudden astonishment, and said: "If that is the case, I will have no more of it." We cannot get beyond the ancient words, "Wine is a mocker."

Let any man with capital enough—it does not take much—*to simply wait*, start a saloon in the most temperate village, and he can surely build up a trade. There are the idlers who sit around the grocery in more or less unprofitable talk, but ultimately get tired of each other and go home. They have wasted time, but no cash. They are not tempted to gorge themselves on crackers and herrings. The saloon-keeper makes it pleasant for them to drop in there. It is light and warm. There are no customers to bother them, and no ladies to put a restraint on anything they choose to say. The proprietor "'treats" them to an occasional glass. It is the cheapest of advertisements. Their sluggish brains are stimulated. They suddenly find a motive in life. They can get stimulus without exertion. A shamefaced "honor" requires them to buy something of the man who keeps open a place for them, and who has actually given them some of his wares. A few evenings make them sure customers. A crowd attracts a crowd. Others will drop in because they are there. Any man who wants to see them on any business must look there for them. Boys are inclined to linger where men gather. Games of cards, checkers, etc., are introduced to increase the attraction. Every man who has learned to drink invites his friends to the saloon. The tired laborer, coming home in the hot evening, sees before him the sign, "Ice Cold Lager Beer." The saloon man stands in his door, talks of the hot day and the hard work, and invites him in to rest and take a cool drink. "It will make you feel better." And it does—for the time. That man will come again. In a little while he will not be able to go home without his beer. If he does he will be miserable all the evening.

A good supper does not restore his energies, nor the quiet of his home rest him as it used to do. The disease of alcoholism is established. When winter comes the appeal changes from "Ice Cold Beer" to "Hot Tom and Jerry," which flushes the whole surface of the body, with its deceitful warmth, leaving the vital organs rapidly to chill, demanding more of the stimulant to throw the blood to the surface again. With a retinue of such customers the saloon is fairly started. With its profit of four hundred per cent. on the original cost of the liquor, it has become a paying business. Abolish it now, and its regular patrons will go to distant cities to get their drink, or smuggle it secretly in. Then shallow economists talk of the "demand." There is a demand, *but it has been created by the supply.* This thing can be done in any town within one year, unless stopped by law or fought by the most vigorous and united efforts of churches and temperance societies that have a very strong hold on the community—and often in spite of the very utmost that they can do.

This explains the furious opposition of liquor men to the laws of Prohibition States. They parade the figures of the amount of liquor they smuggle in, and of the "dives" and "joints" that flourish in Kansas, Iowa, and Maine. Then they "agitate" for a repeal of the law, and pour out money like water to get it repealed. We protest that, on their statement of the case, this is not possible for human nature. Here is a Chicago distiller who finds by his books that he is sending more liquor into Iowa than into any license State of equal population. There is no drawback of license. If he sells direct to consumers, he gets retail prices. *What on earth does he want that law repealed for?* From the case, as he states it, there is no conceivable reason. From the real facts there is every reason. There are hundreds of towns and villages where boys are growing to manhood without ever tasting liquor—where men go on their way without ever wanting it. In those places, the "bootlegger" would be more apt to get another man's boot than to sell any out of his own. Every liquor-dealer knows that by establishing legalized saloons in such towns he can within a year create a demand which will be permanent and increasing. The "trade" can afford to spend a million to create that demand in

Iowa or in Maine. They are ready to do it. It would be a good business investment.

Even in the cities where the law is most poorly enforced, legal selling would immensely increase the sale. We indignantly deny that slander upon American boyhood and manhood, that it "wants to do a thing as soon as you make a law against it." The man who says that is not to be trusted anywhere. He simply advertises himself as of rascally instincts, or accustomed to rascally society. Does the law against murder fill our boys with a raging desire to kill somebody? Does the law against stealing make honest clerks itch to get their hands into their employers' till? Are we likely to have an increase of defaulting cashiers now they know they can be extradited from Canada? Every one who knows decent boys and young men knows that, while they regard the absence of law as permission, they will be kept back by self-respect and regard for the opinion of others from visiting unlawful places unless under the influence of strong persuasion, generally attended with a previous undermining of moral principle. The ambitious clerk in a nice store is not going to be seen by his employer or his customers sneaking into a cellar for a drink of whiskey. He is not going to know that fact about himself. But open one on the same block, as elegant in all its appointments as the store he keeps in; have its doors swing open from the sidewalk; let him see men of fashion and influence going and coming there, and the whole case is changed. It may be literally true in the beginning that he goes there "to see a man"—to collect a bill, close a bargain, make an appointment. It has become one of the regular places of business of the city, and he readily drifts in. So far from its being a recommendation of any so-called "restrictive" law that "it abolishes the dives," that is the worst thing that can be said about it. If liquor must be sold, let it be sold only in "dives." Let the old topers drink themselves to death there if they must. The boys and young men of the better class will be saved. With them the "dives" will be the strongest temperance argument. The shrewd and temperate Spartans used to call in their slaves at times and make them drink while their sons, without tasting the liquor, looked on at the disgusting spectacle, and imbibed a life-long contempt for drunkenness and all that would produce it. The "dives"—if they must exist—may be the Helots of our civilization, and save all our boys who have not the spirit of a slave. But the legalized and gilded saloon is capable of awakening in the best of them a demand else unknown, but which, once awakened, shall become a destructive madness.

It is for this that the liquor traffic is "agitating." It is for this that it is using all its "pull" upon subservient politicians. For this it is using its hold upon the daily press to trumpet far and wide "The Failure of Prohibition," thus preparing public opinion for its repeal. For this it is working underground with its vast corruption fund. The liquor barons are not satisfied with their unparalleled gains—as no avarice ever yet was satisfied. They must have this whole land for their camping-ground from sea to sea.

These are not the words of a dreamer in the study. D. R. Locke, the renowned "Nasby," the editor, politician, and man of the world, said in his pamphlet on "Prohibition :"

"The vast brewing establishments of Milwaukee, Cincinnati, Toledo, and Rochester have millions invested in this business, and their success in the introduction of their beer may be measured by their wealth. They are the richest corporations in the country, and no instances are known where, with fair business management, they have not amassed enormous fortunes.

"They keep energetic men travelling all the time establishing saloons. In the city of Toledo, with 90,000 population, they have 800, and the number is constantly and rapidly increasing. A corporation cannot break ground in the suburbs for a factory that the brewer's agent is not there to purchase a lot upon which to erect a saloon, and the moment an addition to the city is platted, a saloon is the first building that goes up. They know every workingman and the wages he gets, and they demand their share of it, and generally get it.

"Did they confine their operations to the cities it would not be so bad, but they do not. They have invaded the country, and there is scarcely a hamlet or cross-roads in which they are not represented. With millions of capital, with an energy that is wonderful, with all the zeal that cupidity inspires and feeds, they are everywhere. There is not a family that they do not threaten, nor one that is outside their influence.

"It is this aggressive feature of the trade which has awakened a demand for the interposition of the law to prohibit instead of restraining. Heavy taxation of the traffic has no effect, for the profits of the business are so great that no taxation has ever been reached that they could not laugh at. The profit on beer is enormous, and they have a safeguard against taxation in this, that they make their own prices and they have possession of their customers."

District Secretary, Edward Ellis, of the American Baptist Home Mission Society, said, in a public meeting:

"I have been trying for ten years to get ahead of the saloon, and never yet have succeeded. I have gone to towns that were only shanties, and have found it there. I have gone to towns that were only in tents, and have found it there. I have gone to towns that were only in wagons, and there I have found some wagon selling whiskey over the tail-board. Everywhere the saloon was ahead of civilization and the Gospel."

The Brooklyn *Eagle* (Democratic) makes the following statements:

"The brewers are at fault. Hunt the statistics of the output of malt liquor during the past five years, and they will explain the increase in the number of saloons. Why, if I told you that of the sixty groggeries now in operation in this parish over thirty were owned by brewers you wouldn't believe me, yet such is the case. They operate in this way: For instance, if a man is a good fellow, genial and popular in the section in which he wishes to open, he needs little or no money to start a saloon. The funds are furnished by the firm, who only stipulate that the saloon-keeper shall as long as he is indebted to them sell their beer. The brewer takes a mortgage, of the iron-clad chattel description, on the stock and fixtures, and so stands to lose but very little. He always has the best of the bargain, as such customers pay more for their beer than those who are not under obligations to the maker of it.

"It has long been known that of the 3,500 saloons in Brooklyn less than one-third are owned by the individual operating them. The Sixth Ward saloon-keeper is right. If Father Fransioli and the other good priests of St. Peter's, together with local temperance reformers generally, want to secure less rum-selling they must make their fight against the principal and not the agent."

THE CONCENTRATED NATIONAL LIQUOR TRAFFIC IS ONE VAST ORGANIZED TEMPTATION. It is like a wild beast waiting, watching for victims, especially for boys, with their unformed characters, strong energies and passions, and their prospective earning power. This traffic, with its uncounted millions of capital and its half million closely organized workers, is watching around all our cities, villages, and homes—its "business" to destroy by creating a fire of demand that shall burn to the lowest hell.

All the original tendencies of alcoholic drinks are artfully reinforced by those who furnish the supply, that they may create a quicker and more overmastering demand. Says "Nasby":

"The man who comes to stopping at a place of this kind every night and taking one glass, within a week finds a half dozen necessary. And the seller helps him along the downward road as rapidly as possible. There is always upon the counter a plate of pickled codfish, or red herrings cut into proper lengths, or pretzels covered with salt—all thirst-provokers—and they actually put salt into the beer, that the desire for the pleasant liquor may be increased. Beer becomes a necessity to him before he is aware of it, and his fate is fixed. The seller can count upon so much a day from him as certainly as though he had it in his till.

Just as this volume goes to press, there comes to hand the New York *Times* of May 5th, with the following story strikingly illustrating the claims of this chapter. A great crowd visited Rockaway the first Sunday in May, but for some reason "preferred to wander through the paths" rather than visit the saloons. As the afternoon wore on, "a hurried consultation" was held. An insignificant shed suddenly took fire. The church bells were rung. The fire department was summoned.

"Meanwhile all Rockaway turned out. The crowd of visitors hastened to the scene of the conflagration, the report having reached the upper section of the beach that the Seaside was in flames. When the mob reached the shed, somebody with rare presence of mind stamped out the fire. But the crowd was there, and they turned into the saloons and hotels in a manner highly gratifying to the proprietors. The firemen, hungry with the exertion of drawing hook and ladder through the sand, attacked the sandwiches. Extra men were required to tap the beer. The faces of the innkeepers relaxed into broad smiles, and they congratulated the firemen upon their prompt appearance, speculating meanwhile upon what the danger might have been had a hurricane been blowing.

"It is safe to conjecture that the Fire Marshal will never ascertain the cause of yesterday's fire."

It is not good political economy for the State to allow a demand to be created for a product which is only an economic curse.

CHAPTER XI.

THE TRUE RESTRICTION.

"'Shall the throne of iniquity have fellowship with thee, which frameth mischief by a law?' A law framed to protect evil is a method of framing mischief by a law. A law which assumes that a thing is wrong, and yet tolerates it; which attempts only to check and regulate it, without utterly prohibiting it; which aims to derive a revenue from it for the purpose of government; which makes that, which is morally wrong legal, is one of those things in human affairs with which the throne of God can have no fellowship."—*Rev. Albert Barnes.*

"The evil [intemperance] ought not to be permitted to grow in order that the police may be called in to repress it. Prevention is not only better than cure, but prevention is a duty, and cure is a lame, halting attempt to undo an evil which we have wilfully permitted."—*Cardinal Manning.*

The restriction of the liquor traffic is encompassed with some insuperable difficulties which many of its most earnest advocates utterly fail to consider. When temperance men are not satisfied with High License and similar policies which are offered as restrictive measures, they say, "You are so impracticable!" "What do you want?" Well, let us consider a moment

WHAT TEMPERANCE MEN DO WANT.

1. First, then, temperance men want to reduce intemperance. This is certainly a quiet and reasonable statement.

Now note the following

PARALLEL PROPOSITIONS:

2. Intemperance is in direct proportion to *the amount of liquor consumed.*

3. Any restriction which reduces intemperance will reduce *the amount of liquor consumed.*

4. Any restriction which does not reduce *the amount of liquor consumed* neither can be nor ought to be acceptable to temperance men.

2. The income of distillery, brewery, and saloon is in direct proportion to *the amount of liquor consumed.*

3. Any restriction which reduces intemperance will *reduce the income* of distillery, brewery, and saloon.

4. Any restriction *which does not reduce the income* of distillery, brewery, and saloon *cannot* reduce *intemperance,* and neither can be nor ought to be acceptable to temperance men.

Any one who will carefully study these parallel propositions will see that

THE DIFFICULTY IS IN THE PROBLEM,

ex hypothesi, as mathematicians say; that is, it is in the very terms of the original proposition, and must infallibly appear in any conclusion that can be worked out from them. For temperance means the reducing of intemperance, *and of all that produces it.* But,

5. Any restriction which *reduces the income* of distillery, brewery, and saloon will be

BITTERLY CONTESTED BY LIQUOR-DEALERS,

and will be almost as hard to enforce as Prohibition—perhaps harder, as it is more difficult to make a building burn quietly and moderately than to put out the fire altogether. Therefore, when any brilliant genius fancies he has discovered a " restriction which will be at once ' popular ' with liquor-dealers and ' satisfactory ' to temperance men," he had better quietly hide away his discovery and turn his energies to the invention of perpetual motion, which has been the occupation of unbalanced minds in all ages, and is likely to be sooner accomplished and more beneficial to the human race. For, to put

THE MATTER IN A NUTSHELL,

| Temperance men want to abolish intemperance, because it is the ruin of humanity. | Liquor-dealers do not want to abolish intemperance, because that would be the ruin of their business. |

No human mind can unite these irreconcilable things in one policy, acceptable to both temperance people and liquor-dealers.

Many well-meaning temperance people supported High License in the States where it has been adopted, or it never could have been adopted. Many such, in other States, not aware how the experiment has failed where already tried, now favor the system in States where it has not been tried. They look upon it, and are strenuously urged to regard it as part of a system of gradual approaches toward complete Prohibition. But the trouble with all these gradual approaches is that they do not approach. They are not steps toward the extinction of the traffic, but after years of trial they leave it richer, stronger, more firmly intrenched, with no decrease of drunkenness in the interval. There is, however, a restriction which will meet all the requirements of honest but cautious temperance men ; which will at once stamp out the saloons in the rural districts ; which will greatly reduce their number in large towns, and put those which remain under such restraints that the sale of liquor in the whole place will be diminished from about fifty to seventy-five per cent., and which will put the traffic in the way of gradual extinction even in large cities. It meets all the requirements of the demand for "restriction with a view to ultimate Prohibition."

IT IS PROHIBITION.

Its enemies say, "You cannot enforce it in the great cities." We know we cannot as fast as we would. We have to admit that the resistance will be stubborn and the victory slow. The result there at first will be just restriction, but the best restriction ever introduced. The traffic will be outlawed, its debts uncollectible. Palatial saloons will vanish. Great breweries and distilleries will be closed. Capital will be shy of taking any risks in the business, and will soon be diverted beyond recall into other channels. Saloon-drinking and saloon-treating will become unpopular, and be practised only by those whose respectability is below par.

Prof. A. R. Cornwall, of Aberdeen, S. D., says, "The saloons of Omaha are gilded hells; in Council Bluffs they are in old rookeries and back alleys, and are hated and despised by all respectable people. They have no power to attract or tempt the better class of young men."

A prominent merchant of Kansas told us this incident from his own experience. "I had a nephew in Ohio," he said, "who was getting to be a pretty wild boy. His mother wanted me to take him out with me, and see if I couldn't save him. He worked in our store about two weeks, and seemed to be doing very well. Then, one morning, a gentleman came to me, and said, ' Mr. ——, I am obliged to inform you that that new clerk of yours has been drinking beer in the back room of ——'s drug-store.' I thanked my informant, and, after he was gone, called my nephew into the private office, and stated the case to him, and said to him, 'This cannot be allowed. If it happens again, it will mean dismissal. I cannot protect you, for my partners insist that a man who will sneak away to get a drink of liquor contrary to law is not to be trusted in any capacity, and they will not have him in our employ.' 'Uncle,' said he, 'that's the first drink I've taken since I came here, and they've spotted me. You can depend on me. I won't do it again.'" He kept his word, and has become a temperate, trusted, and prosperous man.

What "restrictive" law could have been so effectual as that? If the saloons in that city had been cut down to one hundred, or to ten, *and those legalized*, it would not have been against the young man's honesty or respectability to visit one of those legalized saloons. The fatal thing was to visit an outlawed "joint."

Another instance fell under the writer's own eye. It was in a village which had lately adopted Local Prohibition. The saloons were still fighting the ordinance, though professing to sell no liquor. Two men from the country drove in at a flying rate behind a good horse, straight to a door of a saloon. They sprang out, hitched the horse, and started to enter. Just then they spied a fine, tall, square-looking young fellow coming up the sidewalk. They hailed him, shook hands heartily, said something to him which I did not hear, but all three turned and started back to the saloon. In the door stood the idle barkeeper. As the three crowded to the door, he said something to them which produced visible consternation. All stopped short with very blank faces, and consulted together. While they stood irresolute, the barkeeper leaned forward and said a word or two; then, with a slight beckoning motion, turned and went through the saloon into a back room. One of the older men nudged the other. Both laughed and started to follow. One of them, as he did so, laid his hand on the young man's shoulder, saying, "Come on!" The young man straightened himself up to his full height—a splendid figure as he stood there—shook his head decidedly, turned on his heel and walked swiftly away, while the other two, a little less jolly, went in, and soon came out furtively wiping their mouths.

That is the effect. Honest, self-respecting young men are not going to adopt sneaking devices to do an outlawed act. They will honor the law more than they will covet a drink.

Meanwhile all the country around will be under Prohibition. The cities will be in a state of siege. Leading merchants will find the purchasing power of temperance communities. In ten years the country boys will be trained to temperance habits and principles, and will be finding employment in the cities and rising rapidly to places of trust and influence. In ten years more they will be leading business men. Before a generation is past the boys from the country will be among the chief men in the cities. Then the siege will end. The city will be captured. Prohibition will prohibit. The laws against the liquor traffic will be enforced as well as the laws against all other crimes—with some failures and evasions, but with a vast sum of good, and doing more for the city's peace and protection than all other laws combined.

Prohibitory laws will prohibit at once where immediate Prohibition is possible, and where complete Prohibition cannot be at once secured, these same laws will operate as a most effective restriction, continually tightening toward absolute Prohibition.

If it is objected that these laws will be a dead letter in the interval before final enforcement, we answer that they will not be dead with live, honest officers to enforce them, any more than the Union armies were dead when it took them four years to put down secession; and the educational effect was far better than if secession had been "regulated" by any process during those four years, in the hope that by tolerating it awhile the nation would be made ready for its "ultimate" suppression. In general, the way to do a thing ultimately is to begin doing it immediately.

Those who urge so earnestly that it is folly to pass a law till public opinion is educated up to it, forget the power of

LAW AS AN EDUCATOR.

A gentleman, waiting in a city drug-store for a prescription one Sunday, overheard the following conversation through the telephone: "Can you give me —— Blank's drug-store? Say, Sam, can't you come over? What are you doing? Well, don't you do it! It's against the law! Do you hear? Well, there's a law against it! You're liable to be pulled for it! Never mind what he says! You may get yourself and the firm into trouble. Do you understand? You don't know but he's come just on purpose to get you into a scrape. Well, you quit! Tell him you won't do it, and send him off. Now I know what I'm talking about. I'll stop when I come down in a few minutes. Now be sure and let that alone!"

Then to the listener he said, "He's a young fellow who has just come here and don't know the law against selling liquor on Sunday. A man is trying to get him to put up some whiskey for him, and somebody must put him on his guard."

We often speak of Sunday laws as "inoperative," "a dead letter," etc. Yet here was one, with no official to enforce it, forming opinion across the city through a telephone. It is a fact that a great part of the public idea of right and wrong depends upon what is legal or illegal. Had there been no law on the subject, I can imagine either of those young men selling whatever spirits were called for, and saying to any remonstrance, "Why not? There's no law against it that I know of—" nay, even adding, "We *have to furnish* what customers call for." The whole burden of obligation would have been shifted to the other side. Now, it is no small gain that the young, inexperienced, and thoughtless should have set up before them a plain bar of statutory provision framed by legislators who are presumed to be thoughtful men, careful of the morals of the community.

Lecturing in every school-house on the farmer's right to his land and crops, and the injustice of having his growing grain trampled by hunters and dogs, would not do one-half as much to form public opinion as the law which allows him to tack a shingle to a tree to warn off trespassers, and to prosecute all who disregard it. Boys and idlers reason about it, "What do they have such a law for?" "Why, suppose you had a nice field of wheat or corn that you'd worked hard for. How'd you like to have it all tracked and trampled to let some fellow get a few birds?" "Well, I suppose it's fair enough. You can't blame a man for protecting his land." That law is educating every boy and man in the community. It carries the accumulated sense of right of all landholders to every passer-by in a tangible form.

Take away that law, and the hunter with his dogs and gun says: "Who's going to hinder me, I'd like to know?" and he is bold from the sense of the

TACIT SANCTION

of the community. Take away the law against any practice, and the average judgment of the community is that "there is no harm in it." Law calls attention to the matter, forces all concerned to think about it, and if there is evil in it, forces the public conscience to recognize it. That is a gain. Then, if the law effectually abates, or even reduces an evil, those who did not at first approve it come to do so, as the gain and improvement are forced upon the public attention.

All this is true of the liquor traffic. It is too often viewed as a final settlement of the question to say that no law can be enforced which is not sustained by public sentiment, and it is forgotten that a law which has a just basis is

A MIGHTY FORMER OF PUBLIC SENTIMENT.

Hon. Robert C. Pitman, LL.D., Associate Justice of the Superior Court of Massachusetts, says:

> "Government, in the discharge of its proper duties, should not only frame its laws so as (to quote Mr. Gladstone) 'to make it as hard as possible for a man to go wrong, and as easy as possible for a man to go right,' but it is bound to set before him a true ethical standard. . . . When the State writes 'Criminal' over the doorway of the most elegant drinking-saloons, as well as over the lowest grog-shops; when it places at the bar of justice the tempter by the side of his victim, and when it stamps every package of liquor as a dangerous beverage, meriting destruction as a public nuisance, it has done much to warn the young and unwary, and to turn their feet aside from the downward path."

This restriction by absolute prohibitory law will make all partial restrictions easier. Consider

1. *Sunday Closing.*—This is the great contest in Cincinnati at this time of writing. The difficulty is that there is a traffic which is *legal six days in the week.* The vast stocks of liquor on hand are legal property. The proprietors and bartenders are doing a legal business. They have a host of regular customers whose appetite does not shut down on Saturday night, and who have more leisure and more money on Sunday than on any other day: *The Western Broker* (liquor paper), of Chicago, thus graphically describes the situation :

"The saloons were closed in Duluth Sunday, the 16th, for the first time, and were kept relentlessly shut until 12 o'clock Monday morning. Do the people who never took a drink in their lives ever pause to think what such a statement as this means? Here on the sidewalk are torpid stomachs craving for the invigorating cocktail, unstrung nerves that just one more whiskey would put in perfect tune, and aching brains that think of nothing but brandy and soda ; in the saloon are barrels and bottles of aqua vitæ, and, tantalizing thought! only a door prevents their use. A similar situation has been depicted by Coleridge in that passage in the 'Ancient Mariner,' where he uses the famous, vivid lines : 'Water, water everywhere, but not a drop to drink.' Just substitute whiskey for water, and then you have it."

The peculiar hardship is, that *the whiskey is in there,* "with nothing but a door between." The temptation to violate the law is tremendous. Determined officers can stop the open sale, but the "side-door sale" is a more difficult matter, especially when—as is often the case— the saloon-keeper's family-rooms open into the saloon, and the only thing visible is that he receives a large number of callers that day. But outlaw the whole traffic, make those liquors cease to be property, make them liable to be confiscated wherever found, enact a "search and seizure clause." Then those great stocks of liquor will disappear. There will be no vast capital and no army of dealers to fight your Sunday-closing law. If men are found drunk and traced to a certain place, it is not necessary to prove that the liquor was sold to them there, nor that the owner kept his saloon open that day. The offence is in having a saloon at all. The police can search the premises and seize the liquors for evidence of that, and abate the whole business as a nuisance. With all we hear of lax enforcement of Prohibition in Kansas, we do not hear of any carnival of Sunday selling. The chief facilities for selling liquor on Sunday are removed by outlawing the liquor traffic on all days. This is to stop the worst disorder, and to stop the heaviest drain upon the resources of the wage-workers, as the liquor men declare their Sunday sales are twice those of any other day.

2. *Take Local Option.*—Here is a community with so strong a Prohibition sentiment that they can close their own saloons. Near by is another town with so strong an anti-Prohibition sentiment that the enforcement of Prohibition is very difficult. Under Local Option what happens? Why, men go from the town which has closed the saloons, buy liquor in the town where the saloons are open, and come home drunk. *There is nobody to punish for that sale.* The man who sold it had a legal right to sell it, so long as the buyers were not actually intoxicated on his premises. The only thing the Prohibition town can do is to fine and imprison the drunken man, which is chiefly to punish his family, and perhaps have them to support at the expense of the sober men. The Prohibition officers cannot touch the sale in the non-Prohibition town. But outlaw that traffic by State law, and that

sale can be followed up, and the dealer in the adjoining town be made to smart for it if detected. That is Local Option with a fighting chance.

3. *Selling to Minors.*—It is extremely hard to prove this upon a dealer *who has a legal right to sell to men* all the time. Some old toper may have given the boy a drink out of his own glass. But if no man has a right to sell to anybody, and boys are found to have been drinking, it is not very difficult to find where they got their liquor and punish the offender. The illicit dealers, as a rule, become very shy of the juvenile class. Numbers of parents testify that "Kansas is the grandest place to bring up boys" for this very reason. Thus the destruction of forming manhood is largely prevented, and the "Harvest of Death" is stayed.

All partial restrictions are made easier by the one crowning restriction of Prohibition.

CHAPTER XII.

WHO WILL ENFORCE THE LAW?

"Your poor-houses are full, and your courts and prisons are filled with victims of this infernal traffic, and your houses are full of sorrow, and the hearts of your wives and mothers; and yet the system is tolerated. Yes! and when we ask some men what is to be done about it, they tell you, you can't stop it! and yet there is Bunker Hill! and you say you can't stop it—and up yonder is Lexington and Concord, where your fathers fought for the right and bled and died—and you look on those monuments and boast of the heroism of your fathers, and then tell us we must submit to be taxed and tortured by the rum business, and we can't stop it! No! and yet your fathers—your patriotic fathers—could make a cup of tea for his Britannic Majesty out of a whole cargo—and you can't cork up a gin jug! Ha!"—*Father Taylor, "The Sailor Preacher," in a temperance meeting at Charlestown, Mass.*

A CORRESPONDENT of the Chicago *Standard*, the leading Baptist journal of the West, writes to that paper as follows:

"Do not let us look too much upon men in authority as the enforcers of the law. It belongs to the citizen to see that the laws are enforced. We are a republic. Every citizen is a part of the police-power for enforcing the law. Upon citizens, male or female, rests the enforcement of our State laws."

The liquor laws of Illinois to which he refers forbid the "keeping a disorderly house," "selling to minors, persons intoxicated, or in the habit of getting intoxicated," etc. The writer we have quoted holds that these laws, properly enforced, would be almost equivalent to Prohibition, and that the enforcement belongs to the citizen.

He has put a widespread opinion into admirable statement. It is clear, definite, unfaltering, uncompromising. Such a statement, right or wrong, is always an ultimate gain to the cause of truth.

But when we come to ask, Is it true? three decided objections arise:

1. It is impracticable.

Let us apply it to the very laws in question, and see what headway "the citizen," "male or female," would be likely to make in enforcing them. Enforcement of law includes the detection, the arrest, and the punishment of its violators. How much can the citizen do to detect illegal selling? I have seen two boys under sixteen years of age pass me and go into a saloon with laugh and bravado. If I had followed them, what could I have done? No liquor would have been sold to them while I was there, and means would speedily have been taken to make it too hot for a recognized temperance man to remain. An unrecognized citizen who was merely seeking evidence, would soon be "spotted," and hustled out in some kind of disagreeable row that would threaten not only bodily injury, but a stain upon his name. A detective could show his badge, and back it up, if need be, with a revolver. The majesty of law would be recognized as his shield. The "citizen" would be looked upon as only a vile "informer," for whom nothing was too bad.

Add to this that the ordinary upright citizen has too much else to do. The best man is the busiest man. All his feelings and habits of life, too, make it practically impossible for him to linger in dens of vice and shame. If he were to try it, he would be so plainly ill at ease that he might as well wear a placard, saying, "This is a Temperance Man." Then his ignorance of the tricks and devices of the criminal class would make him a child in their hands, as the novice always is in the hands of the professional. But when we extend the "citizen's" action to "male or female," the supposition becomes too wildly impossible. Women have braved the physical and moral filth of the saloon for moral influence, though, even then, with very limited success. The Crusade, as an appeal to saloon-keepers, collapsed in the nature of things, though as an appeal to God its prayers are fast fulfilling. But woman in the saloon to enforce the laws against the proprietor, would be like woman entering a tiger's den to put a stop to his carnivorous habits. Even when her husband comes home drunk from the saloon and beats her, and smashes their little stock of crockery and furniture, she cannot ordinarily claim the damages the law allows, unless her husband will go on the stand and swear against the man who sold him the drink, with the knowledge that no saloon-keeper in that city will ever sell him another drink. Experience proves that the drinking man cannot be prevailed on to give such testimony one time in ten thousand. The hands of the individual citizen are tied from any effectual detection of crime.

The case is even worse with the arrest and punishment of criminals. If I see men engaged in manifest gambling in another man's parlor—see the cards played, and the heaped-up gold and silver appropriated by the winner—I cannot enter to arrest the proprietor or the players. By crossing the threshold I should make myself a trespasser and put myself in the wrong, instead of righting the wrong I had witnessed.

If I see the door of a saloon ajar on Sunday, can I go

in, arrest the proprietor, drag him to the police-station and club him into submission if he resists ? Can I bring him to trial before me, and fine him or send him to the workhouse ? I am absolutely estopped from all this. The utmost I can do is to call a policeman's attention to that open door, and, if he arrests the proprietor, appear as a witness against him. If the police judge sets aside my evidence, holding that the proprietor had simply gone in to black his shoes, I cannot overrule his decision and inflict a penalty. So far from its being true, that " upon the citizens, male or female, rests the enforcement of our State laws," " the citizens, male or female," are absolutely forbidden to execute our laws, and would lay themselves liable to prosecution if they should attempt it.

2. The existence of executive officers is against this theory of citizen enforcement.

A nurse, worried by the care of a fretful child, exclaimed, " People ought to take care of their own children !" " In that case," replied her mistress, " what should I want of you ?" If " the citizens, male or female," have to enforce their own laws, what do they want of this great army of paid officials ? The sublimity of insolence has never been so perfectly attained as by this claim of men appointed, paid and sworn to do a certain work, that it belongs to the people who pay them to do the work themselves if they want it done ! There is only one thing more amazing, and that is, that they have been able to get their claim accepted by the citizens, who are at once defrauded and defied ; and that ministers, philanthropists, and editors should become the mouth-pieces of recreant officers, to instruct the people that these men are not to be expected to do what they are sworn and paid to do !

Thus the executive usurps the legislative function, and the police department becomes a Court of Appeals to set aside such laws as it pleases, without needing any legal knowledge or study as qualification for the work. Members of the Legislature say to the people, "We have given you a good law. Now, see that you enforce it." A year passes. The law is defiantly violated before the very eyes of the officers of the law. The people form "law and order leagues," which cannot do the enforcing, but might be termed "punching-up societies," to get the men to do the work who ought to do it—and they punch in vain. Then the delinquent officials calmly say, "This law is a dead letter. A law which is not enforced is demoralizing to the public conscience, and should, therefore, be repealed!"

This is the very essence of kingship, when the executive dispenses at pleasure with the enactments of the legislative power. Richard the Lion-Hearted or Henry the Eighth never attempted anything more. For attempting so much, Charles the First was beheaded, and James the Second banished; and if the Prince of Wales were to try it, when he comes to the throne, he would make a short and everlasting end of royalty in England. But we, after having broken the yoke of George the Third, calmly submit to be braved by mayors, prosecuting attorneys and chiefs of police, whom we have made out of nothing to be petty kings.

It is time to re-divide the functions of government, and have it clearly understood that the executive is not co-ordinate with, but subordinate to the legislative. The Legislature has power to incorporate in any law heavy penalties upon executive officers who fail to enforce it, as has been done by the Legislature of Kansas in the "iron-clad" prohibitory law, which has been in force for some four years, and stands unchallenged. The executive has no review of legislative measures which have once been duly enacted into law. General Grant, with his clear common-sense, said on a notable occasion, "Whether the law is good or bad is none of my business. It is law, and I have nothing to do but to enforce it. If a law is bad, to enforce it vigorously is the quickest way to get it repealed." In a word, the business of the executive officer is simply to execute. He has no other reason for his existence.

3. The essential principle of republican government is opposed to this theory of individual enforcement of law.

The author we have quoted says : "We are a republic. Every citizen is a part of the police-power for enforcing the law."

This is the deadliest argument against his theory. *Because* we are a republic, the enforcement of law does not rest upon the individual citizen. A republic differs from a democracy in being representative. As truly as it can be said, "Every citizen is a part of the police-power," it can be said, Every citizen is a part of the law-making power of the nation. But how do the people make laws in a republic? Solely by their representatives. Pure democracy was seen when all the people (*demos*) of Athens crowded into the Agora, and by the show of hands enacted laws. We have repudiated that system for sufficient reasons. In the long run, better laws will be made by representatives, at their worst, than by a mob at its best. Hence, in our system of government, the individual citizen never votes directly upon a law.* The way "the people make the laws,"

---
* The people may vote directly upon a constitutional amendment,

is by voting for representatives pledged to pass certain laws, or believed to favor them. If these representatives break their pledges and refuse to pass the laws they were elected to pass, can the people crowd into the halls of legislation to make the laws after all? That would be Jacobinism in its wildest form, such as Napoleon suppressed at the cannon's mouth. In a true republic, if the representatives fail to pass appropriate laws, the people's only remedy is to elect other representatives, who will do what the people want done.

The case of the enforcement of laws is precisely the same. The whole action of the people in enforcing the laws is representative, exactly as in making them. Sometimes the people forget this. An atrocious murder is committed. All the citizens crowd together and hang the murderer. That is direct enforcement of law by the individual citizen. But all thoughtful men deplore it as contrary to the principles of our Government and the best interests of society. Direct enforcement of law by the individual citizen is called mob law, or lynch law, and tends strongly toward barbarism. The whole theory of our institutions is that the people shall execute the laws, *exactly as they make them*, by their representatives. It would be just as competent for our legislators to say, "If you want better laws, come and make them," as for our executive officers to say, "If you want your laws enforced, go and enforce them." If the representatives of the people for the enforcement of law fail to enforce it, the remedy is the same as if the representatives of the people for the enactment of law fail to enact it. Put in representatives who will. Non-enforcement of law is

but that has no force *as law*, till their representatives in the Legislature pass suitable statutes to carry it into effect.

not an argument for the repeal of the law, but for the repeal of the non-enforcing officers. Private citizens are not called upon to become detectives or patrolmen, in order to cover the remissness of the proper officers. The citizen's business is not to dog the delinquent officer, nor goad him, nor coax him, *but to remove him*, and put in his place a man who does not need to be goaded, coaxed, or watched. The sharpness of private interest does this infallibly. Into a mill near my residence, the proprietor walked one night, and found his watchman asleep. He did not appoint a subsidiary watchman to keep that one awake, nor sit up nights to do it himself. He paid that man off the next morning and put in a new man the next night. The sleeper will never watch in that mill again. A little of this firm common-sense in government would at once better our whole Administration. True, the citizen cannot deal thus directly with appointed officers, but he can always strike them through the appointing power, which is elective. It would be most wholesome for every appointing officer to know that he would be held strictly accountable both for the capacity and the integrity of his appointees.

Especially does it become teachers of public morality to lay responsibility where it belongs, and to teach that the enforcement of law belongs to the officers of the law, and that when they are false to their trust and their oaths, they become chief of violators and worst of criminals, and should be pursued by the withering denunciations of platform, pulpit, and press, and hurled from power by the suffrages of all honest men.

It should be clearly borne in mind that the prospect of enforcement is not increased by weakening the law. If Chicago had made her laws so mild that the dynamite murderers could not have been punished, unless some one had seen the man throw the bomb, and had examined it beforehand, so that he could swear that it was an explosive bomb, and if the penalty had been a $5 fine, would Chicago have had less of dynamite since? Why, if that had been done, every judge who sentenced a criminal, every banker who refused a loan, every merchant who discharged a clerk, every officer who arrested a vagrant, and every housekeeper who reprimanded a servant-maid would have been in danger of the deadly explosive. The law that could punish the concocters and abettors of murder, and punish them with death, was a law that could be enforced to some purpose. Weakening law is not a protection against non-enforcement. Herein is our answer to a different argument, which is commonly couched under the alluring phrase,

"ENFORCING THE LAWS WE HAVE."

Every little while some one comes out with this as a brand-new discovery. "If you would only enforce the laws we have we should do very well. If you can't or won't enforce the laws we have, what's the use of clamoring for new laws?" Well, it is said that an enterprising Connecticut man, whose ancestors drove a thriving business in wooden hams and nutmegs, has invented a new umbrella, to be called "the lending umbrella." It is made of brown paper and willow twigs. It has all the qualities of an umbrella, except keeping the rain off. You lend it to your friend, and if he comes in dripping and complaining, you ask, "If you won't use the umbrella I lent you, what's the use of my lending you another?" The laws we have in the license States "won't hold water," as the lawyers say. Temperance men try them, spend $200 to get the saloon-keeper fined $5, and grow discouraged. The law has all the properties of a temperance law, except stopping the sale of liquor. But that happens to be the very thing we want it for.

The answer to all this plea is very simple. The weaker the law, the harder it is to enforce it; the stronger the law the easier it is to enforce it. The law against counterfeiting is a strong law. It makes the possession of counterfeit money in any quantity a presumption of guilty intent. It makes the possession of counterfeit plates and dies a crime. Premises can be searched for them. They can be seized where found and the owner arrested, and the tools used in evidence against him. The penalties are very heavy. The offender who is convicted is put where he will not need to be convicted again very soon. Hence violations of the law are extremely few. Now, tone that law down. Allow any man to hold all the counterfeit money he pleases. Allow engravers to make all the counterfeit plates and dies they please, to advertise them in the papers, and have stores where they can sell them as freely as chromos. Require evidence that a man has actually passed some of the money before you can convict him, and let counterfeiters be eligible for the jury. Make the penalty for the offence about a fortieth part of what it will cost to convict the offender. Then tell the public, "If you can't enforce the laws you have, what sense is there in your demanding stricter ones?" The answer would be, "*So that we can enforce them.*"

Laws that allow anybody to manufacture liquor, keep it in stock, and to sell it to everybody except drunkards and minors, or on Sunday, or inside the imaginary lines of certain counties or townships, and that make saloon-keepers eligible on the juries that try liquor cases, will always be too weak to be successfully enforced. But a good strong law, like the Murray Law of Kansas, can be enforced with comparative ease. That celebrated law, after defining* the duties of "all sheriffs, deputy sheriffs, constables, marshals, police judges, and police officers of any town or city," declares:

> "If any such officer shall fail to comply with the provisions of this section, he shall, upon conviction, be fined in any sum not less than one hundred nor more than five hundred dollars, and such conviction shall be a forfeiture of the office held by such person; and the court before whom such conviction is had shall, in addition to the imposition of the fine aforesaid, order and adjudge the forfeiture of his said office."

Similarly, the same law provides (Sec. 11):

> "If any county attorney shall fail, neglect, or refuse to perform any duty imposed upon him by this act, he shall be deemed guilty of a misdemeanor, and upon conviction thereof *be fined* in any sum not less than one hundred dollars nor more than five hundred dollars, *and be imprisoned* in the county jail not less than ten days nor more than ninety days; *and such conviction shall operate as a forfeiture of his office*," etc.

This is going to the root of things, holding the officers of the law also amenable to the law. Public officers in Kansas are not much in the habit of telling the people that their laws *cannot* be enforced. Further provision is made in the event of such failure on the part of the county attorney for the attorney general of the State to enter the county, appoint as many assistants as necessary, see the law enforced, and collect the same fees which the county attorney would do for like service.

If Missouri, Texas, and Nebraska had the same law, Kansas would soon stamp out the last remnants of the liquor traffic. We can enforce the laws we have when we have the laws we ought to have.

---

* Laws of Kansas, 1885, Chapter CXLIX., Sec. 7.

CHAPTER XIII.

MAINE.

"The people of Maine are industrious and provident. Wise laws have aided them. They are sober, earnest, and thrifty. Intemperance has steadily decreased in the State since the enactment of the prohibitory law, until it can now be said with truth that there is no people in the Anglo-Saxon world among whom so small an amount of intoxicating liquor is consumed, as among the 650,000 inhabitants of Maine."—*James G. Blaine.*

THE celebrated "Maine Law" was passed in 1851, now nearly forty years ago. Has it been a success? We will take first the testimony of the late D. R. Locke (Nasby), of the Toledo *Blade*, who made a tour through the State of Maine for the express purpose of satisfying himself in regard to this matter. He says: *

"This is the strength of Prohibition. In Portland there are no delightful places fitted up with expensive furniture, no cut-glass filled with brilliant liquors, no bars of mahogany with silver railings, no great mirrors on the walls, no luxurious seats upon the floor—nothing of the sort. Drunkenness there has no mantle of luxury thrown over it, and the mask of sociality has been ruthlessly torn from it. If you want to get drunk in Portland, you go where the material is for that purpose, and that only. You must go and find it—it is not trying to find you.

"Who have taken the place of these 300 rumsellers of thirty years ago? Bakers, shoemakers, tailors, milliners, and people of that class. There are no houses vacant, and there is a better class of houses than ever. The effect of Prohibition upon the material pros-

---

* "Prohibition." By Petroleum V. Nasby, p. 12. National Temperance Publication Society.

perity of the city is marked. The workingmen own their own houses, their newspapers are better sustained, they have book-stores, art-stores, and all that sort of thing, which a whiskey city of the same population never did sustain; the small trades are all flourishing, and, despite the disadvantages the city labors under by reason of climatic and other conditions, it is one of the most prosperous municipalities in the United States. There was once $1,500,000 paid annually for rum. That money now goes into the comforts of life, and there is still a wide margin left for luxuries.

"In the country towns of Maine the effect is still more marked. The farmers, when liquor was out of sight, did not want it, their children grew up without knowing the taste of the destroyer, and comfort and prosperity have everywhere taken the place of slovenliness and unthrift.

"The best argument I found in Maine for Prohibition was by an editor of a paper in Portland, who was, for political reasons, mildly opposed to it. I had a conversation with him which ran something like this:

"'Where were you born?'

"'In a village about sixty miles from Bangor.'

"'Do you remember the condition of things in your village prior to Prohibition?'

"'Distinctly. There was a vast amount of drunkenness, and consequent disorder and poverty.'

"'What was the effect of Prohibition?'

"'It shut up all the rum-shops, and practically banished liquor from the village. It became one of the most quiet and prosperous places on the globe.'

"'How long did you live in the village after Prohibition?'

"'Eleven years, or until I was twenty-one years of age.'

"'Then?'

"'Then I went to Bangor.'

"'Do you drink now?'

"'I have never tasted a drop of liquor in my life.'

"'Why?'

"'Up to the age of twenty-one I never saw it, and after that I did not care to take on the habit.'

"That is all there is in it. If the boys of the country are not exposed to the infernalism, the men are very sure not to be. This man and his schoolmates were saved from rum by the fact that they could not get it until they were old enough to know better. Few men are drunkards who know not the poison till after they are twenty-one. It is the youth that the whiskey and beer men want.

"Thousands upon thousands of men from other States who are slaves to the drink habit, and so securely held by it that they cannot of their own power resist, go to Maine that they may live where it is impossible to procure the stuff which makes the meat it feeds on. While liquor can be procured anywhere in Maine, if one chooses to go to the trouble and expense necessary, its procurement is so hedged about with difficulty that the victim who really desires to free himself of his appetite generally succeeds. The help that Prohibition gives him is enough to turn the scale, and he is enabled to let it alone till his restored stomach and new blood give him will-power enough to do something for himself. It makes a difference with the man suffering for want of liquor whether he can step into a bar-room on every corner and take the one drink for present relief, or whether he has to go to as much trouble as would pay off a mortgage on a farm to get it. Hundreds go to Maine for a month or two and come back rejoicing in the thought that they are free. That they do not keep free is owing to the unfortunate fact that they come back to places where liquor is free, and they fall."

Undoubtedly there is another side to this picture.

The New York *World* in a Lewiston, Me., special despatch says:

"In the Maine cities a political pull is the secret of success in the rum business. Lewiston's story is the story of them all. One of the richest men in town is Henry Hines. He is a wholesale and retail liquor-dealer, and makes no bones of it. He owns three or four retail shops. They are raided only once in a great while, and then by his consent. He controls 200 votes and that is the secret of it. He gets the best of the other dealers because the officers don't dare to arrest him. He gives the Democratic Committee a large contribution in cash, but votes his men on the Republican side. In the rural regions the law is as successfully enforced as the law against stealing or any other crime."

Undoubtedly the Liquor League is working to secure Resubmission and Repeal in Maine, as they have done in Rhode Island. The prize is an inviting one. To be able to say, "Maine, after forty years' trial, has repealed

Prohibition," would be an argument to discourage many of its firmest friends, and to give hope and energy to all its enemies. The first step to repeal is non-enforcement. For that the liquor traffic is now working. They can afford to pay heavy fines. They can afford to have great stocks of liquor confiscated. If they can sell enough to produce manifest drunkenness and disorder, they can lead thousands to believe that the law is useless. Then they can spend great sums to trumpet all these incidents through the press, and one fact repeated a thousand times comes to seem to the people a thousand facts. They can hold up the example of High-License States, and appeal to human cupidity by most plausible arguments.

They say, "You see the liquor is sold and will be. No law can stop it. But if you would put a High License on every saloon, you might raise millions of money which would reduce your taxes." Average human nature has not yet got far enough from barbarism to pay taxes cheerfully. Every man wishes to shift the burdens of government upon somebody else. If you can really persuade him that he is shifting them upon the liquor traffic, he feels a degree of complacency that is as much like virtue as a counterfeit dollar is like the genuine. To put money into his pocket, and at the same time persuade himself that he is doing a public service, is an exquisite satisfaction. If you attempt to show him that the liquor traffic increases taxes more than the license reduces them, he answers, "But it is sold any way. It increases the taxes any way." This is the state of mind the liquor traffic is moving earth and—another region—to produce in the State of Maine.

Will it succeed? There are some possibilities that it

may. There are conscienceless politicians of national ambition. While the temperance vote is strongest in Maine, the liquor vote controls both the great national parties. To please the liquor men is to widen the outlook of ambition beyond the State lines into the national field. There are also politicians who are susceptible to downright bribery, and the liquor men know how to place money "where it will do the most (Satanic) good." The only remedy is for the people of every city and town in Maine to settle it that every official who does not enforce the law shall be *politically dead in Maine*. That will give a quietus to villainous ambition, for the man who is dead in his own State cannot be a live quantity in the nation.

For officers who really mean to fight the liquor traffic, the only effectual weapon is imprisonment of every offender, wherever the law allows it. Now that the national liquor power is concentrating upon you, they will laugh at any fines and confiscations you can inflict. What is $100 or $500 to a trade that is raking in every year its thousand millions? They will pay the offender's fine, and start him again with a new stock of liquors, and charge it to current expenses. But when you imprison a man, that has to be paid *in propriâ personâ*. The National Liquor-Dealers' Protective Association does not wear the stripes or go to the stone pile. It would take a high conscientiousness and a good cause to lead individuals to bear this to advance a national movement, and saloon-keepers have not been conspicuous as martyrs. Let the officials of Maine inflict imprisonment with an unsparing hand for every liquor offence that will bear it. Let the people of Maine demand that this shall be done, and fling out of office every official who will not do it. Three months of this discipline will silence all the boastful stories about "getting all the liquor you want in Maine."

In this the farmers must co-operate. The towns and cities must not be left to fight alone. Every non-enforcing officer of any city who aspires to a State office must be squarely defeated by the rural vote. Let every city officer know that if he pleases the liquor men in his city he can never get an office outside of his city. If the law is not strong enough at any point, let the rural vote rise like the waves of a great sea, concentrating on one object, to send men to the Legislature who will make that law stronger. How much it is to have boys grow up without knowing the taste of liquor, and able to say : " Up to the age of twenty-one 1 never saw it, and after that I did not care to take on the habit !"

Admit, if you will, all that is claimed about drunkenness in Bangor, how much it is for boys to grow up in ten thousand rural homes hating and despising drunkenness, and with not the slightest craving for the liquor which creates it !

We are prepared to believe that the picture could not now be made as favorable in Portland, Lewiston, Augusta, and Bangor as when Mr. Locke wrote. We believe the decline to be the result of a great conspiracy of the national rum power working with the aid of officials who can be influenced by pecuniary rewards or political advantage. We believe that to defeat this conspiracy the good and true yeomanry of Maine must arise to a new crusade to restore their law to energy and power, and, if anywhere it is weak, to bring the law up to the need of the times.

But, admitting all this, we still have evidence that the

Maine Law is accomplishing incalculable good, and that its failure would be a vast misfortune to the State.

Ten years ago Governor Dingley, in a message to the Legislature, wrote: "The great improvement in the drinking habits of the people of this State, in the past thirty or forty years, is so evident that no man who has observed the fact can deny it. Secret drinking has not taken the place of open drinking."

A year later Governor Perham stated: "Probably less liquors are drunk in Maine than in any other place of equal size in this country, perhaps in the civilized world."

Hon. William P. Frye, ex-Attorney General of Maine, declared: "I do unhesitatingly affirm that the consumption of intoxicating liquor in Maine is, to-day, not one-fourth as great as it was twenty years ago. In the country portions of the State, where there stood at every four corners a grocery or a tavern, and within a circuit of two miles from it were unpainted houses, broken windows, neglected farms, poor school-houses, broken hearts, and ruined homes, the law has banished almost every grocery and tavern, and introduced peace, plenty, and happiness."

These are the words of Judge Davis, of the Supreme Court: "The Maine Law, even now, is enforced far more than the license laws ever were."

General Dyer, Inspector General of the State Militia, Bangor, asserts: "The law has materially improved the moral and social condition of the people, reducing crime and poverty."

The following is the resolution passed by the Republican Convention held June, 1882, the largest ever held in Maine by any party:

"We refer with confidence and pride to the general record of the

Republican Party in support of the policy of prohibiting the traffic in intoxicating liquors, the wisdom and efficiency of which legislation, in promoting the moral and material interests of Maine, have been demonstrated in the practical annihilation of that traffic in a large portion of the State ; and we favor such legislation and such enforcement of law as will secure to every portion of our territory freedom from that traffic. We further recommend the submission to the people of a Constitutional Prohibitory Amendment."

In the year 1884 a Prohibitory Amendment was added to the Constitution of the State by a majority of more than 3 to 1—70,783 voting for the Amendment, and only 23,811 against it, giving most conclusively the popular verdict in its favor after thirty years' experience.

The aggregate receipts of Internal Revenue—which are chiefly for liquor and tobacco—decreased in Maine from $514,636.28 in 1863 to $50,286.45 in 1887.* Since that time this poorly-paying State has been consolidated with the District of New Hampshire, and the name of Maine has disappeared from the Internal Revenue list.

But, some one will ask, "Have not the Internal Revenue receipts for the whole country decreased also in the same proportion?" By reference to the same official table, it will be seen that the total receipts of Internal Revenue for the whole nation have *increased* from $41,003,192.93 in 1863 to $118,837,301.06 in 1887. Evidently some special cause has been at work in Prohibition Maine, and that cause would seem to be Prohibition.

There is not now a distillery or brewery in the whole State. How much this means is not always considered. It means that there is not a citizen of Maine who has capital in liquor production within the State, or large

---

* Annual Report of Internal Revenue for 1889, pp. 290-293.

stocks of liquor on hand of which he desires to force the sale in the community.

The following summary of economic results for twenty-five years is from Dr. Dorchester's "Liquor Problem in All Ages," p. 546:

"In August, 1882, Hon. J. G. Blaine . . . said: 'The condition of Maine is prosperous to-day—never more so in the sixty-two years since the State was admitted into the Union.' In the last twenty-five years the progress of the people in all forms of material prosperity has been great. The valuation of the property of the State has increased in that time from $100,000,000 to $225,000,000. In 1857 Maine had eleven savings-banks, with aggregate deposits and accrued profits amounting to $919,571.85. In 1882, Mr. Blaine says, 'There are fifty-five savings-banks, and their aggregate deposits and accrued profits are to-day about $30,000,000, and, perhaps, in excess of that sum.' In 1857 there were only 5,000 savings-bank depositors; in 1882 there were nearly 90,000."

This means prosperity among the common people—young men, clerks, workingmen and women, farmers, etc. They are the patrons of savings-banks. The greater the number of such depositors, the greater general prosperity. The workingman with a deposit in the savings-bank is not helpless in case of sickness or accident. He is not a slave to a tyrannical employer. In this view it is very significant that the number of depositors had increased so vastly, from 5,000 to 90,000, or eighteen times. That is to say, *eighteen people were able to lay up something in 1882, where one had been able to in 1857.* While the number of people able to deposit something in the bank had become eighteen times greater, the amount they were able to deposit had become more than thirty times as great, increasing from $900,000 to $30,000,000. The population of the State in 1860 was 628,279, and in 1880, 648,936, giving an increase in population of only about three and one-half per cent. in the twenty-five years, while the savings-bank deposits have increased more than twenty-seven hundred per cent., and the number of depositors has increased seventeen hundred per cent. Is it any wonder the liquor men think ".Prohibition a failure," when they see those $30,000,000 locked up in savings-banks which might just as well have been spent in the saloon ? Is it any wonder they are fairly raving to break over, and get hold of those savings-bank deposits, and the constant daily earnings of the people who have been able to lay up all that money ? The liquor traffic feels that it is a kind of robbery to have kept all this cash out of their hands so long. This is the prize they are striking for, and which is deemed worth unlimited expense and uncomputed lying. But from the standpoint of the welfare of the people and the happiness of human homes and hearts, who shall say how much it means to have those $30,000,000 in the savings-banks, and *not* to have had them in the saloon ?

CHAPTER XIV.

KANSAS.

"Kansas has abolished the saloon. The open dram-shop traffic is as extinct as the sale of indulgences. A drunkard is a phenomenon. The bar-keeper has joined the troubadour, the crusader, and the mound-builder. The brewery, the distillery, and the bonded warehouse are known only to the archæologist."—*Senator Ingalls, in The Forum, August,* 1889.

"What do you think of this? Kansas is a Prohibition State. She has but one penitentiary, with 996 prisoners. Texas, on the other hand, has no Prohibitory Law, and, while having 100,000 less people than Kansas, has two penitentiaries, containing 3,000 inmates."—*Good Health,* 1889.

The State which had been the first battle-ground in the anti-slavery struggle was the first to pass a Prohibitory Constitutional Amendment. That amendment was passed in the year 1880, and went into effect with appropriate legislation, May 1st, 1881. There were many defects in the earlier laws, but these have been gradually removed until, in 1887, the Murray Law made Prohibition effective in fact, as well as in name, over the greater part of the State. The border towns are exposed to an illicit trade from neighboring States, and in a few cities officials yet wink at quiet violations of the law. The decision of the Supreme Court (in the case of George A. Bowman and Frederick W. Bowman *vs.* The Chicago and Northwestern Railway Company, March 19th, 1888) allowing liquors to be imported and delivered to consignees in the original packages also leads to a considerable trade which the State has no power to prevent.

Yet the testimony is very strong in favor of the value and efficiency of the law.

The following tables of official testimony as to the workings of Prohibition in Kansas, and covering 97 of the 106 counties of the State, are made up of replies to questions submitted by *The Voice* since February last to the county officials of Kansas without regard to their political affiliations or previous knowledge of their views on Prohibition. The first table consists of replies from 83 counties in answer to questions sent to the Probate Judges; the second of replies to questions sent to the County Treasurers, the treasurers of 47 counties replying. Every reply, favorable or unfavorable to the workings of Prohibition, received by *The Voice* to these questions given at the head of the table, is printed below.

The evidence is overwhelming as to the success of the Prohibitory Law. From the 97 counties heard from 94 report positively that there are no open saloons; three qualify their answers, but do not claim that there are saloons in their counties. Ninety-two replies state that drunkenness and the consumption of intoxicants have greatly diminished; that the loss of revenue from former saloon licenses has been more than made good by the decreasing burdens of pauperism and crime under Prohibition, and by the directing of the money formerly spent in saloons into the legitimate channels of trade. Not a man claims that business has been injured by Prohibition. Of the 83 replies received in answer to the question, "Would you advise the re-establishment of the saloons under a High License Law?" 77 answered most emphatically "No," 4 "Yes," while 2 qualify their answers.

This table practically covers the State of Kansas, and demonstrates conclusively that the assertion, "Prohibition don't prohibit," has its foundation in imagination instead of fact.

The first table of answers of Probate Judges was published in *The Voice* of June 13th, 1889. It is given complete on the following pages, but the questions and answers are divided into two sets to adapt it to the size of this volume.

In making the summaries on the following pages it has been impossible to give more than a mere skeleton of each letter. Below we print a few of the letters in detail:

DRUNKENNESS REDUCED NINETY PER CENT.

J. B. Dill, Probate Judge of Jewell County, Mankato: "Absolutely there is not an open saloon in the State to my knowledge. There is not one now in this county of 20,000 inhabitants, and there has not been any in existence since the law went into effect. Drunkenness and the amount of liquor consumed for beverage purposes have, in my opinion, been reduced fully ninety per cent. The loss of the license revenues has certainly been more than made good by a great lessening of the burdens resulting from pauperism and crime and by an increase of legitimate business; honest statistics are very decidedly favorable to Prohibition in this regard. I would by no means consent to the return of the saloons, breweries, and distilleries under a High License Law, and I am confident that a very great majority of the voters and tax-payers of Kansas would join me in saying, *a thousand times No!*" Added to this letter is the following indorsement: "We, the undersigned citizens of Mankato, Kan., heartily indorse the above statement. —J. P. Fairchild, for the Bank of Mankato; George S. Bisbop, Vice-President of the First National Bank; A. Bailey, Register of Deeds; O. H. Durand, Superintendent of Public Instruction; E. A. Ross, Clerk of the District Court; A. B. Peters, M.D., Judge."

"MILLIONS IN IT."

B. R. Porter, Probate Judge of Anderson County, Garnett: "I am well acquainted in Johnson, Miami, Lima, Allen, and Anderson counties. They have no saloons. There are no saloons in Eastern

PROHIBITION DOES PROHIBIT.

OFFICIAL TESTIMONY FROM 97 COUNTIES OF KANSAS.

There is Not an Open Saloon in the State; Drunkenness and the Consumption of Intoxicants have Greatly Diminished; Crime, Pauperism and Taxes have Decreased; Many Jails are Empty, and Police Court Expenses have been Lessened; Business has been Benefited and the Prosperity of the State Increased by Prohibition; Kansas will Never Return to the License System.

County.	Name of Probate Judge.	1. How successfully has Prohibition closed the saloons in your part of the State?	2. To what extent, in your judgment, has it diminished drunkenness and the consumption of intoxicants for beverage purposes?
Allen	J. L. Arnold.	Not place in county where man can buy Intoxicants.	Consumption intoxicants too small to estimate.
Anderson	B. R. Porter.	No saloons in Eastern Kansas.	90 per cent.
Atchison	P. W. Bean.	They are all closed.	The consumption at least 50 per cent.
Barton	B. F. Ogle.	Successfully and entirely.	Consumption three-fifths less than under our Option Law.
Barber	Loren Edwards.	No open saloons that I know of.	More than one-half in all places outside large cities.
Bourbon	B. J. Waters.	A complete success.	Drunkenness almost disappeared. Consumption confined to few who import it.
Brown	T. R. Dickason.	An entire success; no open saloons.	From two-thirds to three-fourths.
Chase	S. A. Breese.*	Not a saloon within 100 miles from here.	Drinking reduced 99 per cent.
Chautauqua	J. V. Beckman.†	Saloons are closed.	Nine-tenths without doubt.
Cheyenne	Justin Badgerow.	No saloons in this county.	One-half.
Clark	J. D. Whitfield.	Changed saloons into drug-stores.	Increased drinking.
Clay	John T. Woods.	No saloons, and but one "permit" in county.	Almost entirely diminished drunkenness.
Cloud	W. V. B. Shaefer.	Entirely closed them.	500 per cent.

County	Name	Response	Effect
Coffey	W. H. Bear.	Not a place in county authorized to sell.	Almost totally.
Crawford	James A. Smith.	Effectually in this part of the State.	One-half, perhaps nine-tenths.
Davis	S. H. Nikirk.	Saloons all closed.	Drunkenness diminished 50 per cent; less drinking.
Decatur	J. R. Conquest.	Entirely closed; only 2 drug-stores with "permits" in county.	75 per cent.
Dickinson	B. W. Peck.	No saloons in county.	Not more than one-tenth the drinking there would be with saloons.
Douglas	John Q. A. Norton.	All saloons absolutely closed.	About 90 per cent.
Edwards	Chas. H. Hatch.	Not a saloon in our county; but 1 drug-store with "permit."	Very little used; law as well enforced as any.
Finney	J. W. Weeks.	Effectually.	At least 75 per cent.
Ford	D. W. Moffitt.	No saloons; "joints" hunted and driven out.	To very great extent; wild carouse under license unknown.
Franklin	J. A. Purdy.	Not a saloon in our county.	Intoxicated man a "seven days' wonder."
Garfield	J. E. T. Kephart.	Not an open saloon in this part of Kansas.	Not one case drunkenness under Prohibition to 25 under license.
Gove	A. C. Hennessy.	In smaller towns of State not a saloon in operation.	Diminished to a great extent.
Graham	S. Van Wyck.	Very successfully.	Diminished very materially.
Grant	(Geo. C. Underwood.	They are all closed.	Diminished about four-fifths.
Gray	J. R. Brady.	Not a place in this county where intoxicants can be procured.	100 per cent.
Greeley	A. K. Webb.	Completely; not a saloon in county.	90 per cent.
Greenwood	Allen Emmerson.	Not a saloon in this part of State.	See but one drunken man where we used to fifty.
Harvey	D. Felger.	Not an open saloon in county.	Not less than 50 per cent.
Haskell	A. P. Herninger.	Open saloons unknown in Kansas; not even a "permit" in county.	Fully one-half.
Jefferson	David Smith.	Not a saloon in county.	Drunkenness fully 75 per cent.
Jewell	J. B. Dill.‡	Absolutely not an open saloon in State.	Fully 90 per cent.
Johnson	J. L. Howard.§	Wholly exterminated them.	50 per cent.
Kingman	C. C. McMurphey.	Not a saloon in our part of State.	Very seldom that a drunken man is seen.
Kiowa	Alfred A. Mullin.	Not a saloon in this part of State.	Drunkenness almost wiped out.

* Postmaster, Cottonwood Falls.
† County Attorney.
‡ To the answers of Judge Dill is appended the following document:

"We, the undersigned citizens of Mankato, heartily indorse the above statement:

"BANK OF MANKATO, J. B. FAIRCHILD,

"A. BAILEY, Register of Deeds.
"E. A. ROSS, Clerk of the District Court.
"GEORGE BISSOP, Vice-Pres. First National Bank.
"O. H. DURANT, Supt. Public Instruction.
"A. R. PETERS, M.D., Judge."

§ County Superintendent of Schools.

186 ECONOMICS OF PROHIBITION.

PROHIBITION DOES PROHIBIT—Continued.

COUNTY.	Name of Probate Judge.	1. How successfully has Prohibition closed the saloons in your part of the State?	2. To what extent, in your judgment, has it diminished drunkenness and the consumption of intoxicants for beverage purposes?
La Bette	T. J. Calvin.	Not a place in county where drop can be bought.	Almost entirely.
Lincoln	F. H. Dunham.	No saloons open or otherwise in county.	Practically to a minimum.
Linn	Enoch Estep.	Not a saloon in this part of State.	None used except brought into State under "original package" guise.
Logan*	H. C. Chapman.	No saloons in Logan County.	Fully four-fifths less liquor consumed than with saloons.
Lyon	W. J. Combs.	I know of no saloons in Kansas.	One-tenth, taking into consideration increase in population.
Marion	C. R. Foote.	Absolutely.	Not less than 75 per cent.
Marshall	G. Goodwin.	No open saloons in our county; but plenty places where it can be bought.	A difficult question; where it used to be bought by glass it now comes in by barrel.
Meade	W. D. Hudson.	All saloons absolutely closed.	At least 75 per cent.
Miami	J. C. Collins.	Completely; no saloons in county.	90 per cent. Practically no drunkenness.
Mitchell	M. M. Rowley.	There are no saloons here.	Not one drunken man seen where 50 under license.
Morris	W. A. McCollam.†	No saloons in this county.	No drunkenness; except in very old cases, no drinking as rule.
Norton	Jesse Taylor.	Totally; we have no saloons.	99 per cent.
Nemaha	Geo. H. Benedict.‡	No saloons in county; no government "licenses" in county seat; population, 2,500.	Nineteen-twentieths.
Neosho	J. L. Denison.§	Not a saloon or licensed drug-store in county.	More than three-fourths. If neighboring States adopt Prohibition our success complete.
Ness	R. B. Linville.	No open saloons in this part of State.	Cannot answer definitely; that not so many persons drink is probable.
Norton	Samuel Means.	Not a place where liquor can be bought openly.	Not one-tenth drunkenness we had under license.
Osage	Geo. W. Doty.	Very successfully.	Two-thirds.
Osborne	B. M. Ramy.	Completely; not a saloon in this section.	Almost entirely.

KANSAS.

County	Name	Violations	Effect
Ottawa	W. D. Thompson.	No saloon in county; positively no violations of law.	75 per cent.
Phillips	N. Poling.	No saloon in county; positively no violations of law.	Diminished drunkenness at least three-fourths.
Pottawatomie	C. B. Huffman.	Saloons all closed in this part.	Reduced nine-tenths.
Pratt	J. A. Gardner.	Not an open saloon in Kansas.	Entirely eradicated in this part of State.
Rawlins	W. H. Siddons.	Every saloon closed in this part of State.	At least four-fifths.
Reno	S. A. Atwood.	Every saloon closed in this part of State.	Drunkenness fully three-fourths.
Republic	C. A. Northrop.	Fully; have to send to Missouri for liquor. No attempt to run saloons in the State.	Drunkenness at least 50 per cent; drinking very largely.
Riley	Geo. C. Wilder.	Saloons all closed in this county.	Greatly decreased; many think nine-tenths.
Rooks	John Mullin.	Completely; not an open saloon in county.	Not one-tenth drunkenness prior to Prohibition.
Rush	G. G. Wade.	All saloons in this part of State closed.	Decreased about 60 per cent.
Russell	J. G. Vogelgesang.	Not a saloon in county or that I know of in this part of State.	No intoxicants used as a beverage. Haven't seen ten drunks in five years.
Saline	C. E. Lamkin.	Closed every saloon in this part of State.	More than three-fourths.
Scott	B. F. Rochester.	Yes; not a saloon or "joint" in county.	About 70 per cent; perhaps more.
Sedgwick	W. T. Buckner.	Prohibition abolished open saloon.	Fully one-half.
Seward	I. F. Poston.	Partial success.	But very little, if any.
Shawnee	A. R. Quinton.	No saloons in the county.	Not one drunk where formerly 20 in Topeka.
Sherman	H. S. Kulon.	Absolutely no saloons in this part of State.	At least 75 per cent. Rarely see intoxicated person.
Sheridan	S. O. Wanzer.	No saloons and but one drug-store with "permit" in county.	Scarcely such a thing known as drunkenness.
Smith	J. W. Henderson.	This county never had a saloon.	Great majority young men growing up without drinking.
Stafford	J. F. Guernsey.	Entirely so.	None; sold now in quantities.
Stanton	S. C. Garner.	Not a saloon in this county.	At least 75 per cent.
Sumner	J. T. Sanders.	A decided success.	At least 90 per cent; probably 98.
Thomas	Joseph E. Loeb.	No saloons here, or in neighboring counties.	An intoxicated person never seen.
Wabaunsee	L. Richards.	Not an open saloon in State.	No liquors used except ordered from Missouri.
Washington	J. R. S. Birch.	I know of no saloon in the State.	To a very great extent.
Wichita	K. J. Shields.	Not single saloon in Western Kansas.	Almost entirely eradicated it.
Wilson	H. G. White.	Closed every saloon in this part of State.	Diminished at least 60 per cent; few old topers ship from Missouri.
Woodson	C. C. Clevenger.	No saloons in this part of State.	Fully one-half. Old topers send to Missouri.

*The answers of Judge Chapman, of Logan County, are also signed by K. E. Wileockson, County Attorney, N. G. Perryman, Sheriff; L. B. Fells, County Treasurer, and W. Jones, County Clerk.

† Ex-Probate Judge.
‡ Deputy Clerk of District Court.
§ County Attorney.
‖ Attorney at Law, Fredonia.

PROHIBITION DOES PROHIBIT—Continued.

County.	Name of Probate Judge.	1. How successfully has Prohibition closed the saloons in your part of the State?	2. To what extent, in your judgment, has it diminished drunkenness and the consumption of intoxicants for beverage purposes?
Chase	F. P. Cochran.*	Closed all saloons.	Some old-timers still send abroad for liquor.
Cherokee	Frank Hoover.†	Saloons are closed.	Drinking diminished.
Ellis	Geo. Philip.	A great many closed.	Diminished 90 per cent.
Hamilton	A. F. Reed.	Closed them all up.	Very greatly.
Harper	B. E. Shawhan.‡	Closed every saloon.	At least 90 per cent.
Hodgman	H. S. Booth.	There are no saloons.	Liquor little used.
Jackson	V. V. Adamson.	No saloons.	Decreased from 75 to 80 per cent.
Jasper	John E. Johnston.	Saloons and "club-rooms" closed.	Drinking decreased at least 75 per cent; rare to see drink.
Lane	Abe Frakes.	Have found saloons in some parts of State.	Drunkenness increased.
McPherson	P. T. Lindholm.	No saloons; law enforced to full extent.	Intoxicants used very little.
Montgomery	M. F. Wood.	Not a place sells liquor.	Decreased more than 90 per cent.
Pawnee	P. H Forbes.§	Every saloon closed; law strictly enforced.	Seldom see drunken man.
Rice	J. C. Seward.	All closed.	Very little drunkenness.
Stevens	N. Campbell.‖		Socially elevating.
Trego	Chas. H. Gibbs.	All saloons closed; no "club-rooms."	Cannot state.

From County Treasurer.

County.	Name of Probate Judge.	3. In your judgment has not the loss of the revenue from former saloon licensees been more than made good by the decreasing burdens of pauperism and crime resulting from Prohibition; and by the directing of the money formerly spent in the saloons, now into legitimate channels of trade?	4. Would you advise the re-establishment of saloons, breweries, and distilleries in Kansas under a High License law, as a means calculated to benefit the social and business interests of the State?
Allen	J. L. Arnold.	Yes, most positively.	No.
Anderson	B. R. Porter.	Yes, emphatically.	No; the idea is preposterous.
Atchinson	P. W. Bean.	To first clause, do not think so; to second, merchants greatly benefited by Prohibition.	I would I would rather have 40 open saloons than 20 "joints."

KANSAS.

County	Name	
Barton	B. F. Ogle.	It has; our jails empty, crime largely reduced.	would not now; was formerly liberal on this subject.
Barber	Loren Edwards.	Yes.	Would not in rural districts. High License might do away with perjury in cities.
Bourbon	B. J. Waters.	It has; under Prohibition our city has prospered as never before.	I would not; our people will never again establish saloons.
Brown	T. B. Dickason.	No amount of money can compensate for evils of saloons.	Nothing could induce me to recommend their re-establishment.
Chase	S. A. Breese.¶	Pauperism and crime reduced at least 50 per cent.	No; many formerly opposed now favor Prohibition.
Chautauqua	J. V. Beekman.**	It most certainly has.	Forever opposed to re-establishment of saloons.
Cheyenne	Justin Badgerow.	Yes.	I would not.
Clark	J. D. Whitfield.	Yes.	Yes, by all means.
Clay	John T. Woods.	Yes, a thousand times.	No, indeed; Prohibition is a success.
Cloud	W. V. B. Shaefer.	Yes, sir; expense running criminal courts, county, less than one-tenth what it was under the license.	No, sir, I would not.
Coffey	W. H. Bear.	It certainly has.	No, a hundred times no!
Crawford	James A. Smith.	Yes, emphatically.	No.
Davis	S. H. Nikirk.	Taxes are now higher.	Very high license might be preferable. Am not a Prohibitionist, but acknowledge it has done good in this State.
Decatur	J. R. Conquest.	It has; Oberlin County seat, population 1,000, no police or marshal.	Not by any means.
Dickinson	B. W. Peck.	Loss of revenue not more than $3,000; saving to families at least $50,000.	Most emphatically no; formerly strong Anti-Prohibitionist.
Douglas	John Q. A. Norton.	Yes, by a big majority.	No.
Edwards	Chas. H. Hatch.	Not a pauper in the county.	I would not; those who would are a small minority.
Finney	J. W. Weeks.	That is my impression; our city and county jails empty.	No.
Ford	D. W. Moffitt.	Crime diminished wonderfully; this city,†† from having most unsavory reputation, now exceedingly quiet.	No.
Franklin	J. A. Purdy.	Emphatically yes.	No, sir; would be great calamity to our prosperous State.

* County Attorney.
† Deputy County Treasurer.
‡ Clergyman, answered for the County Treasurer.
§ City Attorney Larned; answers fully concurred in by S. F. Mercer, Probate Judge.
‖ City Clerk, Hageton.
¶ Postmaster, Cottonwood Falls.
** County Attorney.
†† Dodge City.

PROHIBITION DOES PROHIBIT—Continued.

County.	Name of Probate Judge.	3. In your judgment has not the loss of the revenue from former saloon licensees been more than made good by the decreasing burdens of pauperism and crime resulting from Prohibition; and by the directing of the money formerly spent in the saloons, now into legitimate channels of trade?	4. Would you advise the re-establishment of saloons, breweries, and distilleries in Kansas under a High License law, as a means calculated to benefit the social and business interests of the State?
Garfield	J. E. T. Kephart.	Yes.	No.
Gove	A. C. Hennessy.	It has; many former habitual drunkards now sober and industrious.	I would not; but three criminal cases now pending in county.
Graham	S. Van Wyck.	It has.	Not under any circumstances.
Grant	Geo. C. Underwood.	I do; pauperism and crime diminished.	By no means.
Gray	J. R. Brady.	More than made good.	No, never.
Greeley	A. K. Webb.	It has.	I certainly could not, knowing what Prohibition has done for people and business of Kansas and Iowa.
Greenwood	Allen Emmerson.	Yes, more than 100 times.	No, sir.
Harvey	D. Felger.	Yes; seldom hear such pleas as saloon for revenue.	No, never.
Haskell	A. P. Herninger.	Yes, sir.	No, sir, not by any means.
Jefferson	David Smith.	Most assuredly; only occupant our jail for 18 months was a "bootlegger."	Never; no man will ever say resubmission in Kansas.
Jewell*	J. B. Dill.	It certainly has.	A great majority of Kansas voters unite with me in saying a thousand times no!
Johnson	J. L. Howard.†	Yes.	No.
Kingman	C. C. McMurphey.	Our burden for pauperism very light; do not think Prohibition increases taxation.	Would work more harm than benefit.
Kiowa	Alfred A. Mullin.	Yes, yes, yes; no doubt about it.	No, never.
La Bette	T. J. Calvin.	Revenue from saloons never paid. Decrease of pauperism and crime from Prohibition beyond conception.	Not by any means; Prohibition is the secret of our unparalleled increased population.
Lincoln	F. H. Dunham.	Most assuredly yes.	Most emphatically no.
Linn	Enoch Estep.	Yes, doubly so.	No; and this sentiment increasing every day.

County	Name	Response 1	Response 2
Logan‡	H. C. Chapman.	Loss more than made good.	People of Kansas want no saloons; law rightly enforced.
Lyon	W. J. Combs.	Yes.	No.
Marion	C. E. Foote.	Yes, several times over; great many poor men now own homes.	By no means; would be a curse socially and burden to business.
Marshall	G. Goodwin.	Not the case in this section, being so near the Nebraska line.	I certainly should. I consider the saloons, under proper restrictions, less evil than perjury.
Meade	W. D. Hudson.	It has.	No.
Miami	J. C. Collins.	It has; police judges very little to do compared formerly.	I would not. Many who opposed law bitterly now favor it.
Mitchell	M. M. Rowley.	Crime diminished three-fourths by police judges' docket; jails empty.	No; Kansas is very much benefited socially and in business by Prohibition.
Morris	W. A. McCollam.§	The gain financially has been great.	By no means; Prohibition already a success; every year adds to its favor.
Morton	Jesse Taylor.	Yes.	No.
Nemaha	Geo. R. Benedict.‡	Yes, merchants formerly opposed Prohibition now favor; say trade increased.	No; have less crime and fewer paupers under Prohibition.
Neosho	J. L. Denison.¶	Yes; crime and pauperism have diminished.	By no means; Prohibition come to stay.
Ness	R. B. Linville.	Do not know.	No.
Norton	Samuel Means.	More than made good; court and poor-house expenses greatly reduced.	Never.
Osage	Geo. W. Doty.	Yes.	No.
Osborne	B. M. Kany.	Much more than made good; crime, pauperism, taxes, less.	No, never; our boys safe, girls not insulted by bloated beasts.
Ottawa	W. D. Thompson.	Yes, yes.	Not by any means.
Phillips	N. Poling.	More than twofold made good by decreased crime.	I would not.
Pottawatomie	C. B. Huffman.	Revenue of saloons amounted to nothing compared with decreased cost of crime.	Not by any means; nearer total Prohibition more we want it.

* To the answers of Judge Dill is appended the following document: "We, the undersigned citizens of Mankato, heartily indorse the above statement:
"BANK OF MANKATO, J. B. FAIRCHILD,
"A. BAILEY, Register of Deeds,
"E. A. ROSE, Clerk of the District Court,
"GEORGE BISHOP, Vice-Pres. First National Bank,
"O. H. DURANT, Supt. Public Instruction,
"A. B. PETERS, M.D., Judge."

† County Superintendent of Schools.
‡ The answers of Judge Chapman, of Logan County, are also signed by K. E. Wilcockson, County Attorney; N. G. Perryman, Sheriff; I. B. Felts, County Treasurer, and W. Jones, County Clerk.
§ Ex-Probate Judge.
‖ Deputy Clerk of District Court.
¶ County Attorney.

PROHIBITION DOES PROHIBIT—Continued.

COUNTY.	Name of Probate Judge.	3. In your judgment has not the loss of the revenue from former saloon licenses been more than made good by the decreasing burdens of pauperism and crime resulting from Prohibition; and by the directing of the money formerly spent in the saloons, now into legitimate channels of trade?	4. Would you advise the re-establishment of saloons, breweries, and distilleries in Kansas under a High License law, as a means calculated to benefit the social and business interests of the State?
Pratt	J. A. Gardner	It has; not criminal case or pauper in county.	No, sir.
Rawlins	W. H. Skiddone	Thousands saved to poor families.	No, sir.
Reno	S. A. Atwood	Yes, beyond a doubt.	No.
Republic	C. A. Northrop		Not under any circumstances; Prohibition would receive 2 votes to 1 formerly.
Riley	Geo. C. Wilder	Undoubtedly; legitimate business increased; crime, pauperism decreased.	Man in Kansas seriously suggesting such thing would be counted fit subject asylum for imbeciles.
Rooks	John Mullin	No doubt of it.	Not by any means.
Rush	G. G. Wade	Yes, more than made good.	No, never.
Russell	J. G. Vogelgesang	Yes.	No.
Saline	C. E. Lamkin	It has, and can be proven by court records and officials.	I would not; if resubmitted would not receive respectable minority vote.
Scott	B. F. Rochester	Yes.	Never, no, never.
Sedgwick	W. T. Buckner	More than made good.	No; formerly favored High License.
Seward	I. F. Poston	Not the case here.	No; would suggest Local Option and High License.
Shawnee	A. B. Quinton	It has; taxes not higher than before.	No.
Sherman	H. S. Rulon	Much more.	By no means; neither in pecuniary nor moral sense.
Sheridan	S. O. Wanzer	Yes, sir, I do; no pauperism here.	Most emphatically no.
Smith	J. W. Henderson	Most emphatically yes.	I would not.
Stafford	J. F. Guernsey	I hardly think so.	I most certainly would.
Stanton	S. C. Garner	Yes, most emphatically.	No, never.
Sumner	J. T. Sanders	Yes; prior Prohibition 15 saloons, 15 policemen; now, one marshal, little to do.	No, sir; better class all vie in upholding our law.

County	Name	Response	Notes
Thomas	Joseph E. Leh.	Yes, yes, yes, yes!	No, no, no, never; liquor can absolutely not be had here.
Wabaunsee	L. Richards.	Very much more.	Decidedly no.
Washington	J. R. S. Birch.	Yes, tenfold.	No, decidedly.
Wichita	E. J. Shields.	It most certainly has.	Most emphatically no!
Wilson	H. O. White.*	Taxes lighter, fewer prosecutions criminals, decrease pauperism.	By no means; cannot afford to take money from legitimate trade to support useless parasites.
Woodson	C. C. Clevenger.	Yes; inmates poor-houses, asylums, jails, penitentiaries decreasing, population increasing.	No.
Chase	F. P. Cochran.†	Yes; taxes decreased 50 per cent., criminal practice fully two-thirds, pauperism largely.	
Cherokee	Frank Hoover.‡	Lessened taxes; money formerly spent in saloons now directed into legitimate trade.	
Ellis	Geo. Philip.	Guess not.	
Hamilton	A. F. Keel.	Naturally; our jail empty.	
Harper	B. E. Shawhan.§	Yes; pauperism decreased; but 2 prisoners in jail in 12 months.	
Hodgman	H. S. Sooth.	Yes; decreases taxes, diminishes pauperism and crime.	
Jackson	V. V. Adamson.	Yes, crime less each year, pauperism at low ebb.	The series of questions sent to these county officials did not include the question at the head of this column; but their replies to the preceding questions leave no doubt as to their objection to the re-establishment of the liquor traffic in Kansas.
Jasper	John E. Johnston.	Yes; taxes decreased for police purposes; less crime; pauperism decreased 75 per cent, proportion to population.	
Lane	Abe Frakes.	Dull as thunder.	
McPherson	P. T. Lindholm.	Yes; crime decidedly decreased.	
Montgomery	M. F. Wood.	About 50 per cent.; business increasing; helped poorer classes.	
Pawnee	P. H. Forbes.‖	Yes; taxation and crime decreased; business benefited.	
Rice	J. C. Seward.	Yes; pauperism undoubtedly decreased.	
Stevens	N. Campbell.¶	Less crime, if anything; pauperism decreased.	
Trego	Chas. H. Gibbs.	Crime diminished; in no sense derogatory to business.	

* Attorney at Law, Fredonia.
† County Attorney.
‡ Deputy County Treasurer.
§ Clergyman, answered for the County Treasurer.
‖ City Attorney, Larned; answers fully concurred in by S. F. Mercer, Probate Judge.
¶ City Clerk, Hugoton.

Kansas. The Murray Law is effectual. Ninety per cent. is the measure of decrease in drunkenness and drinking. I say emphatically, Yes!—the former saloon revenue has been more than made good by the benefits accruing from Prohibition. High License, if advocated, would be considered preposterous. The great body of our voting population would no more re-establish the saloons, breweries, and distilleries than they would advocate the use of crude carbolic acid for gravy! The saloon in Kansas has gone and gone forever; we *know* that we are better off in every way, morally, financially, and religiously. 'Tis true liquor is brought in from Kansas City and other points in Missouri, and it is used slyly. Sometimes men sell it on the sly. This business is called 'bootlegging.' At our last term of the District Court one man was convicted for selling in this way, and he was fined $100 and given a jail sentence of thirty days. I have been a resident of Anderson County for four years, and during that time I have not seen more than half a dozen drunken men, nor do I know of a single crime committed by a man while drunk in this county, except a case or two of assault and battery that I heard of. 'Resubmission' was the party cry of the Democrats and a few whiskey Republicans up to about two years ago. That cry is no longer heard in the land. In Eastern Kansas no man advocating resubmission could possibly be elected to a township or county office. There are 'millions in' Prohibition. Let any State try Prohibition for ten years, even to the extent that we of Kansas have tried the law, and it will never return to 'the trade' again. There are millions in it for any State or people."

THE POLICE FORCE REDUCED.

B. J. Waters, Probate Judge of Bourbon County, Fort Scott: "Prohibition is a complete success. My feeling is so strong that I wish I could go to Pennsylvania to tell the people some facts. Drunkenness has almost entirely disappeared in our city, notwithstanding the fact that our population now is nearly three times greater than when Prohibition went into effect. The consumption of intoxicants as a beverage now is confined to the few who import liquor for their private use. There is no place in our city or county where liquors of any kind can be purchased, even for medicinal purposes. *Since the abolition of the liquor traffic our city has prospered as she never did under the saloon system. When Prohibition went into effect we had a population of only about 5,000, with 22 saloons. We now have 15,000, and our police force is not so large as in the days of the saloon.*

The good resulting from the effects of Prohibition has been so great that I am fully convinced that our people will never favor the re-establishment of the saloon, either by High License or any other method."

"AN ENTIRE SUCCESS."

T. B. Dickason, Probate Judge of Brown County, Hiawatha: "I do hope that Pennsylvania will do herself justice at the coming election, and she can do that only by adopting the Prohibition Amendment. Prohibition is an entire success. There are no open saloons that I can hear of in this part of Kansas. Drunkenness and drinking have been reduced from two-thirds to three-fourths. If the General Government would prohibit the issuing of stamps to all who have not obtained local permits, the sale of intoxicants would be materially lessened. No amount of revenue from the saloons can compensate for the misery coming from the sale of intoxicants. There are many more happy families in Kansas to-day than there would be under saloon rule and ruin. Seeing the good that has been done by our law, nothing could induce me to recommend open saloons under any circumstances whatever. By refusing to tolerate saloons, Kansas got rid of a bad class of men and gained better classes."

VERY SEVERE AGAINST RUMSELLERS.

W. H. Bear, Probate Judge of Coffey County, Burlington: "There is not a saloon or other place in this county that is authorized to sell intoxicating liquors of any kind. Drinking and intoxication have disappeared almost totally. Public sentiment here is hardening and growing more severe against rumsellers all the time. No! a hundred times no! I would not under any circumstances agree to the establishment of High License in Kansas."

DODGE CITY RECLAIMED.

D. W. Moffitt, Probate Judge of Ford County, Dodge City: "Crime has decreased wonderfully under Prohibition in this part of Kansas. Dodge City used to have a most unsavory reputation—perhaps the worst reputation of any city in the United States; but now it is exceedingly quiet and very moral. Saloons are an unknown quantity. Joints' are being hunted from cover to cover and driven out. The amount of liquor consumed has been decreased to a very great extent. The wild carouses so frequent in the days of open saloons are entirely unknown now. We would never receive the saloons back upon the terms of High License."

ONLY ONE PRISONER IN EIGHTEEN MONTHS.

David Smith, Probate Judge of Jefferson County, Oskaloosa: "Not a single saloon is running in this county, which has the distinction of being the county first settled in the State. Oskaloosa is only twenty-five miles from Leavenworth. If drunkenness has not been diminished fully seventy-five per cent. in Kansas, why all this whining and howling by the liquor-dealers of Kansas City, St. Louis, and elsewhere? For proofs of the material benefits conferred upon Kansas by Prohibition, see Governor Martin's letter of last year, and Governor Humphrey's recent letter. Never would we agree to take the saloons back. Do you remember how the Democrats fought for resubmission in this State in the face of ever-increasing majorities, until last year not a man or a paper in the State even hinted at it, either before or after the campaign began? And in the face of that 80,000 Republican majority last fall, do you suppose anybody will ever say resubmission again in Kansas? *For eighteen months the only occupant of our jail was a bootlegger*, who took the risk of sneaking in an occasional jug in a small square box by express from Kansas City, and, filling his little bottles, doled the poison out to a few old topers. If old souks choose to order jugs of whiskey by express, concealed in boxes, they may do so a few times, but they soon become ashamed of the practice. The great and crowning glory of our Prohibitory Law is the abolition of the open saloon, where drunkards are so easily manufactured out of the young men and boys through tippling and treating. Our boys are no longer tempted. I have five boys, and can truthfully say I have no fear that they will acquire the drink habit. Can any father in New York or Pennsylvania say as much?"

GREAT NEWS FROM TOPEKA.

A. B. Quinton, Probate Judge of Shawnee County, Topeka (the State capital): "From my own knowledge I declare that there are no saloons in this county of about 65,000 population, and I have every reason to believe that there is no open saloon in any part of the State. A drunken person is a rare thing in Topeka's Police Court, which I presume is an average court. It does not have one case of drunkenness where formerly twenty would stand charged. The loss of the liquor revenue has been more than made good. Our taxes are not higher than before in any particular, unless made so by some special improvement tax. No, I would not advise a return to saloons under High License."

"PROHIBITION IS TOTAL."

Jesse Taylor, Probate Judge of Morton County, Richfield : "Prohibition is total in this part of the State. We have no saloons. I think drunkenness and tippling have been reduced by ninety-nine one-hundredths. I am no crank,·but I know what Prohibition has done for Kansas, and I would not favor receiving the saloons again under High License."

THE POLICE COURT HARDLY PAYS ITS RENT.

W. M. Rowney, Probate Judge of Mitchell County, Beloit : "There are no saloons here. They have been closed for the last four years. Possibly there are places in back rooms where certain persons can get liquor, but boys and young men do not enter them, and they are less likely to become drunkards than they would be with licensed saloons. There is not one drunken person seen now in this part of the State where fifty were seen when saloons were licensed. I do not believe one gallon of liquor is consumed now where ten were consumed during the reign of the saloons. *Since the Prohibition Amendment went into effect the docket of the Police Judge of this city has been comparatively free from cases of 'drunks.' When the saloons were open about three-fourths of all the cases in the Police Court were 'drunks,' and many of the other cases originated from the use of liquor. The Police Court now scarcely pays the rent of the office. Our jails are empty, and crime is on the decrease.* A large majority of the people of Kansas are very well satisfied with the law. Kansas has been very much helped socially, and from a business point of view, by Prohibition, and the people do not care to return to High License."

FROM A VERY PROMINENT JUDGE.

T. J. Calvin, Chairman of the House Committee on Temperance in the Kansas Legislature of 1879 and 1881, and now Probate Judge of La Bette County, Oswego : "The statements made in the East about Prohibition in Kansas are conscienceless. I notice that one statement says : 'It is a common-sense proposition that if you take from a State a large portion of the revenue necessary for its maintenance, such deficit in revenue must be made up by increased taxes on the remaining revenue-paying property of the State.' I reply, It is a common-sense proposition that if you take from a State the open saloon, there will be no use for a large police force to preserve order, which more than absorbs the revenue, to say nothing of the court expenses arising from saloons. The revenue from saloon licenses was never enough to support the police force. The decrease of pauperism and crime since Prohibition came into effect is really beyond conception. It is not true that Prohibition has increased taxes. Taxes are less in Kansas than they were before Prohibition. The rate per cent. of tax depends on the valuation. In Kansas, property is assessed at only about one-fourth its actual value. As to the claim made by the liquor men that more people pay the United States special tax in Kansas under Prohibition than under license, I have some facts to state. From 1881 to 1887 there were a great many 'bootleg' saloons in Kansas, and the operators procured United States 'licenses' and sold on the sly. But why don't the liquor statisticians refer to the figures of United States 'permits' for Kansas since the law of 1887 went into effect? Kansas men know why. There has been a great decrease. In La Bette County, having 30,000 population, there is not a United States license issued, and this is due to the law of 1887. The early Prohibition statutes of Kansas were imperfect, but the present law is a success. Besides, it must be remembered that a great many of the so-called United States 'licenses' are issued to drug stores. Let me ask, if Prohibition is not a success in the States where it has been tried, why is it that those States are so strongly in favor of Prohibition? Why is it that every rum-sucker is opposed to it and every temperance man is for it? If any person has doubts about the success of Prohibition in Kansas, let him come and visit the cities of this State and try to buy liquor. He will quickly find out that Prohibition prohibits. In this part of the State it has entirely closed the saloons. There is not a place in the county of La Bette where liquor can be bought. *I will give any man $10 who will furnish proof of the purchase of so much as one drop in this county. In the whole county, with its 30,000 inhabitants, it would be impossible to find an intoxicated man by diligent search in a week's time.* Occasionally you will find an old toper who has been to Missouri for rum, but such cases are few. *Prohibition is the secret of the unparalleled increase of population and wealth of Kansas in the last eight years. Every respectable citizen of Kansas is proud of the results of the Prohibitory Law, and if the question were voted on again there would be a majority of not less than 100,000 in favor of the law.*"

NO DRUNKENNESS—INCREASED ENTERPRISE.

W. A. McCollam, ex-Probate Judge of Morris County, Council Grove: "There are no saloons in this county, and none in the adjoining counties, I think. There is essentially no drunkenness in sight. The cases that come to light are exceptional. The gain financially has been very great. The high taxation found in most cities results from the increased enterprise of a hopeful people. They are constantly building water-works, street-railways, electric-light establishments and school-houses. Propositions for the repeal of Prohibition and the enactment of High License would find little favor. Prohibition is already a success, and every year promotes its perfect operation."

GROWING IN FAVOR EVERY YEAR.

John C. Collins, Probate Judge of Miami County, Paola: "Prohibition prohibits completely here. There is no saloon in Miami County. The Prohibitory Law is enforced as well as any of the criminal laws. I think intoxication and drinking have been diminished fully ninety per cent. There is practically no drunkenness in this county, and the vice is especially rare among young men. The Police Judges have very little to do, although in former days they had enough. No political party can succeed in Kansas that favors re-establishing the saloons. The law is a success and grows in favor every year."

A. K. Webb, Probate Judge of Greeley County, Tribune: "Prohibition has closed the saloons completely in this part of Kansas. Not one is now to be found in Greeley County. In my judgment, drunkenness and the amount of intoxicants consumed have been decreased ninety per cent. To your third question I reply, 'It has.' I certainly could not advise a return to the liquor traffic under High License, knowing as I do what Prohibition has done for the people of Kansas and Iowa and for business."

J. W. Gardner, Probate Judge of Pratt County, Pratt: "Prohibition has closed every saloon in the State. It has entirely eradicated drunkenness in this part of Kansas and banished intoxicants as beverages. *This is a county of 13,000 population. The county owns a Poor Farm worth $12,000. There has not been a single person sent to the Farm for more than a year. There is not a criminal case on the docket for the May term of Court.* No, sir, I would not advocate a renewal of the legalized liquor business in Kansas under High License. Drinking intoxicants is unpopular in this State."

Joseph E. Lesh, Probate Judge of Thomas County, Colby : "We know no such thing as a saloon here. There never has been a saloon in our thriving city since it was organized, May 8th, 1885, and there are no saloons in any of the neighboring counties. The Prohibition laws are strictly enforced, and Prohibition is a complete success in Northwestern Kansas. Drunkenness and drinking have been diminished to such an extent that an intoxicated person is never seen. I do not doubt that if the Prohibitory Law were not enforced there would be occasional drunkenness, causing misery to women and children. The citizens of Thomas County let liquor alone, buy wholesome things, and live to make their wives and children happy. Yes! Yes! Yes! Yes! as you say, the revenue from license has indeed been more than made good by a great decrease in pauperism and crime and by a growth in lines of legitimate business. No! No! No! No! Never will we let the miserable saloons start up again in Kansas; never, for any license fee. We are determined to enforce the Prohibitory Law and keep out the saloons. High License is no benefit, socially or financially, to any country. We are so much opposed to the rum traffic that in our county we do not even permit the sale of liquors for medicinal or mechanical purposes. Liquor is absolutely unobtainable here. Such wines as are needed for sacramental purposes are obtained by special orders from Kansas City or St. Louis."

J. T. Sanders, Probate Judge of Sumner County, Wellington : "This county has a population of 40,000, but there is not a place in it where a drink of liquor of any kind can be legally procured. A very few low, disreputable people known as bootleggers are occasionally found peddling rum, but they are now very scarce. The violations of the Prohibitory Law are but slightly in excess of the violations of laws against theft, forgery, and other crimes. The decrease in drinking and drunkenness since the Prohibitory Law went into effect has been not less than ninety per cent., probably as much as ninety-eight per cent. A drunken man is seldom seen now, and when seen, public sentiment brands him as a criminal. Before Prohibition was enacted, drunkenness did not debar a man from entrance to society. A man who drinks to excess has no standing whatever now; he takes his place with thieves and other criminals. *Under license we had 15 saloons in this city of 10,000 inhabitants, and the same number of marshals, police officers, etc. Now we have but one mar-*

shal and he finds but little to do. When the saloons were licensed the Police Judge made quite a large salary; now the office is worth only $25 per month. Inveterate drunkards are reformed, and pauperism and crime have been diminished to the extent that the sale of liquor has decreased. Perhaps you will wish to know how I can with such positiveness declare that drunkenness and drinking have been decreased ninety to ninety-eight per cent. in Sumner County. I will tell you. I have resided here for ten years. I used to be the agent of two leading express companies, which brought in nearly all the beer and the greater part of the whiskey used. Under the license law we delivered from 75 to 200 cases of beer per day. Now it is very seldom that a case of beer or a gallon of whiskey enters the city—probably not more than four cases per month are received here. We have in the county only three drug-stores that are permitted to sell liquors for lawful purposes, and their sworn statements of liquors of all kinds sold for mechanical, scientific, and medicinal purposes, for the month of April, showed only 583 sales. Yet the county, as I have said, has 40,000 inhabitants. Besides, it lies on the border of Oklahoma, and there was a great rush through it in April to the land of rattlesnakes and malaria, and many of the emigrants did their best to persuade the druggists to make unlawful sales. The better people in Kansas, both Republicans and Democrats, all vie with each other in praising the Prohibition Law."

Samuel Means, Probate Judge of Norton County, Norton: "There is not a place in Norton County where any one can buy liquor, wine, or beer openly. There is not a single drug-store where the stuff is kept and can be purchased legally. There may be bootlegging going on, but it is done on the sly—very slyly. If liquor and beer are shipped in from Nebraska and Missouri they are shipped clandestinely. I am confident that we have not one-tenth the drunkenness that prevailed before Prohibition. I honestly think that the decrease in expenses for pauperism and crime, as well as the increase in legitimate lines of trade, have more than made good the saloon revenues. The court expenses are greatly reduced. *We have now in the Poor-house only three persons; before Prohibition came the county paid out from $5,000 to $7,000 annually to keep the poor.* I would never advise a return to the old saloon system, and we do not intend to return under any circumstances."

C. B. Huffman, Probate Judge of Pottawatomie County, Westmoreland: "I think I can safely say that there is not an open saloon in the State of Kansas. Some of the saloon men fought the law as long as they had means to fight with, and they found it was a defensive warfare, whose inevitable result was to put the fighters into jail for a considerable time. They have quit fighting now. Prohibition has reduced the consumption of liquor nine tenths. Assertions to the contrary are false, and are made by men whose only object is to injure the cause of temperance. A drunken man is not seen now where ten were seen before the law was passed. Men who could not support their families decently when we had license, are now getting houses of their own. *The saloon revenue paid to the State and counties under the license law was insignificant compared with the decrease in crime and the reduction of costs in criminal cases. Our jail has not a sing'e occupant now, and the last occupant was there for violating the Prohibitory Law. I heard a very prominent criminal attorney say at the last term of Court here that his business had been ruined.* What falsehoods the liquor men spread in the East about Kansas! As for the statement that taxation has increased, it is utterly untrue. The revenue from the manufacture and sale of intoxicating drinks never did and never will pay the expenses of criminal prosecutions caused by their use. There is one of these Eastern misrepresentations that is particularly villainous. It is the one about the so-called United States 'liquor-dealers' license.' The reason there are so many of these so-called 'licenses' in Kansas is this: Whenever any petty bootlegger wants to engage in the business, he procures a Government 'license,' and perhaps the very first little bottle that he pulls from his boot-top is discovered by persons interested in the enforcement of the law and causes his arrest and punishment. I think it is very wrong for the General Government to grant 'revenue' licenses in a State where the sale is prohibited, unless the person applying holds a permit duly given by the local authorities; and even then it is a piece of meanness for a great and rich Government to keep up a system which enables the liquor men to make such misrepresentations of statistics, to say nothing of the meanness of sanctioning the sale of the accursed beverage, and making money that way. If the question of Prohibition were resubmitted to the people, not one-fourth of them would vote for re-establishing the old traffic. The nearer we come to total Prohibition, the more we want it."

G. C. Underwood, Probate Judge of Grant County, Ulysses: "The saloons are all closed, and the Prohibitory Law was the means of closing them. If the people are in favor of the law, the saloons can be closed every time. In this county drunkenness and drinking have been diminished four-fifths; and there would be still less drunkenness if topers did not ship liquor in under false names from other States. Prohibition lessens pauperism and builds schoolhouses and churches instead of poor-houses. It elevates the people to a higher plane of morality. I would by no means say any word that could be construed to mean a willingness to accept the traffic again upon any conditions. The benefits from Prohibition are so many that I cannot enumerate them. Under it there is no chance for minors to get liquors. We do not have the crimes that prevail among people who tolerate the whiskey traffic. My experience teaches me that taxes decrease instead of increase under Prohibition. Before the Prohibitory Law went into effect my taxes (in Bourbon County) were $3.25 per $100. I have not paid so high a rate at any time since. This year the tax-rate (on a low assessment) is $3 per $100 in Grant County, and the school-tax alone accounts for one-half of the total. As for the United States liquor-dealers' 'permits,' I want to say that at this time there is only one in the whole of Grant County, and it is held by a druggist."

J. R. S. Birch, Probate Judge of Washington County, Washington: "There is not a saloon, to my knowledge, within the State. Drunkenness and the amount of liquor used have been reduced to a very great extent. *The saloon revenue has been made good ten times over by a decrease in the burdens resulting from pauperism and crime, and by putting money into legitimate lines of trade.* No, decidedly, I would not advise bringing back the saloons under High License." [This letter was received since the last issue of *The Voice* went to press, and therefore was not included in the table printed a week ago.—ED. *The Voice.*]

G. G. Wade, Probate Judge of Rush County, La Crosse: "All saloons in our part of the State are closed. In my judgment, the Prohibitory Law has diminished drunkenness and the consumption of intoxicants here about sixty per cent. Some liquors are smuggled into this county for individual use. In this county the saloon revenue is more than compensated for by benefits resulting from the law. No, never would I advise re-establishing saloons, breweries, and distilleries under High License."

TESTIMONY OF COUNTY TREASURERS.

The following table is made up of replies to a series of questions sent by *The Voice* in February, 1889, to every County Treasurer in the State of Kansas as to the working and effects of the Prohibitory Law in that State.* It contains every reply—favorable or unfavorable—received by *The Voice* up to the time of putting this table in type. The following is a condensed summary of the replies to the questions in following table:

SUMMARY.

QUESTION I.—To what extent is the Prohibition Law successfully enforced in your section?—43 replies, and only 1 answers that the law is not successfully enforced; 1 says "occasionally violated;" 1 answers "eighty per cent.;" and 1 "fairly well."

QUESTION II.—What can you say of its effect in closing up the saloons?—45 replies; 37 say that all saloons are closed; 1 replies "excellent;" 1, "good from every standpoint;" 2, "good;" 1, "few open saloons;" 1, "a great many closed;" 1, "makes saloons out of drug-stores;" and 1, "have found saloons in some parts of the State."

QUESTION III.—To what extent has it diminished drunkenness and the use of intoxicants for beverage purposes?—46 replies, 38 of which agree that it has diminished drunkenness and drinking from fifty to ninety-nine per cent., or "almost totally;" 1, that it has "lessened some;" 1, "lessened drinking among the young;" 1, "confined to jugs from Missouri;" 1, "drunkenness caused by contact with Missouri" (a High-License State); 1, "not diminished;" 1, "none;" 1, "cannot state;" while 1 replies that it has "increased drunkenness."

QUESTION IV.—What is the effect of Prohibition on business interests, and the attraction or repulsion of capital for investment?—45 replies, 28 of which declare that Prohibition has been decidedly beneficial; 6, "that it has had no bad effect;" 6, "that they see no difference;" 1, "cannot tell;" 1, "that times are hard, but not due to Prohibition;" 1, "dull as thunder;" 1, "has destroyed values;" and 1, "like a bombshell in an army."

---

* For special provisions of "The Murray Law" in regard to enforcement, with penalties against non-enforcing officers, see p. 170.

QUESTION V.—Has money which was formerly spent in the saloons been directed to legitimate channels of trade?—42 replies, 33 of which answer yes ; 1, " presume so to great extent ;" 1, " about fifty per cent.;" 1, " in some cases ;" 1, " where dives are closed, yes ;" 1, " yes, except what goes to license States ;" 1, has " no observation ;" 1, notices " no visible effect ;' 1, " guess not ;" and 1, " no."

QUESTION VI.—Has Prohibition tended to increase or decrease taxes?—44 replies, 21 of which reply to decrease ; 4, " that taxes have not increased ;" 7, " see no change ;" 6, " cannot say ;" 1, " tended to increase at first ;" 1, " small increase ;" 1, " increased slightly ;" and 3, " increased."

QUESTION VII.—What has been the effect of Prohibition on criminal conditions?—45 replies, 33 answering most emphatically that crime has decreased ; 1, " very good ;" 1, " good everywhere ;" 1, " good ;" 1, " jail full of convicted whiskey sellers ;" 2, " can see no difference ;" 4, " cannot say ;" 1, " crime not reduced ;" and 1, " criminals increased from liquor prosecutions."

QUESTION VIII.—Has pauperism increased or decreased under Prohibition?—45 replies, 30 of which answer "decreased ;" 1, " no paupers here ;" 1, " pauperism at low ebb ;" 1, " no paupers ;" 1, " decreased, if any ;" 1, " not increased ;" 1, " about the same ;" 1, " no effect ;" 1, " no change ;" 1, "little change ;" 4, " cannot say ;" 1, " increased, but Prohibition nothing to do with it ;" and 1, " increased, some fools lay it to Prohibition."

QUESTION IX.—What effect has Prohibition on the growth of the State in number and character of population?— 43 replies, 28 of which declare that it has been beneficial to the growth and character of the population ; 1, " most glorious ;" 1, " very good ;" 2, " good ;" 1, " better than ever before ;" 1, " excellent ;" 1, " never more prosperous ;" 1, the " places of drunkards filled by good citizens ;" 2, " no effect ;" 1, " decreased foreign immigration more than made up by natives of good character ;" 4, " cannot say."

With but two or three exceptions the opponents of Prohibition will find little satisfaction in these official replies from 47 Kansas counties.

As before, the questions and answers are given in full, but in two sets, to accommodate them to the limits of these pages.

HOW PROHIBITION DOES PROHIBIT IN KANSAS.

TESTIMONIES FROM THE COUNTY TREASURERS OF THAT STATE AS TO THE WORKING AND EFFECTS OF THE LAW.

The Saloons are Closed up; Intemperance, Pauperism, and Crime have Greatly Diminished; Taxation has Generally Decreased; Business Interests have been Benefited in Many Ways and the Number and Character of the Population have Greatly Improved under Prohibition.

County.	Name of County Treasurer.	1. To what extent is the Prohibition law successfully enforced in your section?	2. What can you say of its effect in closing up the saloons?	3. To what extent has it diminished drunkenness and the use of intoxicants for beverage purposes?	4. What can you say as to the effect of Prohibition on business interests, and the attraction or repulsion of capital for investment?	5. In your observation has money which was formerly spent in the saloons been directed under Prohibition to legitimate channels of trade?
Allen	E. H. Funston.*	....	No saloons.	No drunkenness.	....	....
Atchinson	T. J. Emlen.†	Well.	Not an open saloon.	Even prohibits cider.	Very good.	Most certainly.
Barton	Fred. E. Walker.‡	None whatever.	Makes saloons out of drug stores.	None.	Like bomb-shell in army.	No.
Bourbon	F. H. Miller.§	Almost to the letter.	All closed.	Diminished 90 per cent.	Bank deposits doubled, collections 100 per cent. easier.	Yes.
Brown	O. C. Hill.¶	Fairly well.	No open saloons.	Diminished 75 per cent.	Salutary.	Yes.
Chase	F. P. Cochran.**	Fully.	Closed all saloons.	Some old-timers still send abroad for it.	Attracted capital, been of great good.	Yes.
Chantauqua	J. D. McBrian.††	Well as any other criminal law.	Closed entirely.	Diminished 75 per cent.	On the whole favorable.	Yes.
Cherokee	Frank Hoover.§	Occasionally violated.	Closed.	Drinking diminished.	No detriment.	Beyond a doubt.

County	Name				
Clark	W. C. Dugan,*	Almost a clean sweep.	Have no saloons.	At least 75 per cent.	Good; capital not repulsed.	Yes, except what goes to license States.
Clay	G. H. Fullington.	Fully.	No open saloons.	Diminished drunkenness 75 per cent.; drinking 50 per cent. Greatly diminished.	Decidedly good.	It has.
Cloud	D. M. Stockhouse.	Well as any other.	Saloons all closed.		Capital greatly increased.	In-It has.
Coffey	M. L. Barber.‡‡	Successfully as any.	Closed entirely.	Diminished 90 per cent.	Attracted men of solid means.	Of Yes, sir.
Davis	C. B. Stebbins.	Like other laws.	No open saloons.	Diminished 66⅔ per cent.	Invites capital and It has. best classes.	
Ellis	George Philip.	Fairly.	Great many closed.	Diminished 60 per cent.	No difference.	Guess not.
Graham	S. Q. Wilson.	Fairly well.	No open saloons.	Fully one-half.	Not affected.	Think it has.
Greenwood	J. E. Rosel.	Very successfully.	All saloons closed.	Intoxication very rare	No capital repelled.	Yes.
Hamilton	A. F. Keel.	Almost entirely.	Closed them all up.	Very greatly.	Cannot tell.	Naturally.
Harper	B. E. Shawhan.§§	Well as other criminal laws.	Closed every saloon.	At least 90 per cent.	Attracted men of capital.	Yes.
Hodgman	H. S. Sooth.	Well as any law.	No saloons.	Little need.	Attracts best men.	Yes.
Jackson	V. V. Adamson.	90 per cent.	No saloons.	75 to 80 per cent.	Capital coming to us.	Yes.
Jasper	John E. Johnston.	As well if not better than any other.	Saloons and "club rooms closed."	Drinking at least 75 per cent. Rare to see drunk.	Attracted the best capital.	Yes.
Jefferson	C. Hosford.	Prohibits in fact.	No saloons what- ever.	All drunkenness caused by contact with Missouri.	Attracts capital except for breweries.	Yes, sir.
Kingman	A. B. Moore.	None allowed to sell.	No open saloons.	Drinking unpopular.	No business injured except liquor business.	Where "dives" closed answer invariably yes.
Labette	W. H. Porter.	Well enforced.	Good, from standpoint.	Drunkenness diminished 66 to 75 per cent.	Times are hard, some fools lay it to Prohibition.	Presume to great extent.

* Member of Congress, Iola.
† Questions referred to the editor of the Atchinson *Globe*, who replied by calling Prohibitionists "Pharisees," St. John's "hypocrite and political abortion," and Prohibition "venerable flapdoodle," which "has destroyed values, increased taxation, not diminished the consumption of liquor or reduced the criminal calendar."
‡ Special Life Insurance Agent.
§ Deputy County Treasurer.
‖ Assistant County Treasurer.
¶ Mr. Hill's answers concurred in by T. B. Dickason, for 14 years Probate Judge of Brown County.
** County Attorney.
†† Clergyman.
‡‡ Ex-County Treasurer and ex-Member Legislature.
§§ Pastor M. E. Church.

HOW PROHIBITION DOES PROHIBIT IN KANSAS—Continued.

COUNTY.	Name of County Treasurer.	1. To what extent is the Prohibition law successfully enforced in your section?	2. What can you say of its effect in closing up the saloons?	3. To what extent has it diminished drunkenness and the use of intoxicants for beverage purposes?	4. What can you say as to the effect of Prohibition on business interests, and the attraction or repulsion of capital for investment?	5. In your observation has money which was formerly spent in the saloons been directed under Prohibition to legitimate channels of trade?
Lane	Abe Frakes.	....	Have found saloons in some parts of State.	Increased drunkenness.	Dull as thunder.	....
Marshall	W. H. Smith.	Well as other laws.	Excellent.	Fully 80 per cent.	Brings best men in.	Yes, not a hungry child in city
McPherson	P. T. Lindholm.	To full extent.	No saloons.	Intoxicants used very little.	See no difference.	Yes.
Miami	J. W. Bryar.	Fully.	Good.	Nearly 100 per cent.	For the better.	Yes.
Mitchell	R. W. Lundy.	Well as any other.	Good.	Think 75 per cent.	Good; capital does not hesitate to come	Yes.
Montgomery	M. F. Wood.	Excellently.	Not a place sells.	Decreased more than 90 per cent.	Business increasing.	About 50 per cent.
Morris	P. J. Potts.	No whiskey sold except secretly.	No saloons.	Largely decreased.	Beneficial unquestionably.	In some cases.
Norton	F. M. Snow.	No open violation.	Saloons closed.	Decreased 90 per cent.	No question; capital safest when no drunkenness.	It has.
Osage	R. H. McClair.*	Fully as any.	No saloons in county.	Almost entirely driven out drunkenness.	Business nearly doubled. Capital had with ease.	Very decidedly so.
Osborne	J. A. Beeman.	A glorious success.	No saloons or "joints."	Almost totally.	Benefited immensely.	Certainly has.
Ottawa	T. Lord.	Can't buy drink in county.	No saloons.	Not seen drunken man in year.	No visible effect.	Certainly.
Pawnee	†P. H. Forbes.‡	Strictly.	Every saloon closed.	Seldom see drunken man.	Beneficial.	Yes.
Rice	J. C. Seaward.	As other laws.	All closed.	Very little drunkenness.	No disadvantage.	Yes.

KANSAS.

COUNTY	Name of County Treasurer.	6. Has Prohibition tended to increase or decrease taxation in the cities and towns of your vicinity? and to what extent?	7. What has been the effect of Prohibition on criminal conditions as evidenced from records of courts, prisons, and from personal observations?	8. Has pauperism increased or decreased under Prohibition?	9. What effect has Prohibition had upon the growth of the State in the number and character of its population?	10. Name any other advantageous results, which in your observation have come from or accompanied Prohibition.
Rooks	George N. Michel.	Well as any law.	Closed every saloon.	Confined to jugs from Missouri.	Getting people of means.	Has generally.
Rush	A. R. Hockensmith.§	Fairly well.	Few open saloons.	Lessened some.	Attracts capital rather than otherwise.	No visible effect.
Shawnee	W. A. Giebhardt.‡	Satisfactorily.	No saloons.	....	Good.	Yes.
Sheridan	W. S. Quisenberry.	....	....	....	....	....
Smith	T. Woods.	Fully.	Never had a saloon.	Lowered drinking among young.	No effect.	No observation.
Stevens	N. Campbell.¶	....	....	....	....	....
Thomas	Charles H. Hovey.	Well as most laws.	Not a saloon or drug store where liquor can be bought.	Very few use liquor.	Much money applied to debts that would have gone for drink.	Yes.
Trego	Charles H. Gibbs.	All saloons closed.	No "club rooms."	Cannot state.	In no sense derogatory.	....
Wabaunsee	J. B. Fields.	Stops boys drinking.	No saloons.	Diminished drunkenness greatly.	Notice no change.	Yes.
Washington	J. O. Young.	Strictly.	All closed, no liquor in drug stores.	Decreased 75 per cent.	No bad effect.	Yes.
Allen	E. H. Funston.**	No change.	Less crime.	Decreased.	Increased, population improved.	No wife-beating.
Atchinson	T. J. Emlen.††	....	....	....	....	....

* County Clerk.
† Mr. Forbes's answers fully concurred in by S. F. Mercer,
‡ Probate Judge, Pawnee County.
§ City Attorney, Larned.
‖ County Superintendent of Schools.
¶ Chief Clerk to Secretary of State.
⁋ City Clerk, Hugoton.
** Member of Congress, Iola.
†† Questions referred to the editor of the Atchison *Globe*, who replied by calling Prohibitionists "Pharisees," "St. John a 'hypocrite and political abortion,'" and Prohibition "venerable flapdoodle," which "has destroyed value, increased taxation, not diminished the consumption of liquor or accompanied the criminal calendar.

HOW PROHIBITION DOES PROHIBIT IN KANSAS—Continued.

COUNTY.	Name of County Treasurer.	6. Has Prohibition tended to increase or decrease taxation in the cities and towns of your vicinity? and to what extent?	7. What has been the effect of Prohibition on criminal conditions as evidenced from the records of courts, prisons, and from personal observations?	8. Has pauperism increased or decreased under Prohibition?	9. What effect has Prohibition had upon the growth of the State in the number and character of its population?	10. Name any other advantageous results, which in your observation have come from or accompanied Prohibition.
Barton......	Fred. E. Walker.*	Decreased.	Not a crime from drink in 6 years.	No paupers here.	Doubled; much better class.	Churches greatly improved.
"	F. H. Miller.†	No effect.	None that I can see.	Decreased.	No effect.	....
Bourbon	G. Hornaday.‡	Reduced 20 per cent.	Crime reduced 90 per cent.	Decreased largely.	Nearly doubled.	Invaluable help every way.
Brown	O. C. Hill.§	To decrease.	Decreased 50 per cent.¶	Decreased.	Largely increased; better class.	Better schools.
Chase.......	F. P. Cochran.¶	Decreased fully 50 per cent.	Criminal practice decreased fully two-thirds.	Largely decreased.	Sober and industrious, constantly increasing.	Instead of want and wretchedness, peace and plenty.
Chautauqua,	J. D. McBrian.**	Strongly to decrease.	Decreased 40 per cent.	Decreased materially.	Very good.	....
Cherokee...	Frank Hoover.†	Lessened.	Decreased, especially murders.	About the same.	Decreased foreign immigration more than made up by natives of good character.	Promotes order, good morals; prevents vote-buying.
Clark	W. C. Dugan.	Decreased just the cost of whiskey prosecutions.	Good every way.	Decreased.	Most glorious.	Good every way.
Clay	G. H. Fullington.	Decreased decidedly.	Crime materially decreased.	Decreased.	Never more prosperous.	More churches and schools.
Cloud......	D. M. Stockhouse.	Decreased county; increased city more than offset by increased business.	Jail almost empty, criminal docket greatly reduced.	Decreased.	Quite phenomenal and of better classes.	Place of saloons, reading rooms and gymnasiums.
Coffey......	M. L. Barber.††	Decreased about 1 per cent.	Jails empty, only 1 arrest in 12 months.	Decreased 33⅓ per cent.	Increased 400,000.	Good morals and property increased.

KANSAS.

County	Respondent	Cost of government	Jail/Crime	Pauperism	Population/Character	Other remarks
Davis	C. B. Stebbins.	Cost running city government less than under license.	Reduced.	Decreased.	Increased faster since than before Prohibition.	Law grows in favor every year.
Ellis	George Philip.	Increased.	No difference.	Increased, but Prohibition nothing to do with it.	Cannot say.	Rid of a good many "bums."
Graham	S. G. Wilson.	Slightly decreased.	Very good.	Decreased.	Great increase in numbers and character.	Done away with treating.
Greenwood	J. E. Rossel.	Cannot say.	Cut down 25 per cent.	Decreased.	Stimulated growth; population not excelled.	Labor more industrious, and better fed.
Hamilton	A. F. Reed.	Cannot tell.	Our jail empty.	Cannot tell.	Wonderful growth since Prohibition.	
Harper	B. E. Shawhan.‡‡	Decreased, if anything.	But 2 prisoners in jail in 12 months.	Decreased.		
Hodgman	H. S. Sooth.	Decreased.	Diminishes.	Judge it decrease.	Increased growth. Brought best class.	No man elected unless avowed Prohibitionist.
Jackson	V. V. Adamson.	Not increased.	Crime less each year.	Pauperism low ebb.	Invited best men of nation.	Advanced socially, morally and financially.
Jasper	John E. Johnston.	Taxes decreased, for police purposes.	Less crime.	Decreased 75 per cent proportion to population.	Better than ever before.	Vices and temptations fewer.
Jefferson	C. Hosford.	Decreased.	Not an occupant in county jail during 1888.	Cannot say.	Attracts better class.	
Kingman	A. B. Moore.		Jail full of convicted whiskey sellers.	To decrease.	Character population improved.	
Labette	W. H. Porter.	Cannot answer.	Few crimes from whiskey.	Pauperism increased, and some fools lay it to Prohibition	No effect.	Increased sobriety.
Lane	Abe. Frake.					

* Special Life Insurance Agent. † Deputy County Treasurer. ‡ Assistant County Treasurer. § Mr. Hill's answers concurred in by T. B. Dickeson, for 14 years Probate Judge of Brown County. ‖ Answered by M. L. Gaelich, Clerk of District Court. ¶ County Attorney. ** Clergyman. †† Ex-County Treasurer and ex-Member Legislature. ‡‡ Pastor M. E. Church.

HOW PROHIBITION DOES PROHIBIT IN KANSAS—Continued.

COUNTY.	Name of County Treasurer.	6. Has Prohibition tended to increase or decrease taxation in the cities and towns of your vicinity? and to what extent?	7. What has been the effect of Prohibition on criminal conditions as evidenced from the records of courts, prisons, and from personal observations?	8. Has pauperism increased or decreased under Prohibition?	9. What effect has Prohibition had upon the growth of the State in the number and character of its population?	10. Name any other advantageous results, which in your observation have come from or accompanied Prohibition.
Marshall....	W. H. Smith.	Not increased taxation, but length of tax roll.	Fallen off about 50 per cent.	Largely decreased.	Excellent.	Homes improved.
McPherson..	P. T. Lindholm.	Cannot say.	Decidedly decreased	Cannot say.	Increased numbers and benefited character.	Former opponents of Prohibition now for it.
Miami......	J. W. Bryan.	Cannot say.	Greatly diminished.	Decreased.	Character decidedly better.	....
Mitchell	R. W. Lundy.	Unchanged.	Crime decreased wonderfully.	Decreased.	Growth of State all could be desired.	Character population unsurpassed.
Montgomery	M. F. Wood.	Tended to increase at first.	Great falling off of drunkenness and disorder.	Helped poorer classes.	Good.	....
Morris......	P. J. Potts.	Certainly not increased.	Cannot say.	Naturally creased.	Bridgs in better class.	....
Norton	F. M. Snow.	Decreased.	Cannot say.	Decreased.	Cannot say.	....
Osage.	R. H. McClair.*	Tax rate no greater with extensive improvements.	Marked decrease.	Population doubled, paupers decreased one-half.	Character population decidedly improved.	....
Osborne	J. A. Beeman.	Reduced 2 per cent.	Little litigation from drink.	Decreased.	Rapidly increased and better class.	Hundreds of poverty-stricken drunkards sober and industrious.
Ottawa	T. Lord.	No difference.	Diminished, seldom any one in jail.	No paupers.	Cannot state.	No saloon power in politics.

KANSAS.

County	Name				Remarks
Pawnee	†P. H. Forbes.‡	Decreased.	Greatly decreased.	Not increased.	Growth unprecedented under Prohibit'n.
Rice	J. C. Seaward.	Cannot say.		Undoubtedly decreased.	Given us a better class.
Rooks	George N. Michel.	Less than in 1880.	No crime from drink	Decreased.	Places of drunkards filled by good citizens. Done more for Kansas than any other one thing.
Rush	A. R. Hockensmith.§	Lessened.	Lessened.	Decreased.	Improved quality and quantity. Increased number of Prohibitionists.
Shawnee	W. A. Gebhardt.‖	About the same.	Good.	Decreased.	Cannot state. Larger per cent. can read and write.
Sheridan	W. S. Quisenberry.				Prohibition not a success in any respect.
Smith	T. Woods.	Increased.	Cannot say.	No effect.	Good effect. People endorse it more fully than at first.
Stevens	N. Campbell.¶	Small increase.	Less crime.	Decreased, if any.	Socially elevating, politically demoralizing.
Thomas	Charles H. Hovey.		Cannot say.	Cannot say.	Very beneficial, both to number and character. People would have been poorer but for Prohibition.
Trego	Charles H. Gibbs.	No perceptible change.	Diminished.	No change.	Attracted industrious and moral citizens.
Wabaunsee	J. B. Fields.	Increased slightly.	Criminals Increased from liquor prosecutions.	Little change.	Growth last 3 years more than 10 years before. Much good socially and morally.
Washington	J. O. Young.	Not affected.	Lessened 25 per cent.	Decreased.	Brings better class. Good effect on young.

* County Clerk.   § County Superintendent of Schools.
† Mr. Forbes's answers fully concurred in by S. F. Mercer, Probate Judge, Pawnee County.   ‖ Chief Clerk to Secretary of State.
‡ City Attorney, Larned.   ¶ City Clerk, Hugoton.

To these tables we may add the testimony of ex-Governor Martin, of Kansas, delivered while he still held the executive office.

GOVERNOR MARTIN'S ADDRESS.

The following address was delivered by Governor John A. Martin, at the annual meeting of the Kansas State Temperance Union, in Representative Hall, Topeka, June 12th, 1888:

During the past four years I have had, I think, a fair opportunity to learn what has been accomplished in this State. I have visited nearly every section of it, and have talked with officers or citizens of every county. I have watched, with interest, the course of events, and the development of public sentiment touching the temperance question. I certainly have no reason to misrepresent the condition of affairs in Kansas. I have never made any secret of the fact that I voted against the Prohibition Amendment, and I cannot, therefore, be suspected of a desire to vindicate my own original judgment when I declare, as I do, that in my opinion this State is to-day the most temperate, orderly, sober community of people in the civilized world. I realize fully the force of this statement, and am prepared to sustain it here or anywhere.

First. I assert in the most positive language, that the temperance laws of Kansas are enforced as earnestly, as fully, and as effectively as are any other laws on our statute books, or as are the criminal laws of any other State in the Union.

Second. I do not believe that there is to-day an open saloon within the limits of the State of Kansas; nor do I believe that such a saloon has existed, within the borders of this State, for more than a year past. I do not mean to say that intoxicating liquors are not sold in Kansas. But I do assert, with emphasis and earnestness, that the open saloon, as it existed here at the State capital three years ago, and as it is known to-day in all other States where the liquor traffic is legalized or licensed, has been banished from Kansas utterly.

Third. I assert that whenever or wherever liquors are sold in Kansas at all, they are sold just as other crimes are committed—namely, in secret—just as houses are robbed, or horses are stolen, and by men who live in daily and hourly terror of the law.

Fourth. I affirm that, as a rule, arrests of those who violate our temperance laws are as swift and certain, and their punishment, when arrested, as sure and full as are arrests and punishments of any other class of law-breakers or criminals.

Fifth. I believe and declare that, as a result of the enforcement of our Prohibitory Laws, and the banishment of the open saloon, fully nine-tenths of the drinking and drunkenness prevalent in Kansas eight years ago, has been abolished; that thousands of men who were then almost constantly under the influence, more or less, of intoxicants, are now temperate and sober; and that in thousands of homes all over this State, where want, wretchedness, and woe were then the invited guests of drunken husbands and fathers, plenty, peace, and contentment now abide.

Sixth. I assert that, in every town and city throughout the State, arrests for drunkenness are annually decreasing, notwithstanding the fact that their populations are steadily increasing.

Seventh. I affirm that public sentiment in nearly every section of Kansas has been steadily strengthening in favor of rigid temperance laws and their rigid enforcement, and that this growing sentiment is due to the plainly apparent and now generally conceded fact that our temperance laws have largely abolished drinking and drunkenness, and the poverty, wretchedness, and crime of which the open saloon is the fruitful and certain cause.

Eighth. I assert that this development of public sentiment has made drinking unfashionable. The abolition of the saloon has practically abolished the American habit of treating. Young men in Kansas no longer regard drinking as an assertion of manhood. They know that the use of intoxicating liquors is more or less a bar to confidence, employment, or preferment, and especially to political preferment. The way to office does not lead, as it did eight or ten years ago, through the open saloon. The saloon as a potential factor has been eliminated from our political system. Society does not make excuses for nor coddle the men whose breath smells like a distillery. Men of confirmed drinking habits are, as a rule, ashamed to be seen drinking, and the bad example of their habits is thus not flaunted before the public eye, to seduce and debauch young boys and callow youth. All these things have had their influences, and have wrought the happiest results in making drinking not only unfashionable, but, in large measure, unpopular and discreditable, and the effects are plainly seen in the marked society of a Kansas assemblage of any character, civil, military, or political. Public sentiment is often more powerful than statutes, and, in Kansas, law and public opinion unite in regarding sobriety as the highest virtue of manhood.

The enemies of all temperance laws are constantly asserting that Prohibition is a failure; that more liquor is used in Kansas than was used when the saloons were open; and that drinking and drunkenness have not been reduced.

I avail myself of this occasion, also, to make some suggestions which, it seems to me, are worthy of consideration by your organization, and by all friends of temperance in Kansas.

Wherever and whenever the laws are not honestly enforced, the local judicial officers—that is, the county attorneys and sheriffs—are the responsible parties. It is practically impossible for any one to sell intoxicating liquors as a beverage, in any town or city in Kansas, if the county attorney and sheriffs of the county do their duty. These officers co-operating together can make the illegal selling of liquor impossible. A sheriff who is indifferent or hostile to the laws, can largely nullify any efforts of a county attorney to enforce them, and *vice versa*. These are the two officers who, above all others, have the absolute power, if they have also the will, to abolish liquor selling. Both should be in harmony with the spirit of our laws, and resolve to see that they are obeyed, or liquor selling cannot be wholly prevented. Of course the police force of any city can do a great deal to suppress the liquor traffic, but even a police force earnestly endeavoring to accomplish this result, can be thwarted in its endeavors by a county attorney and sheriff who will wink at or encourage violations of the law.

In nearly every county in Kansas, I am glad to say, the local judicial officers are in sympathy with the spirit of our laws, and prosecute, with vigor and sincerity, all who violate them. In only a few counties are the sheriffs or county attorneys opposed to the Prohibition Law, and so do little or nothing to enforce its provisions.

What is needed in Kansas is not more laws on this subject, nor more rigorous laws, but simply a sincere and vigorous enforcement of the laws we have. It is a mistake to change or modify laws at every session of the Legislature, and the friends of temperance should not make such a mistake.

In conclusion, I want to thank the officers and members of your organization for the generous and helpful support they have given me as the executive of the State. It is natural, I know, that men and women devoted, as you have been and are, to a great cause, should at times imagine that everything was not being done that could be done to promote its success. Great reforms move slowly. Great results are never accomplished in a brief time. In Kansas we are attempting to abolish a business that has been legalized or licensed for centuries ; a business whose large pecuniary profits tempt thousands of men ; a business that has, to sustain it the appetites, hereditary or cultivated, of tens of thousands ; a business that custom, sentiment, and even law, has regarded as a necessary evil.

The wonder is, therefore, not that so little has been accomplished, but that so much has been done to banish from this great commonwealth this monstrous evil. I have endeavored to state the accomplished results, as briefly and as clearly as is possible, and I feel confident that the facts I have summarized—and they are facts beyond dispute—will be a source of joy and pride to every honest, sensible, practical friend of temperance in this State.

In answer to this mass of testimony we have seen nothing on the other side that deserves serious consideration. It might be said of it all, as was strikingly shown under oath in one case, that the informant's knowledge of liquor selling in Kansas increases directly as the square of his distance from the State. Undoubtedly liquor can be procured in Kansas, and undoubtedly horses can be stolen there. To have done either is more discreditable to the man who has done it than to the law which forbids it. Mr. Maynard says :

"The Kansas saloons of to-day, the 'joints,' have few things in common with the legalized gin palaces, the sumptuous bar-rooms of other States. I have seen the interiors of some of them, and I know whereof I speak. The flashing mirrors, the polished furniture, the cut-glass bottles, the sensuous pictures, the music, the troops of noisy, coarse, and brazen men and women—none of these things are found in the Kansas saloon. The place itself you will have great difficulty, in most instances, in finding, unless, as the phrase goes, 'you know the ropes.' Entrance to a 'joint' must be sought through the medium of diplomacy, of whispers, winks, signal raps, and passwords. If you are a stranger in a town where 'joints' exist, and you are anxious to gain an entrance to one, the best thing for you to do is to 'fall in,' so far as you dare, with the most disreputable gang you can find about. If you can succeed in overcoming any suspicion which may exist as to your own disreputableness, you may be shown the way into a 'joint.' You will be taken, perhaps, to some tumble-down building in a back alley, into a secret room connected with a blacksmith-shop or a livery stable, in a dark hole underground, or up into a dingy garret, always being sure everywhere as you approach these places that the coast is clear. And when, at last, the raps being given and the bolts drawn, you find yourself in a 'joint,' you begin to realize what a desolate, ugly, repulsive place a saloon is when it is stripped of all those glittering accessories which are designed to seduce the weak and unwary to indulgence in drink, a place where the liquor traffic stands forth by itself in all its bare and hideous reality. A small, dimly lighted, dirty room, a rude wooden bench or two, a few chairs, a few ordinary glasses and black bottles on a shelf, a jug of whiskey, and a cask or two of beer—these are the surroundings and the outfit of the average 'joint.' The stock of liquors on hand is always very limited, for it is not considered wise to invest a large amount of capital in liquids which are liable to be confiscated any day and spilled in the gutter. In most cases the stock on hand is so small that it can be whisked out of sight in a moment if necessity demands it. A single jug of whiskey or a case of beer is considered sufficient to start a 'joint.' And, as I have already intimated, there is a notable absence in these places of those sights and sounds so common in our legalized 'joints' in other States. The glitter and flash, the coarse laughter, the maudlin song, the loud oath, the shouting and brawling, the jostling, swaggering crowds of boys and men, passing in and out, none of these things are to be seen or heard around the Kansas saloons. They are not the political centres of the community, the sources of local governmental power and inspiration, places for the concoction of political schemes, rendezvous of thieves, gamblers, procuresses, and all other persons who live at the expense of the peace, virtue, and industry of their fellow-men. They are none of these things, because there is no occasion or incentive for them to become such. Those who frequent them sneak in and out with as little delay and as little noise as possible. Business is carried on in subdued tones, and glasses are clinked very lightly, if at all.

"Liquor cannot be obtained in any way or anywhere except by the methods of the sneak-thief or the midnight marander. If you must have the stuff, you must crawl for it, and make common cause with the vilest of the earth."

When a man boasts that he has "got all the liquor he wanted" in Kansas, we are driven to certain conclusions as to his character and associates. He is not the best kind of a witness to anything. In conversation with a leading merchant of Topeka, he remarked to the author, "Our business men will not employ a clerk who is known to visit joints, for we do not trust him. We hold that a man who will break that law will break any other law." We have not too much confidence in a man's keeping the law of veracity after he has been drinking in all the "joints" of Kansas.

From Leavenworth, which perhaps resisted as hard and as long as any city, we have the following testimony :*

HOW THE CITY DIDN'T "GO TO THE DOGS."

Seven years ago, when the saloons had full swing, it was almost impossible to borrow money on Leavenworth real estate ; now some of the best companies in America have agents here soliciting loans. In the two years since the saloons were closed one of our banks has added $150,000 to its capital. Two new banks have been established. The Riverside Coal Mine has been sunk by Kansas City capitalists, and is now giving employment to 180 men. A coal mine is being sunk by a company of 480 workingmen, who have subscribed a capital of $50,000 ; and this mine will be down to coal by the beginning of March.

Mr. Harkness, of the Standard Oil Company, and others, have bought 1,600 acres of land and are opening a coal mine which will employ 600 men. A new flour mill has been built. The real estate transfers for the last two years amounted to $2,324,000.

The Leavenworth *Standard*, a Democratic paper opposed to Prohibition, said, January 2d :

"This year we have had what might be called a boom in small dwellings, and in the latter part of the year, in large brick buildings. Two hundred and nine buildings have been put up, at a cost of

---

* See *The Voice* of January 31st, 1889.

$208,389. The remaining seven buildings are the Union Depot, Santa Fé Freight and Passenger Depot, the public building, and the hospital at the Soldiers' Home, which will cost $635,000, making a total for the year in buildings of $861,391.

The 209 buildings spoken of are nearly all workingmen's dwellings. The money that would have been spent for whiskey last year, if the saloons had been open, was put into homes. I have lived here for thirty years, and in all that time have never seen brick buildings going up in the winter; but this winter men are at work erecting houses.

All the citizens declare that Leavenworth was never so prosperous, and even our most conservative business men admit that they would not have the saloons again. The increase of business has been such under Prohibition and the condition of all classes (especially the poor) has improved so much, that if a vote were taken now upon the Prohibition issue in Leavenworth the vote in favor of the saloons would be so small that it would hardly be worth counting.

DECREASE OF CRIME.

Official statistics support all the above statement about the improvement of Leavenworth under enforced Prohibition. Attorney-General Bradford gives these figures of commitments to the penitentiary from Leavenworth County: 1886 (open saloons), 36; 1887 (closed saloons), 13; first half of 1888 (closed saloons), 5.

Rev. Sumner T. Martin, of Leavenworth, in a letter to *The Voice*, testifies to the beneficial results of Prohibition. He says that some liquor is undoubtedly sold secretly, but that conditions are steadily growing better. He attributes the success of the law largely to the Metropolitan Police system.

The Cincinnati *Journal and Messenger* of March 13th, 1890, contains the following testimony from Chief Justice Horton, of the Kansas Supreme Court:

"Prohibition has now been the law in Kansas for eight years; it is a law at present, it will continue to be the law in future. Resubmission is called for only by the enemies of the law; its friends, who are in a large majority, do not desire resubmission. They do not wish to bear, as tax-payers, the expense of resubmission; they are not anxious for the presence of whiskey orators and whiskey newspaper correspondents, for the most part non-residents of the State, and with no permanent interest in Kansas, going about defaming people of the State, exaggerating present evils that greater evils may come. The people of Kansas do not care to have the State again made the scene of the expenditure of money by liquor-dealers' associations; nor do they wish the jointist or 'boot-legger,' who still lurks and skulks in Kansas, to believe that there is, or is to be a suspension of judgment in his case. *There are thousands of children in Kansas who have now arrived at the years of observation and discretion who have never seen a saloon.** It is the intention of the great majority of the voters in Kansas that while these children remain in Kansas they never shall see one. It is the determination of this majority, a majority which is being daily re-enforced, that the word 'saloon' shall never meet the eyes of the children as they file out of the doors of the public school. With the education these children are receiving, it is absolutely certain that when they become voters they will sustain the doctrine of Prohibition."

To which we will add the following testimony from a letter to the Chicago *Lever*, dated August 12th, 1889:

THE DRUNKARD'S PARADISE.

WHAT PROHIBITION IS DOING IN KANSAS—MERCHANTS TESTIFY OF ITS EFFECT ON BUSINESS—THE GREATEST MARVEL OF THE AGE.

As for Kansas, the merchants are satisfied with the law as it stands, and while it is not absolutely perfect, it is better than the open saloon, and takes away the public example and temptation, so that many people who drank from habit when liquor was in sight, now that it is so hard to procure have entirely abandoned it and never give it a thought.

A MERCHANT

in one of the towns of Kansas related to the *Lever* correspondent a fact which is a fair sample of most towns in the State when saloons were in full blast. He had a few former customers who always brought in turkeys and other products of their farms and sold them.

---

* The author personally knew of the following incident: A bridal couple from the interior of Kansas stopped to visit with friends of ours in Ohio, and neither of them had ever seen a saloon or a drunken man till they were married and started East on their wedding journey.

Instead of filling their orders as made up by their good wives, the proceeds went to the saloons, and it was often the case that the merchant had to advance them money to get some of the most necessary articles to take home. Now things are changed. These same customers never think of trying to hunt up places where liquor may be obtained, but sell what they have, buy and pay for what they want to take home, and have money jingling in their pockets on the way home.

No! These merchants and their customers would not favor a return of the saloon.

A CIGAR DRUMMER

from Missouri, says when he strikes Kansas, coming in at Atchison or Leavenworth, until he leaves it at Galena, near Joplin, Mo., he does not know what to do with his surplus change, and he is overloaded with money all the time he is in the State. Just as soon as other localities are reached where his customers expect to be treated, his spare change begins to lessen. So many instances might be cited in favor of the present law, and the great and good thinking people of Kansas could not be induced to return to the old system of open saloons, no more than the South could be brought back to the idea of slavery again.

THE PEOPLE

of Kansas do *not* want resubmission. They are satisfied with the present law until it can be amended and put in the best possible form. The merchants say the law is better than the open saloon. That the farmer, the mechanic, and the laborer now have more money, and their families are better off in every respect than under the old law, is not to be denied.

There are very few open saloons in the State. There are places where it is possible to get beer and whiskey, but it has to be done in such a roundabout way that it is not resorted to by the many that otherwise patronize open saloons.

From an economic standpoint, the Prohibitory law of Kansas is one of the greatest marvels of the age.

The following statement was signed by one hundred and fifty-three of the most prominent citizens of Kansas —men thoroughly representing the wealth, intelligence, and professional, commercial, and religious interests of the State :*

"We, the undersigned, citizens of Kansas and familiar with the operation of the laws prohibiting the traffic in intoxicating liquors, declare that Prohibition has been a moral and FINANCIAL BENEFIT to Kansas. These laws are as well enforced, and in many portions of the State even better enforced than other criminal laws. There has been an enormous decrease in the consumption of liquors and in the amount of drunkenness. During the eight years since Prohibition was enacted our population has greatly increased, BUSINESS HAS PROSPERED, poverty and crime have diminished, and the open saloon has disappeared. A very small per cent. of our people are opposed to this policy. The great majority of the citizens of Kansas are well satisfied with the results of Prohibition, and would not on any account think of returning to our former system of license."

Among the signers the following names appear :

Irwin Taylor, Assistant-Attorney-General ; W. A. Johnston, Associate-Justice of the Supreme Court ; D. M. Valentine, Associate-Justice ; Lyman U. Humphrey, Governor of Kansas ; Albert H. Horton, Chief Justice ; E. Wilder, Treasurer, R. B. Gemmell, Superintendent of the Telegraph, A. A. Robinson, Second Vice-President and Manager, and E. B. Purcell, Director of the Atchison, Topeka and Santa Fé Railroad Company ; Peter McVickar, President of Washburn College ; N. C. McFarland, late Commissioner of the General Land Office ; R. B. Spillman, Judge of the Twenty-first District ; George T. Fairchild, President of the State Agricultural College ; N. Green, ex Governor of Kansas ; John A. Martin, ex-Governor of Kansas ; J. B. Anderson, President of the First National Bank of Manhattan ; John F. Hensley, President of Emporia College ; J. W. X. Ninde, Bishop of the Methodist Episcopal Church ; J. C. Miller, Pastor of the Presbyterian Church, Winfield ; F. J. Sauerber, Pastor of the First Presbyterian Church, Emporia ; Charles B. Graves, Judge of the Fifth District : Henry Booth, Speaker of the House of Representatives and Department Commander of the Grand Army of the Republic ; A. R. Taylor, President of the State Normal School ; John

---

* See *The Voice* of May 30th, 1889.

S. Park, Pastor of the First Presbyterian Church of Wamego and Moderator of the Synod; J. A. Lippincott, Chancellor of the State University; D. C. Milner, Pastor of the Presbyterian Church of Manhattan; Z. A. Smith, Editor of the Leavenworth *Times*; John Cooper, Superintendent of the City Schools of Manhattan; Robert Crozier, Judge of the District Court, Manhattan; H. F. Sheldon, Mayor of Ottawa; A. Dobson, President of the Bank of Ottawa; George Sutherland, President of Ottawa University; M. L. Ward, Professor of Mathematics and Political Science in Ottawa University; P. P. Elder, ex-Governor of Kansas and ex-Mayor of Ottawa; Horace J. Smith, President of the First National Bank of Ottawa and Representative from the Sixteenth District; John P. Harris, President of the People's National Bank of Ottawa and late State Senator; John A. Frow, Clerk of the District Court of Franklin County; George T. Anthony, Collector and ex-Governor of Kansas; A. W. Benson, Judge of the Fourth Judicial District; J. T. Coplan, Cashier of the First National Bank of Atchison; D. Martin, ex-District Judge; George Storch, President of the United States National Bank of Atchison; Henry Elliston, State Senator; T. M. Pierce, County Attorney of Johnson County, Olathe; William R. Smith, City Attorney of Atchison; Frank Royse, Chairman of the Democratic County Central Committee (county not stated); Noble L. Prentis, formerly Editor of the Atchison *Champion*; D. R. Anthony, formerly Editor of the Leavenworth *Times*; J. F. Tufts, Assistant Attorney-General for Atchison County under the provisions of the Prohibitory law, from August, 1886, to January, 1889; C. O. French, Judge of the Sixth District; W. M. Rice, Representative from the Twenty-second District; A. H. Sargent, Police Judge of Fort Scott; A. G. Robb, Presiding Elder, Fort Scott; J. A. Hyden, Presiding Elder, Independence District; H. W. Chaffee, Presiding Elder, Ottawa District; B. Kelly, Presiding Elder, Emporia District; J. A. Motter, Presiding Elder, Leavenworth District; S. E. Pendleton, Presiding Elder, Atchison District; J. R. Madison, Presiding Elder, Marysville District; G. S. Dearborn, Presiding Elder, Topeka District; A. S. Embree, Presiding Elder, Manhattan District; H. A. Gobin, President of Baker University; George T. Thompson, Editor of the Manhattan *Nationalist*; G. A. Atwood, Editor of the Manhattan *Republican*; A. Schuyler, W. B. Johnson, F. A. Cook, and J. C. B. Scott, Professors in Kansas Wesleyan University; J. H. Lockwood, Presiding Elder, Salina District; Thomas Anderson, ex State Senator; R. H. Bishop, Justice of the Peace for eighteen years, etc.

Mr. L. A. Maynard, of the New York *Observer*, who made a special tour through Kansas for the study of Prohibition, has recorded his observations in a very calm, complete, and, withal, readable pamphlet entitled "The Truth About Kansas." He shows that the Prohibitory law has injured certain kinds of business. For instance, he says :*

"The police judge at Fort Scott was one of those who thought the law had injured business. It certainly has injured his business, for the records show that in 1874, when Fort Scott had almost one-third of its present population, the office of police judge was worth $2,400 a year. Now it is worth only $800, and the amount is growing smaller every year. The same loss has been experienced in the police business all over Kansas. I was told of a man at Topeka engaged in the *manufacture of steel cells*, for jails, who says that *his business has been ruined in Kansas*, and he is going to 'move out.' I also saw in the Labor Commissioner's office at Topeka a complaint from a *barrel manufacturer* that the demand for barrels had '*fallen off terribly*' since the coming of Prohibition. Such 'losses' as these, I believe, are the only ones that Kansas has actually sustained as the result of Prohibition."

On the other hand, he says :

"The men who make complaint about the loss of revenue from the liquor-shops are too short-sighted and narrow-minded to see that the loss is being made up to them many times over by a decrease in expenditures for police regulation, for the care and punishment of criminals, and by the increase of thrift and economy among the laboring classes, and by the sounder and healthier tone of all branches of business. Tradesmen generally have a better trade than they had in saloon days, and their bills are paid more promptly. *This is the universal testimony.*"

Of this he gives such instances as the following :

A RAILROAD MAN'S VIEWS.

Mr. E. B. Purcell, a Director of the Atchison, Topeka and Santa

---

* "Truth About Kansas," page 24.

Fé Railroad, and one of the leading business men of the State, says:

"In my opinion the Prohibitory law of the State has been a great success from a business point of view.'... I know personally of numbers of men in the neighborhood of my own town who before the Prohibitory law went into effect were squandering their earnings on drink, and who but for Prohibition would be to-day, I believe, without a home or a dollar in the world. But these men are now sober and industrious and have comfortable homes. I believe that railroad men in this State generally share my views as to the success of the law. I have heard many express the same opinion. The amount of liquor brought into the State under the present law and the amount of money sent out are grossly exaggerated. I do not believe it is one-tenth of what it was before Prohibition."

VIEWS OF STATE COMMISSIONER OF LABOR STATISTICS.

I found Mr. Frank H. Betton, Commissioner of the Bureau of Labor and Industrial Statistics, at his desk in the capitol building at Topeka. He said, in substance, that he had no doubt that the Prohibitory law had been highly beneficial to the laboring classes in the State. His investigations and his personal observations confirmed him in that view. More men were earning their own homes now than ever before. The workingmen were better clothed and better fed. They do better on the same wages here than they do in towns where liquor is openly sold.

IDEAS OF AN EDUCATOR.

Professor D. Bemiss, Superintendent of City Schools at Fort Scott, said:

"I am certain that the Prohibitory law has been helpful to the cause of education in Kansas. We have very few children kept from school because of poverty; very few require aid from the city in the shape of books because of poverty. I am certain, also, that the law is influencing the character of recent emigration to our State. I chose this State myself on that ground, and I know of others in this region who have come here for a similar reason. To make Prohibition perfectly successful here we need a national law forbidding the shipment into the State of intoxicating liquors. This is our chief difficulty."

WHAT A BANK PRESIDENT SAYS.

"It seems to me the sentiment of business men here is all one way on this subject of Prohibition. I am quite certain that it is here in Hutchinson. The law has been a help to us in every way, morally and financially. I do not believe you could find a citizen of this city who would own up that he wanted the saloons back here again. We closed the saloons in Hutchinson before the Prohibitory law went into effect. *I have a boy twelve years old who has never seen a saloon.* You might be in town six months and never see a man under the influence of liquor. There is some whiskey brought in here, but it is not one-twentieth part of what would be here if it was not for Prohibition. The amount shipped in is growing less all the time. The liquor traffic will be wiped out altogether before long."— *President of First National Bank of Hutchinson.*

VARIOUS OPINIONS.

"We seem to have *got rid of the dead-beats* in this town since the Prohibitory law went into effect. We find that the poorer class of people pay their bills more promptly than they used to in saloon times. We could give you the names of men who spent about all their wages in those days in the saloons, but who are now paying for their own homes and living comfortably."—*Manager of Topeka Coal Company, Topeka.*

"I can see a great difference in the condition of the poor in this city since the Prohibitory law went into effect. I have been visiting among the poor here for the last fifteen years, and there never was so little destitution as at the present time, although our city is three times as large as it was ten years ago. I note a great change in the home surroundings of the men who formerly drank. They live in better shape and their children are better clothed. I know the law has been a great blessing to this city."—*Mrs. Has Clark, City Missionary at Fort Scott.*

"I can see a marked improvement in the habits of railroad men. They do not drink near as much as they used to, and their morals are better. Prohibition, in my opinion, is a good thing for us all, and especially for labor."—*Railroad Fireman.*

"Some of our men say that their wages go a great deal further here in Topeka than they did in places where they could drop into the saloons occasionally. They cannot afford to send off and get liquor, and so they go without it. We do not have any trouble with drunken men here."—*Street car Starter at Topeka.*

Mr. Maynard gives, from a personal interview, the following :

VIEWS OF GOVERNOR HUMPHREY.

"As to my views on the Prohibitory law, I can do little more than to reiterate the sentiments which I expressed in my recent biennial message. I said then, and I repeat it now, that the records of courts and of prisons, from the city 'calaboose' to the penitentiary, show a diminution of crime and a falling off in our prison population, bearing the most incontestable evidence of the efficiency of the present state of the law and of the prohibitory policy which the law is designed to enforce. And I will say further, at this time, that, in my judgment, if the question of Prohibition was now resubmitted to the people of this State, it would be carried by a hundred thousand majority. The law is as well enforced as any other law upon our statute-books. It does not entirely prohibit the sale of intoxicants in the State; neither do the laws against stealing and other crimes entirely prohibit. Considering all the circumstances of the case, the law has been a marvellous success. The business of selling intoxicating liquor as a beverage is sinking lower and lower in the estimation of the people. Drunkenness is fast becoming an unknown vice with us. I have noted the fact that at political conventions and other large gatherings, which I have attended in this State in the past two years, an intoxicated man is an extremely rare sight. At a soldiers' reunion, which I attended last year, lasting three days, *I did not see one man under the influence of drink.* The office of police judge in our towns and cities is becoming a mere sinecure. The business of the criminal courts is falling off every day."

AN IMPORTANT DOCUMENT.

Disinterested Testimony—Prohibition as a Financial Benefit.

The following extract is from the annual report of Stockholders' Committee of the Farmers' Loan and Trust Company, of Kansas. It pays a most remarkable tribute to Prohibition as a financial benefit to a State. The men who sign this document are all residents of Boston, and they have no personal interest in making the statement they do except that they can make more money out of loans in a Prohibition State than under license:

"Believing it to be a matter of financial interest and otherwise to our stockholders, we digress somewhat to treat upon a question which has been and is agitating the moral, social, religious, and political welfare of all sections of our common country. We have no motive other than to apply the deductions therefrom obtained to the value of your Kansas investment.

"Noting the practical effect of Prohibition upon the people of the State, our observations lead us to believe that this movement is a grand success in Kansas, which adds, and will continue to add, value to all the lands in the State.

"Whatever makes human existence less burdensome, reduces taxation, prevents crime, and destroys pauperism, is sure to give tangible and material wealth to any State. From a personal interview with General S. B. Bradford, Attorney-General of the State, we have learned the following startling facts regarding the beneficial effects of Prohibition:

"In Atchison County, in 1885, 23 persons were sent to the penitentiary for crimes. In January, in 1886, all the saloons in that county, 60 in number, were closed. During 1886 the number of persons sent to the penitentiary was but 13; in 1887 but 6, and in the first half of 1888 but 1 person.

"In Leavenworth County the saloons were closed in March, 1887. In 1886 there were 36 persons sent to the penitentiary; in 1887, 13, and during the first half of 1888, 5.

"In Ford County, including Dodge City, the saloons were closed in the fall of 1886. In 1886 14 persons were sent to the penitentiary; in 1887, 6, and during the first half of 1888, 2.

"There are at present 104 less persons in the penitentiary than one year ago. The jails of the State are practically empty.

"The average of convicts is one-third less than four years ago.

"In four years of Prohibition, grand larceny has decreased 15 per cent., and crimes against persons have decreased 25 per cent.

"There is to-day one pauper to every 1,350 persons. In 1880, the last year of the dram-shop act, there was one pauper to every 750 persons. There is not a barrel of bonded liquor in the State, and there is not a distillery in the State.

"WE LOOK UPON THE ABOVE FACTS, VOUCHED FOR BY SUCH HIGH AUTHORITY, AS A STRONG ARGUMENT IN FAVOR OF LOANS IN A STATE ADVANCING SO RAPIDLY IN MORAL AS WELL AS MATERIAL PROGRESS. . . .

"All of which is respectfully submitted.

"LEVI S. GOULD,
"F. G. HOBSON,
"A. C. GOSS,
"Q. E. RANKIN,
"*Stockholders' Committee.*"

The following testimony is from the *Western Baptist* of Topeka, Kan., and, so far as we know, has never been challenged :

NO SALOONS.

Topeka has more churches than any city of the same size in the country. It has not a single saloon or drinking-place, and probably this cannot be said of any other city in the Union having as large a population. Four years ago there were one hundred and forty saloons in the city, doing a flourishing business. It was claimed that it would be impossible to clean them out entirely ; but a crusade was inaugurated against them by the county officials, which in less than a year closed every drinking-place in the city. Before the whiskey element became convinced that the law would be enforced, over $25,000 in fines were collected from saloon-keepers for violation of the Prohibitory law, and more than thirty of them served out sentences in the county jail. It is now absolutely impossible to buy a drop of liquor in Topeka as a beverage. There has been a very noticeable decrease in the amount of crime since the law went into effect; though the city has doubled in population, the number of arrests by the police is not as great as when the saloons were open. Persons who violently opposed the Prohibitory law now admit that it has been a blessing to the city of Topeka. Speaking of the closing of the saloons, County Attorney Curtis said : "At one time there were one hundred and forty saloons open in Topeka ; their average sales per day were not less than $30 each, which would make $4,200 spent daily for liquor. This amount came largely from the working people. To-day not one dollar of that amount is spent for whiskey. Where does it go to? It goes for food and clothing for the wife and children. I know of scores of instances where families were suffering for food because the father gave his wages to the saloon-keeper. Now they are living in a cosey home of their own ; they have all the necessities of life, and, indeed, a few of the luxuries ; the children, who were once poverty stricken and living in rags, are now attending the public school, and the father will tell you he is the happiest man in the State, and that Prohibition rescued him."

With such facts before him, the true economist would smooth such a traffic's way to oblivion and multiply the motive-power. Crowd all steam upon Prohibition and lay a broad track for it wherever humanity dwells. Let the business of the police judge, the steel-cell manufacturer, and the barrel-maker decline, and that of the grocer, the clothing dealer, the educator, and the house-builder advance, till ours shall become a nation of homes over which the saloon's baleful shadow shall fall nevermore !

CHAPTER XV.

IOWA.

"Four-fifths of this State is without a saloon. Not a distillery is left in the State and not to exceed a dozen breweries are left. Bootlegging is confined to the lowest criminal tramp element. Seventy-five per cent. of our jails are without a prisoner. Grand juries are without business. Criminal expenses are greatly reduced. Bank deposits have largely increased. Lawyers are without practice. Politicians are no longer fearful about examining the question. Popular opinion is growing stronger day by day in favor of the law. These things are attested by the Iowa ministers, teachers, Governor, State officials, three fourths of the editors, and a myriad of other witnesses."—*President B. F. Wright, of Iowa State Temperance Alliance.*

The people of Iowa passed a Constitutional Prohibitory Amendment on June 27th, 1882. "The vote on the amendment in the State was: For it, 155,436; against it, 125,677; majority in favor, 29,759. In this vote 46,000 more ballots were cast than in the general election for Governor, in 1881.* . . . But a sad reverse came upon the friends of the Prohibitory Amendment, and it was lost on account of clerical errors in the Legislature passing it." This caused it to be set aside by the Supreme Court. This has been a source of weakness to the present time, the law not established in the Constitution being largely the foot-ball of conflicting parties, liable to be repealed by any legislature.

---

* See "Liquor Problem in All Ages," pp. 420-22. A thrilling narrative.

A Prohibitory law was passed by the Legislature, and went into effect July 4th, 1884.

Of the effect of this law, after three years' trial, Governor Larrabee testifies as follows in a letter published in the *Keosauqua Republican*, and sent direct to the author of these pages from the Executive Office :

A LETTER FROM GOVERNOR LARRABEE.

EXECUTIVE OFFICE, DES MOINES, IA., June 30, 1887.

Messrs. Sloan & Rowley, Keosauqua, Ia.

DEAR SIRS : Your letter of the 28th inst., requesting certain information relative to the Prohibitory law of this State and the manner in which it is enforced has been received.

In reply I have to say that our Prohibitory law is being enforced in eighty-five of the ninety-nine counties of the State, as well as the laws against other crimes, all malicious reports to the contrary notwithstanding. In the fourteen remaining counties, situated principally along the Mississippi and containing large towns abounding in foreign population, the law is but partially enforced, and in a few instances is even defiantly violated. These places are, however, gradually yielding to a public sentiment in favor of general enforcement, which is rapidly growing even in the eastern part of the State.

Prohibition has certainly not injured any business interest except that of the saloon-keeper, nor has it driven any good citizens from our borders. It is true we have lost since the adoption of the Prohibitory law several thousand incurable vendors of liquor and perhaps a few hundred incurable topers, but we have every reason to congratulate ourselves upon such a loss. Hon. G. W. Ruddick, Judge of the Twelfth Judicial District and one of the oldest and best judges of the State, in an official report, dated June 11th, 1887, makes the following statement : " The jails in this district are now idle, and in eight terms of court held by me since January 1st there has been but one indictment presented, and I think the grand juries have been reasonably diligent. Much of the criminal element has certainly emigrated."

Hon. John W. Harvey, Judge of the Third Judicial District of this State, also makes an interesting statement concerning the influence of Prohibition on crime. He has been judge four years and a half. In 1883 he sentenced 31 persons to the penitentiary; in 1884, 23; in 1885, 20; in 1886, 14, and during the first six months of 1887, 3. These were divided among counties as follows: Decatur, 9; Ringgold, 6; Taylor, 8; Page, 11; Montgomery, 28; Adams, 2; Union, 20; Clarke, 6; Wayne, 1. The latter county has been in the district only since January. Judge Harvey says: "I am frequently asked what is the cause of this decrease in crime during the last four years. My answer is, the enforcement of the Prohibitory liquor law. And it seems to me that the above figures prove this beyond a doubt. The first year I was on the bench the saloons were running; the second and third years they were running in some localities; but the fourth year I do not believe there was a saloon in the district. I am satisfied that there was not an open saloon. Red Oak, in Montgomery County, and Creston, in Union County, were the last places in the district to give up the saloons, and the record from these two counties shows the result. The result from these counties is not because they have a larger population than the other counties of the district. Page has a much larger population than either of these counties. In the counties where the law has been best enforced there has been the least crime. During the last year it has not been an uncommon thing, as in this county (Decatur) at the last term, for the grand jury to adjourn without finding an indictment.

"At first, under the present pharmacy law, some of the druggists were disposed to take advantage and abuse the trust imposed in them, but a number of convictions and fines and the revocation of a number of pharmacy permits by the Pharmacy Board, has had a wholesome effect, and I believe that a great majority of the druggists in this district are now disposed to obey the law."

Hon. William P. Wolf, of Tipton, Speaker of the House of Representatives in the Twentieth General Assembly, writes as follows concerning the progress of Prohibition in his county: "When open saloons were running in Tipton, breaches of peace and other crimes were much more frequent than now. The records of the courts will show that aside from the prosecutions for violation of the liquor law, prosecutions in Cedar County for other crimes have fallen off more than sixty per cent. from what they were when saloons were running, for the reason that crimes are less frequent. It is no argument that the law in some cases is evaded and secretly violated. The traffic in Tipton is driven into the dark, and the liquor law is not violated there oftener than the law against theft. Where the officers have enforced the law the feeling in its favor is certainly stronger than ever, many who had opposed it being now opposed to its repeal. It is much stronger in the State than when it was passed, because enforcement has taken away many arguments before used against it. If submitted to-day as a non-partisan question, it would carry by a much larger majority than before, and its strength must increase."

As regards the internal revenue of a State, it is no indication whatever of the amount of liquor consumed in that State, for the tax on liquors is paid by the manufacturer, and not by the consumer. For several years one of the largest distilleries in the country was in operation here manufacturing for export only. From that institution alone was collected by far the greater part of the internal revenue of Iowa. It has long been a disputed question whether this distillery could be operated under the Prohibitory law, and about three months ago, on a final test in the district court, it was ordered closed.

It is true, both shooting and murder have occurred under the Prohibitory law. A minister at Sioux City and a constable at Des Moines were killed in the attempt to enforce the law, but these crimes were in both instances committed by those who had always defied the law.

It would be useless to undertake the task of contradicting all the false reports put in circulation by unscrupulous men. Officers may, in a few instances, have shown a lack of discretion in the performance of their official duties, but this in the minds of candid men will not affect the merit of the law. The law is steadily gaining in public favor, and Prohibition is beyond doubt the settled policy of Iowa. Could the Prohibitory law at the present time be submitted to our people for their ratification, I am confident it would be endorsed by a majority of from sixty to eighty thousand votes

Very respectfully,
WILLIAM LARRABEE.

Governor Larrabee's letter is so compact that it will be well to call special attention to the most important points. In regard to the alleged non-enforcement, the Governor says :

"The Prohibitory law is being enforced in eighty-five of the ninety-nine counties of the State, as well as the laws against other crimes, all malicious reports to the contrary notwithstanding. In the fourteen remaining counties, situated principally along the Mississippi and containing large towns abounding in foreign population, the law is but partially enforced, and in a few instances is even defiantly violated. These places are, however, gradually yielding to a public sentiment in favor of general enforcement, which is rapidly growing even in the eastern part of the State."

There is the process. The law puts these large towns practically in a state of siege, with enforced Prohibition all around them, constant information of its benefits coming from better governed counties within the State, which force conviction on business men and win their confidence, thus creating a steadily rising public sentiment within the cities, out of which enforcement at length will come.

Since Governor Larrabee's letter was written Sioux City, where the martyred Haddock fell, has wheeled into line, with closed saloons and the great Arensdorf Brewery converted into an oatmeal factory. It is sometimes said that the advocates of Prohibition are not willing to take anything unless they can get all. They were willing to take eighty-five of the ninety-nine counties of Iowa and wait and work for the other fourteen, and they are going to take them before long.

As to the general effect upon the State, the Governor says :

"Prohibition has certainly not injured any business interest except that of the saloon-keeper, nor has it driven any good citizen from our borders. It is true we have lost since the adoption of the Prohibitory law several thousand incurable vendors of liquor and perhaps a few hundred incurable topers. But we have every reason to congratulate ourselves upon such a loss."

Is there any other State that would care to take this consignment of exiles and consider it an element of prosperity ?

As to the effect on crime, Governor Larrabee quotes Judge Ruddick, of the Twelfth Judicial District, as follows:

> "The jails in this district are now idle, and in eight terms of court held by me since January 1st there has been but one indictment presented, and I think the grand juries have been reasonably diligent. Much of the criminal element has certainly emigrated."

From Speaker Wolf, of Tipton, he quotes the following:

> "When open saloons were running in Tipton, breaches of the peace and other crimes were much more frequent than now. The records of the courts will show that, aside from prosecutions for violations of the liquor law, prosecutions in Cedar County for other crimes have fallen off more than sixty per cent. from what they were when the saloons were running, for the reason that crimes are less frequent. It is no argument that the law in some cases is evaded and secretly violated. The traffic in Tipton is driven into the dark, and the liquor law is not violated there oftener than the law against theft. Where the officers have enforced the law, the feeling in its favor is certainly stronger than ever, many who were opposed to the law being now opposed to its repeal."

With all which the Governor's concluding sentence heartily agrees:

> "The law is steadily gaining in public favor, and Prohibition is beyond doubt the settled policy of Iowa. Could the Prohibitory law at the present time be submitted to our people for their ratification, I am confident it would be endorsed by a majority of from sixty to eighty thousand votes."

This was in 1887. Have not two years' more experience spoiled it all? Let us see. Just before the last session of the Legislature, in 1888, the district judges of the State wrote to Governor Larrabee, and out of twenty-four all but three declared that crime and drunkenness had been decreased to a great extent, and they would oppose any attempt to substitute a High License and Local Option law. Several of the judges opposed Prohibition when it was first enacted, but the beneficial results apparent from it caused them to change their minds.

Judge Harvey, of the Third District, writes:

"I am not aware that there is a saloon in the district. Prohibition has reduced crime at least one-half and the criminal expenses in like ratio."

Judge Lewis, of the Fourth District, testifies:

"The law is as well enforced as any other, and has decreased criminal expenses at least two-thirds."

Judge Wakefield, also of the Fourth District, writes:

"I am satisfied that our city (Sioux City, so long contested), having during the past year enjoyed a season of great prosperity and growth, has aided materially in the change of affairs here. *As the saloons were driven out other business came in to occupy the vacant places.*"

Judge Granger, of the Thirteenth District, writes:

"The closing of the front door of the saloon, whereby it is destroyed as a place of social resort, has cancelled nine-tenths of the drunkenness."

Yes, certain inveterate topers and stray drummers will "get whiskey" anywhere, even by the most degrading means. But the better class of men will not drink unless they are sustained by a considerable public opinion, by custom, and by the presence of many whom they respect and like. Prohibition saves all the best and most hopeful among the endangered classes. To "destroy the saloon as a place of social resort" is a great thing to do. Its complete extermination is then not far away.

We are able to quote a still later letter from Governor Larrabee, dated February 6th, 1889, in which he says:

"The Prohibitory law of Iowa has much more than answered the expectations of its former most hopeful advocates. . . . There has been a steady growth in our population, and the census of 1890 will probably show in Iowa at least 2,000,000 inhabitants. The vote at the last election showed an increase of 65,329 votes over the Presidential election of 1884—a larger increase than the election of 1884 showed over that of 1880.

THE BANKING BUSINESS

of a State is, perhaps, as fair a barometer of business as can be found. The number of banks in the State has increased from 186, in 1883, to 244, in 1888 ; deposits have increased from $27,231,719.74 to $39,935,362.68, in 1888.

"I think more than half of the jails in the State are empty at the present time. There are ninety-eight less convicts in our penitentiaries than there were three years ago, notwithstanding the growth of the population.

"Tramps are very scarce in Iowa. There are evidently few attractions for them here. Probably more than three thousand of their recruiting stations have been closed in Iowa during the past five years.

THE WIVES AND MOTHERS

of the State, and especially those of small means, are almost unanimously in favor of the law. *The families of laboring men now receive the benefits of the earnings that formerly went to the saloons.*"

That is the real trouble. That is why the law is hated, and a stupendous effort made to overthrow it. Why should these "wives and mothers"—these "families of laboring men"—be spending the money on which the saloon elsewhere has a perennial mortgage ? These $39,000,000 in banks, too, which might be in breweries and distilleries !

But from the point of view of human happiness and welfare, the testimony is all one way. From *The Voice* of June 6th, 1889, we are permitted to take the following table, which, as in previous cases, we give in two sections, on account of space :

THE SUCCESS OF IOWA'S LAW.

TESTIMONIES FROM THE PROSECUTING ATTORNEYS COVERING 58 COUNTIES OF THE STATE.

I.—IN NEARLY EVERY INSTANCE THE OPEN SALOON HAS BEEN UTTERLY ABOLISHED; DRUNKENNESS, PAUPERISM, AND CRIME HAVE GREATLY DECREASED.

COUNTY.	Name of County Attorney.	Name of Post-Office.	1. How successfully has Prohibition closed the saloons in your part of the State?	2. To what extent, in your judgment, has it diminished drunkenness and the consumption of intoxicants for beverage purposes?
Adair	D. A. Illtes.†	Greenfield.	All saloons closed in this section of State.	Decrease drunkenness quite perceptible.
Adams	John W. Bixby.	Corning.	Closed all saloons in county.	Not in the least; people send to Nebraska and Illinois for liquor.
Audubon	H. W. Hanna.	Audubon.	All closed in this county.	Fully one-half.
Buchanan	H. W. Holman.	Independence.	Not place in county where drink can be bought openly.	Fully 90 per cent.; not half dozen arrests drunkenness 18 months in this city 8,500 population.
Buena Vista	M. J. Sweeley.	Storm Lake.	Not an open saloon in this section of State.	Fully one-half; Prohibition unquestionably a success.
Butler	F. Lingenfelder.	Greene.	Very successfully.	25 per cent.
Calhoun	E. C. Stevenson.	Rockwell City.	Effectually closed every saloon in county.	50 to 75 per cent.
Cerro Gordo.	Joseph J. Clark.	Mason City.	The open saloon is a thing of the past.	From two-thirds to three-fourths.
Cherokee	A. R. Molyneux.	Cherokee.	Not an open saloon in county; the traffic practically stamped out.	Drunkenness three-fourths; consumption largely decreased judging from decreased crime.
Clay	A. C. Parker.	Spencer.	The saloons have been successfully closed and are kept closed.	At least 50 per cent.
Crawford	P. F. C. Lally.	Denison.	No open saloons; Prohibition enforced in this county.	Diminished enormously.

IOWA.

County	Name	Place		
Dallas	D. W. Woodin	Adel	No open saloons in county.	Drunkenness more three-fourths. Iowa had 6,000 saloons before Prohibition; now less than 400.
Delaware	Eli C. Perkins	Delhi	Know of no saloons in this part of the State.	Diminished 90 per cent.
†Des Moines	James D. Smyth	Burlington	Old and well-regulated saloons generally closed up; but worst class small places bad as ever; difficult to find parties conducting them.	Not at all.
‡Dubuque	Alphous Mattews	Dubuque	Not at all.	None in this county; has decreased public and increased private drinking.
Emmett	John G. Myerly	Estherville	No places in vicinity where intoxicants sold in open violation of law.	One-half in small towns.
Fayette	D. W. Clements	West Union	Prohibition generally a success in State. Have seen no open saloons in long time.	Consumption Intoxicants largely decreased.
Floyd	S. W. Woodhouse	Rockford	No saloons in this county.	Very little.
Franklin	W. D. Evans	Hampton	Utterly and absolutely.	From 80 to 90 per cent.
Fremont	William Eaton	Sidney	No saloons in the county.	Prohibition a success in this county.
Greene	Z. A. Church	Jefferson	Not a single saloon in county; law more successful than against larceny.	At least 90 per cent.
Grundy	R. J. Williamson	Grundy Centre	Open saloons largely closed.	Not as much beer, but more whiskey; individuals send out of the State for liquors.
Hamilton	G. F. Tucker	Webster City	Have no saloons in this part of Iowa.	Diminished 95 per cent.; whatever liquor drank shipped from other States.
Hancock	J. K. Wichman	Garner	Saloons in this part of Iowa almost entirely closed.	Diminished one-half; some people send out of the State for liquors.

* From Clinton County Mayor C. W. Chase, of Clinton, population 18,000, replies, that " Saloons in Clinton have been closed," but that liquors are brought in to some extent over the border. "The effect of closing the saloons here has been to improve the social condition of society, lessen crime and police duty, and certainly is no detriment to business."

* From Woodbury County Judge C. R. Lewis, of Sioux City, population 25,000, reports : " Saloons all closed in this district, including nine counties." " Drunkenness very largely decreased; drinking more than half." " Never so prosperous as under Prohibition; taxes decreased; crime decreased more than one-half; pauperism decreased."

* From Keokuk, a city of 16,000 in Lee County, W. F. Blake, a prominent citizen, reports: " Every brewery, saloon, and liquor-selling pharmacy has been closed." " The closing of the saloons has had a remarkable effect upon the peace, good order, and prosperity of the city. There has been a decrease of 65 per cent. in the number of criminal commitments. Retail tradesmen say laboring men buy more supplies than ever before."

* From John T. Scott, Brooklyn, County Attorney of Poweshiek County: 1. " No open saloons in county." 2. " Three-fourths at least." 3. " Yes, fourfold." 4. " Never."

* From M. Atkinson, Bedford, County Attorney of Taylor County: 1. " Effectually." 2. " Seldom see intoxicated person." 3. " Without doubt." 4. " No."

† Clerk of District Court.

‡ See explanation for these counties on pages 249-251.

THE SUCCESS OF IOWA'S LAW—Continued.

County.	Name of County Attorney.	Name of Post-Office.	1. How successfully has Prohibition closed the saloons in your part of the State?	2. To what extent, in your judgment, has it diminished drunkenness and the consumption of intoxicants for beverage purposes?
Hardin	H. L. Huff.	Eldora.	No saloons in county; before Prohibition we had 50.	Diminished in this part at least 80 per cent.; not 1 drunk to dozens before Prohibition.
Harrison	J. S. Dewell.	Mo. Valley.	We consider it a *success* here.	Diminished three-fourths; many so-called "respectable" people ship liquor from other States.
Henry	A. W. Kinkead.	Mount Pleasant	Not an open saloon in county; generally true over State.	Very largely.
Howard	W. K. Barker.	Cresco.	Every saloon closed in this part of State. No liquor sold openly and very little clandestinely.	Drunkenness about 50 per cent.; consumption between 80 and 90 per cent.
Humboldt	C. A. Babcock.	Humboldt.	Entirely closed them.	Fully one-half. If liquor not shipped to individual from other States drunkenness not noticed.
Jasper	W. G. Clements.	Newton.	Entirely successful in this part of the State.	Diminished fully three-fourths according to police court records.
Jefferson	J. M. Illnkle.*	Fairfield.	Not a saloon in our city; formerly 15.	Prior to Prohibition almost a daily thing have cases of drunkenness in court. For two years past as Mayor have had but 7 or 8 cases.
Johnson	C. S. Ranck.	Iowa City.	Open saloons few in this county; but believe many places where liquor can be had.	Do not believe diminished drunkenness; those who wish get liquors from other States.
Jones	F. O. Ellison.	Anamosa.	Very successfully; not a saloon in county; three years ago about 25.	Fully from 40 to 50 per cent.; drunkenness an uncommon occurrence.
Lucas	J. C. Copeland.	Chariton.	Not an open saloon in county; no "bootleggers".	50 per cent.
Madison	John A. Gulher.	Winterset.	No open saloons in this Congressional District, containing the capital.	Very largely; few cases drunkenness compared with license States.

IOWA.

County	Name	Town	Saloons	Drunkenness
Mills	E. B. Woodruff	Glenwood	No open saloons in county.	Drunken men very rare; though old topers send out of State for liquor.
Mitchell	W. L. Eaton	Osage	Completely; not a saloon in county, though some liquor shipped in from Minnesota.	To a large extent. Drunkenness exceedingly rare.
Monona	Chas. E. Underhill	Onawa	Completely closed them.	Diminished at least four-fifths.
O'Brien	J. B. Dunn	Sheldon	All saloons closed in county for over three years.	Over one-half.
Osceola	O. J. Clark	Sibley	Closed every open saloon in Northwestern Iowa.	More than 90 per cent. here.
Page	T. R. Stockton	Clarinda	Entirely successful; saloons all closed in county.	At least 75 per cent.
Palo Alto	Thos. O'Connor	Emmettsburg	Saloons closed in the county.	Very little; much liquor shipped in from Illinois and Wisconsin.
Pocahontas	Byron J. Allen	Pocahontas	Prohibition has practically closed liquor traffic in this State. No saloons in this part.	Safe to say 95 per cent.; a drunkard is a rare thing.
Polk	J. K. Macomber	Des Moines	All saloons closed in central Iowa. No open saloons in Des Moines, with 40,000 population.	Amount liquor sold very small compared with days of license; very little drunkenness here.
†Scott	J. W. Stewart	Davenport	The law a dead letter in this city.	Consumption increased at least 25 per cent.; of vile, adulterated liquor at least 100 per cent.
Story	George W. Dyer	Nevada	Prohibition closed all saloons this part of State.	At least 75 per cent.
Union	P. C. Winter	Afton	Not an open saloon in this part of State.	Not one case of drunkenness where were 100 before Prohibition.
Washington	Charles J. Wilson	Washington	No saloons in this part of State.	Very much decreased.
Wayne	C. W. Steele	Corydon	Absolutely and without question.	In our county seven-tenths; especially true of consumption.
Winnebago	C. L. Nelson	Forest City	Not an open saloon in this or neighboring counties.	Scarcely such thing as drunkenness here; before Prohibition you could not pass through street without seeing drunks.
Winneshiek	John R. Kaye	Calmar	When I came here, January, 1887, between 60 and 70 saloons; now not one.	Decreased tenfold.
Worth	Frank Forbes	Northwood	No attempt to run saloons in this part of State.	Fully 80 per cent., and we are within 4 miles of Minnesota line.
Wright	R. H. Whipple	Dows	Successfully closed in this and surrounding counties.	Not one-tenth drunkenness was before Prohibition; a few old topers still ship liquors into State.

* Mayor of Fairfield. † See explanation for these counties on pages 249–251.

THE SUCCESS OF IOWA'S LAW.

TESTIMONIES FROM THE PROSECUTING ATTORNEYS COVERING 58 COUNTIES OF THE STATE.

II.—Former Revenue from Saloon Licenses More than Made Good by Increased Prosperity under Prohibition; Iowa will Never Return to License.

County.*	Name of County Attorney.	Name of Post-Office.	3. In your judgment has not the loss of the revenue from former saloon licenses been more than made good by the decreasing burdens of pauperism and crime resulting from Prohibition; and by the directing of the money formerly spent in the saloons, now into legitimate channels of trade?	4. Would you advise the re-establishment of saloons, breweries, and distilleries in Iowa under a High License law, as a means calculated to benefit the social and business interests of the State?
Adair	D. A. Illes.†	Greenfield.	It has.	No, I would not.
Adams	John W. Bixby.	Corning.	I think not.	I would; our law will not prevent drinking.
Audubon	H. W. Hanna.	Audubon.	Yes.	No!
Buchanan	H. W. Holman.	Independence.	Yes, emphatically; litigation fallen off 25 per cent.	No, sir; every business except law and liquor more prosperous under Prohibition.
Buena Vista	M. J. Sweeley.	Storm Lake.	Yes; criminal litigation decreased here 75 per cent.	No; Iowa will never take such a backward step.
Butler	F. Lingenfelder.	Greene.	Yes.	No.
Calhoun	E. C. Stevenson.	Rockwell City.	Yes, undoubtedly.	No. No! No!!
Cerro Gordo	Joseph J. Clark.	Mason City.	Yes, beyond all question; crime greatly decreased, jails nearly all empty.	No; people Iowa overwhelmingly against license.
Cherokee	A. R. Molynew.	Cherokee.	Yes; costs criminal prosecutions wonderfully decreased.	Not under any circumstances.
Clay	A. C. Parker.	Spencer.	Unquestionably this is true.	No.
Crawford	P. E. C. Lally.	Denison.	Crime decreased a good deal; business benefited a good deal.	So long as adjoining States make liquor and railroads are allowed to ship it in, I would favor very High License. I am an Anti-Prohibitionist.

IOWA.

County	Correspondent	City		
Dallas	D. W. Woodin.	Adel.	Yes; pauperism and crime decreased under Prohibition.	No; High License would be long step backward.
Delaware	Eli C. Perkins.	Delhi.	Yes, more than 100 times.	Prohibition a success in 22 of 99 counties. We don't want saloons or High License here.
‡Des Moines	James D. Smyth.	Burlington.	I do not think so.	Yes.
‡Dubuque	Alphons Mattews.	Dubuque.	Revenue smaller cities entirely cut off.	Believe a judicious license law would be the best.
Emmett	John G. Myerly.	Estherville.	It has not.	I would not; merchants now receive money formerly went to saloons.
Fayette	D. W. Clements.	West Union.	Pauperism and crime decreased, though population increased; many jails entirely emptied.	
Floyd	S. W. Woodhouse.	Rockford.	Can see no effect.	NO.
Franklin	W. D. Evans.	Hampton.	Yes; Prohibition stronger than ever.	No; such a suggestion regarded in this part of State as sheer nonsense.
Fremont	William Eaton.	Sidney.	Yes; criminal costs reduced at least 75 per cent.	No; Prohibition growing in strength and effectiveness.
Greene	Z. A. Church.	Jefferson.	Yes; county jail empty most of the time.	No; no successful argument can be made against workings of this law.
Grundy	R. J. Williamson.	Grundy Centre	Cannot tell.	Yes and no; depending on restrictions.
Hamilton	G. F. Tucker.	Webster City.	Yes; positive knowledge that loss saloon revenues been many times made good.	Never, unless I wanted to disembowel the business interests of the State.
Hancock	J. E. Wichman.	Garner.	Much more than made good by increased prosperity of former drinkers and the greatly decreasing burdens pauperism and crime.	I would not; license only benefit legal fraternity; business interests much better served by Prohibition.

* From Clinton County Mayor C. W. Chase, of Clinton, population 16,000, replies, that "Saloons in Clinton have been closed," but that liquors are brought in to some extent over the border. "The effect of closing the saloons here has been to improve the social condition of society, lessen crime and police duty, and certainly is no detriment to business."
* From Woodbury County, Judge C. H. Lewis, of Sioux City, population 25,000, reports: "Saloons all closed in this district, including nine counties." "Drunkenness very largely decreased." "Never as prosperous as under Prohibition; taxes decreased; crime decreased more than one-half; pauperism decreased."
* From Keokuk, a city of 16,000 in Lee County, W. E. Blake, a prominent citizen reports: "Every brewery, saloon, and liquor-selling pharmacy has been closed." "The closing of the saloons has had a remarkable effect upon the peace, good order, and prosperity of the city. There has been a decrease of 65 per cent. in the number of criminal commitments. Retail tradesmen say laboring men buy more supplies than ever before."
* From John T. Scott, Brooklyn, County Attorney of Poweshiek County: 1. "No open saloons in county." 2. "Three-fourths at least." 3. "Yes, fourfold." 4. "Never."
* From M. Atkinson, Redford, County Attorney of Taylor County: 1. "Effectually." 2. "Seldom see intoxicated person." 3. "Without doubt." 4. "No."

† Clerk of District Court.
‡ See explanation for these counties on pages 249–251.

THE SUCCESS OF IOWA'S LAW—*Continued.*

COUNTY.	Name of County Attorney.	Name of Post-Office.	3. In your judgment has not the loss of the revenue from former saloon licences been more than made good by the decreasing burdens of pauperism and crime resulting from Prohibition; and by the directing of the money formerly spent in the saloons, now into legitimate channels of trade?	4. Would you advise the re-establishment of saloons, breweries, and distilleries in Iowa, under a High License law, as a means calculated to benefit the social and business interests of the State?
Hardin......	H. L. Huff	Eldora.	Yes; greatly overbalances saloon revenues; less crime and expenses under Prohibition.	No; many formerly opposed to Prohibition now favor it.
Harrison ...	J. S. Dewell.	Mo. Valley.	No question that this is true in all rural parts and smaller cities; as to few larger cities much dispute.	I would not; never; no benefit to be derived from saloons.
Henry.......	A. W. Kinkead.	MountPleasant	Think so.	No.
Howard.....	W. K. Barker.	Cresco.	Pauperism decreased; not one crime now where 3 under license; families drunkards provided for.	No; Prohibition has come to stay. Was formerly opposed to Prohibition
Humboldt..	C. A. Babcock.	Humboldt.	Yes, emphatically, yes!	No, emphatically, no! No decent, unprejudiced person would answer otherwise.
Jasper	W. G. Clements.	Newton.	Yes; records show not one-fourth crime before Prohibition. Our jail empty year at time.	No, we would not return to saloons; I formerly doubted the propriety of Prohibition.
Jefferson....	J. M. Hinkle.*	Fairfield.	I think so. Our city never so prosperous as in last 3 or 4 years; less suffering and better financial condition.	I would not; Iowa in better condition than if Prohibition had not been enacted.
Johnson.....	C. S. Ranck.	Iowa City.	Do not think Prohibition has decreased burdens of pauperism and crime.	Would prefer $1,000 license with Local Option.
Jones........	F. O. Ellison.	Anamosa.	Most emphatically yes; our jail empty most time; no criminal cases 2 or 3 terms court; law and liquor business only onee that suffer.	No; saloon too expensive an evil for business unen to tolerate.
Lucas........	J. C. Copeland.	Chariton.	Yes; not one-fourth criminal business formerly; our jail unoccupied last 2 years.	No.

IOWA. 247

County	Name	City	Response
Madison	John A. Guiher.	Winterset.	Revenue from license never paid one-tenth expenses saloons. Merchants say they are benefited by Prohibition. I would not; license not one feature to commend it.
Mills	E. B. Woodruff.	Glenwood.	Yes! No!
Mitchell	W. L. Eaton.	Osage.	Yes, completely emptied our jails; have not one-tenth crime formerly. No; scarcely a license man in town.
Monona	Chas. E. Underhill.	Onawa.	A decided benefit financially. No, indeed; *Prohibition of untold benefit to Iowa.*
O'Brien	J. B. Dunn.	Sheldon.	No question about it; prison statistics conclusively show it. No, not by any means.
Osceola	O. J. Clark.	Sibley.	Decidedly yes! Where we used to have 35 to 40 criminal cases not more than 2 now, often none. Most certainly not! I was formerly an active Anti-Prohibitionist.
Page	T. R. Stockton.	Clarinda.	Emphatically yes. With the same emphasis I answer no!
Palo Alto	Thos. O'Connor.	Emmettsburg.	Taxes are higher. High License is what we should have.
Pocahontas	Byron J. Allen.	Pocahontas.	It undoubtedly has; our criminal statistics show it. Never.
Polk	J. K. Macomber.	Des Moines.	Yes, decidedly. Not in Iowa.
†Scott	J. W. Stewart.	Davenport.	A thousand times no; Prohibition has never been enforced here. I would by all means; you cannot prohibit the use of intoxicants any more than the social evil.
Story	George W. Dyer.	Nevada.	Certainly it has; not one criminal prosecution where there were 10 before Prohibition. No; it makes no difference how high the license.
Union	P. C. Winter.	Afton.	I say yes. No.
Washington	Chas. J. Wilson.	Washington.	Approximately correct. I would say no.
Wayne	C. W. Steele.	Corydon.	Yes; the decrease in court expenses is extremely large. No; the day of the saloon is past.
Winnebago	C. L. Nelson.	Forest City.	Hundreds of dollars saved in court expenses by Prohibition; several times Grand Jury met and adjourned, nothing to do. Not in Iowa or any other State.
Winneshiek	John B. Kaye.	Calmar.	It has; Prohibition gaining friends from all parties. No; though I voted against the Amendment, I am satisfied law can be enforced.
Worth	Frank Forbes.	Northwood.	Not criminal case in district court for 2 years; that alone more than makes good loss of revenue from saloons. No!
Wright	R. H. Whipple.	Dows.	Yes, more than made good. I would not; Prohibition come to stay in Iowa; public opinion strengthening in its favor.

*Mayor of Fairfield. † See explanation for those counties on pages 249–251.

The above replies from the county attorneys of Iowa, covering fifty-eight of the ninety-nine counties of that State, have been received by *The Voice* in answer to a series of questions similar to those which elicited the remarkable letters from probate judges of Kansas, published in *The Voice* of May 23d. In this instance, as in the case of Kansas, *The Voice* had no previous knowledge of the political affiliation or views on Prohibition of the persons addressed, and all the replies, favorable and unfavorable, are included in the table. The same letter accompanied these questions as was sent to the judges of Kansas.

While the replies from the county attorneys of Iowa do not exhibit the striking unanimity of opinion in favor of the Prohibitory law as did the answers of the Kansas probate judges, they nevertheless show that Iowa's short experiment in Prohibitory legislation is regarded as a success. All over the State drunkenness, pauperism, and crime are reported to be greatly diminished. Several of these lawyers who formerly opposed and voted against the law now declare themselves its enthusiastic supporters, and this in the face of their admissions that criminal and other litigation has greatly decreased under the operation of Prohibition.

A striking feature of the report, and indicating the necessity of national law to protect the States in their endeavors to rid themselves of the liquor traffic, are the replies from eight or more counties that, while the saloons have been closed up and abolished, liquor is nevertheless shipped in from license States in violation of the Iowa law.

The following is a summary of the replies in the table:

SUMMARY.

QUESTION I.—How successfully has Prohibition closed the saloons in your part of the State?—58 replies, 54 of which assert positively that there are no open saloons ; 2, that the law is not at all enforced ; 1, that open saloons are few ; 1, that old and well-regulated saloons have been closed up, but small ones remain because of difficulty of finding and convicting the owner.

QUESTION II.—To what extent has Prohibition diminished drunkenness and the consumption of intoxicants for beverage purposes?—58 replies, 50 replying that it has decreased drunkenness, and the consumption of liquors in per cents. varying from 40 to 99 per cent. ; 2 say " very little ;" 3, " not at all ;" 1, " diminished beer drinking, increased whiskey drinking"; 1, " increased"; 1, " don't believe diminished." A considerable proportion of the answers to these questions, it will be noticed, complain that liquor is shipped in from other States to individuals.

QUESTION III.—Has not the loss of revenue from former saloon licenses been made good by the decreasing burdens of pauperism and crime, and the directing of the money formerly spent in the saloons into legitimate channels of trade?—58 replies, 49 answering yes ; 7, no ; 2 cannot tell.

QUESTION IV.—Would you advise the re-establishment of the saloons, breweries, and distilleries of Iowa under High License?—54, replies, 46, no ; 5 yes ; 3, qualified.

Of the unfavorable reports contained in the table, *The Voice* gives the following explanation :

THE TRUTH ABOUT THE WORKINGS OF THE LAW IN THE REBEL CITIES.

The letters show that while the law has greatly benefited nearly the entire State, there are a few cities in which the full advantages of it have not been reaped. Particularly for the cities of Burlington, Dubuque, and Davenport, the reports from the county attorneys are unfavorable. It should be remembered that these officials are elected by the influence of political machines, and in counties where the politicians are especially subservient to the rumsellers the county attorneys are not likely to be friendly to the law.

In order to get additional and unbiassed testimony for the three cities named, we telegraphed to well-known citizens for brief statements of the facts, with intelligent explanations. The following answers have been received :

BURLINGTON, IA., May 31 (*Special Dispatch*).—Under High License we had, in Burlington, 5 breweries, 3 wholesale liquor houses, 39 " permit" dealers, and 80 saloons. Under Prohibition there are not more than 30 saloons in operation, and all the other places have been driven out. There is not one barrel of liquor in Burlington now where there were hundreds.

All the saloons not being closed, the full benefits of Prohibition have not been obtained. For this the political influences are responsible, all the civil officers—judges, mayor, policemen, constables, and justices of the peace—holding their places by the favor of the liquor men. The saloons that are still running here are operated by outside dealers, and suits are pending against them.

This is a river city of about thirty thousand population. The German element is large, but the situation is steadily improving under Prohibition. The extensive vineyards and the large beer-gardens that were operated as Sunday resorts, where drunkenness and debauchery reigned, are things of the past. A German anti-Prohibitionist, who was mayor for four years during the license system, says that drinking has decreased thirty per cent. ; that the saloon-keepers used to violate all laws, both of God and man, especially the Sabbath law, which they now observe, and that the criminal and pauper expenses during the sway of High License were so great that little, if anything, was left to the city.

T. W. Barkyte, a banker and an anti-Prohibitionist, states that many who formerly spent their money in the saloons are now depositing it in the banks. The city is orderly, the police judge and half of the police force could be dispensed with, and hundreds who voted against the Amendment are now enthusiastic friends of the law. It has been successful beyond our hopes. The ex-saloon-keepers are asking for High License. More building is going on in Burlington than in any of the other river cities.

MRS. M. H. DUNHAM.

DUBUQUE, IA., May 31 (*Special Dispatch*).—When Iowa voted for Prohibition by thirty thousand Dubuque went against it seven to one. Naturally in a city intensely opposed to the measure at the beginning, the most favorable results have not been gained. A large number of the citizens are foreigners, who have considerable investments in saloons and breweries, and ever since the law was enacted Dubuque has been a rebel city.

But even in Dubuque the future has an ominous look for the liquor men. There is not a saloon-keeper or brewer or any one directly interested in the liquor business who would not gladly have our present law exchanged for any form of license, high or low. The breweries could not be sold for twenty cents on the dollar. The saloon-keepers are beginning to understand that Prohibition has come to stay, and many admit that they cannot resist the law much longer.

The progress of the struggle against the violators has been hindered by delays in settling questions of law. Many new questions arose, and some of them had to go to the United States Supreme Court. They have been disposed of now, not for Iowa alone, but for other States that may handle the saloons by Prohibitory law ; and such States need not experience the delays encountered in Iowa.

It is in no sense true that Prohibition has been demoralizing in Dubuque. The city, because of peculiar circumstances, has not enjoyed the benefits coming from the law in almost all other quarters, that is all. She has gone on as before, taking license money from the saloons, as before. While those parts of Iowa where the law is enforced are striking object-lessons of the benefits of Prohibition, Dubuque demonstrates the folly and worthlessness of anything short of enforced Prohibition. Thus her record does not show a striking decrease in crime, although crime is not on the increase.

J. T. ADAMS.

DAVENPORT, IA., May 31 (*Special Dispatch*).—Although the law is violated in Davenport by the connivance of the politicians, it is so far successful that the records show no increase in arrests for crime. The responsibility for violations lies upon Democrats and Republicans alike. Both parties try to control the liquor vote.

E. W. BRADY.

These three cities are the worst spots in Iowa. Excepting a very few other cities, they are the only bad spots. On the other hand, Prohibition has been conspicuously successful in cities just as important as Burlington, Dubuque, and Davenport—notably in Des Moines, Sioux City, and Keokuk. All the reputable testimony that is received goes to prove that Prohibition works magnificently over nearly the whole of the vast territory of the State.

D. W. Clements, County Attorney of Fayette County, writes :

"MEN HERE WHO FORMERLY SPENT MUCH MONEY IN THE SALOON AND OBTAINED THEIR WEARING APPAREL AND THEIR SMALL QUANTITIES OF GROCERIES ON CREDIT LARGELY NOW BUY FOR CASH. THE MERCHANT RECEIVES THE MONEY FORMERLY SPENT IN THE SALOONS AND THE FAMILY GETS THE BENEFIT."

J. K. Macomber, County Attorney of Polk County (including Des Moines, the State capital), writes :

"There is very little drunkenness here. IT IS DECIDEDLY TRUE THAT THE SALOON LICENSE REVENUE HAS BEEN MORE THAN MADE GOOD BY A LARGE DECREASE IN THE AMOUNT OF CRIME AND THE DIVERTING OF MONEY THAT WOULD OTHERWISE GO TO THE SALOON INTO OTHER CHANNELS OF TRADE. I would not advise a repeal of Prohibition and a trial of High License in Iowa."

HOW PROHIBITION

TESTIMONIES FROM THE JUDGES OF

THE SALOON IS PRACTICALLY A THING OF THE PAST; DRUNKENNESS, HAVE BEEN BENEFITED; TAXATION, IF ANYTHING, HAS TENDED TO IMPROVED UNDER PROHIBITION.

NAME OF JUDGE.	Judicial District.*	1. To what extent is the Prohibition law successfully enforced in your section?	2. What can you say of its effect in closing up the saloons?
Scott M. Ladd	Fourth.	Well as most laws.	No saloons here.
C. H. Hewis	Fourth.	Almost absolutely universally.	No saloons in district, 9 counties.
G. W. Wakefield.	Fourth.	About as other criminal statutes.	Saloons closed.
O. B. Ayers	Fifth.	Saloons stay closed.	Not a saloon in district, 6 counties.
J. H. Henderson.	Fifth.	Well as other criminal statutes.	Not a saloon in district, 6 counties.
J. K. Johnson	Sixth.	Well as other criminal statutes.	Closed all saloons in district, 6 counties.
D. Ryan	Sixth.	Generally.	Not a saloon in this precinct.
Walter I. Hayes†	Seventh.	Practically not at all.	Temporarily closed, but begin again.
S. M. Weaver	Eleventh.	Thoroughly.	No saloons in this district, 8 large central counties.
Geo. W. Ruddick	Twelfth.	Well as others for prevention of crime.	Closed except in large cities.
J. W. Sweney‡	Twelfth.	In 85 of 90 counties well as other criminal laws.	Closed saloons in nearly all parts of State.
L. O. Hatch	Thirteenth.	....	No open saloons in this district, 6 counties.
H. E. Deemer	Fifteenth.	Well enforced except 1 county adjoining Omaha	No saloons in this district (8 counties) except one.
J. H. Macomber.	Sixteenth.	Fairly well in more than three-fourths of State.	Quite successful.

* Just before the last session of the Iowa Legislature a number of the Judges of that State wrote to Governor Larabee giving their opinions of the working of the Prohibitory law. We give below testimonies from districts not covered by the above table:

Hon. Henry Bank, Jr., Superior Court Justice: At the September term, 1887, District Court of Keokuk, for the first time not a criminal case before court.

Hon. H. C. Traverse, Judge 2d District: No saloons in but 1 of 8 counties in this district; crime diminished. Would have downed saloons long ago but for protection of Federal Courts.

Hon. J. W. Harvey, Judge 3d District: Law well enforced; no saloons; reduced crime and criminal expenses one-half.

SUCCEEDS IN IOWA.

THE DISTRICT COURTS OF THAT STATE.

Pauperism, and Crime have Greatly Decreased ; Business Interests Decrease ; While the Character and Happiness of the People have

3. To what extent has it diminished drunkenness and the use of intoxicants for beverage purposes ?	4. What can you say as to the effect of Prohibition on business interests, and the attraction or repulsion of capital for investment ?	5. In your observation has money which was formerly spent in the saloons been directed under Prohibition to legitimate channels of trade ?
Drunkenness remarkably reduced.	Very favorable.	Yes, largely.
Drunkenness very largely; drinking more than one-half.	Never as prosperous as under Prohibition.	Yes, to quite large extent.
Diminished.	Business has not suffered.	Goes to building homes.
Largely decreased.	Increased business on the whole.	Yes.
Very much.	No bad effect. In opinions of most, good	Money now saved ; people more prosperous.
Very largely.	Not much effect either way.	Yes, but can't say to what extent.
Drunkenness much less frequent.	Do not think capital repulsed.	Not advised.
Not at all.	No material difference.	Practically same as before.
Drunkenness decreased three-fourths.	For the better ; no capital driven away.	Merchants find trade with laboring men much more satisfactory.
Diminished drunkenness three-fourths.	Some cases reduced rents, some liquor men gone to other States.	Don't know.
Decreased more than 90 per cent.	No business injured except saloons and breweries.	It has ; and to the acquirement of homes.
Social drinking very common ; a few drunkards sobered up.	....	....
Diminished drunkenness at least 75 per cent.	Legitimate business has not suffered.	Yes.
A great deal.	No damage to any business except perhaps the lawyers.	It has.

Hon. Marcus Kavanagh, Jr., Judge 9th District : Crime decreased over 50 per cent.; Prohibition added largely to individual happiness.
Hon. W. F. Conrad, Judge 9th District : Crime largely diminished ; cost of courts very much lessened.
Hon. Lot Thomas, Judge 14th District : Reducing crime and criminal expenses; well enforced as other criminal laws
Hon. J. D. Giffen, Judge 18th District : Law seems to work well in this district.
† Member Congress 2d Congressional District Impeachment charges brought in 1886 against Hayes for refusing to enforce Prohibition while on the Bench were sustained by the Legislature.
‡ Member Congress, 4th Congressional District.

HOW PROHIBITION SUC-

Name of Judge.	Judicial District.*	6. Has Prohibition tended to increase or decrease taxation in the cities and towns of your vicinity? and to what extent?	7. What has been the effect of Prohibition on criminal conditions as evidenced from the records of courts, prisons, and from personal observation?
Scott M. Ladd...	Fourth.	Think municipal taxes heavier.	Lower grade offences decreased.
C. H. Hewis.....	Fourth.	Decreased.	Decreased more than one-half.
G. W. Wakefield.	Fourth.	Increased, not due to Prohibition.	Fewer arrests.
O. B. Ayers.....	Fifth	Not increased.	Crime decreased fully one-half.
J. H. Henderson.	Fifth.	To decrease.	Very marked decrease.
J. K. Johnson...	Sixth.	Decreased court and criminal expenses compensate for loss of license fees.	Decreased three-fourths in four years.
D. Ryan.........	Sixth.	To decrease.	Decreased over one-half in these 6 counties.
Walter I. Hayes†	Seventh.	No difference.	No distinct effect.
S. M. Weaver...	Eleventh.	Not increased; local police expenses, etc., materially decreased.	Lessened; jail population less than for many years.
Geo. W. Ruddick	Twelfth.	Perhaps increased in towns and cities.	Very favorable; crime much reduced.
J. W. Sweney‡..	Twelfth.	Enormously decreased municipal and county expenses.	Little criminal business; most jails empty for months.
L. O. Hatch	Thirteenth.	....	No change as to crimes per se.
H. E. Deemer...	Fifteenth.	Remains about same.	Decreased 50 per cent. Many jails untenanted.
J. H. Macomber.	Sixteenth.	Municipal taxes perhaps increased, but merchants benefited on the whole.	Decreased.

* Just before the last session of the Iowa Legislature a number of the Judges of that State wrote to Governor Larabee, giving their opinions of the working of the Prohibitory law. We give below testimonies from Districts not covered by the above table:
   Hon. Henry Bank, Jr., Superior Court Justice: At the September term, 1887, District Court of Keokuk, for the first time not a criminal case before Court.
   Hon. H. C. Traverse, Judge 2d District: No saloons in but 1 of 8 counties in this district; crime diminished. Would have downed saloons long ago but for protection of Federal Courts.
   Hon. J. W. Harvey, Judge 8d District: Law well enforced; no saloons; reduced crime and criminal expenses one-half.

CEEDS IN IOWA—Continued.

8. Has pauperism increased or decreased under Prohibition?	9. What effect has Prohibition had upon the growth of the State in the number and character of its population?	10. Name any other advantageous results which, in your observation, have come from or accompanied Prohibition.
Decreased.	Attracts sober and better element.	Clears State of criminals and "bummers."
Decreased.	Constantly improving every way.	Benefit to working classes.
Probably comparatively decreased.	Population steadily increases.	Think have smallest per cent. illiteracy in nation.
Largely decreased.	Next census will show large, healthy growth.	Criminal and poor expenses largely decreased.
Decreased.	Salutary.	People more peaceable, contented and prosperous.
Materially decreased.	Think population bettered.	Very many advantages from Prohibition.
Cannot say.	Not time to tell yet.	....
Some increase, but not due to Prohibition.	Probably tended to keep out some foreigners.	There are none.†
Certainly not increased.	Growth healthy; lost none but saloon keepers.	With each year of Prohibition opposition becomes less.
Decreased.	Slightly retarded growth, but better classes not driven away.	....
Very materially decreased.	Character population better; only liquor-dealers have left.	Many business men, formerly opposed, now favor Prohibition.
....	....	....
Increased quite perceptibly.	Losing some of worst classes; gaining best.	Saloon out of politics; bummers gone, fewer rogues.
Decreased.	Dozens of moral lepers left for Nebraska,§ but no good citizens.	Labor more hopeful; supplies families better.

   Hon. Marcus Kavanagh, Jr., Judge 9th District: Crime decreased over 50 per cent.; Prohibition added largely to individual happiness.
   Hon. W. F. Conrad, Judge 9th District: Crime largely diminished; cost of courts very much lessened.
   Hon. Lot Thomas, Judge 14th District: Reducing crime and criminal expenses; well enforced as other criminal laws.
   Hon. J. D. Giffen, Judge 18th District: Law seems to work well in this district.
   † Member Congress 2d Congressional District. Impeachment charges brought in 1886 against Hayes for refusing to enforce Prohibition while on the bench were sustained by the Legislature.
   ‡ Member Congress 4th Congressional District.
   § A $1,000 High License State.

The above table is made up of replies received to a series of questions sent out by *The Voice* about March 1st to all the district judges of Iowa. It contains every reply, fourteen in all, favorable or unfavorable, which has been received to the questions, these replies covering nine of the eighteen judicial districts of the State. In a foot-note are appended some testimonies from judges residing in districts not covered by the above table. The following is a summary of the replies given in the table:

SUMMARY.

QUESTION I.—To what extent is the Prohibition law successfully enforced in your section?—13 replies, only 1 of which intimates that the law is not well enforced.

QUESTION II.—What can you say of its effect in closing up the saloons?—14 replies, 9 of which answer that all saloons are closed; 1, "quite successful;" 1, "no saloons in district except in 1 of 8 counties;" 1, "closed saloons in nearly all parts of State;" 1, "closed except in large cities;" and 1, "temporarily closed but soon begin again."

QUESTION III.—To what extent has it diminished drunkenness and the use of intoxicants for beverage purposes?—14 replies, 12 of which affirm that drinking and drunkenness have been greatly diminished; 1, "not at all;" while 1 asserts that social drinking is very common, though a few drunkards have been sobered up.

QUESTION IV.—What has been the effect of Prohibition on business interests, and the attraction or repulsion of capital for investment?—13 replies, 5 of which reply that the result has been favorable; 5, that business has not been injured except saloons and possibly lawyers; 2, that they see no special effect either way; while 1, that in some cases rents have been reduced on account of liquor men moving away.

QUESTION V.—Has money which was formerly spent in the saloons been directed to legitimate channels of trade?—13 replies, 9 of which answer yes; 1, "money now saved;" 2 do not know; 1, "practically same as before."

QUESTION VI.—Has Prohibition tended to increase or decrease taxes?—13 replies; 4, "decreased;" 5, that taxes have not inoreased; 1, "increased, not due to Prohibition;" 1, "increased, but merchants benefited on the whole;" while 2 think municipal taxes may be higher.

QUESTION VII. —What has been the effect of Prohibition on criminal conditions? - 14 replies, 12 of which reply that crime is much decreased, while 2 can see no change.

QUESTION VIII.—Has pauperism increased or decreased under Prohibition? -13 replies, 10 answering "decreased;" 1, "not increased;" 1, "cannot say;" 1, "some increase, not due to Prohibition."

QUESTION IX.—What effect has Prohibition on the growth of the State in the number and character of population?—13 replies, 10, that the effect has been good; 1, "not time to tell yet;" 1, "probably tended to keep out some foreigners;" and 1, "slightly retarded growth, but better classes not driven away."

Thus it will be seen of these answers to *The Voice's* questions from nine of the eighteen judicial districts of Iowa practically but one can be construed as unfavorable to the working of the law; while in the foot-notes are favorable testimonies from judges in at least six of the remaining districts.

The following extracts from letters of the district judges to Governor Larrabee give more fully their approval of the law and their reasons for it. Several of these judges opposed Prohibition when it was first agitated, but the beneficial results apparent from it caused them to change their minds, and in their letters to the Governor they objected to efforts for repeal. Judge Carson, of the Fifteenth District, wrote:

"When in the Senate I favored Local Option, but I am now satisfied that the [Prohibition] statute should stand. My belief is that the effect has been very favorable in the reduction of criminal offences, especially those growing out of brawls and quarrelling."

So heartily did the judges commend the law that only three of the twenty-four from whom opinions have been quoted answered unfavorably. The following are extracts from the letters, as published lately in the Lincoln (Neb.) *New Republic:*

Judge H. C. Traverse, of the Second District:

" We would have had the saloon down long ago if the federal courts had not stretched their protecting hands over the heads of such fellows as ' Stormy Jordan.' As it is, there is only one county (Wapello) out of the eight counties comprising this district where open saloons are in operation. *My experience is that wherever saloons are closed crime is diminished.*"

THE FEDERAL COURTS A HINDRANCE.

Judge D. Stewart, of the Second District:

" I would not advise the repeal of the Prohibitory liquor law. I am satisfied that this district would have been entirely rid of saloons and breweries for the past year or two if the inferior federal courts had not interfered with the State courts."

Judge J. W. Harvey, of the Third District:

" I am not aware that there is a saloon in the district. It [Prohibition] has *reduced crime at least one-half, and the criminal expenses in like ratio.* I would not and do not favor the repeal of the law."

Judge C. H. Lewis, of the Fourth District:

" *The law is as well enforced, as any other, and has decreased criminal expenses at least two-thirds.*"

Judge S. M. Ladd, of the Fourth District:

" There is a great decrease of cases triable before justices, but not much change in the number of higher offences."

Judge G. W. Wakefield, of the Fourth District:

" I am satisfied that our city [Sioux City], having during the last year enjoyed a season of great prosperity and growth, has aided materially in the change of affairs here. AS THE SALOONS WERE DRIVEN OUT, OTHER BUSINESS CAME IN TO OCCUPY THE VACANT PLACES."

Judge O. B. Ayres, of the Fifth District:

"I have no doubt but that the Prohibitory law has reduced criminal offences and the expenses of the courts in this district very largely, and I certainly would not advise a repeal of it."

Judge J. K. Johnson, of the Sixth District:

"There can be no doubt that the effect of the Prohibitory law has been to reduce very materially crime and *criminal expenses* in this district."

INDIVIDUAL HAPPINESS PROMOTED.

Judge Marcus Havanagh, of the Ninth District:

"*It* [Prohibition] *has decreased crime over fifty per cent. and added largely to individual happiness.*"

Judge W. F. Conrad, of the Ninth District:

"As to the operation of the law, my observation is that it has largely diminished crime in this district and very much *lessened the costs* of maintaining the courts."

Judge S. M. Weaver, of the Eleventh District:

"Crime generally is very much lessened."

Judge John B. Cleland, of the Twelfth District:

"The action of the law has been beneficial, and tended to lessen criminal business and *expenses.*"

Judge C. T. Granger, of the Thirteenth District:

"The closing of the front door of the saloon, whereby it is destroyed as a place of social resort, has *cancelled nine-tenths of the drunkenness.*"

Judge Lot Thomas, of the Fourteenth District:

"As to the effect of the Prohibitory law in this district, I am satisfied that it is reducing crime and, as a consequence, criminal expense. *In this district the law is as well enforced as are any of the other criminal laws of the State.* In my judgment, it would be a grave mistake to attempt to repeal the law or to substitute Local Option or High License in its place."

Judge H. E. Deemer, of the Fifteenth District:

" The Prohibitory law is working nicely in every county in this district except in Pottawatomie, and I think there it is having a good effect and gaining ground rapidly. *It is a noticeable fact that there the criminal docket is much larger, in proportion to the number of inhabitants, than in other counties.*"

REPEAL WOULD BE A CALAMITY.

Judge A. B. Thornell, of the Fifteenth District:

" The Prohibitory law has been very effective in all places in this district except at Council Bluffs. *I should regard its repeal as a calamity,* and have no suggestions to offer in its stead."

To all this we would add:

GOV. LARRABEE'S FAREWELL MESSAGE TO THE LEGISLATURE.

The Governor on the Splendid Achievements of Prohibition—The State is in Every Way the Better for the Law—Figures Showing Decrease in Crime, etc.

DES MOINES, IA., February 17, 1890.—Governor Larrabee's farewell message to the Legislature has just been made public. The following are a few extracts from the Governor's remarkably strong statements:

" Thousands of those who voted against the Constitutional Amendment, in the belief that such a law would prove a dead letter, are now convinced that it can be enforced, and demand its retention. Sioux City, Des Moines, Cedar Rapids, and Ottumwa have banished the saloon, and yet are among the most prosperous cities in the State.

" The benefits which have resulted to the State from the enforcement of this law are far-reaching indeed. It is a well-recognized fact that crime is on the increase in the United States, but Iowa does not contribute to that increase. While the number of convicts in the country at large rose from one in every 3,442 of population in 1850 to one in every 860 in 1880, the ratio in Iowa is at present only one to every 3,130. THE JAILS OF MANY COUNTIES ARE NOW EMPTY DURING A GOOD PORTION OF THE YEAR, AND THE NUMBER OF CONVICTS IN OUR PENITENTIARIES HAS BEEN REDUCED FROM 750 IN MARCH, 1886 TO 604 ON JULY 1, 1889. IT IS THE TESTIMONY OF THE JUDGES OF OUR COURTS THAT CRIMINAL BUSINESS HAS BEEN REDUCED FROM 30 TO 75 PER CENT, AND THAT CRIMINAL EXPENSES HAVE DIMINISHED IN LIKE PROPORTION.

"There is a remarkable decrease in the business and fees of sheriffs and criminal lawyers, as well as in the number of requisitions and extradition warrants issued. We have less paupers and less tramps in the State in proportion to our population than ever before.

"BREWERIES HAVE BEEN CONVERTED INTO OATMEAL MILLS AND CANNING FACTORIES, AND ARE OPERATED AS SUCH BY THEIR OWNERS.

"The report of the Superintendent of Public Instruction shows an increased school-attendance throughout the State.

"THE POORER CLASSES HAVE BETTER FARE, BETTER CLOTHING, BETTER SCHOOLING, AND BETTER HOUSES.

"THE DEPOSITS IN BANKS SHOW AN UNPRECEDENTED INCREASE, AND THERE ARE EVERYWHERE INDICATIONS OF A HEALTHY GROWTH IN LEGITIMATE TRADE. MERCHANTS AND COMMERCIAL TRAVELLERS REPORT LESS LOSSES IN COLLECTIONS IN IOWA THAN ELSEWHERE.

"It is safe to say that not one-tenth, and probably not one-twentieth as much liquor is consumed in the State now as was five years ago. The standard of temperance has been greatly raised, even in those cities where the law is not yet enforced. Many a man formerly accustomed to drink and treat in a saloon has abandoned this practice in deference to public opinion.

"Our courts show a marked improvement in dealing with this question, nearly all of the judges being now disposed to enforce the law, whether they are in sympathy with it or not. In those counties where the law is not enforced the fault lies almost invariably with the executive officers."

It would not be fair to dismiss the matter without considering

GOVERNOR BOIES *vs.* GOVERNOR LARRABEE.

Governor Larrabee, after four years' experience as Governor, gives *specific facts* from the records. Note this: The number of convicts, said Governor Larrabee, in Iowa in 1880 was one to 860 of population; in 1889 it was one to 3,130. "It is the testimony of the judges of our courts," he said further, "that criminal business has been reduced 30 to 75 per cent., and that criminal expenses have been reduced in like proportion."

Compare with these specific statements the strongest assertions made by Governor Boies, and see how weak the latter are in fact. He says:

"It is a patent fact, known to every one who has taken the pains to inform himself, that in many of our cities [no names given], containing as they do a large fraction of our population, the only effect of the law has been to relieve the traffic in these liquors from legal restraint of every kind.

"There is not a large city in the world where the demand for intoxicating liquor as a beverage is not supplied by either a legalized or illicit traffic therein, nor has there been nor will there be.

"In my judgment, the chief obstacle to the enforcement of this law lies in the fact that in and of itself it is a cruel violation of one of the most valued of human rights."

In Governor Boies's argument there is practically nothing to answer, because in the whole speech from which these are extracts he gives absolutely no statistics. It is all *a priori* argument against Prohibition—very old at that—and unsupported inferences therefrom. As a specimen of his inferences, take the following:

"It is equally notorious that in the large cities of the State where the open saloon has been closed [an admission that there is some 'legal restraint!'] a secret traffic sufficient to supply all the wants of the trade has immediately followed."

This is unsupported assertion. "It is notorious"— which by no means shows that it is true, when the class of witnesses who make it "notorious" is considered. But if the "secret traffic" is "sufficient to supply all the wants of the trade," what is "the trade" worrying about? Why do they want to pay a license when they can sell all they like for nothing? Such argument is an insult to the intelligence of rational men.

How it is possible to get liquor in Iowa a little story will show. The author heard a well-known lawyer of Ohio relate this incident in the presence of a number of persons who can be called on to substantiate it if needful. He said:

"After I had been at the hotel about a day and seen no liquor, I began to want some very much. I went to the landlord and asked him where I could get a drink of whiskey. He replied, 'We don't sell any. It's against the law.' In a moment or two he turned to me, and said, 'Step this way, Mr. ——, I would like to speak with you.' I followed him up two flights of stairs and down a long hall, till at last he knocked at a door, and said, 'There's a gentleman in there who would like to speak to you, Mr. ——;' then turned and walked off. In a minute the door opened, and a man said, 'Come in here!' I went in, and he locked the door, took out the key and put it in his pocket. Then he went to a dark closet and took down a black bottle and a dirty glass, poured out a drink, and handed it to me, saying, 'There, drink that quick, and get out of this!' Soon as I was outside the door he turned the key behind me. I was so disgusted that I felt as if I never wanted another drink of whiskey as long as I lived. But I did go for it several times afterward, and *every day I had to go to a different room.*"

Now if any one claims that there will be as much selling and drinking on such a system as by open, licensed, splendid saloons, he simply shows that he is doing his best to make out a very bad case.

But Governor Boies continues :

"*It must be apparent to unbiassed minds* that in these localities, at least, the sale of intoxicating liquors as a beverage has not been diminished by our Prohibitory law, but instead thereof that it has been greatly increased, *if* want of legal restraint of any kind will produce that effect."

Not an attempt to produce one figure in evidence! "The Statistics of Ifs" would be a good name for this conclusion. If the Governor had facts he would give them. If there were facts to be had, he would have found them. Since he gives not one fact, that is the very best proof that there are no facts on his side. But the Governor's idea of "a want of legal restraint of any kind" is sufficiently comical. It seems that *to absolutely forbid a thing by law* is complete "want of legal restraint." For instance, think of "the want of legal restraint of any kind" on burglary and highway robbery! It is evident these crimes *must* be vastly increasing in Iowa. We have not heard of any instances, but it *must* be so, "*if* want of legal restraint of any kind will produce that effect." To think of those absolutely unlicensed and unregulated burglars and highwaymen and the terrible increase of their crimes that *must* be going on!

But life is too short and too serious to spend on such logic. When the Governor will give us some facts, they shall have respectful attention. Till then, the statistics of Governor Larrabee and the district judges and other attested facts stand exactly where they would if Governor Boies had not spoken. In the realm of facts his speech is an absolute blank, and as such may be dismissed from consideration.

The jails remain just as empty, the number of convicts in the penitentiary just as small, the dockets of the criminal courts just as blank, and the bank vaults just as full as if Governor Boies had never delivered his inaugural. We remember that Governor Glick started on just such a track in Kansas in 1882. But Governor Glick is gone and the law of Kansas stands stronger than ever. We are dealing with economics, and we have one very refreshing piece of economics to deal with.

The following item appeared in the Indianapolis *Journal*, April 3d, 1889:

"The State of Iowa seems to be in a highly sound and solvent financial condition. The State Treasurer has just called in $75,000 of outstanding warrants and $220,000 more will be called for April 25th. When the last named batch is paid off the floating indebtedness of the State will be reduced to less than $75,000, which may be increased some during the summer by current appropriations, but will be wiped out by the fall taxes, leaving the State out of debt by January 1st, 1890."

We next quote the following from *The Voice* of June 6th, 1889:

> KEOKUK, IA., May 31. (*Special Correspondence.*)—A most notable demonstration of the unparalleled commercial prosperity that attends Prohibition wherever it is well enforced, is the cancelling of the interest-bearing debt of the State of Iowa. The State Treasurer has issued a call for outstanding warrants, covering $95,000, the last remnant of the interest-bearing debt of the State. The call expires on June 25th.
>
> This is a gratifying surprise to the people of Iowa, for it was never expected that the debt would be wiped out so soon. The news that the last dollar was to be paid off electrified the whole State House force, from the janitors up to the Governor, and occasioned much comment among the lawyers in attendance at the Supreme Court.
>
> And this is how Prohibition is " ruining Iowa."

Now we are informed that this has actually been done, and Iowa stands in the list of States in the new *World* almanac, with " Funded Debt—None."

When it comes to such a pass that a State has no debt, and is running short of convicts, it is high time something should be done. No doubt a " well-devised" system of High License would soon change all this.

CHAPTER XVI.

RHODE ISLAND.

"HEADQUARTERS OF THE RHODE ISLAND
PROTECTIVE TRADE ASSOCIATION,
June 6, 1889.

"*Dear Sir:* On the 20th of this month the election will take place in this State on the question of repealing the Constitutional Prohibition Amendment now in force. The time for work is very short, and we are urgently in need of funds to carry on this campaign, and strongly appeal to you to aid us in this crisis. *The final overthrow of the Prohibitory party in Rhode Island is almost assured at this election,* but we find that the liberal contributions of our friends here are inadequate to meet the demands of the occasion. We therefore send this appeal to our friends abroad for financial aid to assist us in making the fight. Whatever sum you may feel disposed to contribute, please send *at once* to Mr. P. F. Madigan, Treasurer, who will acknowledge the same in our behalf. Very respectfully yours, P. F. Madigan, Thomas Grimes, Edward Smith, Patrick Maroney, P. H. Hogan, John J. Maguire, D. W. Sheehan, Hugh Gorman & Co., P. O'Connor, William F. Grimes, Charles H. Stebbins, A. J. Donahue, Committee of the R. I. Protective Trade Association.

"J. J. MORGAN,   "JAMES HANLEY,
"Secretary.   "President."
—*Circular of Liquor Dealer's Association.*

AFTER a very spirited contest a Prohibitory Constitutional Amendment was adopted, April 7th, 1886, by the following vote:

For the Amendment............15,113
Against   "   9,230

The vote for the Amendment was more than three-fifths of those voting at the election, as the Constitution requires it to be, in order that an amendment may prevail. But the total vote was light, being but 24,343, while the vote for Governor the same year was 26,869, and the vote for President in 1884 was 32,771. The success of the Amendment was a complete surprise to the liquor men, and doubtless the light total vote gave them hope. Rhode Island contains a large foreign population, and is on the highway between the two great liquor centres of Boston and New York. The area of the State is so small that enforcement of a Prohibitory law, with license States all around, is peculiarly difficult. The State is almost all border. To add to the difficulty, the Legislature appointed General Charles R. Brayton, an avowed enemy of Prohibition, as the chief of a State Special Police for the enforcement of the law. How the law would be enforced in such circumstances was easy to predict, and the predictions were fulfilled. There was that steadily weakening enforcement of law which more than anything else makes it contemptible. The law itself was imperfect in many important respects. Yet, with all this, the effect of Prohibition was extremely favorable. The following statement is given in the *Political Prohibitionist* for 1888 :

DECREASE OF ARRESTS AND CRIME IN PROVIDENCE.—The city of Providence is the stronghold of the liquor traffic in Rhode Island. The results gained in that city are much less favorable than those obtained in other parts of the State. The table below shows the number of arrests for offences growing out of the liquor traffic, and the total number of arrests in Providence during the first six months of Prohibition (July, 1886, to January, 1887) as compared with the arrests during the corresponding months of 1885, when the city was under license. The city had the same chief of police during the two years, so that it cannot be claimed that the decrease of arrests under Prohibition is due to a less efficient administration of the law:

CASES REPORTED BY POLICE.

	License. 1885.	Prohibition. 1886.	Decrease.
Assault	96	71	25
Breaking and entering	20	13	7
Brawlers, revellers, and disorderly persons	103	69	34
Common drunkards	60	29	31
Disturbances suppressed	1,000	638	362
Drunkenness	2,457	1,423	1,034
Larcenies	350	305	45
Vagrancy and sturdy beggars	108	49	59
Total	4,194	2,597	1,597
Arrests for all kinds of crimes	3,398	*2,262	1,136

That is, during the first six months of Prohibition, drunkenness was decreased almost one-half, and crime of all kinds one-third in the chief city. In the rural districts the results would, of course, be better still. What this reduction of drunkenness and crime means it is not easy to estimate in cash. The reduction of court and police expenses, the increase of wage-earning power, the avoidance of the sicknesses which result from excess and exposure, must count up to a heavy sum on the credit side. These figures show at once why the law was so bitterly hated. "What!" it will be said, "a law hated *because* it reduces drunkenness and crime?" Exactly that. For that shows that less liquor was consumed; which means that less liquor was sold. Wherever that is the case, the combined Liquor Power of the nation, and all its adherents on the platform and in the press will storm at and curse that law. That it works for the general prosperity of the community is so much proof that it is a bad law for the liquor trade. If men have not been getting drunk, it shows that they have

---

* Including 236 arrests for violation of the Prohibitory law.

not bought so much liquor as they might have done. If they have spent money for groceries, clothing, and shoes, that is so much that they have not spent for drink. If the money has been deposited in banks, it is because it was not deposited in saloons. All the mighty agencies of the liquor traffic will be exerted to break down such a law. Its merits are its faults.

In Rhode Island the economic benefit of the law was plainly shown.

At a legislative hearing on the question of the resubmission of the Prohibition Amendment an address was made by Mr. Walter B. Frost, a prominent Providence journalist, in reply to the claims of the Resubmissionists that Prohibition has "disarranged business," "depreciated the value of real estate," is "incapable of enforcement," and is "injurious to the best interests of the State." Mr. Frost's unanswerable figures—all taken from official sources—put an entirely new face upon the Providence situation.

Mr. Frost said :

"Every business man who has signed that petition [for resubmission] will admit that the volume of bank clearings, taken year in and year out, give a fair indication of the condition of business ; that when business is dull or 'disarranged' the volume of bank transactions decreases, and that when business is brisk and the city is prosperous the clearings increase in volume. Let us take the figures for the last three years under High License, and compare them with the three years of Prohibition. In 1883 the clearings amounted to $237,148,800. In 1884 they were $217,448,300, a decrease of $20,000,000. In 1885 the clearings figured $216,465,200, a decrease of a million since the previous year, and a net decrease of $21,000,000 in the three years.

BANK CLEARINGS UNDER PROHIBITION.

"In 1886 Prohibition was voted. That year business was 'disarranged' to the extent that the bank clearings at once jumped up to $232,688,200, an increase of $16,000,000, instead of the regular decrease of the previous three years. In 1887, when the law was fairly well enforced, the clearings rose to $244,977,100, another increase of $12,000,000. In 1888, when the law was not enforced as well, the increase was only $4,000,000, but still an increase, the figures being $248,669,640. In other words, during the last year of license the volume of business in this city had actually decreased $20,683,600, compared with three years previous, while during the third year under this amendment the bank transactions had increased $32,204,440 over the last year of license. These figures are taken from the news columns of the Providence *Journal,* and cannot be discredited by these petitioners.

THE SAVINGS BANKS.

" These Resubmissionists will also admit that the condition of the savings banks forms a very fair criterion from which to judge the prosperity of the masses, or the lack of it, and consequently the condition of business. I will apply the same test to the volume of savings banks deposits which I applied to the bank clearings. In 1882 the amount due depositors in all the savings banks of this State was $48,320,671.80. Three years later the deposits had grown to $51,816,390.42, an increase of $3,000,000 in the last three years of license. On November 21st, 1888, the amount due depositors had increased to $57,699,884.94, or $6,000,000 accretion during the rule of Prohibition—an increase over the three license years of 100 per cent.

PROSPERITY OF A PETITIONER'S BANK.

" The total number of individual depositors in 1882 was 112,472; in 1885 the number was 116,381—an increase of 4,091. In 1888 the depositors numbered 123,102—an increase of 6,721 during Prohibition as against 4,091 during a corresponding time under license. The largest bank in this city is the Providence Institution for Savings, of which Colonel William Goddard, one of these petitioners for resubmission, is the honored president. In 1882 the depositors in Colonel Goddard's bank numbered 26,988; in 1885 they numbered 27,879—an increase of only 991 in the last three years of license, when business was presumably 'arranged' to the satisfaction of these petitioners. Under the beneficent rule of Prohibition the depositors in this bank have increased to 30,241—an increase of 2,361 —a nearly 300 per cent. increase over the showing of the three license years. Gentlemen of the committee, these figures were not 'cooked up' for this occasion, but were taken from a volume published by authority of the State and prepared by Almon K. Goodwin, State Auditor.

"In view of these figures, which prove that from some cause or other the beginning of the great prosperity of this State was coincident with the adoption of Prohibition, for competent business men to assert that the Amendment has 'disarranged business' is as foolish as it is false.

REAL ESTATE AND PERSONAL PROPERTY.

'Then, again, they assert that the Amendment has 'depreciated the price of real estate.' In what section of the city or State has this depreciation occurred? Why is it that the assessors of taxes have not learned of this falling off in values? The facts of the case are that the value of real estate in this city has increased $8,000,000 since 1885. The exact figures are, as furnished by the Assessors' office: 1885, $92,887,400; 1888, $100,915,860. Somebody may say that the valuation has been raised arbitrarily to provide for greater revenue, and that this accounts for the increase. That argument would not hold, however, in regard to personal property. The valuation of the personal property in this city in 1885 was $31,314,600; in 1888 it had grown to $35,837,840, an increase of $3,500,000, or 11 per cent. in three years.

"It is a fact patent to everybody that it is almost impossible to secure a store in the business part of Providence; that rents are increasing every year, and that vacant houses are the exception and not the rule in any portion of the city. I will assert without fear of contradiction that not one of these Resubmissionists would sell a foot of his property in the business portion of Providence at the assessed value of three years ago.

"Mr. Chairman, I am not one of those who are ready to admit that Prohibition has been altogether a failure in this State, even with the lax enforcement which it has experienced. The enemies of Prohibition are constantly asserting, and its friends are too ready to admit that Prohibition, as it has so far existed, has increased drunkenness rather than decreased it. Statistics prove that this is not true; and even if it were true, it would be no proof that this Amendment 'is incapable of enforcement.' Because the State of Rhode Island possesses an old and miserable State House, and has never had a better one, is no proof that she never will have a better one. Because the city of Providence, at the rate it is now filling the cove, would still have a cove a hundred years hence, is no argument that the cove can never be filled. I know and you know, gentlemen of the committee, that it can be filled in two years. Prohibition has been enforced. What has been done can be done again.

DECREASE OF ARRESTS.

"As bad as the situation is and has been in the city of Providence, there has been progress. Prohibition has been law in this State two years and six months on January 1st last. The arrests for drunkenness and disorderly conduct in Providence during that period were 9,323. The last two years and a half under license showed arrests for the same causes amounting to 11,304—a falling off of just 2,000 in two years and a half. A law that will accomplish so much simply by its deterring effect, and in the face of flagrant inactivity on the part of the police—such a law is not 'incapable of enforcement.'

"The New York *Tribune* of January 9th, 1887, commenting editorially on the fact that arrests for drunkenness had fallen off more than 40 per cent. in the first six months of Prohibition, says : 'A law that accomplished that much is a good law. We would be glad to have in this city a measure that would reduce the amount of crime —pocket-picking, burglary, arson, "boodling" or what not—as largely as the Prohibition act has decreased drunkenness and its attendant evils in Providence, and no one would deny the value of such a law.'

"A law which has accomplished so much cannot truthfully be said to be ' injurious to the best interests of the State.' "

The world knows the rest of the story. In order to win the liquor vote, against the protest of numbers of the best citizens, the Legislature, on May 31st, 1889, voted to resubmit the Prohibitory Amendment to popular vote on June 20th, allowing less than three weeks for discussion. A stringent ballot-reform law had been passed by the previous Legislature, providing for a secret ballot and the severe punishment of bribery. This law was to go into effect on June 1st. The Legislature which resubmitted the Prohibitory Amendment, at the same time amended the ballot-reform law, so that it should not take effect till June 30th, ten days after the vote on Prohibition. The fact that such means were needed to secure its repeal is very good testimony to the excellence of the law

Of this whole proceeding, Hon. Henry B. Metcalf, a prominent member of the Republican Party of Rhode Island, said :

"I think the characterization of the recent action of the General Assembly of Rhode Island as 'outrageous' to be fully justified by facts. I cannot imagine any valid defence or apology therefor. The meanness of the conditions of the act, allowing no time for discussion, suspending the action of the new ballot law and fixing the election at the worst possible time for farmers, would disgrace a Tammany caucus. The active friends of the Amendment are weary, have but very little available money, and have no well-united organization for prompt and effective work. But a good deal has been begun during the last twenty-four hours that promises good results, although distinct plans are not yet formulated. If we can awaken the people we can and will win. By Wednesday or Thursday next I am expecting, rather confidently, to be able to report considerable progress. I shall throw my entire strength into the work, but have to regret the limitations of it.

"That this experience will lead to better organization for future work I have no doubt, but now we must strike without much organization, and depend upon fervor rather than wait for the machinery or method that is so needful."

The repeal of the Prohibitory Amendment, in such circumstances, simply shows the power of unscrupulous political combinations. All the facts we have on the economic conditions indicate valuable results for public order and financial prosperity from even very imperfect Prohibition.

Since the return to High License, a great cry of distress is going up from the State. The Pawtucket *Gazette* and *Chronicle*, a strong Republican daily paper, says, in its issue of October 18th, 1889 :

"The citizens of Rhode Island cannot have forgotten the rather profuse assurances that were given them only a few months ago, that when the demon of Prohibition should have been exorcised from the body politic, once more would the State of Rhode Island rejoice in a government by law.

"Nor will they readily forget with what unction the advocates of a repeal of Prohibition deplored the demoralizing influences of a law that was at variance with public opinion and, therefore, incapable of enforcement, thereby destroying popular respect for all law.

"If we mistake not, the proposed conditions of righteousness have been fulfilled, and law has been made in entire harmony with that class of public opinion represented in the demand for repeal of Prohibition.

"Who says that law is either enforced or respected to-day in either Pawtucket or Providence? Is liquor being sold only according to law in either city? How many law-breaking liquor-sellers have been arrested?

"There are laws and ordinances against drunkenness, and it is the sworn duty of officials to enforce these laws and ordinances. Is one drunken man arrested out of every ten that reel by our policemen?

"Will somebody tell us the conditions under which law may be permitted to be enforced? Or is it best to annul all law?"

The *Gazette and Chronicle* in its same issue makes this significant remark :

"Political prostitution is one of the choice outgrowths of the beautiful and 'restrictive' rum law."

The same paper said, September 20th :

"More drunken men were seen on our streets during the past week than were seen here in the three years of the non-enforced Prohibitory law."

The Pawtucket *Record* said, about the same time :

"It has been said or written that Prohibition was detrimental to business. Yes, we think it did injure the rum business ; at any rate, it appears to be prospering under the beneficial influence of license."

The Newport *Daily News* said, September 28th :

"Drunkenness is increasing, and it appears to be the general sentiment of the community that no more liquor licenses should be granted. Men under the influence of liquor, but not in any way unable to reach their destination, are seen on any hand by the police and others."

The Newport *Enterprise* (*Ind.*) said in its issue for October 3d :

"They [the people] went back to license, and before the winter is out they will find things worse than ever. There will be about seventy rum-shops now ; and it is a poor place that does not take in $60 a week. That is $4,200 a week for all, and *a quarter of a million a year spent in Newport for intoxicating liquors that ought to go to grocers, bakers, butchers, and other respectable s'ores.* The tradesmen will see the beauty of license and rum this winter when they try to collect their bills. The city will get $25,000, and ten times that amount will go into the pockets of the rumsellers, who will send half of it out of the State, and spend more of the other half in buying up the houses of honest citizens ruined by bad debts that might have been paid if men had drunk less rum. There is no need of electioneering ; the drunken men reeling round the streets will do all that, and if Local Option is put before the people in the spring, it would not surprise us to see it carried, to stay. Wait !"

CHAPTER XVII.

ATLANTA.

"Not a dollar of capital has gone from our city, or is going, unless it's liquor capital. We want all that sort of capital to go."—*Senator Colquitt in Brooklyn, N. Y., February 23d, 1886.*

"Take the fact of owning houses. Artemus Ward says: 'A man may die for his home, but who ever heard of a man dying for his boarding-house?' I say to you here, it's the poor man's home, and the poor man's home alone, that has stood time and again between Jay Gould and Vanderbilt and the enraged mob of American workingmen. It is the conservatism of the home-owning wage-worker that has kept Socialism out of the admirable labor organizations. In the last two years there have been six hundred and eighty-seven citizens who have become home-owners, against one hundred and fifty-three in the two years previous — citizens owing no man and owning no man as master, wearing the collar of no faction, free-born American citizens, not quibbling about personal liberty, but standing with wife and little ones, honest and independent, above penury and degradation! [Applause.]—*Henry W. Grady.*

THE city of Atlanta, Ga., with a population of some 75,000, has now tried Low License, Prohibition, and High License. In November, 1885, the city voted for a Prohibitory ordinance, which took effect July 1st, 1886. By the construction of this law, however, the wholesale liquor houses did not shut up till some six months later, and a few wine rooms selling so-called "native wines" were allowed to continue in operation. But the saloons were abolished July 1st, 1886. Prohibition continued in force till January 1st, 1888. The beneficial effects of the law were very marked, as will be seen by the following striking despatch

FROM ATLANTA'S MAYOR.

REFUTATION OF REPORTS IN NORTHERN PAPERS—QUIET STREETS AND HAPPY HOMES—DECREASE OF CRIME AND GENERAL PROSPERITY.

During the campaign of 1886, despatches were extensively published for political effect in Northern papers charging that the Prohibitory law in Atlanta was practically a nullity, and that the " jug trade" had become about the only important industry of the city. To meet these statements, *The Daily Voice* telegraphed to Mayor Hillyer, who replied as follows :

" ATLANTA, GA., October 26.—I wish to say that in the bar-room days drunkenness was common and not always noticed. The police were less attentive and many escaped arrest. Now, if a man gets drunk, or partly drunk, it attracts attention. The police are active and vigilant, and arrests are nearly certain to follow any indications of illicit sale. The figures in the police office show that the arrests for disorder and drunkenness last Saturday and Sunday were 22 ; the corresponding days in 1885 such arrests numbered 31, and in 1884, 25. Many of the cases occurring at present are chargeable to the use of domestic wine, which is not prohibited, and which, it is said, is often ' doctored.' The figures in the express office show that hardly one jug or demijohn is shipped per one thousand inhabitants, and all exaggerated reports are to be condemned. The good effects of Prohibition here are apparent. Trade in all branches, except the whiskey traffic, is prospering. There is marked improvement in the habits, the morals, and the happiness of the people. Increased prosperity is admitted and rejoiced in, both as to private and public affairs. The attitude of the newspapers throughout the Union is greatly to be deprecated. Scores and hundreds of facts prove the efficacy of the law. Atlanta now has peaceful streets and happy homes, with sober husbands, sons, and brothers, with plenty to eat and to wear, where before there were broken hearts, fear of domestic outrage, and sometimes actual want. The great daily press abroad says nothing of the great good that has resulted, but if a hand truck load of jugs is seen (which is no great matter to sixty thousand people) this must be magnified into a ' jug train,' and the whole press of the United States made to ring with it.

"There is not one-tenth as much of intoxicants drunk in Atlanta now as there was a year ago, possibly much less than that. Formerly the advocates of bar-rooms were numerous and powerful, now nobody advocates their restoration. Formerly the *temperance issue* was High License; now, the *very most that the opponents to total Prohibition would contend for* is High License. The bar-room nuisance has gone out from Atlanta forever, and we would like all the world to know it.

"We are determined to give total Prohibition a fair trial under the law, and are greatly strengthened and encouraged with it so far. Our people are already practically united in the belief that the bar-room will never come back. I only wish that the outside world could see the truth as we have it demonstrated here. They would thus escape the danger of being misled by the many exaggerated and prejudiced rumors that are published in other States on the subject.

"GEORGE HILLYER,
"*Mayor of Atlanta.*

The mayor's hopes were not realized. Prohibition in Atlanta was succeeding too well. There was the greatest danger that it would disprove the favorite proposition of the liquor-dealers and their sympathizers, that "Prohibition could never be enforced in a large city." It was enforced in Atlanta, and the city was prosperous and rejoicing. Something must be done. It must be remembered that the whole liquor power of the nation is one, concentrated in one National Liquor Dealers' Protective Association. This tremendous power concentrated upon the city among the Georgia mountains. The nation almost held its breath to watch the unequal contest. Henry W. Grady, brave, eloquent, and true-hearted, toiled and plead for Prohibition with all his matchless power. The Atlanta *Constitution*, of which he was editor, had a divided influence, his partner being for High License. But on June 21st, 1887, one year after Prohibition had taken effect in Atlanta, the *Constitution* printed the following editorial :

"A GREAT EVENT."

"The election at which Prohibition was put on trial in this city is entitled to a place among great events. No election of a local nature was ever before held in a city of 60,000 people in which more was involved. The changes proposed by it were so radical as to be almost revolutionary. Over 100 business houses were to be closed. Nearly 500 men were to be forced to give up a chosen employment. The city treasury was to be left with $40,000 less revenue. Trade amounting annually to millions was to be turned away from the city. Many large business houses were to be left unrented. Of course, a movement proposing measures so radical met with the most spirited and determined opposition. Many of our best citizens regarded it with outspoken disfavor.

"It was said that Prohibition in a city so large as this was impracticable; that it would not prohibit; that the trade would be injured; that taxes would be increased; that the stores in which the liquor business was carried on would not be rented for other purposes; that the same amount of whiskey would be drunk with the law as without it, the city would only miss the revenue; that it would be a death-blow to Atlanta's progress.

"It has now been eighteen months since the election, and twelve months since the law went into effect. We are prepared thus from observation to note results.

PROHIBITION DOES PROHIBIT.

"Prohibition in this city does prohibit. The law is observed as well as the law against carrying concealed weapons, gambling, theft, and other offences of like character. If there had been as many people in favor of carrying concealed weapons, theft, gambling, etc., as there were in favor of the retail of ardent spirits twelve months ago, law against these things would not have been carried out as well as it was against the liquor trade. In consideration of the small majority with which Prohibition was carried and the large number of people who were opposed to seeing it prohibit, the law has been marvellously well observed.

BUSINESS IMPROVED UNDER THE LAW.

" Prohibition has not injured the city financially. According to the Assessors' books, property in the city has increased over $2,000,000. Taxes have not been increased. Two streets in the city, Decatur and Peters, were known as liquor streets. It was hardly considered proper for a lady to walk these streets without an escort. Now they are just as orderly as any in the city. Property on them has advanced from 10 to 25 per cent. The loss of $40,000 revenue consequent on closing the saloons has tended in no degree to impede the city's progress in any direction. Large appropriations have been made to the water-works, the public schools, the Piedmont Fair, and other improvements. The business men have raised $100,000 to build the Atlanta and Hawkinsville Railroad. The number of city banks is to be increased to five. The coming of four new railroads has been settled during the year. *Fifteen new stores containing house-furnishing goods have been started since Prohibition went into effect. These are doing well.* More furniture has been sold to mechanics and laboring men in the last twelve months than in any twelve months during the history of the city. The manufacturing establishments of the city have received new life. A glass factory has been built. A cotton-seed oil mill is being built worth $125,000. All improvement companies with a basis in real estate have seen their stock doubled in value since the election on Prohibition.

FORMER SALOONS NOW OCCUPIED BY TRADESMEN.

" Stores in which the liquor trade was conducted are not vacant, but are now occupied by other lines of trade. According to the real estate men more laborers and men of limited means are buying lots than ever before. Rents are more promptly paid than formerly. More houses are rented by the same number of families than heretofore. Before Prohibition, sometimes as many as three families would live in one house. The heads of those families now not spending their money for drink are each able to rent a house, thus using three instead of one. Workingmen who formerly spent a great part of their money for liquor, now spend it in food and clothes for their families. The retail grocery men sell more goods *and collect their bills better* than ever before. Thus they are able to settle more promptly with the wholesale men.

INCREASED SALES OF LEGITIMATE GOODS.

"A perceptible increase has been noticed in the number of people who ride on street cars. According to the coal-dealers, many people bought coal and stored it away last winter who had never been known to do so before. Others, who had been accustomed to buying two or three tons on time, this last winter bought seven or eight and paid cash for it. A leading proprietor of a millinery store said that he had sold more hats and bonnets to laboring men for their wives and daughters than before in the history of his business. Contractors say their men do better work, and on Saturday evenings, when they receive their week's wages, spend the same for flour, hams, dry goods, or other necessary things for their families. Thus they are in better spirits, have more hope, and are not inclined to strike and growl about higher wages.

IMPROVEMENT IN THE SCHOOL CHILDREN.

"Attendance upon the public schools has increased. The Superintendent of Public Instruction said in his report to the Board of Education, made January 1st, 1887 :

"' During the past year it has become a subject of remark by teachers in the schools and by visitors, that the children were more tidy, were better dressed, were better shod, and presented a neater appearance than ever before. Less trouble has been experienced in having parents purchase books required by the rules, fewer children have been withdrawn to aid in supporting the family, the higher classes in the grammar schools have been fuller, and more children have been promoted to the high schools, both male and female, than ever before in the history of the schools. All these indications point to the increased prosperity of the city and to the growing interest in the cause of education on the part of the people.'

"There has been a marked increase in attendance upon the Sunday-schools of the city. This is especially noticeable among the suburban churches. Many children have started to the Sunday-schools who were formerly not able to attend for want of proper clothing. Attendance upon the different churches is far better. From fifteen hundred to two thousand people have joined the various churches of the city during the year.

THE MARKED DECREASE IN CRIME.

"The determination on the part of the people to prohibit the liquor traffic HAS STIMULATED A DISPOSITION TO DO AWAY WITH OTHER EVILS. *The laws against gambling are rigidly enforced.* A considerable stock of gamblers' tools gathered together by the police for several years past was recently used for the purpose of making a large bonfire on one of the unoccupied squares of the city. The City Council has refused longer to grant licenses to bucket shops, thus putting the seal of its condemnation upon the trade in futures of all kinds.

"All these reforms have had a decided tendency to diminish crime. Two weeks were necessary formerly to get through with the criminal docket. During the present year it was closed out in two days. The chain-gang is almost left with nothing but the chains and the balls. The gang part would not be large enough to work the public roads of the country were it not augmented by fresh supplies from the surrounding counties. The city government is in the hands of our best citizens. . . .

"Our experience has demonstrated to us beyond a doubt that a city of sixty thousand inhabitants can get along and advance at a solid and constant rate without the liquor traffic."

HENRY W. GRADY'S SPEECH.

For two years the Prohibition policy had been maintained in Atlanta, but in the summer of 1887 the liquor men began to take steps for repeal. By November of that year a hot fight was raging. The vote on repeal was to be taken in the latter part of that month.

The *Constitution* was then under the joint management of Mr. Grady and Evan P. Howell. Mr. Howell was an uncompromising Anti-Prohibitionist. Mr. Grady was in the height of his new-made national reputation as a political orator. He was young and ambitious, and he knew full well the dangers besetting public men who meddled with Prohibition. The great Prohibitory Amendment campaigns had just closed in Texas and Tennessee, with crushing majorities for the bar-rooms. *The national liquor power had announced that the next thing on their programme was to obtain the repeal of the Prohibitory law in Atlanta.*

Every selfish interest seemed to dictate a conservative course for Mr. Grady in the Atlanta campaign. But he made an independent study of the whole situation, became convinced that Prohibition had done great good, and on the evening of November 3d made a speech which electrified the city and was one of the most thrilling and convincing arguments for Prohibition ever delivered.

The force of this speech was in its eloquent and pathetic presentation of practical testimony about the improvement of the poor under the reign of Prohibition, the great decrease in the number of distress warrants, the disappearance of the practice of garnisheeing wages, the change of sentiment among business men in favor of Prohibition, the increase in the number of school-going children, the decrease in crime, etc.*

FROM GRADY'S SPEECH—DISTRESS WARRANTS.

Here is a part of what Mr. Grady said on the subject of distress warrants:

"Mr. George Adair rents houses to thirteen hundred tenants. He states that he has issued in the last year one distress warrant where he issued twenty, two years ago. [Applause.] I claim to be an intelligent man with some courage of conviction; but I pledge you my word, if that one fact were established to my satisfaction I would vote for this thing if I never heard another word on this subject. Have you thought what that means—a distress warrant? It means eviction; it means the very thing that is to-day kindling the heart of this world for poor Ireland. It means eviction! It means turning woman and her little children out of the home that covers them, and to which they are entitled. I was astonished at Colonel Adair's statement. Mr. Tally, who rents six hundred or eight hundred houses, says: 'I used to issue two or three distress warrants—four or five--a month. I have not issued a single one in eighteen months.' [Applause.] Now, both of them are Prohibitionists. Let me try you with Harry Krouse. He was an Anti-Prohibitionist. He said: 'My distress warrants averaged thirty-six to the year, and I have not issued one in twelve months.' I said:

"'Then, my friend, I don't carry your conscience, but how can you be an Anti-Prohibitionist?'

"'I ain't. My knowledge of the thing, day by day, among people I used to pester and evict has changed my convictions, and I am a red-hot Prohibitionist.'

"I went down to Mr. Scott, who did not vote for Prohibition, and asked him. He said: 'I have issued as many as twenty-five distress warrants in a month, and I have issued six in the last eighteen months, and five were to get people out of houses because they were obnoxious to the neighbors. I have issued one single distress warrant for failure to pay rent.'

---

* Prohibition Leaflet, "Atlanta's Three Policies."

"I said: 'You didn't vote for Prohibition.'

"He said: 'I did not believe it was practicable.'

"I asked: 'What do you think now?'

"He said: 'I am going to vote, and vote for Prohibition.' [Applause.]

"Mr. Roberts was a Prohibitionist. He is a square man and an intelligent man, and is running for Council, which is a good sign. [Laughter and applause.] He says: 'My testimony is the same. I formerly issued two or three distress warrants every month, and I have not issued one in twelve months.'

THE TERRORS OF EVICTION.

"Have you ever thought about a woman being turned out of her house—the little cottage that covers her and her children? Can you picture—you who live in comfortable homes filled with light and warmth and books and joy—can you think of these people—human beings, our brothers and sisters, the poor mother, brave though her heart is breaking, huddling her little children about her, and the father, weak but loving, and loving all the deeper because he knows his weakness has brought them to this want and degradation, and little children, those of whom our Saviour said: 'Suffer them to come unto me and forbid them not'—there asking, 'Mamma, where will we sleep to-night?'—can you picture that and then their taking themselves up and the woman putting her hand with undying love and faith in the hand of the man she swore to follow through good and evil report, and marching up and down the street—this pitiable procession—through the unthinking streets, by laughing children and shining windows, looking for a hole where, like the foxes, they may hide their poor heads?

"My friends, they talk to you about personal liberty, that a man should have the right to go into a grog shop and see this pitiable procession—now stopped—parading up and down our streets again. They talk to you about the shades of Washington, Monroe, and Jefferson. I would not give one happy, rosy little woman, uplifted from that degradation—happy again in her home, with the cricket chirping on her hearthstone and her children about her knee, her husband redeemed from drink at her side—I would not give one of them for all the shades of all the men that ever contended since Cataline conspired and Cæsar fought!"

At the end of this sentence there was tremendous

cheering. Men and women waved their handkerchiefs, some of them standing up.

GOVERNOR BROWN'S RENT ROLL AS AN ISSUE.

"All of it means simply this, that where Mr. Adair, renting to all sorts of people, issued twenty distress warrants a year ago, he issues one now; it means that out of every twenty families evicted two years ago there are nineteen happy in their homes to-night. [Applause.] And yet we are told we must vote to restore the old order because it has reduced Governor Brown's rental column $5,000 a year!" [Applause.]

At the end of this sentence the scene was almost indescribable. Thousands of handkerchiefs waved as before, men held up their hats on walking sticks and whirled them in the air. The cheering was almost deafening.

"My friends, I don't believe that statement, to begin with. I do not believe his rent income is fairly and permanently diminished $5,000 a year; and if it is, he is my friend, and I congratulate both him and myself on the fact that he is able to stand it. I say this in no spirit of sarcasm or criticism, but I do say if there is a law, if there is a governmental theory, if there is, may it please you, an untried experiment that will shelter one honest woman and two unconscious children in their homes, it is our duty to vote that law and this Government's duty to enforce it, though it should cut it down $25,000. [Tremendous applause.] And the reason for that is not based in communism, but in humanity. If the Government owes any duty to the individual, it is that every man, woman, and child that leads an honest life is entitled to food and shelter; and if there is a difference to be found between diminishing the luxury of the rich, or protecting the poor in their birthright, it is manliness and humanity and good government to let the rich suffer. [Applause]

"Now, I have talked to you about the rent, about the house that a man and his wife live in; I have shown you, not by my own assertion, but by the statements of the only experts in the city—the real estate men, who for years have handled from three thousand to four thousand houses—I have shown you, I say, that where twenty suffered before, nineteen are protected under 'Prohibition that don't prohibit.' What would we have with Prohibition that did prohibit?"

Upon other aspects of the improvement of the poor, Mr. Grady said, in part:

NO MORE GARNISHEEING.

"The next step is to get our employers and ask their testimony. I went to Mr. Boyd, of Van Winkle & Co., and he said: 'Where I formerly had ten or fifteen garnishments at a time to answer, I now have none.'

"The garnishment, next to the distress warrant, is the most iniquitous form of debt collection. It means that the law lays its hand on a man's wages and holds them in its grasp, though his little children may clamber about his knees and cry for bread.

"Mr. Boyd is a Prohibitionist; let me give you Grant Wilkins. He is a man of profound convictions. You can cut him up into postage-stamps and he will not deny a thing he thought was right. He said he was one of the most violent, if that word may be used, of the Anti-Prohibitionists. He said: 'I have told them I was not going to attend their "Anti" meetings, that I did not intend to have anything to do with it this time; I came to that conclusion simply because I work two hundred and twenty men, and I see what Prohibition has done for them, and I believe my duty requires I should let it alone. My foreman goes to their homes and sees them; they live better, their houses are better, they have shoes where they were shoeless, and they have plenty to eat where they formerly barely lived. I have had thirty garnishments at once in my shop, and I have been running seven months, and I have not answered one single garnishment.'

"That is the first time in a long and pleasant friendship that I have known Grant to acknowledge he was wrong. I could absolutely weary you with testimony like that. [Cries of 'Go on!']

CONVERTED AGAINST THEIR CONVICTIONS.

"There is a man—I cannot give his name, Colonel Maddox knows him—he is a member of the Anti-Prohibition Committee; he is one of the largest manufacturers in this city, and, as a rule, his associates are against Prohibition. He went into Colonel Maddox's office, and Colonel Maddox slapped him on the shoulder and said:

"'Hello, Anti.'

" ' No, sir; not much.'

" ' You are printed that way,' said Colonel Maddox.

" ' It's wrong,' he said.

" What changed him? The marked and undoubted improvement in the working people. He said :

" ' My wife and I rode out Decatur Street the other day. I looked at the street and the improved condition down there, and said : " My dear, I am a Prohibitionist from this time forward." ' He was converted against his convictions.

" Mr. Riordan was an Anti-Prohibitionist in the last race. He came into Colonel Maddox's office—by the way, Colonel Maddox's office seems to be a sort of a place for them to come. Mr. Riordan says : ' I was an Anti-Prohibitionist on principle'—a personal liberty man, I suppose—' but I work from sixty to one hundred men, and I have seen a change that as an honest man I dare not disregard, and I am for Prohibition.'

" Ladies and gentlemen, how can you answer such as that? I am not a profound lawyer. I don't know how much personal liberty I have got. Sometimes I wish I had more [looking with a smile at Mrs. Grady, who sat in the audience]. That is purely a personal matter to which we need not allude further. I don't want any profound knowledge of law that clouds my brain and judgment when such facts appeal to me !"

In conclusion, Mr. Grady said :

INCREASE IN THE SCHOOL POPULATION.

" There are eight hundred and twenty-nine more children in attendance at the schools this year than last. How do you account for that? [Laughter.] It has been two years since Prohibition was adopted, and there are eight hundred and twenty-nine more children in the schools. That means one of two things, and you can take either horn of the dilemma : either there are more people here or there are more people able to send to school.

DECREASE OF CRIME.

" My friend, Mr. Hooper Alexander, whom I once at the polls irreverently called Hoopee, has sent me a note in which he says :

" ' I see you are on statistics. If it is worth noticing, I can add a few. I examined the city court criminal docket this afternoon, and it shows a marked and steady increase in misdemeanors from 1881 to 1885 ; a falling off of 20 per cent. in 1886 ; the record of 1887 shows 313 indictments against 675 in 1885 and 440 in 1886.'

"Mark that An increase to 1885, and in 1886 there was a decrease from 675 cases to 440. That was with the experiment only half tried. The present docket extends from 1881 to 1887. Crime in 1887 less than half that of 1885, and less than any year of the docket. There was scarcely a case of vagrancy for a year past.

PERORATION.

"I assume to keep no man's conscience ; I assume to judge for no man ; I do not assume that I am better than any man, but that I am weaker. But I say this to you, I have a boy as dear to me as the ruddy drops that gather about this heart. I find my hopes already centring in his little body, and I look to him to-night to take to himself the work that, strive as I may, must fall unfinished at last from my hands. Now, I know they say it is proper to educate a boy at home ; that if he is taught right at home he will not go wrong. That is a lie to begin with, but that don't matter. I have seen sons of some as good people as ever lived turn out badly. I accept my responsibility as a father. The boy may fall from the right path as things now exist. If he does, I shall bear that sorrow with such resignation as I may ; but I tell you, if I were to vote to recall barrooms to this city, when I know it has prospered in their absence, and that boy should fall through their agency. I tell you—and this conviction has come to me in the still watches of the night—I could not, wearing the crowning sorrow of his disgrace and looking into the eyes of her whose heart he had broken—I could not, if I had voted to recall these bar-rooms, find answer for my conscience or support for my remorse. [Applause] I don't know how any other father feels, but that is the way I feel, if God permits me to utter the truth."

Then, looking over the vast audience, stilled to hear the voice of the speaker, Mr. Grady said with great earnestness and eloquence :

"The best reforms of this earth come through waste and storm and doubt and suspicion ; the sun itself when it rises on each day wastes the radiance of the moon and blots the starlight from the skies, but only to unlock the earth from the clasp of night and plant the stars anew in the opening flowers. Behind that sun, as behind this movement, we may be sure there stands the Lord God Almighty, Master and Maker of this universe, from whose hand the spheres are rolled to their orbits, and whose voice has been the harmony of this world since the morning stars sang together." [Tremendous, loud, and long-continued applause.]

To this speech no adequate reply was ever made. For a time it seemed that the advocates of Prohibition were sure to sweep the field. They were confident of carrying the election. But thoughtful men were anxious *because the Liquor Power did not show its hand.* It was not to be supposed the liquor men would let such an election go by default. Because they made no sign the danger was all the greater. They had some deep scheme, the deeper because it was still. In fact, it was so shrewd, so artfully conceived, that no one appreciated what it was till it was sprung upon the people in the full tide of victory.

A correspondent wrote on November 29th: "Everything seemed to promise glorious victory for the Prohibitionists until Thursday (November 24th). There never was a body of earnest men more sanguine of a brilliant success than the Prohibitionists of Atlanta. Never for a moment did they think of less than 800 majority. The entire registry list had been canvassed. The Prohibitionists had secured pledged voters enough to carry the day by a handsome majority.

"This confidence lasted until Thursday. On that day the 'Antis' assumed a more confident air. They began to claim majorities. *It was whispered around that they had plenty of money.* The negro vote had become more solid.

"'Yellowstone Kit,' a vendor of patent medicines, who had been plying his work here for some time among the negroes, had

BY WELL-DIRECTED CHARITIES,

and by working upon their superstitions, gained a wonderful influence over them. He had attracted but little notice from the whites. Suddenly it was announced that he had quit selling patent medicines and taken to making Anti-Prohibition speeches. Everybody at once realized that he was a powerful factor in the contest, for the negroes actually feared him, and almost worshipped him. He rode through the streets at night followed by thousands of them yelling like wild men. They lifted him from his carriage, and from the sidewalks listened to his wild harangues. The scenes beggared description. On Friday night the 'Antis' made the first grand demonstration on the streets, with 'Yellowstone Kit' for their central figure. He rode up the main streets attended by thousands of negroes. To this mountebank's power over the ignorant voters is largely due the result."
"Yellowstone Kit" was the hand of the Liquor Power, by which it scraped up all that was ignorant, superstitious, and purchasable, and hurled it in a solid mass against the beneficent law.

Very influential, too, was a placard representing Abraham Lincoln striking the fetters from a slave, and protesting against Prohibition as an invasion of liberty. Great pains have been taken to find in Mr. Lincoln's works and in the reminiscences of those who knew him anything resembling the words thus attributed to him, but in vain. The evidence is strong that they were effective with the negroes, who were not scholars, but dearly loved the memory of the great emancipator. So Prohibition was defeated by 1100 majority, and a system of High License took its place.

The license was made as "restrictive" as possible. The fee for selling all kinds of liquors was put at $1,000; that for beer and wine only at $100, with severe provisions against the most common abuses of the traffic. The law is remarkably good for a license law. It has now been in force for two years, giving time to study its effects.

In the summer of 1888, about six months after the return of the bar-rooms, the Atlanta *Commonwealth* gave the following interviews with tradesmen of the city:

"W. R. Heath, 336 Decatur Street (groceries), when asked how his trade since the return of the bar-rooms compared with the corresponding period of the previous year, answered:

"'Trade is off 50 per cent. The majority of my customers are colored people. During Prohibition whiskey was hard to get; they were compelled to send away for it, and that involved a good deal of trouble. My customers stayed sober and paid their debts then; now whiskey is convenient, and drunkenness and the chain-gang are the consequences. I know four colored men who were sober and industrious during Prohibition, now they are drunk and in the chain-gang half their time.

"'During Prohibition I credited these men, and they paid promptly; now their credit is gone, and the bar-rooms and Judge Anderson get all the cash. I was and am and ever will be a Prohibitionist.'

"The next house we entered was a large grocery house. We saw the senior member of the firm, and to our question, 'How is trade?' he replied: 'Trade is not near so good as it was a year ago.'

"'What is the cause?'

"'There is only one cause that I can see—namely, the bringing back of bar-rooms. I do not know what effect the bar-rooms have on other business, but they have certainly injured the retail grocery trade. I voted for Anti-Prohibition last election, but I shall unhesitatingly vote for Prohibition next time, for Prohibition benefited the town. I ask you not to give my name.'

"Stowers, White & Co., 362 Decatur Street (furniture on the instalment plan): 'Business not so good, collections much worse;

cause—spending money in bar-rooms which should be applied to the payment of debts.'

"J. H. Smith (Anti), 361 Decatur Street, was not in. His chief clerk, N. A. Landford, a Prohibitionist, gave us the following information : ' Business has fallen off from last year one third. Let me show you our books. Now take Mr. ——, a white man, a good mechanic. During Prohibition he paid us every Saturday night, and his account amounted to $5, never less than $3 ; now his trade amounts to $2, and occasionally $4, and for the past two weeks he has paid us nothing.

"' Now here is a colored man who always paid during Prohibition ; never allowed his account to become past due. In April we had shut him off owing us $44 40. What is the cause ? Close at hand is a bar-room, and drunkenness is common—men who during Prohibition were never seen under the influence of drink now staggering by here.'

"J. F. Hudgins, 358 Decatur Street : ' Business has fallen way off from last year. Why, on Saturday nights last year we could hardly wait on the trade ; now the bar-rooms are crowded and my place looks lonely. Where people spent $8 to $10 with me last year they now spend twenty-five to fifty cents. My cigar and tobacco trade has entirely fallen off. They go to the bar-rooms for such now.'

"' Mr. Hudgins,' we said, ' you were formerly in the business in Macon ; from your own experience do you think bar-rooms benefit a town ?'

"' *The bar-room business benefits the man who runs the bar, and injures everybody else*—injures the patrons thereof directly and the community indirectly. The first step in the drunkard's career is taken in the bar-room. I have seen hundreds of them take the fatal step, some of them in my own bar-room. I never saw a man worthy the name of a man who liked the business. Whiskey is not only a curse to the man who drinks, but also to the man who sells. I have shut down on some of my best customers on account of drinking. I am a Prohibitionist now more than ever.'

"A. J. Divine (colored), 188 Decatur Street (retail groceries), says : ' Business was better since last January ; there was more money in circulation till a bar-room started near me. I voted and worked for Anti-Prohibition. I am now a Prohibitionist for two reasons : 1. They placed a saloon right by me—this is injuring my trade ; people are buying whiskey with money they formerly spent with me for groceries. 2. During the last campaign the Anti Prohibitionists struck no line of demarcation ; they promised to do what was right. I am no social equality negro, but I voted to bring whiskey back to Atlanta, because I was promised that the colored man would have the same rights in obtaining that whiskey that the white man has. Well, I made a mistake, for if you go into one of these bars for a drink they tell you to get out, that they don't sell to niggers.'

"Adamson & Son do a large grocery business at 264 Decatur Street. Young Mr. Adamson was in, and seemed to be suffering from the effects of a meeting at the court-house the night before. He announced to the reporter that we had 'downed' his crowd, but that they would not get left again. He said business was about the same—if anything a little better. 'I don't see,' said Mr. Adamson, 'that the voting back of whiskey has in any way affected my business. I am an Anti, because I think the sale of liquor benefits Atlanta.'

"Thompson & Waley, grocers, 265 Decatur Street, said they didn't sell as much nor get paid for as much as last year. People find other places more attractive. 'Close at hand is the Bell Street Compress, giving employment to quite a number. On Saturday evenings, last year, you never saw the wives of these men assembling on the street corner ; now, every Saturday evening, you see women waiting on the corner to keep their husbands from going to the bar-rooms to spend their money. Put me down as a Prohibitionist confirmed in the faith.'

"W. S. Shields runs a butcher shop on Decatur Street. He says he does not do one-half the business he did a year ago. Saturday night's trade is not near one-half. The cause, he says, is people drinking liquor. 'There are $300 due me now by people who paid promptly during Prohibition. Put me down as against bar-rooms.'

"Y. S. Crow, corner Decatur and Bell streets, Anti-Prohibitionist, said : ' My business is a little better. Cause, bringing back liquor to the town.'

"Tate & Son (colored), 220 Decatur Street, dry goods and groceries. They own the store in which they do business and also a large platform on the Richmond and Danville Railroad. J. E. Tate, the son, made the following statement :

"'Business has fallen off 50 per cent. from last year. Cause, liquor being voted back. This is the main cause. People who spent their money for groceries before now spend it in the bar-rooms. Collections are very poor. Why, we have lost more money since whiskey has returned than we did during the two years of Prohibition. I have been neutral; did not vote. I am a Prohibitionist from now on. Why, I know men who during Prohibition made $3 and $4 a day, who since whiskey has returned have not supported their families. They hang around bar-rooms, and do not think of working. Some of them are white men, and some colored. I rarely saw a woman drunk during Prohibition; now I see them frequently. Last week I saw three drunken women pass my store, one right after the other. Bar-rooms and whiskey are a curse to my race.'

"T. J. Buchanan (retail groceries), Decatur Street, said: 'Business not so good as last year. Ran two stores last year, now I run only one. I have investigated the matter, and find from my books that my business has fallen off 25 per cent. There may be other causes for this state of affairs, but the most tangible one to me is "Personal Liberty and Red Liquor." Money is being diverted from the proper channels of trade into the tills of the bar-rooms.

"'During Prohibition I invariably sent up-town and got $100 in silver change for Saturday's trade. When a customer came into my store they would frequently offer me a five-dollar bill to change; now five-dollar bills are scarce. They may be here, but if they are the bar-rooms change them, and we only get the remnants.

"'I know of cases of men who kept sober during Prohibition, worked steadily, and made a good living for their families, but who are now drinking and carousing while their families are suffering for the necessaries of life. Close at hand is a man, a good mechanic, naturally kind-hearted and honorable, a good husband and indulgent father, but cursed with a love for whiskey. During Prohibition this man remained sober and provided well for his family. Himself, wife, and children were pictures of happiness, and he was laying up money. Now he neglects his work, spends his money in the bar-rooms, and his wife and family have to suffer. They are now the very pictures of misery, and all on account of the bar-room, whose allurements are fast ruining a man who is capable of making himself and others happy. The saloon-keeper is benefited at the expense of the ruin of an entire family. I want Prohibition, and when it comes again I want it to stay.'

"J. A. Bachelor, who keeps a grocery store at 236 Decatur Street, said: 'Business about the same as last year. Bringing back bar-rooms has not affected my business; there are dead-beats now who do not pay, and there were dead-beats who would not pay during Prohibition. I voted Anti before; I am undecided now; have no idea I shall vote at all when the question comes up again.'

"John T. Hagan runs a grocery store at 190 Decatur Street; he also runs a soda and mineral water bottling establishment. To the question, 'How is business?' he responded: 'Grocery business is not one-fourth and soda water not one-tenth what it was last year. The grocery business has fallen off because people spend their money for whiskey and have nothing left for groceries. The soda water trade is injured by beer drinking.'

"The next place visited was a large grocery store which does, perhaps, the largest retail business on Decatur Street. The gentleman interviewed had conscientious scruples about having his name appear in print, but had no objection to giving his opinions and to state facts. He emphatically declared that sales were not near so large nor collections near so good as they were a year ago. 'Men spend money for whiskey which they formerly spent with us. Whiskey gets them into trouble, then come fines, perhaps imprisonment. The time spent in attending court and in the chain-gang represents so much money that these men spent for groceries with us last year.

"'There is another grievance,' he said. 'We do not now have as good a class of trade as we had last year. People do not like the complexion of Decatur Street, and they stay away. Bar-rooms have caused all this. We voted for Anti-Prohibition before, but were there another election we would vote for Prohibition.'

"M. L. Bridwell, coal and wood, 219 Decatur Street, stated that he voted the Anti-Prohibition ticket last time. Has very decided opinions on 'restriction and High License;' did not care to have them published. His sales were about the same, but *his collections much worse* than last year.

"R. J. Mosler, crockery and fancy goods, 132 Decatur Street, said he had located in his present store April 20th, 1887. 'Trade was better then than it is now. I think bar-rooms have injured my business. I am a Prohibitionist and ever expect to be.'

"I. H. Hoge, groceries, 124 Docatur Street, said: 'I sell as many goods as last year, but find it *much harder to collect*. I have had a large colored trade. I sold them goods on credit last year and got paid for them I have had to shut down on several of them; they can't run an account with me and also one with the whiskey shop. They will pay their whiskey account and leave me out in the cold. Bringing back bar-rooms to Atlanta has injured my business. I am a Prohibitionist and expect to remain one.'

"Morris & Murphy, wholesale and retail grocers, 113, 115, and

117 Decatur Street. Mr. Murphy said: 'Sales much larger; collections good. Bar-rooms have not affected my business; I attribute this entirely to hard work, strict attention to my own business, and leaving other people's business strictly alone.'

"Terry & Brown (groceries), 107 Decatur Street: 'Our cash trade is about two-thirds of what it used to be. Credit trade about the same. *Collections powerfully dull.* Bar-rooms unquestionably injure business. A man need not be a Solomon to see that money spent for whiskey cannot be spent for groceries, and that a man who earns barely enough to support his family must curtail his grocery bill when he spends part of his earnings with the bar-rooms. I never voted, but I know that Prohibition is much better than the condition of things prevailing now.'

"Hanye & Dunlap, grocers, 85 and 87 Decatur Street: 'Our cash trade has fallen off; our credit trade has increased, because we have extended our territory. Bar-rooms have hurt our cash trade and forced us to cut off, since January 1st, forty credit customers who, during Prohibition, came up every Saturday night and paid their accounts. Since whiskey came back they spend their money for drink. Bar-rooms had not been established a week before we began to feel their effects in the demoralization of our trade. We are Prohibitionists.'

"S. A. & J. A. Morris, 133 to 137 Decatur Street (wagon yard and grocery store): Mr. S. A. Morris, on being asked about business, replied: 'We are selling many more goods than this time last year; the re-establishment of bar-rooms has not helped our business. I do not think it has affected our business one way or the other. I think there are too many bar-rooms in Atlanta now, and entirely too many on Decatur Street. Our cash sales are larger.' Mr. S. A. Morris is one of the Anti members of the City Council.

"Before leaving Decatur Street we called on Messrs. Mack & Sugarman, dealers in clothing and gents' furnishing goods. To our question regarding business, Mr. Sugarman replied: 'Business is not so good as during Prohibition. People spend their money in the bar-rooms now instead of in the clothing stores. During Prohibition colored people wore good clothes and good shoes; now you see the same people with ragged clothes and worn-out shoes. Saturday night's trade, which was formerly so good, is now way off. I am a Prohibitionist now. My partner, Mack, says he is an Anti, but he is not.'"

Up to the present time the police statistics are as follows:

AS TO CRIME.

Under Prohibition alone, imperfect as it was, arrests in Atlanta decreased as follows:

Year.	Liquor law.	Population.	Total arrests.	Population to 1 arrest.
1883	Low License	49,517	5,578	8.8
1884	"	53,812	5,824	9.2
1885	"	56,837	6,305	9.0
1886	Six months Prohibition	60,000	5,578	10.7
1887	Prohibition	65,000	6,138	10.3
1888	High License	70,000	7,817	8.9
1889	"	75,000	10,379	7.2

DRUNKENNESS MORE THAN DOUBLED BY HIGH LICENSE.

The arrests for drunkenness alone for the first nine months of $1,000 High License, compared with the same months during the last year of Prohibition, are as follows:

	Total arrests.		Arrests for drunkenness.	
	1887. Prohibition.	1888. $1,000 License.	1887. Prohibition.	1888. $1,000 License.
January	349	575	59	190
February	382	571	85	184
March	400	667	63	216
April	468	650	78	139
May	540	642	73	151
June	541	623	70	108
July	567	733	80	156
August	699	724	84	171
September	578	620	92	195
Totals	4,524	5,805	674	1,519

Note a few striking sentences, eloquent in their simplicity.

The dealer in furniture says: "The first Saturday night after the return of the bar-rooms our trade decreased $28, which are now about one-half what they were." Here is one reason why the home is wretched where the saloon is prosperous. The money that is spent for whiskey cannot be spent for furniture.

The coal and wood dealer reports: "When the bar-rooms were closed, I sold them half a ton at a time; now, 25 and 50 cents worth." Did you ever have an invalid or a tender babe in your family? What would you say to starting in for a day on 25 cents worth of coal, not knowing when you could buy any more?

Nearly unanimous are such reports as these:

"They now buy a cheaper class of goods—want cheapest every time."

"There has been one continuous demand for cheaper goods ever since the bar-rooms returned." That means discomfort in the home and loss to the tradesmen at the same time.

Most striking, too, is the "bad debt" report:

"Harder to collect from workingmen now than during Prohibition. Bad debts increasing with these people."

"Bad debts have increased tenfold; collections impossible."

That is the tribute which the honest tradesman pays to the liquor-dealer. The saloon-keeper gets his money.

He says of his business:

"They do not ask for credit, but pay as they go." He has only to threaten not to sell, and he can wring from the mad appetite of his victims their last cent. The groceryman, the butcher, the furniture dealer, and the shoe-dealer can trust and wait, and wait in vain.

In December, 1889, *The Voice* addressed inquiries to prominent business men of Atlanta, whose replies are presented in the following table:

TABLE OF REPLIES FROM 47

NAME AND BUSINESS.	1. Have you noticed since the return of the open barrooms to Atlanta any increase or decrease in the average amount of your sales to the workingmen, as compared with sales to the same class of people under Prohibition? If so, which? and to what extent?	2. Do you sell more or less on average to workingmen for cash than you did under Prohibition — in other words, have your credit sales to this class of people proportionately decreased or increased? and to what extent?
1 AMORDUS, M. F.—*Lumber*	Do not think condition of workingmen affected.	Do not believe business affected either way.
2 ATKINS, J. W. & E. C. W. —*Wholesale Hats.*	We are in wholesale business exclusively.	....
3 BAKER, D. J.—*General Merchandise.*	A decrease of 20 per cent.	I sell 50 per cent. less for cash.
4 BECK & GREGG—*Wholesale Hardware.*	Being wholesalers, have little to do with workingmen.	....
5 BROOKS, B. C., & BRO.—*Furniture.*	We can truthfully say that first Saturday night we had decreased $28 in our sales, which are now about one-half.	We sell for cash about one-fourth now what we did under Prohibition.
6 BROOKS, J. W., & Co.—*Retail Grocers.*	I have experienced a considerable decrease — at least 20 per cent.	I sell 50 per cent. less for cash than under Prohibition.
7 BUCHANAN, T. J.—*Family Groceries.*	A decrease of 25 per cent.	Sell considerably less for cash.
8 BURGE, C. H. — *Retail Groceries.*	A decrease, especially to workingmen.	Cash trade fallen off about 25 per cent.; credit increased about the same.
9 DANIEL, J. C.—*Boots and Shoes.*	A decrease of about one-half.	Sell less; the demand for credit greatly increased.
10 DRAPER, W. W. —*Wholesale Boots and Shoes.*	Our city patrons — some Anti-Prohibitionists — tell us the bar-rooms have cut off their trade.	Answered under No. 1.
11 EVINS, JOHN C.—*Furniture.*	When bar rooms returned I felt it very seriously in falling off of trade.	My trade is good, but there is less ability and less disposition to pay now than during Prohibition.

BUSINESS MEN OF ATLANTA.

3. Do you notice that it is easier or harder now to make collections in Atlanta than it was under Prohibition? In other words, does the number of "bad debts" have a tendency to increase or decrease?	4. Do you find the working people now purchasing generally a cheaper or a better class of goods than under Prohibition? If so, give some examples of what they buy now compared with formerly.	5. In your opinion would it or would it not be a benefit to business generally if the money now spent in the saloons should be spent for clothing, fuel, furniture, etc., and the other comforts and necessaries of life?	
....	....	Prohibition cannot be enforced.	1
....	Our best information is that poor people and laboring class took much better care of families, paid their grocery and other bills more promptly during Prohibition than before or since.	....	2
In my trade collections are much harder.	Cannot say.	Money spent for liquors is a complete loss.	3
....	....	It certainly would.	4
We used to collect from $75 to $100 a week, now we can get only from $25 to $40, and very hard to do that.	They buy the cheapest and mostly second-hand goods.	Yes, sir.	5
Collections from the laboring class are not nearly so good as during Prohibition.	About the same class of goods.	Answering from personal experience, it would undoubtedly be better.	6
Much harder to make collections. Many formerly spent earnings for provisions now buy on time and spend money in bar-rooms.	No marked difference.	Undoubtedly. Re-opening bar-rooms greatest evil that ever befell us.	7
Much harder to make collections now than during Prohibition.	They now buy a cheaper class of goods; want cheapest every time.	In my opinion our cash sales would increase tenfold if the bar-rooms were closed.	8
Much harder; bad debts increase more rapidly, although I am more cautious than during Prohibition.	Cheaper goods purchased now; under Prohibition they bought shoes worth from $2 to $3; now from $1 to $1.50.	Most emphatically it would.	9
Think collections not as good.	Know nothing.	Certainly would be a benefit.	10
It is much harder to collect now. When bar-rooms returned my collections fell off fully 25 per cent.	There has been one continuous demand for cheaper goods ever since bar-rooms returned. I sell on average 25 per cent cheaper goods.	Would be a great benefit to the entire community.	11

TABLE OF REPLIES FROM 47 BUSI-

Name and Business.	1. Have you noticed since the return of the open barrooms to Atlanta any increase or decrease in the average amount of your sales to the workingmen as compared with sales to the same class of people under Prohibition? If so, which? and to what extent?	2. Do you sell more or less on average to workingmen for cash than you did under Prohibition — in other words, have your credit sales to this class of people proportionately decreased or increased? and to what extent?
12 FINCHER & FINCHER—Retail Groceries.	Our trade with the drinking classes is about half what it was during Prohibition.	They want more credit and pay less, most of them nothing.
13 GILBERT, H. C.—Groceries.	My trade was better during Prohibition.	I sell less; credit sales are on the increase.
14 GRAMLING, H. S.—Dry Goods.	A decrease, I think, of 20 per cent.	We refuse more now than we did during Prohibition.
15 HUGHES & LAW—Hats and Gents' Furnishing.	Can't see any difference.	No increase.
16 *HENTSCHEL, C.—Groceries.	About 200 per cent. increase.	I sell more for cash.
17 †HENTSCHEL, WILLIAM—Clothing, Gents' Furnishing.	Some increase in some businees, a large fall off in others.	I do not credit.
18 HOGAN, W. J.—Retail and Wholesale Grocer.	Business generally better in Atlanta, but do not attribute it to open saloons, but to rapid growth of city and better crops.	Credit sales to laboring class have increased.
19 HOLBROOK, A. L., & Co.—Retail Groceries.	At least 10 per cent. less.	Our credit sales have increased some; would be much larger, but we refuse; demand for credit much increased.
20 HUFF, H. T.—Coal and Wood.	When the bar-rooms were closed I sold them half ton at a time; now 25 and 50 cents' worth.	Sell less; can't credit at all.

* C. Hentschel, who signed himself "Groceries" in answer to our questions, is put down in the body of the Atlanta City Directory as "Groceries and liquors." He has also the following half-page display advertisement on page 28 of the Atlanta Directory: "Carl Hentschel, Dealer in Imported and Domestic Wines, Brandies and Whiskies and Other Liquors—Fresh Beer always on Draught—Fancy Groceries, Fine Tobacco and Cigars—54 and 56 Decatur St., Atlanta, Georgia."

† There are five Hentschels in the Atlanta Directory—four of whom are directly

NESS MEN OF ATLANTA—Continued.

3. Do you notice that it is easier or harder now to make collections in Atlanta than it was under Prohibition? In other words, does the number of "bad debts" have a tendency to increase or decrease?	4. Do you find the working people now purchasing generally a cheaper or a better class of goods than under Prohibition? If so, give some examples of what they buy now compared with formerly.	5. In your opinion would it or would it not be a benefit to business generally if the money now spent in the saloons should be spent for clothing, fuel, furniture, etc., and the other comforts and necessaries of life?	
Collections are much harder now.	Many buy nothing, their wives having to support them.	It would benefit our business very much.	12
It is harder to make collections since return of bar rooms.	Cheaper.	It would.	13
... ...	Cheaper. Hosiery, formerly 25c., now want 10 to 15c.; flannels, formerly 85c. to 50c., now want 20c to 80c.; shoes, formerly $1.50 to $2, now $1 to $1.50.	It would.	14
Noticed no difference.	Noticed no change.	Think it would be.	15
My collections much better now.	Better goods are bought now than before.	Would be best for money to be spent for food, clothing, etc. But parties spending money for whiskey, best buy by drink than gallon, as under Prohibition.	16
Cannot say.	About the same. Have more money to buy with.	I think the saloons best; men formerly bought by gallon, now buy by drink.	17
Bad debts have noticeably increased.	Notice no difference.	Money spent for drink would greatly benefit business, and none others think otherwise except those directly or indirectly in liquor business.	18
Harder to collect now from workingmen than during Prohibition; bad debts increasing with these people.	Do not see much difference as to quality; but quantity and cash is less.	We most assuredly do; workingmen do not live as well now as under Prohibition.	19
Harder to collect from that class that spend money in saloons.	Colored people buy the cheapest things they can get; during Prohibition bought the best.	It would. Prohibition the best thing that could happen to a town or place.	20

engaged in the liquor business: the saloon-keeper above described; August Hentschel, wholesale dealer in lager beer; Gottlieb Hentschel, saloon at 40 Decatur Street; Paul Hentschel, barkeeper for Gottlieb Hentschel, boards at 881 Wheat Street; and William Hentschel, dry goods, 52 Decatur Street (next door to C. Hentschel's saloon), who also boards at 881 Wheat Street. These facts may help to account for the unfavorable opinion which William Hentschel, "Clothier and Gents' Furnisher," holds with reference to Prohibition.

TABLE OF REPLIES FROM 47 BUSI-

Name and Business.	1. Have you noticed since the return of the open barrooms to Atlanta any increase or decrease in the average amount of your sales to the workingmen, as compared with sales to the same class of people under Prohibition? If so, which? and to what extent?	2. Do you sell more or less on average to workingmen for cash than you did under Prohibition — in other words, have your credit sales to this class of people proportionately decreased or increased? and to what extent?
21 Johnson, W. E.—Fresh and Smoked Meats.	A very decided decrease, almost 50 per cent. or quite.	I sell less for cash; could sell more on credit, but know can't pay now as did under Prohibition.
22 Kalb, Frederick G.—Groceries and Produce.	My sales less than during Prohibition on account laboring classes buying inferior goods.	My credit sales, if allowed, would increase greatly; but credit being refused, they buy cheaper goods.
23 Kelly, C. H., & Co.—Wholesale Grocers.	....	I don't sell any to workingmen.
24 Kimball, J. H., Sn., & Co.—Dry Goods and Clothing.	Our trade is at least 20 per cent. less since the return of the bar-rooms.	The demand for credit is much greater; men perfectly responsible before return of bar-rooms will not pay at all now.
25 Kilpatrick, J. W.—Grocer.	Decrease.	Sell about 25 per cent. less.
26 King Hardware Co.—Hardware.	....	....
27 Kirke, Thomas & Co.—Hardware.	None.	About the same.
28 Lyon, J. A.—Grocer	My sales have decreased at least 15 per cent.	Credit sales increased; cash sales decreased.
29 McDonald, N. D., & Co.—Booksellers and Binders.	No change from a gradual increase.	No change.
30 Maucu, M. M.—Wall Paper and Paints.	Don't see working people in my line of trade.	Cannot tell.
31 Morris & Murphey—Wholesale Grocers.	....	....
32 Neal, John—Furniture.	Sales decreased about one-third.	Credit sales increased largely.
33 Phillips & Co.—Furniture and Money Broker.	Have made no calculation as to the difference.	During Prohibition we gave such large credit that it will take all Anti-Prohibition to collect.

NESS MEN OF ATLANTA—Continued.

3. Do you notice that it is easier or harder now to make collections in Atlanta than it was under Prohibition? In other words, does the number of "bad debts" have a tendency to increase or decrease?	4. Do you find the working people now purchasing generally a cheaper or a better class of goods than under Prohibition? If so, give some examples of what they buy now compared with formerly.	5. In your opinion would it or would it not be a benefit to business generally if the money now spent in the saloons should be spent for clothing, fuel, furniture, etc., and the other comforts and necessaries of life?	
Much harder to collect now; almost impossible to collect from workingmen who visit bar-rooms.	They bought better meats than now, and much more liberally. Now they buy the cheapest they can get.	It would be of incalculable benefit to all other business except the whiskey trade. I know the good it did us.	21
The number of bad debts increases as more money is spent for liquor.	During Prohibition the working class indulged in luxuries, but now confine themselves to bread and meat.	Of course.	22
I find it a great deal harder to collect than in time of Prohibition.	I have noticed no difference.	I know the working people were in a much better condition during Prohibition.	23
Much harder, debts increasing.	The demand for cheaper goods has increased. This effect is felt on all conditions and professions.	Much better.	24
Bad debts increased.	Purchase cheaper goods than formerly.	Would benefit business in my opinion.	25
....	....	Money spent for whiskey lost to other lines of trade; whiskey makes men unable to earn money, thus bringing double loss to business.	26
See no difference.	Our trade never better.	Undoubtedly.	27
Bad debts have increased tenfold; collections impossible.	Neither; only less in quantity.	Yes! Yes!! Yes!!! Yes!!!!	28
No change to note.	We can note no change.	Saloons seem but as other mediums of circulation.	29
....	Don't know any difference.	Of course it would.	30
....	....	We are Anti-Prohibition folks.	31
Much harder to make collections. Bad debts increased.	Purchase cheaper goods, imitation instead of genuine.	A thousand times better; but Prohibition don't prohibit.	32
Bad debts are decreasing slowly—as we put on the hydraulic pressure.	Selling about the same class of goods.	It would be beneficial if all saloon customers would spend money with us; but it will never be as long as rye is made.	33

TABLE OF REPLIES FROM 47 BUSI-

Name and Business.	1. Have you noticed since the return of the open barrooms to Atlanta any increase or decrease in the average amount of your sales to the workingmen, as compared with sales to the same class of people under Prohibition? If so, which? and to what extent?	2. Do you sell more or less on average to workingmen for cash than you did under Prohibition — in other words, have your *credit* sales to this class of people proportionately decreased or increased? and to what extent?
34 PRICE & FOSTER—*Shoes*..	We found it easier during Prohibition to sell good goods than now.	....
35 PRIOR, G. S.—*Groceries*..	My trade confined mostly to customers whom presence of whiskey does not affect.	My opinion is that the working class spend some less with me than during Prohibition.
36 BRIDGER, J. C. — *Coal Merchant*.	A slight decrease.	Credit sales increased.
37 RAGSDALE, I. N.—*Groceries and Provisions*.	My trade not as good as under Prohibition.	More demand for credit than when had no whiskey.
38 RICE, R J.—*Grocer*......	Sales decreased very perceptibly from the first Saturday night	Risky to sell on credit to a workingman who drinks.
39 RICHARDS, S P., & SON—*Books, Stationery and Music*.	Have been unable to discern any effect on our business.	....
40 REDUS, R. R.—*Wholesale Fruits and Fish*.	Perceptible decrease cash sales to workingmen since defeat of Prohibition.	The largest number are now less worthy of credit.
41 REESE, H. O.—*Grocer*....	My sales slightly decreased.	Sell less for cash, time sales increased.
42 RYAN'S SONS, JOHN—*Wholesale, Retail Dry Goods, Boots and Shoes*.	....	....
43 SAWTELL, T. R.—*Wholesale, Retail Butcher*.	Have noticed no change.	About the same.
44 THORNTON & GRUBB—*Books and Stationery*.	....	....
45 TREADWELL, CHARLES—*Furniture Dealer*.	Noticed one-third off in sales.	Cash sales decreased one-third.
46 Vaughan, C. J.—SALOON.	MY SALES TO WORKINGMEN HAVE INCREASED.	THEY DO NOT ASK FOR CREDIT, BUT PAY AS THEY GO.
47 WILSON, R W.—*Gents' Furnishing and Dry Goods*.	Not much difference, if any; return of bar-rooms in my favor.	Credit sales are just as good as under Prohibition.

NESS MEN OF ATLANTA—Continued.

3. Do you notice that it is easier or harder now to make collections in Atlanta than it was under Prohibition? In other words, does the number of "bad debts" have a tendency to increase or decrease?	4. Do you find the working people now purchasing generally a cheaper or a better class of goods than under Prohibition? If so, give some examples of what they buy now compared with formerly.	5. In your opinion would it or would it not be a benefit to business generally if the money now spent in the saloons should be spent for clothing, fuel, furniture, etc., and the other comforts and necessaries of life?	
....	About the same class of goods.	If Prohibition had been continued long enough it would have been a decided benefit to business.	34
Do not notice any particular difference; my house not in neighborhood working people.	Don't notice any difference.	Of course; it could not possibly be otherwise.	35
Bad debts have increased.	Cheaper in my line; now want the cheapest, formerly the best.	Be great benefit to have money diverted from saloons.	36
Think bad debts have increased.	Nearly same, but in less amounts.	Business would be generally better.	37
Harder to collect; men who paid under Prohibition now do not pay at all.	They buy nothing but the barest necessaries.	Would increase business one-third.	38
....	....	Such would certainly be the case in this city as in any other.	39
Collections much harder to make; pretty fair increase "bad debts."	Am not informed.	Undoubtedly; alarming increase of levies and sale of working people's effects over Prohibition period.	40
Harder now to collect; great many cases impossible.	I see no change.	Would be extremely beneficial.	41
....	....	Prohibition campaign most injurious, disgusting proceeding launched on suffering public, paralyzing business, estranging friends.	42
Have noticed no change.	See no change.	It would; whiskey was sold so close to Atlanta that all who wished could send for it.	43
....	....	Yes! Yes!! Yes!!! Yes!!!!	44
Harder to make collections; debts increase.	Purchase cheaper goods, soft wood instead of walnut.	Yes, better State by $2,000,000.	45
I FIND IT EASIER TO COLLECT MY RENTS NOW THAN DURING PROHIBITION.	CANNOT SAY AS TO FURNITURE, BUT FROM WHAT I SEE THEY BUY BETTER GOODS NOW.	I THINK NOT. DON'T THINK FAMILY IN CITY SUFFERS FROM HUSBAND'S DRINKING.	46
Think collections better; Atlanta never more prosperous.	Buy as good goods and as many as under Prohibition.	It would if they would purchase goods with money.	47

SUMMARY OF PRECEDING TABLE.

QUESTION I.—Have you noticed since the return of the open bar-rooms to Atlanta any increase or decrease in the average amount of your sales to workingmen, as compared with sales to the same class of people under Prohibition? If so, which, and to what extent?

Forty replies (excluding 2 saloon-keepers, whose sales are much greater), of which 26 report a decided decrease; 4 report that their trade is not with the workingmen; 6 see no difference; 3, that business is better; 1, increase in some lines of business, decrease in others.

QUESTION II.—Do you sell more or less on an average to workingmen for cash than you did under Prohibition? In other words, have your *credit* sales to that class of people proportionately decreased or increased, and to what extent?

Thirty-seven replies (excluding 2 saloon-keepers, who sell more for cash), of which 27 reply that there are less sales for cash and a greater demand for credit; 6 report no change; 1 does not credit; 1 cannot tell; 1 does not sell to workingmen; 1 gives an evasive answer.

QUESTION III.—Do you notice that it is easier or harder now to make collections in Atlanta than it was under Prohibition? In other words, does the number of "bad debts" have a tendency to increase or decrease?

Thirty-four replies (excluding 2 saloon-keepers, whose collections are much better), of which 26 report that collections are harder or "bad debts" are increasing; 5 notice no difference; 1 cannot say; 1, 'bad debts" decreasing under pressure; 1, collections better.

QUESTION IV.—Do you find the working people now purchasing generally a cheaper or better class of goods than under Prohibition?

Thirty-eight replies (exclusive of 2 saloon-keepers, who find that better goods are purchased), of which 17 reply that cheaper goods are purchased ; 20 notice no difference, except that some find a less quantity is purchased ; 1, "Our trade never better."

QUESTION V.—In your opinion, would it or would it not be a benefit to business generally if the money now spent in the saloons should be spent for clothing, fuel, furniture, etc., and the other comforts and necessaries of life?

Forty-four replies (exclusive of 2 saloon-keepers), of which 38 reply affirmatively ; 1, "Prohibition cannot be enforced ;" 1 "thinks saloons best ;" 1, "Saloons but as other mediums of circulation ;" 1, "We are Anti-Prohibition folks ;" 1, "It will never be ;" 1, "Prohibition campaign injurious."

The answers to Question V are a sufficient explanation for the results set forth in the table. Much of the money that went during the Prohibition period to the retail merchants for food, clothing, furniture, and other necessaries of life is now worse than wasted in the High License saloons.

TESTIMONY OF THE MERCHANTS AS TO THE EFFECTS OF HIGH LICENSE.

The following are samples of the replies received from the business men of Atlanta :

THEY DON'T BUY BY THE HALF-TON NOW.

H. T. Huff, coal and wood dealer : "When the bars were closed in Atlanta the workingmen used to come and buy from me by the half-ton ; now they buy only twenty-five and fifty cents worth at a time. I sell less for cash to workingmen than I did during Prohibition, and I find that it won't do to give credit at all. It is harder now than it was under Prohibition to make collections from the class of people who spend their money at the bars. Among this class it is now the practice to buy the cheapest articles they can get, whereas they used to buy the best while we had Prohibition. I think Prohibition is the best thing that can ever happen to a town or place."

J. C. Daniel, boots and shoes: "I have noticed a decrease in the average amount of sales to workingmen since the legalized bar-rooms returned. It is difficult to state the extent of the decrease, but I should say about one-half. I sell less to workingmen for cash, and the demand for credit has greatly increased. It is much harder to make collections. Bad debts increase rapidly, although I am much more cautious now than I was during the reign of Prohibition. Cheaper goods are purchased now. The working people buy shoes now worth from $1 to $1.50, whereas during Prohibition they bought shoes costing from $2 to $2.50 and frequently $3. Most emphatically, I think it would be a benefit to business generally if the money now spent in saloons were spent for the necessaries of life. I am a Prohibitionist, but I have not put my answer too strong. I am also a Democrat and belong to the Solid South."

SALES TO WORKINGMEN FIFTY PER CENT. LESS.

W. E. Johnson, fresh and smoked meats: "There has been a very decided decrease in my sales to workingmen since the Prohibitory law was done away with—almost or quite 50 per cent. I sell less for cash and could sell more for credit, but I know that the working classes can't pay now as they did under Prohibition. I know from experience. It is much harder to collect money now—almost impossible to collect from those workingmen who visit bar-rooms. As a general thing, these classes bought better meats under Prohibition than they buy now, and much more liberally; they purchased the best then, but now they want the cheapest they can get. Prohibition would be of incalculable benefit to all lines of business except the whiskey trade. I know this because we have experienced it and know the good it did us."

W. J. Gramling, dry goods: "The decrease in my sales to workingmen since the return of the open bar-rooms is, I think, about 20 per cent. We refuse credit now more than we did during Prohibition. The working people buy cheaper grades of goods; for instance, under Prohibition they bought hosiery worth twenty-five cents, and now they want ten and fifteen-cent hosiery; for flannels they would pay thirty-five to fifty cents, but now they pay twenty to thirty cents; they used to buy shoes worth $1.50 to $2, but now they give only $1 to $1.50. It would be a good thing to throw the money now spent in the saloons into other lines of trade, if that could be arranged; for the people spend money for whiskey when not able to do so, and hence their families have to do without the comforts of life."

THE BAR-ROOMS HURT HIM "VERY SERIOUSLY."

John E. Evins, dealer in furniture : "When the bar-rooms returned I felt the result very seriously by a falling off of trade, and especially of collections. My trade is good and has been on the increase from the beginning of my business. I sell almost altogether on the instalment plan. There is less disposition and less ability to pay now than there was during Prohibition. It is much harder to collect now than it was during Prohibition. When the bar-rooms returned my collections fell off fully 25 per cent. There has been one continuous demand for cheaper goods ever since the bar-rooms returned. I am selling on an average about 25 per cent. cheaper than formerly. It would surely be a great benefit to the entire community if the money now spent in saloons were properly spent for the necessaries of life."

C. H. Burge, retail grocer : "I find a decrease of sales—especially to the working classes—as compared with sales during Prohibition. My cash trade has fallen off 25 per cent., and my credit trade has increased about that much. It is much harder to make collections now than it was during Prohibition—much harder. The workingmen now get a cheaper class of goods ; indeed, they now want the cheapest every time. In my opinion, our cash sales would increase tenfold if the bar-rooms were closed. The money that was formerly spent for groceries now goes for whiskey."

THE GREATEST EVIL ATLANTA EVER HAD.

T. J. Buchanan, family groceries : "Yes, there has been a decrease of sales to workingmen since the bar-rooms came back—about 25 per cent. I sell less for cash to these classes now, and the extent of the falling off is considerable. It is much harder to make collections now. A great many who formerly spent their money for provisions now buy on time and spend their money in the bar-rooms and leave their grocery bills unpaid. As to the class of goods bought I notice no marked difference. Most undoubtedly it would be of advantage to business generally if the money now spent in the saloons were spent for the comforts and necessaries of life. The reopening of the bar-rooms in our city is the greatest evil that ever befel it."

D. J. Baker, general merchandise : "I have noticed a decrease in my trade with working people since Prohibition ceased—I suppose about 20 per cent. I sell less for cash by 50 per cent. In my trade I find it much harder to make collections. I cannot say that there have been any cheaper goods used in my business, for I don't handle any cheap goods or shoddy stuff. I know that money spent for liquor is a blank—a complete loss to women and children who need it. I can't express my opinion strong enough on this subject."

THE FIRST SATURDAY NIGHT OF LICENSE.

B. C. Brooks & Brother, furniture : "We can truthfully say that on the first Saturday night after the return of the bar-rooms our sales showed a decrease of $28, and that our sales to working people have fallen off about one-half. Our cash sales to workingmen are only about one-fourth what they were under the Prohibitory law. We used to collect from $75 to $100 per week, but now we can get only $25 to $40, and it is very hard work to get that. The working classes now buy the cheapest goods, mostly second-hand."

J. W. Brooks & Co., retail grocers : "I have experienced a considerably decreased trade since Prohibition went out—at least 20 per cent. I sell 50 per cent. less for cash than I did under Prohibition. Collections from the laboring class do not show near so good as they did during Prohibition. I can cheerfully answer from personal experience that it would undoubtedly be better for business if the money now spent in saloons were spent for the comforts and necessaries of life."

BAD DEBTS HAVE INCREASED.

J. H. Kimbrell, Sr. & Co., dry goods and clothing : "Our trade with the working classes is at least 20 per cent. smaller since the return of bar-rooms. The demand for credit is much greater. Men who were perfectly responsible when we had no bar-rooms will not pay at all now. It is much harder to make collections, and bad debts have increased. The demand for cheaper goods has increased. This does not apply altogether to working people, but the same is true to some extent of all conditions and professions. It would be much better for business if there were no money spent in saloons. Let me give you an illustration : On Decatur Street there are twenty-two bar rooms paying $1,000 license and two beer saloons paying $100 license ; add house rents for these places, clerk hire, cost of fixtures, and cost of goods, and an enormous amount of money is represented, for which the consumer gets nothing in return."

"A THOUSAND TIMES BETTER."

John Neal, furniture : "There has been a decrease in my sales of say about one-third to the working people since the bar-rooms came back. We sell less to them for cash, and credit has decreased largely. It is much harder to make collections, and bad debts increase in consequence. The working people are purchasing cheaper goods ; they buy imitation goods instead of the genuine. It would be a thousand times better for the trade if the money spent in saloons were spent for comforts and necessaries."

ALL THE ANSWERS GIVEN, BOTH FAVORABLE AND UNFAVORABLE TO PROHIBITION.

Many more letters containing testimony similar to the above might be given.

All the answers received from the forty-seven business men replying, whether favorable or unfavorable to Prohibition, have been given in the foregoing table, and may be summarized in the following general statements :

1. That sales of goods to workingmen have greatly decreased when compared with the Prohibition period ;

2. That the proportion of credit sales has greatly increased, less being bought for cash ;

3. That under High License "bad debts" have increased and collections are harder to make than they were during Prohibition ; and

4. That business men are selling a cheaper class of goods and taking in less cash than they did in Prohibition days.

The testimony of these replies is overwhelmingly to the effect that the returning saloons under High License have injured business in Atlanta and rendered worse the condition of the poor. It would be difficult to find a fairer test, and the conclusion is inevitable that, leaving moral and humanitarian considerations wholly out of account, merely as a matter of profit and loss, High License as compared with Prohibition is an unqualified financial curse, blunder, and disaster.

And this testimony of injury to business and decreased personal prosperity comes during a period of great general prosperity (1889) in the nation at large, and while Atlanta herself is increasing in population and enterprise.

CHAPTER XVIII.

THE NEW LANDS.

> "What beings fill those bright abodes?
> How formed, how gifted? What their powers, their state?
> * * * * * * * *
> Has War trod o'er them with his foot of fire?
> And Slavery forged his chains, and Wrath and Hate,
> And sordid Selfishness and cruel Lust
> Leagued their base bands to tread out light and truth,
> And scatter woe, where Heaven had planted joy?
> Or are they yet all Paradise, unfallen
> And uncorrupt? existence one long joy,
> Without disease upon the frame or sin
> Upon the heart, or weariness of life?"
> —*Henry Ware, Jr.*

BOTH Dakotas for Prohibition give us a light of hope. Numerous Iowa men have settled there and given their influence for the system they left in their own State. The new laws seem to be stringent, and should succeed, if men, good, true, and brave, stand firmly by them. The young States have done nobly. Just when older States at the East had voted down Prohibition, and the Liquor Traffic, flushed with victory, concentrated upon them, with menaces in one hand and bribes in the other, those stanch pioneers resisted both and voted out the saloon from their borders. It is too soon for statistics, but it is beautiful to think what a civilization may be which is built up from the beginning without the saloon.

Oklahoma has, however, given a practical illustration of the worth of Prohibition which there is no gainsaying. Major J. A. Pickler, one of the Congressmen from South Dakota, made the following statement in Washington, D. C. :

"I was in Oklahoma for two months during the opening of the Territory, as an agent of the Interior Department. Fifty thousand people came into Oklahoma within twenty-four hours, all strangers to each other, as many as a dozen men claiming one town lot on which they had squatted, and four or five claiming the same tract of land. With no laws to govern this people except the general laws of the United States, without a governor, sheriff, or constable, we had perfect peace and order, with no bloodshed whatever for six months. I, as did all thinking men, attributed it to the Prohibition by the Government of any liquor being brought into the Territory. This is a complete demonstration that the National Government can thoroughly and successfully enforce Prohibition. I have no doubt but that it could enforce it in the District of Columbia or any place.

"When you get the United States Government to take hold of the liquor traffic," added Congressman Pickler, "the traffic's life will be short."

Oklahoma is under the laws of the Indian Territory, which are strictly prohibitory. The United States officers examine suspected baggage for liquor, even searching grip-sacks for the contraband article, and throwing out and smashing any bottles of liquor they find. The Chicago *Lever* contains the following :

ST. LOUIS, Mo., August 12, 1889 (*Special Correspondence*).—The *Lever* correspondent has just returned from an extensive trip through the great Prohibition State of Kansas and the Prohibition Territory of Oklahoma, and is more firmly convinced than ever that the United States Government should be the party to take up the cudgel and wield it the same in the States as it does in the Indian Territory and Oklahoma, where Uncle Sam has sole jurisdiction of affairs. This national idea is very plainly demonstrated in the new promised and possessed land of Oklahoma, and the *Lever* representative saw United States regulars go through the grips on the cars at Oklahoma City, before the passengers were allowed to leave the train, and several bottles were broken by being thrown out of the windows. There had been evidences that liquor was being smuggled into the city in that manner, and the officers took in the situation at once.

This process is so effectual that the liquor sympathizers in Congress, in the bill giving Oklahoma a territorial government, made a crafty attempt to nullify Prohibition by the following provision :

"SECTION 7.—That the general statutes of Nebraska, which are not locally inapplicable or in conflict with this act, or in conflict with any law of the United States, are hereby extended to and put in force in the Territory of Oklahoma until after the adjournment of the first session of the Legislative Assembly of said Territory."

This, of course, would have given over the new Territory to High License. To Major Pickler belongs the honor of pointing out and attacking this insidious provision.

In a speech on the Oklahoma bill, printed in *The Congressional Record* for March 4th, he said :

"The Government of the United States has refused to allow the sale of intoxicating liquors in the Territory of Oklahoma. And wisely, Mr. Speaker, did the Government refuse to allow the shipment of intoxicating liquors into this Territory. In my judgment, had liquor been allowed to be sold in that Territory during the settlement, no such record of order and bloodless history of occupancy would have been known as has become the history of Oklahoma.

"It seems to me, Mr. Speaker, that during the coming contests concerning the organization of counties, the locations of county seats, the selection of the capital of the Territory, the election of officers, and, more than all, the exciting contests concerning the ownership of the lands and town lots of this Territory, wherein one man will be dispossessed and the title declared in another, and in the many other exciting scenes and contests that must ensue in the organization of this Territory, it would be far better that the Congress of the United States should continue the policy heretofore pur sued by the General Government of preventing the sale of intoxicating liquors in this Territory until they are organized and have themselves legislated upon this question.

"As I understand it, under the laws of Nebraska, which under this bill govern this people, and to which I object, upon the petition of thirty freeholders a license is granted for the sale of intoxicating liquors. Under this law from three hundred to five hundred saloons will be opened in Oklahoma in a remarkably short time after the passage of this act.

"Mr. Speaker, in the interest of a peaceable organization of that Territory, in the interest of the harmony and good name of this people, who are a grand people, and for whom, after months of intimate intercourse with them, I have the highest respect and regard, I do not believe Congress should permit this great promoter of discord to be brought among them.

"Why not substitute the laws of Kansas instead of Nebraska? I believe one-fourth of the people in that Territory were former residents of Kansas; they are acquainted with the laws of Kansas, and the administration of Kansas laws, and the procedure in Kansas courts. Mr. Speaker, they have acted largely under Kansas laws in their proceedings so far in this Territory. The city of Oklahoma adopted the laws of Kansas in its organization.

"This Territory is in the jurisdiction of the courts of Kansas, the United States Marshals ordered to that Territory to preserve the peace are Kansas officers, and they are the officers who now are in this Territory preserving order. Prisoners arrested therein are sent to Kansas for trial, and from every standpoint it seems to me Kansas laws should be the ones for the present government of this people, and under these laws the sale of intoxicating liquors would be prohibited. And I know it is the desire of the people of that Territory that Congress should protect them in this regard as the Government has in the past."

Subsequently Major Pickler said, in an interview:

"I CANNOT POSSIBLY UNDERSTAND HOW THERE CAN BE ANY OPPOSITION TO LETTING THOSE PEOPLE LIVE IN PEACE, AS THEY HAVE DONE EVEN WITHOUT LAWS. THE FACT IS, THE AMERICAN PEOPLE DON'T SEEM TO NEED LAWS FOR THE PRESERVATION OF GOOD ORDER EXCEPT WHERE THERE IS WHISKEY."

The House of Representatives, on March 13th, 1889,

amended the bill by a vote of 134 to 104, extending the provisions of Section 2,139 (prohibiting the introduction of intoxicating liquors into Indian Territory) to the Territory of Oklahoma. So there is good hope that the new Territory may never know the curse of the saloon. Let us rejoice that Congress has decided to treat white men as well as it does the Indian.

Whatever the future may develop, however, be this remembered to the lasting honor of Prohibition, that fifty thousand men racing into the wilderness, with fierce contentions for title to lands, with not a magistrate among them, were able to settle all without bloodshed or life lost, because they had not a saloon.

CHAPTER XIX.

THE LABORING MEN.

"The labor problem is, after all, only the people's problem."—*J. Lloyd Thomas, in "Liquor's War on Labor's Rights."*

"The use of liquor and its influences have done more to darken labor's homes, dwarf its energies, and chain it hand and foot to the wheels of corporate oppression than all other influences combined."—*R. F. Trevellick, President of National Labor Union and Eight Hour League."*

"When confidence is general, and there is a good prospect that business will run smoothly and profitably, manufacturers begin to enlarge operations, and employers of every kind want more help, and they have to bid up to get it; that would be a natural rise. Such would have been the case at the present time, without doubt, had quiet prevailed; but strikes, turbulence, and boycotts have destroyed confidence, and now a very dull period seems certain. Another illustration of 'killing the goose that lays the golden egg.' Apparent victories by either capital or labor, when gained by artificial pressure, will not be permanent."—*"Common Sense on Labor," by Cupples, Upham & Co.*

THE best definition of republican government ever given was that of Lincoln, in his immortal speech at Gettysburg, "Government of the people, by the people, and for the people."

The laboring men, the working classes, form the vast majority of every people. Their interest is the interest of us all.

Every statesman, every theologian, every republican, every patriot, must find the welfare of the laboring classes a matter of absorbing interest and of transcendent importance. What does the liquor traffic do for them? One answer springs to every one's lips: "It brings them misfortune. It's a curse to them." But in order to deal with the matter adequately, we must go somewhat into the particulars of the curse. How much do our laboring men spend for liquor?

Dr. Dorchester, "Liquor Problem," p. 672, estimates the consumers of liquor in the United States at 15,000,000 out of a population of 59,000,000 in 1886. To get that number he counts one-half the males between fifteen and twenty-one as drinkers, and three-fourths of the male population over twenty years. This is surely too large an estimate. If true, it would make "The Liquor Problem" discouraging, not to say desperate. With this large allowance for consumers, he puts a very moderate allowance for the total cost of liquors—$700,000,000, when, according to Dr. Hargreaves, the cost of liquors to the consumers in 1883 was $944,000,000, from which it has been steadily increasing to the present time.

With these data Dr. Dorchester gets $49.34 as the average cost to each laboring man who drinks.

All who know the habits and circumstances of laboring men know that there are few drinkers among them whose liquor expenses can be brought within $50 a year. A writer in the St. Paul *Pioneer Press* says:

"The remark was made in our presence a short time since that a large proportion of the laboring men of this city spend from twenty to forty cents each day for beer. At the rate of twenty-five cents each day, the sum thus spent in a year would be $78.25, making no account of any used on Sundays."

But all accounts, whether of liquor dealers, or of temperance workers, or of employers of labor, show that Sunday is the heaviest drinking day. This is what might be expected. What makes the imperiousness of the drink habit? The depth of the reaction that follows the withdrawal of the stimulus. It is not the desire of having the liquor, but the horror of not having it. The action of brain, stomach, muscle, all flags for want of the accustomed spur.

With the flagging of energy, there is an abnormal sensitiveness of nerve that makes every small annoyance intolerable. It is of little use to read, or talk, or sing to the man in that condition, or to provide the daintiest dishes. It would take the grace of a saint to make a church service endurable, and the man who drinks six days in the week is not usually a saint. It is not rational to expect him to make his rest day a day of torment. But if he drinks he will drink more than on another day. He has more time to drink, and other men have more time to drink with him. He has nothing else to do. There is less risk if he takes "a drop too much." He will not mash his hand under a trip hammer nor fall into a kettle of molten iron on Sunday. He can take time to sleep it off.

If we allow drinking on the six days, we may be pretty sure it will go on, in some way, on the seventh. The appetite which is roused up to Saturday night is not going to be suddenly balked on Sunday. The only way to make Sunday closing a real success is to begin it on Monday morning, and keep it up all the week.

So the twenty-five cents a day will be at least $91.25 for the year, and more probably will be fifty cents on Sunday, making the yearly amount more than $100. The man who spends that will not be a very heavy drinker, either. Five glasses of beer a day, one after breakfast, one at "eleven o'clock," one after dinner, another after supper, and one more somewhere along in the evening. No one will ever see him drunk, and he will pride himself on his self-control and self-denial. But his hundred dollars will be gone all the same. This is the moderate drinker's outlay.

E. E. Hale gives in the *Chatauquan* of May, 1886, the following estimate:

"On an average in Massachusetts, in 1883, a thousand dollars would be cut up thus:

Groceries	$295.20
Provisions	197.60
Fuel	43.00
Dry goods	20.00
Boots, shoes, etc.	36.30
Clothing	103.20
Rent	197.40
Sundries	107.30
Total	$1,000.00

Now suppose our moderate drinker to be doing better than the average laboring man, and earning his $1,000. In that case he just about spends his "sundries" for drink. That means that he will never become a man of property. He will always be in the grind. He will never own so much as a house and lot. Lord Derby recently gave to English workingmen an impressive lesson on this subject. He said: "They would all, of course, like to be land owners. Estimating the value of an acre of fertile land at £60, the price of a square yard of land would be about threepence." "I wonder," said Lord Derby, "how many workingmen consider that when they order threepenny worth of beer or spirits they are swallowing down a square yard of good agricultural land?"

That for land at $300 an acre. In this country, where choice land can be bought at from $10 to $50, the amount would be much greater. At $16 an acre—for which many good Western farms are now selling—a man would swallow just one square rod of fertile land with every ten-cent drink. Or, to turn the matter another way, the country is full of pretty villages where $200 to $500 will buy a nice lot. For the $100 drink money which the man may save the next year after his lot is paid for, a building association will put up a house for him on the instalment plan. Then he at once saves his rent, $197.40, and can apply that on payment for his house, and it will not be long before it will be his own. This thousands of mechanics actually do in the suburbs of our manufacturing towns. But a workingman cannot drink and do it.

P. A. Burdick, the gifted lecturer, tells the following interesting story:

While engaged in a temperance campaign in the town of B—, I called into a wagon shop to see a man who had signed the pledge, and was introduced by him to one of the wood workers. He was a moderate drinker. During the conversation he said: "I would like to know how it is that Mr. D. has paid for a home worth $1,200, has sent his three children to school for four years, and has a $1,000 United States bond. We have worked here together in this shop for fifteen years. He has received only $2 per day and I $2.50. I can't understand how he has a home and $1,000 at interest and I have neither."

"Don't you save anything of your wages?"

"No; sometimes at the end of the year I am $35 ahead, and sometimes the same amount in debt."

"Have you any children?"

"No."

"Do you drink?"

"Not much; only beer, and I buy that by the quart, so I get it cheaper than by the glass."

"How much do you use a day?"

"You see that pail? Well, I get that full twice each day, and it costs me twenty-five cents a pail. It don't amount to much."

"Do you get your pail filled on Sunday?"

"Yes, just the same as week days."

"Now, if you will multiply 365, the number of days in a year, by fifty cents, you will see that it does amount to something. It amounts to $182.50."

"Well, that is so. I never reckoned it up before."

"Do you use tobacco?"

"Yes, smoke and chew both. I get my box filled every morning, which costs five cents, and smoke three five-cent cigars a day. I wonder how much that amounts to?"

"We can soon tell. It is 365 multiplied by 20, the amount spent each day, and it amounts to $73 a year."

"Then both amount to $255?"

"Yes, sir, you are correct. Is there any other habit you indulge?"

"I don't know whether you would call it a habit, but I never work on Saturday. I take that as a holiday."

"How do you celebrate your holiday?"

"Well, I might just as well make a clean breast of the whole matter: I generally sit in the bar-rooms; play now and then a game of 'Pedro' for the beer to 'amuse the boys.'"

"How much do you think 'amusing the boys' costs you every Saturday?"

"Oh, half a dollar I guess would cover it."

"Did you know it cost you $3 each Saturday instead of fifty cents?"

"No, I can't see it so."

"Let me show you. If you should work every Saturday you would earn $2.50; you would have this amount Saturday night in your pocket. Now if you don't work you are short $2.50. Not only that, but the fifty cents you spend to 'amuse the boys' coming out of Friday's wages. Do you see it?

"Now we will sum up the whole business:

For beer, one year	$182.50
For tobacco "	73.00
For lost time "	131.00
For 'amusing the boys,' one year	26.00
Total	$412.50

"If you had saved this sum every year and put it in a savings bank at six per cent. interest, how much would you have now, do you suppose?"

"I have no idea; I can now see why Mr. D. has laid up money, for he neither drinks, uses tobacco, nor plays cards. He works every day. Will you figure it out, Burdick? I am anxious to know just how big a fool I have been."

I had done all the figuring on a pine board in the shop. He stood looking over my shoulder all the time, muttering to himself. The amount astonished him. It amounted to $9,676.07—enough to astonish any man. He said, "Bring out your pledge, put it all in, liquor, tobacco, and cards! I want the whole or none. Almost

$10,000 I have squandered, and never dreamed I was the only one to blame."

He had the pine board framed and hung up over his work bench. He shows it to every one who comes in, and asks them, "How is it with you?"

There are thousands of men who are thoughtless and careless in regard to their interest, and then curse "ill luck," "fate," etc., where no one is blameable but themselves.

What the actual cost of drink is to men who are not "moderate" may be seen by the following estimate from the New York *World* of February 24th, 1890, giving the expense of what it calls a "jag" on Washington's Birthday:

"Every hotel bar, every club, every saloon was filled all day with those who came to moisten their clay and were in no hurry to quit such pleasant work. Let us look at the cost of a modest Wall Street man's two-day celebration:

WASHINGTON'S BIRTHDAY.

Wine at luncheon	$1 75
Wine at dinner	5 00
Cordials	50
Nips, bracers, cocktails, refreshers, occasional moisteners and sundries before dinner	7 00
Things to drink before bedtime	15 00

SUNDAY.

Bs and Ss	1 00
Revivers, headache-chasers, antipyretics, fog-killers, and brain-dusters	3 25
Wine at meals	3 00
Sober second thought before bedtime	75
Total	$37 25

"These figures are for only one man's drinking. Wall Street men pay more for their jags than club men. A clerk on say $8 a week would pay for his two days' jag about this way:

WASHINGTON'S BIRTHDAY.

Treating, five rounds, say five men each time.... $2 75

SUNDAY.

Working the growler............................ 50

Total $3 25

"The poor mechanic who has a large family to support and feels the necessity of cheering up a bit in honor of G. W., chases the duck, hunts the fox, flies the pigeon, and works the growler at intervals during Saturday and Sunday. It costs ten cents to fill the can, and it makes probably ten trips on Saturday and six on Sunday, so his jag costs only $1.60 for two days. Poor men can't afford cocktails next morning. Possibly the broker and the club man add to the cost of their two days' moisture by three brandies and sodas at $1.50 this morning. At all events, the figures given above are modest and cheap for a two days' jag."

That $1.60 from the "poor mechanic's" meagre wages means untold misery to the "large family" sorely needing every cent.

Laboring men who do not drink should know that every drinking man cheapens the labor of all other men. In the intervals of his sprees he can do for many years almost as good work as a sober man. No employer, however, really wants him, because "there is no dependence to be placed on him." He has one obvious resource. He must live; something is better than nothing; he will sell his labor for what he can get—perhaps two-thirds, perhaps half what would otherwise be its market price. When there are many such men afloat in the community, they bring down the whole price of labor in that community. The sober man asks for reasonable wages. The employer answers, "I can get plenty of men to do the work for half that money." Tell him they will not be steady, and he answers,

"When they fall out, there are plenty more to step in." So the sober man, by no fault of his own, finds his wages cut down nearly, if not quite, to the drinker's level. His chief advantage is that he spends what he does get better. But he does not get what he would if this low-priced labor were out of the market. The drinker, with his recklessness of family and the future, and his spending to the last cent, is a slave. He must take what he can get, and with such treatment as happens to come along with it. The market is full of this slave labor, and sober workmen suffer in consequence, as free labor always suffers where slave labor prevails.

From the moment a man owns a house and lot or has money in the savings-bank he becomes more than a mere laborer; he is a capitalist. He experiences the comfort of poor Richard's quaint saying: "Now that I have a cow and pig every one bids me good-morrow." It is not only better for him but for the country. The man who owns something has a stake in the welfare of society and the maintenance of public order.

A reporter for the Cleveland *Leader* spent a day interviewing Socialist agitators. He found that one of their leaders had given up his connection with them and had not attended their meetings for over two months. "Why did you leave them?" was asked of him. "Well, it cost me too much money, and I couldn't afford it. I had to associate with our members and look after them. They usually stay in saloons, and every time I entered one it cost me ten cents or a quarter. The men frequent saloons because they have no place else to go. They go there and talk over their grievances." Note the fact, which is universal in Chicago and New York as well, that the Communists and Anarchists "usually stay in saloons;" that every man who enters is expected to drink at a cost of "from ten cents to a quarter;" that "they go there and talk over their grievances" while swallowing down, at the rate of a square rod for every drink, the means which might make every one of them a capitalist, with no special "grievances" to talk about. So far from its being the fact that "they go there (to the saloons) because they have nowhere else to go," the real fact is, that they have nowhere else to go because they go there. It is interesting to note where this man, who "could not afford" to be an Anarchist, lived.

"He led the way to the sitting-room, a cosey, well-furnished apartment, and invited the reporter to a seat in an easy-chair beside a burnished base-burner. The reporter was somewhat surprised to find a Socialist in such pleasant environments. The wife was entertaining a group of young friends in an adjoining room, and several bright-faced little children were playing about the premises."

Ah, yes. He "couldn't afford it." But if he had just kept on affording it, he would have swallowed his base-burner and easy-chair and the rest of the pretty things. His wife and children would have been "bright-faced" no longer. They would have moved into some mean dwelling, and he would have gone to the saloon "because he had nowhere else to go," and "discussed his grievances," because they would have been all he had left.

Or look at it in another way. The man who spends all his earnings is constantly on the verge of pauperism. Let us not be hard on those who have to do it—the minister who must keep up the state of a professional man on the pay of a day laborer, the young clerk whose last cent is needed to support a widowed mother and younger children. Such cases are occasion for sympathy and regret. But the voluntary wasting of a surplus is matter for downright condemnation.

If such a man jams his hand, or sprains his ankle, or has an attack of sickness, at once he begins to run in debt. If he has been given to other extravagances, he may retrench, pay his debts, and get square with society again. But if his extravagance has been drink, in that he will never retrench; but the more "blue" his circumstances, the darker his prospects, the more he will drink, as long as there is anything to buy the drink with. So, on the first inroad of misfortune the drinking man goes down a step in the ladder over which there is no return. *When liquor once downs a man it always tightens its grip.*

The use of his surplus for drink is one of the most supremely selfish things a man can do. It is to deny his family everything but bare subsistence. No self-respectful woman would marry him if he were to say at the outset: "I will furnish you lodging, food, clothing, and fire, and I expect to drink up the rest." Yet that is exactly the status to which the wife of many a moderate drinker finds herself reduced, while no one thinks of the family as destitute or suffering, or of the husband as intemperate.

Every last atom of margin goes to the saloon. The man is cross at being asked for an extra penny for home, because he needs it all for the drinks which he don't know how to live without. The very man who has the reputation—in the saloon—of "such a generous fellow," "so good-hearted," will be snappish and savage if his wife asks him for twenty-five cents, because his "good heart" has led him to spend that on himself and "the good fellows" who drink with him. Then if she isn't cheerful, he is pitied—"such a good fellow," and "such a gloomy, melancholy wife." Let him take his hundred dollars of drink-money and spend it in being "a good fellow" *to her* for a spell, and see whether she'll be gloomy. He can get as bright a smile as ever he had in the days of their courtship, if he thinks it worth more than to be slapped on the back by a coarse man whose beer he has just paid for.

Do you say this is moonshine? Well, lovers are fond of moonshine, and in happy homes they never quite outgrow it. Try a little moonshine. Bring all your week's wages home, and then ask your wife to walk down street with you and buy what she most wants, and as you catch glimpses of her face in light and shadow on the way, see if moonshine isn't beautiful.

In my own experience of reform work, where some hundreds of men have been induced to sign the pledge and reform—for a while, at least—the change in the men was not more striking than the brightness, cheer, and youthfulness that dawned upon the faces of mothers and sisters, daughters and wives.

A young father, just as he was going out in the evening, was met by his little daughter, begging, "Oh papa, won't you buy me one of those pretty hoops for half a dollar? All the girls have them, and they are so nice." "Half a dollar for a hoop!" he answered. "You must think I'm made of money. No, indeed; I can't afford it."

The little one began to cry, "Oh papa, if you only could! I want it so much, and all the girls have them."

"Well, I can't help that. I've no money for such things. Get a hoop off that old barrel in the back yard. That will be just as good."

And he lit a cigar and walked off down street. He went into a nice respectable billiard-room, with saloon attachment, of course. A number of pleasant acquaintances were there. He played several games, with the odds rather against him, and had the liquor and cigars to pay for, amounting to a dollar and a quarter. He paid it with smiling good-nature, "like a man," and walked back home in the pleasant summer evening. Near his home he overtook a crying child. It was his little Grace sideling against the wall. The other children had all made fun of her "old hoop," and she was stealing home broken-hearted, trying to hide it from observation. The man had not drank enough to deaden his finer feelings. It came to him with a sharp pang that he had spent on his own pleasure more than twice the money he had just denied his loved little daughter, and sent her out disappointed to be sneered at, crushed and ostracized in her little world. He caught her up in his arms, flung the old barrel hoop to the middle of the street. "It's not too late yet," he said; "come and show me where they keep those hoops, and you shall have the nicest one there is in the store."

"Oh papa, can you? Do you have the money now?"

"Yes," he said; "I have the money now."

The little one went to bed happy, but it was long before the father slept. That tear-stained face and shrinking figure kept coming before him, and he saw how in a thousand ways his "I can't afford it" to his dear ones had simply meant "I want it for my own self-indulgence." The sharp regret made him a temperance man.

Since writing the above, we have come upon the following incident, which the Philadelphia *Methodist* vouches for as "a true story."

"Papa, will you please give me fifty cents for my spring hat? 'Most all the academy girls have theirs."

"No, May; I can't spare the money."

The above request was persuasively made by a sixteen-year-old maiden as she was preparing for school one fine spring morning. The refusal came from the parent in a curt, indifferent tone. The disappointed girl went to school. The father started for his place of business. On his way thither he met a friend, and, being hail fellow well met, he invited him into Mac's for a drink. As usual, there were others there, and the man that could not spare his daughter fifty cents for a hat treated the crowd.

When about to leave he laid a half-dollar on the counter, which just paid for the drinks.

Just then the saloon-keeper's daughter entered, and going behind the bar, said: "Papa, I want fifty cents for my spring hat."

"All right," said the dealer, and taking the half-dollar from the counter, he handed it over to the girl, who departed smiling.

May's father seemed dazed, walked out alone, and said to himself: "I had to bring my fifty cents here for the rumseller's daughter to buy a hat with, after refusing it to my own daughter. I'll never drink another drop."

And he kept his pledge.

It is easy to see how a man who goes on hardening himself in this selfishness for years, denying his family all but bare subsistence for his own gratification, becomes at length capable of denying them even that, when his drinking habits have reduced his income, and the drink has become a mightier need.

This using the surplus for drink means that the wife and mother shall have no domestic help. Why, that hundred dollars would pay the wages of a girl at $2 a week, and save many a burdened woman from a broken constitution and perhaps from an early grave. If she could even hire an occasional day's work. But no, she must drag herself out weak and faint to do the family washing, while the husband genially swallows in five drinks of whiskey the money that would pay a strong woman for doing it. Fine, generous, good-hearted fellow!

The drink-money of the nation would employ—in the proportion in which other money is spent—ninety-four thousand domestic servants and eleven thousand laundresses. Pretty hard for the mother who has been up all night with a sick baby, and then has to wash dishes, cook, sweep, dust, and mend all day, taking care of the baby and feeding it from her own breast besides. How some of that drink-money would lighten her burden!

Then those hundred thousand women who should be employed in domestic work must crowd into the labor market among the men, bringing down wages by the irresistible laws of trade—a heavy economic loss. If the matrons of America were able to employ all the domestic help they really need, that would go far to solve the problem of the starvation wages of women workers.

To spend all he earns as fast as he earns it makes the laboring man perfectly helpless in a strike. The first day that work stops destitution begins. Ten thousand men are ten thousand times worse off than one. If it was only the one, the ten thousand might scrimp a trifle and support him. But when they all stop, they all begin to go down at once. The more men there are on a sinking ship the sooner it will go to the bottom. Hence, Mr. Powderly says: "Strong drink is the greatest enemy the laboring man has. The saloon and not capital has crushed every labor organization that has gone down heretofore, and there is no hope for the laboring man who persists in frequenting drinking places." It is noteworthy that the most successful strike in many years is that of the dock laborers of London, whose leader, John Burns, is an ardent temperance man, and used all his powerful influence to keep the workingmen temperate. The strike was disgraced by no act of violence, and the victory was absolute. They gained all they asked.

If all this is true of the moderate drinker on handsome wages, what must be the case of the host who are not moderate and upon scanty wages?

They are the great majority. From them the liquor traffic derives its chief profits. To sustain its invested capital, its vast establishments, and its present income, the liquor traffic needs drunkards; not, indeed, those who have got where they can't earn, but those who can still work and earn, though they can neither drink moderately nor quit drinking. These are to the liquor traffic what cows are to the dairyman. The cows work all day eating the grass which the dairyman can't eat, and wouldn't if he could. Then they come in at night and deliver him the milk. These mechanics and laborers work all day, and then come and deliver the money to the saloon-keeper, who very likely couldn't do their work if he would, and certainly wouldn't if he could. It's easier to have them work and he get the money.

He has such a mastery over them as no Legree ever had over his slaves. He needs no bloodhounds to keep them from running away.

They see that he is growing rich and they are growing poor, and they know it is their money that is doing it, but they bring it to him faithfully still. While each of them gets for hard work the wages of one man, the saloon-keeper without any work gets the wages of a hundred men. But there is no rebellion. It never occurs to one of them to say, "I'll quit feeding this lazy scoundrel and keep my own money." No, indeed. The bronzed toiler sits down in the den of his lily-handed, iron-hearted master, hands over to him his wife's dinner, and his children's shoes, and the very rent money, which alone stands between him and the street, and talks grandly about his "personal liberty." And the bar-keeper smiles upon him. No wonder! Such an idea of "liberty" will be ranked in history as one of the most amazing delusions that ever gained power over the human race.

Mr. Powdery, in a speech before the General Assembly of the Knights of Labor, said :

"The temperance question is an important one, and I sometimes think it is the main issue. The large number of applications during the past year to grant dispensations to allow the initiation of rum-sellers was alarming. I have persistently refused them, and will enjoin my successor, if he values the future success of the order, to shut the door with triple bars against the admission of the liquor dealer. His path and that of the honest, industrious workingman lie in opposite directions. The rumseller who seeks admission into a labor society does so with the object that he may entice its members into his saloon after the meetings close. No question of interest to labor has ever been satisfactorily settled over a bar in a rum hole. No labor society ever admitted a rumseller that did not die a drunkard's death. No workingman ever drank a glass of rum who did not rob his family of the price of it, and in so doing committed a double crime, murder and theft. He murders the intellect with which the Maker hath endowed him. He steals from his family the means of sustenance he has earned for them. Turn to the annals of every dead labor society, and you will see whole pages blurred and destroyed by the accursed footprints of rum. Scan the records of a meeting at which a disturbance took place, and you will hear echoing through the hall the maudlin, fiendish grunt of the brute who disturbed the harmony of the meeting."

In a circular since issued he uses these emphatic words :

"To our drinking members I extend the hand of kindness. I hate the uses to which rum has been put, but it is my duty to reach down and lift up the man who has fallen a victim to the use of liquor. If there is such a man within the sound of the secretary's voice when this is read, I ask him to stand erect on the floor of his Assembly, raise his hand to Heaven, and repeat with me these words : 'I am a Knight of Labor. I believe that every man should be free from the curse of slavery, whether the slavery appears in the shape of monopoly, usury, or intemperance. The firmest link in the chain of oppression is the one I forge when I drown manhood and reason in drink. No man can rob me of the brain my God has given me unless I am a party to the theft. If I drink to drown grief, I bring grief to wife, child, and sorrowing friends. I add not one iota to the sum of human happiness when I invite oblivion over the rim of a glass. If one moment's forgetfulness or inattention to duty while drunk brings defeat to the least of labor's plans, a life-time of attention to duty alone can repair the loss. I promise never again to put myself in such a position.' If every member of the Knights of Labor would only pass a resolution to boycott strong drink so far as he is concerned for five years, and would pledge his word to study the labor question from its different standpoints, we would then have an invincible host arrayed on the side of justice."

To his words, we may add those of another leader of workingmen, P. M. Arthur, Chief of the Brotherhood of Locomotive Engineers, who says :

"If I could, I would inaugurate a strike which would drive the liquor traffic from the face of the earth."

CHAPTER XX.

THE BEST CUSTOMERS.

"There was every element of trade prosperity present except the buying element, but, unfortunately, that element, instead of applying itself to the purchase of the goods that filled the warehouses, wasted its resources at the public-house: for instance, £24 per head (about $120) were spent yearly in drink, and but 8s. (about $2) on cotton goods, and so the people were in poverty and rags, and manufacturers could find no market for their goods."—*London Economist,* 1876.

If one man absorbs the wages of one hundred men, he does not give back to society their purchasing power. He can only wear one pair of shoes and one suit of clothes at one time. They must wear one hundred pairs and one hundred suits at the same time. He can only live in one house. They must have one hundred. He can only eat one man's rations. They, if they did not spend their money to fatten him, would eat one hundred times as much. If we allow the military rate of five women, children, and aged persons to every able-bodied man, saloon-keeper included, the disparity becomes still greater. It is then 500 to 5. That is, there will be 495 more persons to spend the wage-money in the general market if none of it is spent in the saloon. It seems self-evident that more will be spent and more goods bought.

"Ah, but," says some one, "the saloon-keeper will buy a better quality."

True, and just here is one of the most amusing economic errors in the minds of sensible people. The present writer once applied to a furnishing goods dealer in behalf of a temperance paper.

"Why," said the proprietor, "liquor men are my best customers. Just before you came in a saloon-keeper was here and bought four suits of silk underwear. I don't know a temperance man in town that would do that." "No," we replied; "they don't have so much of other people's money to do it with." But, even so, was that a gain to trade?

Let us say the saloon man paid $16 a suit for his silk underwear. There was $64. Suppose one hundred of his customers had kept their money and bought what they needed. They wouldn't have bought silk, but red flannel at $2 for shirt and drawers, $4 for two suits. That is not much. John Doe would not get much genial courtesy from the store-keeper for a little matter like that. And if Mr. Grossbier came in to look at silk underwear, John might stand and fumble over the pile of red shirts till he was tired.

But, all the same, John is the best buyer, because there are more of him. One hundred workingmen for their red flannel suits will spend $400 against the saloon-keeper's $64 for silk. If the profit on the silk goods is 50 per cent. of the retail price, that will be $32. The profit on the woollens would be 25 per cent. of the selling price, or $100 on the two hundred suits.

That is, there would be more than three times as much profit on the workingmen's trade as on the saloon-keeper's in this single line. True, we must deduct something for clerk hire, for it will take more clerks to sell and handle the two hundred woollen suits than the four silk ones. But *that means employment* for promising young men and prosperity for the community. So it will take more drayage, more railroad transportation, etc., all which means employment and work for somebody, and it will take more than three hundred pounds of wool to make those two hundred suits, employing many more hands in factory, on farm, and all the way along the line. This is but one item. Suppose the same saloon-keeper gets him a custom-made suit for $35, and the workingmen only buy ready-made suits at $12 each. Still their purchases amount to $1,200 against his $35. Even if he indulges quite freely in changes of raiment, still he would hardly buy more than three suits to their one—if they kept their money to buy with. Even at that rate, their purchases would be more than ten times his.

In the food market the difference is still more striking. Bishop Vincent, in his spicy and beautiful " Home Book," p. 526, gives the following incident :

"A coal miner in Pennsylvania quit work on a Saturday night, treated the boys at the saloon, went to the butcher's shop, and stood aside while the saloon-keeper bought a roast for Sunday's dinner and a sirloin steak for Monday's breakfast. The miner took two pounds of liver. The following Monday the miner made a speech to his fellow-miners, and they agreed to buy no beer for a week at the saloon. They kept their word. Next Saturday the miner went to the butcher's shop. The saloon-keeper came in, and the miner stood one side. The saloon-keeper said that, as business had been very dull, he would take liver for his Sunday dinner and Monday breakfast. The miners took roasts and steak. Which is the better for the butcher, the farmer, the merchant —one roast and forty livers, or one liver and forty roasts ?"

The wife of the man who bought the silk underwear will buy a silk dress at, say, $30, with laces and trimmings for perhaps $20 more. How she will be waited on! The workingman's wife—when he don't drink—will buy a simple dress at twenty-five cents a yard. Her modest purchase will be, all told, about $5.

Her custom is not worth much. But let the procession in! One hundred plain dresses—$500 against $30. Still the working classes are far ahead.

Now let us take Dr. Hale's table and double all amounts for the prosperous saloon-keeper, allowing him to spend $2,000 where $1,000 is a fair average income. He will then spend for

Groceries	$590.40
Provisions	395.20
Fuel	86.00
Dry goods	40.00
Boots, shoes, and slippers	72.60
Clothing	206.40
Rent	394.80
Sundries	214.60
	$2,000.00

Now let us take the one hundred workingmen. Many of them will not earn $1,000 a year. Some will earn more. A good stone-mason will earn $4 a day. Numbers of machinists earn their $3 and $4 a day. But we will average the one hundred men at $2 a day for three hundred working days, or $600 each a year. They are quite ordinary people, you see, in very moderate circumstances. But do you observe, they will have $60,000 to spend? This, according to Dr. Hale's table, will be divided as follows:

Groceries	$17,712
Provisions	11,856
Fuel	2,580
Dry goods	1,200

Boots, shoes, and slippers	2,178
Clothing	6,192
Rent	11,844
Sundries	6,438
	$60,000

That is, allowing the saloon-keeper to spend $2,000 where $1,000 is an average income, and allowing each laboring man to spend but $600 where $1,000 is an average income, still one hundred workingmen are worth to trade as much more than one prosperous saloon-keeper, as $60,000 is more than $2,000. To the grocer that means sales—in round numbers—of $18,000, instead of $600; to the boot and shoe dealer $2,000, instead of $75; to the clothing store $6,000, instead of $200; to real estate owners, rents of $12,000, instead of $400. Which is best for the business of that town and for every man in it who has anything to sell?

Let us contrast it in another table:

	100 Workingmen.	1 Saloon-keeper.
Groceries	$17,712	$590.40
Provisions	11,856	395.20
Fuel	2,580	86.00
Dry goods	1,200	40.00
Boots, shoes, etc.	2,178	72.60
Clothing	6,192	206.40
Rent	11,844	394.80
Sundries	6,438	214.60
	$60,000	$2,000.00

It is probably not in human nature for the grocer to help feeling a little more complacency toward the man who buys $600 worth during the year than toward the man whose purchases amount to only $175. But when the hundred workingmen spend almost $18,000, they are the best customers.

The balance of trade is in their hands. On the economic basis only, leaving humanity out of the question, the most important thing is to take care of the workingmen. If you want your town to prosper, look out for the workingmen. See that they get their full pay and that nobody cheats them out of it—that they are neither oppressed, degraded, nor discouraged.

Fire the saloon-keeper and lose his $2,000 in trade. If he offers you $1,000 for a license, send that along with him. You will be $3,000 out, but your grand force of workingmen with their $60,000 will quickly make that good.

"Oh, oh, oh!" exclaims a critic, "you're wild as a hawk. Those men would never spend their $60,000 for liquor. Why, they couldn't. They will have to live somewhere, eat something, and have some kind of clothes on. No ordinary saloon-keeper gets any such income as that would allow, either."

Well, all right. But where does the money go?

Take any one of those men with his $600 a year, temperate and industrious.

He is always respectably dressed, suitably to his work. You never think of pitying him. His wife and children are neatly clad. They are well fed, with color in their cheeks and light in their eyes. His plain little home is comfortable. His pastor or employer can go in and sit down with no sense of wretchedness. What he buys at the grocer's or provision dealer's he buys as independently as a millionaire. They are glad to see him come in. If a fellow-workman is hurt, this man will have a spare dollar to help make up a purse for him.

Now let him take to drink, and in a little while tell me what has happened. A slouchy, ragged, dirty laborer, his wife and children with faces pinched and dress forlorn, his home squalid. His wife steals into the grocery, and a hard gleam comes into the grocer's eyes the moment he sees her. She makes some poor little purchases, and the grocer charges them with a savage resignation, almost wishing he could be harder-hearted. The man shambles into the meat market, and though he comes first, "stands aside," as in Dr. Vincent's story, to let the saloon-keeper buy, and then takes his soup-bone or liver. What has happened? Where has the money gone? The question reminds one of the Hindu problem, Where is the flame of a candle after it is blown out? Query about it as you will, there stands the fact that for all practical purposes the purchasing power of that family is destroyed. I have repeatedly seen this process gone through in less than three years.

Doubtless much is spent for tobacco in the expensive form of cigars along with the drink. Much is gambled away at billiards and cards in the saloon or in some adjoining resort. Much is to be charged to lost labor while on sprees or recovering from them. But the amount spent outright for drink is more than most people are willing to believe. A reformed man remarked to the author not long since: "If I had stopped years before I did I should be better off now. When I was drinking, it was nothing for me to step into a saloon in the morning and spend $5 before I came out." Mr. Sims, in his paper on "Horrible London," says:*

"It is only when one probes this wound that one finds how deep it

---

* Quoted by Gustafson, "Foundation of Death," p. 254.

is. Much as I have seen of the drink evil, it was not until I came to study one special district, with a view of ascertaining how far the charge of drunkenness could be maintained against the poor as a body, that I had any idea of the terrible extent to which this cause of poverty prevails."

Else how do you explain it that a man who has worked for weeks in a Local Option town and is paid $40 on Saturday night goes to a "wet town" over Sunday "on a fearful drunk," comes back about Tuesday, and has to get trusted for a small sack of flour? Such cases are happening all the time, as every well-informed person knows.

So that, as a matter of fact, let the one hundred men whom we have seen to be earning their $600 a year each, and spending $60,000 in the aggregate—let them become confirmed drinkers, and in a very few years their trade will have practically disappeared. Then any live merchant will say: "I wouldn't give ten cents for the trade of the whole batch. I'd rather not be bothered with it." But that trade once meant great grocery stores with piled-up sacks of flour, barrels of sugar and crackers, and all kinds of supplies, and rows of clerks crowding each other to wait on the customers. It meant the meat market full of rows of hams, jars of lard, roasts and steaks and boiling pieces, and busy men behind the counter. It meant drays full of great cases of goods for the bustling dry-goods stores, shoe stores, and hat stores. It meant a comfortable, genial feeling of interest, confidence, and sympathy between employers and workers, buyers and sellers, and that general cheer that comes to everybody when everybody else is prospering.

Well, you've destroyed all that, and it won't take many clerks to wait on your saloon-keeper and his bartenders. Make much of that trade, for it's the most you'll get now. Hang on to his license fee, for you are going to need it badly to jail these laboring men when they "get into trouble" and to support their families while they are in the workhouse. "What fools these mortals be."

CHAPTER XXI.

THE TRADESMEN.

"IF in every eleventh year a fire should be kindled in the United States on the first of January, and continue burning till the last moment in December, and if every particle of our agricultural and manufactured products, as fast as they are produced, should be cast into the flames, and burned up until only the ashes remain, it would not inflict as much injury upon our people as is produced every eleven years by the use and sale of intoxicating drinks. The money expended for these drinks is not only lost, but the drinks entail upon our people the additional evils of vice, wretchedness, crime, and demoralization, that far, very far, outweigh the value of the money expended for them. If the products to the value of the money spent for drinks were only destroyed by fire or flood, it would not deprive our industrious classes of the mental and physical power to replace them, as do the things for which their hard-earned millions are expended. What nation or people, however favored, can long exist and prosper who expend or waste the value of so much labor for poisonous drinks? Can we wonder that we have money-panics, hard times, and stagnation of trade?"—*William Hargreaves, M.D.*

TRADE is the life of civilization. It is of no use to me that there are fifty million bushels of wheat in Dakota. I cannot charter a car to bring me a sack of flour. In fact, the wheat wouldn't be flour after I got it unless it went through a grist-mill. I want some man to buy that wheat by the thousand bushels. I want another man to run a grist-mill, turning out flour by the hundreds of barrels. I want a wholesale grocer to keep a warehouse, from which my retail grocer may order a hundred sacks and send me one when I am ready for it. I want railroads over which that wheat shall be transported before it is ground, and the flour transported afterward. I want laborers to build those roads, trackmen to walk them, engineers and conductors and brakemen to run the trains, coal to feed the engines, iron to make them of, miners to dig out the coal and iron, foundries and furnaces to melt that iron, rolling mills, locomotive and car works, and a host of machinists to make the rails and engines and cars that are to bring me my sack of flour. I need other factories to make the ploughs that break the ground, the drills that sow the wheat, the reapers and binders that harvest it, and the threshing machines that separate the grain. I need horses and wagons to work on the farms, to haul the wheat to the train and the flour across the city, and the delivery wagon that brings it to my door. I need harness-makers to make the harness for those horses, wheelwrights to make the wagons, and teamsters to drive them and to handle the goods. I need millwrights to build the grist-mills and keep them in repair, elevators and warehouses to store the grain and flour, and a good building for my grocer to keep store in. I want thousands of quarrymen to get out stone for those buildings and masons to set the stone, lime quarries to burn the lime for mortar and plastering, brick-yards to make brick by the million, and bricklayers to build the walls. I need carpenters to shape the timbers, build the roofs and floors and the thousands of wooden cottages that all these workmen will live in, and thousands of lumbermen in the forests of Maine and Michigan to fell the trees, and saw-mills to saw the lumber, engines to run those saw-mills, lumber-yards to keep the lumber in, and steamers, barges, and tugs on the lakes to bring it to the lumber-yards.

It sets a large part of the continent astir and employs an army of men to furnish me my sack of flour. The same is true of the chair I sit in, the paper I write on, and every article of furniture, food, and clothing in my house. The dollar and one-half I spend for my sack of flour sets all these thousand wheels of industry in motion, and never rests till part of it reaches the farms of Dakota and part of it the coal and iron mines of Pennsylvania. Nor does it rest then, for the farmers spend it, and the miners spend it, and it starts on again.

The same money is used over and over, like the water in a mill stream. The water comes to the first mill, and rushes through its great wheels, setting every shaft in that mill whirling. But the water does not stay in the wheels. If it did it would do no good. It is as necessary that it should rush out as that it should rush in, and when it comes out it comes with all its power in it. On it goes to turn the wheels of the next mill, and the next, and the next, the same water used over and over again, starting new machinery, giving employment to new hands all along its course. So if the nation saves its thousand millions of drink-money, that will not merely bless millions of homes and satisfy the immediate wants of those now intemperate, but the effect will be felt in all branches of industry. Saving $1,000,000,000 will not nearly describe the benefit, nor can we trace it to all its rich results. That thousand millions will be spent over and over again by each one to whom it comes, perpetually multiplying itself as it pays new labor and skill, which results in new wealth-production.

The immediate objection will be made by many that the same amount expended in liquors will employ just as many persons. The answer is that the liquor trades are a class by themselves, employing a remarkably small number of persons for the value of the product, whether at wholesale or retail. While the percentage of the wholesale value of the product expended for labor in all other industries is 17.87, in the liquor business it is only 10.45. The increase in the cost of liquor to the consumer over the wholesale price is something enormous—viz., from $144,000,000 at the manufactory (in 1880) to $734,000,000 as purchased by the consumers, or an increase of more than 400 per cent. Comparatively a small number of persons are engaged in handling the retail article. Dry goods, groceries, etc., differ greatly in quality and style. They require many persons to show them. They are also bulky, and require many persons to handle them. One thoughtful and innocent lady can tire out a dozen clerks and salesmen in an easy trip down a dry goods store, and leave them laboriously putting away long after she is gone. But liquors are small in bulk and limited in variety. A full supply can be kept behind a single bar, within reach of one man's hand. The appetites of the customers are sharp, clear, and exceedingly definite. The glass of beer is drawn in an instant, and the automatic fixture closes of itself. The whiskey is poured into the glass with a turn of the hand, the cork thrust into the bottle, the change swept into the till, and the sale is made. One man can wait on a crowd and scarcely stir from his place. It needs no package clerk to do up the bundle, no cash-boy to run with the change. The goods are gulped down on one side of the counter, the money is gulped down on the other, and the transaction is complete.

A bushel of corn for which the farmer gets thirty cents requires heavy ploughing, harrowing, planting, and cultivating in the hot sun, and, besides, cutting, binding, husking, loading, and hauling. A bar-keeper will stand in a comfortable room and sell to the farmer thirty cents' worth of whiskey in three minutes, with no other exertion than a sweep of his arm, and on that sale he will make a profit of 400 per cent. above the cost of production. Thus $1,000,000,000 expended for useful articles employ 433,000 persons, while expended for liquor, the same amount will employ but 41,000 persons in its production. Hence, it is easy to see that other trades stand no chance at all beside the liquor trade, and that when men of other callings trade with the saloon-keeper, he must gain a steady and heavy advantage, and that just so fast as he grows rich they must grow poor. By a liberal calculation, based on the brewers' own estimates and the census reports, it appears that the money invested in liquors employs, including all who raise the grain, etc., only one-ninth of the labor which the same amount would employ if spent for grist-mill products. The liquor traffic, therefore, cannot be averaged with any other business in computing the amount of labor employed in proportion to the amount sold.

Another objection will be that we have computed the amount spent for liquors on the retail basis, and the amount spent for other goods on the wholesale basis; that, in reality, the people would not be able to buy all these amounts of other products if they did not drink, because they could not buy at the wholesale prices, and at the retail prices they would get only one-half or at most three-fourths of the amount above given. This objection seems very reasonable at first thought. But on consideration it will appear that we have that amply provided for. In all this computation we have taken into account only the direct cost of the intoxicants, making no mention of the indirect, which, as we have seen, will be at least as much more. This restores the balance. If a man earns $15 a week and spends it on a spree, he will probably lose the next week's work as the result. That will be the same in cost to him as if he had worked both weeks and spent the $30. If he had not drunk the liquor and had worked steadily the two weeks he would have had the $30 to spend for useful articles, and it would have been so spent. So when we have found what the nation's thousand million dollars would buy at wholesale, we have still another thousand millions to compensate the retailers for handling the product and bringing it to every man's hand and door.

Then the money so spent is going to be used over and over again. The grocers will buy dry goods, and the dry goods dealers will buy groceries, and all will need boots and shoes, hats and caps. Everybody is the customer of everybody else. The two thousand millions once paid for useful articles will immediately start on again, keeping the great tide-mill of industry turning still.

Many incidental advantages will be found. The grocer's profits will not be merely in increased sales, but in increased receipts. People eat now. The judgment of charity leads the grocer to trust those who can be trusted with any show of reason. Then the saloon gobbles up the money, and the grocer is left with a string of bad debts.* In one city, the author was told of a single

---

* See Chapter XVII., p. 276, how the business men of Atlanta, over and over, tell of the danger of trusting and the difficulty of collecting "since the return of the bar-rooms."

firm of grocers, doing a large business, who had lost in this way $75,000 in fifteen years. The boarding-house-keepers meet the same fate—one of the most cruel forms of fraud, because most of them are needy and dependent women. A worker in a great machine establishment told me of several young men without families who earned $4 to $5 a day, when they worked, and would drink and gamble it all away as fast as received. "How do they live?" I asked. He answered: "They run up a bill at the boarding-house, and when the landlady won't trust them any longer they go to a new boarding-house, and she never can collect her bill, because they haven't anything. Fellows that live that way have to beat it out of somebody."

Then the community loses it. The landlady cannot buy the new dress for herself, the shoes and hats for her children, the new furniture, carpets, and bedding, the need of which is so manifest. Then, when she has to sell off her furniture to a second-hand dealer for a song, give up her house and leave town, there'll be one less good renter, one less good customer at the grocer's and the provision dealer's, and these men will be wondering what makes the hard times, and think probably it's because the tariff is too high, or not high enough. It is the far-reaching trail of the saloon-keeper.

But would this money be spent for useful articles if not for liquors? The answer is emphatically YES.

One little town I know that adopted local prohibition three years ago. It had then three saloons. There was an immediate change. The loafing crowds in the evenings disappeared. Croakers exclaimed, "The town is ruined." The liquor men urged on the cry and spread it to other places. Certainly the noisy evening crowds no longer thronged the sidewalks. The farmers' horses no longer stood hitched at all the posts through sun and rain and snow, for hours together. Several houses became vacant. One tenant removed his goods at dusk on a Sunday evening, for some mysterious reason, and started for a whiskey town. But soon a clothing dealer took one vacant saloon, tore out the interior, put in elegant fixtures, and a fine stock of goods. A grocer refitted another empty saloon. An enterprising young man started still another grocery on the cash plan, when for a long time there had been "too many groceries." But he prospered, because there was cash in the town to buy with. Soon a dry goods firm bought the building in the rear of their store, took out the partition, and made one room of the two in order to get space for their business. It was not long before they leased still another in rear of that. After the law had existed a year and a half, a Local Option contest in a neighboring town led us to look up the facts. The dry goods firm said: "If this is ruin, we are ready to be ruined right along in the same way for the next ten years. We have never done such a business. You have only to look around our store and see for yourself." On mentioning to them a report that former customers from the country were now taking their trade to other towns, they answered: "None that we know of that we care to keep. On the contrary, we are getting a new run of custom from the country around M—— (a whiskey town), and some of their very best—ladies who want to buy nice and expensive goods, and don't want to go through the kind of crowd that hangs around saloons in order to do it. They are driving down here now. They are coming to our town for their furniture, too." The merchant paused a moment, and then said: "The fact is, there's no money in a crowd that hangs around all the evening because they can get whiskey. *They don't buy anything but whiskey.* There's no money in a gang of farmers sitting around the saloons the best part of the day. If they stay at home and work their farms, then, when they do come to town, they'll have something to buy with."

The coal dealer said shortly: "Never had such good sales and so few bad debts. It stands to reason that if people don't buy whiskey, they'll have some money to buy something else with, and in this climate they're bound to keep warm." The clothing dealer, in the renovated saloon, said: "We've sold $3,000 worth more goods the past year than any year before of the ten years we've been here. If you wish, I'll show you our books." The new cash grocer said: "My business has done splendidly. I have the largest drayage in the place but one. I must get a larger room."

So it went on. Now, after three years, a new town-hall has been built, at an expense of $15,000. Wooden stores are being removed and fine brick buildings put in their places. A new furniture store has been opened and a new brick church built. All the other churches have been newly frescoed, and two of them have put in pipe organs. Fine new residences are springing up at commanding points and old ones are remodelled till they, too, seem new. Almost all the old stores and the majority of private residences have been newly painted, till the town looks like a new place of a higher and happier grade. Painters and paper-hangers cannot keep up with their orders. The former bar-keeper of one of the saloons has engagements as a paper-hanger for weeks in advance, and has built himself a new house. *But that liquor towns are too easily accessible across the borders,* this town would be enjoying almost unqualified prosperity. One of the council said : " Why, we used to pay our night police out of the fines, but now we have no fines to pay him with. We have to pay him out of the taxes. But we can afford to. We make enough more in other ways." The town has no trouble in keeping the back door of the saloons closed on Sunday since it shut the front door the rest of the week. An air of quiet prosperity and happiness pervades the whole town. Prohibition pays and pays well.

CHAPTER XXII.

THE FARMERS.

"REMARKABLE WILL.—A wealthy farmer of —— County has just died, bequeathing his whole property to the saloons and gambling houses of his native town. His four sons are made his executors, and there is no doubt of the entire amount reaching its destination."
—*Tennessee Paper.*

"There is a sore evil which I have seen under the sun—namely, riches kept for the owners thereof to their hurt. But those riches perish by evil travail: and he begetteth a son, and there is nothing in his hand."—*Eccl.* v., 13, 14.

RIDING one day through a fair and fertile valley of Ohio, among thrifty and beautiful farms, one house impressed me with sudden contrast. It was a grand old mansion with verandas before it, shade trees around, but with an indescribable air of decay, as if a blight so many acres square had fallen upon that one estate. The house had once been white, but the paint was worn away, except for a trace here and there, and the wood-work was black from exposure to the weather. The shingles of the roof lay in wind-rows. Quilts and hats and old clothes were stuffed in the broken windows, and some—where, apparently, there were not old clothes enough to fill them—were roughly boarded up. The fence was leaning and the gate was down; boards were entirely gone from the sides of the barn and others hung loose, flapping in the wind. "Who lives there?" I suddenly inquired. My companion gave me a name which told the whole story. The son of a wealthy man, inheritor of a splendid farm, himself a hard and skilful worker, but every little while brutally drunk. Whiskey had the same effect on his windows in the pure, beautiful country that it does upon the windows of the forlorn tenement-houses in the cities. It only needed to have the rest of the farmers like him to make that whole countryside desolate and dreadful.

Not long after I drove out on another road in the same section. There was a house of entirely different construction, a large and once opulent mansion of solid brick. But Desolation had sat down upon it. What ailed the grass? What ailed the trees? The very air around seemed murky and stifling. The pair of bony horses with sore backs, savagely twitching tufts of grass in the door-yard, laid back their ears and hung their under-lips with an air at once disreputable and defiant. Here, too, it only needed a name to tell the whole story— "a man mighty to drink wine, a man of strength to mingle strong drink." Unless something intervenes, neither of these farms will go down another generation in the same family. In fact, I have been told that one of these men is, even now, in the language of the country, "all broke up."

I once knew a very accomplished hostler. He knew Latin, French, and mathematics, and was well versed in English literature. He had graduated at West Point, and had held honorable and responsible positions. Two fine farms had come to him by inheritance. One day he went to a physician and said: "Doctor, I want you to examine my throat." The doctor did so, and replied: "I don't see anything wrong." "Don't you see anything down there?" "Nothing whatever."

"Well, you ought to see two good farms, for they've both gone down there." Think of the toil and sweat, the early rising, the miles tramped behind the plough, the wood-chopping and stump-grubbing, the acres swept by the old hand scythe, the ditches dug and tilled, the rails split and fences built to make out of the wilderness those two good farms for the heir to pour down his throat, or, more strictly, to give to the saloon-keeper for no consideration whatever.

A touching poem expresses the same thought:

SIGNING THE FARM AWAY.

Fine old farm for a hundred years
  Kept in the family name;
Corn-fields rich with golden ears
  Oft as the harvest came;
Crowded barn and crowded bin,
And still the loads kept coming in—
Rolling in for a hundred years;
And the fourth in the family line appears.

Orchards covered the slopes of the hill;
  Cider—forty barrels they say,
Sure in season to come from the mill,
  To be tasted around Thanksgiving Day!
And they drank as they worked and ate,
Winter and summer, early and late,
Counting it as a great mishap
To be found without a "barrel on tap."

But, while the seasons crept along,
  And passions into habits grew,
Their appetites became as strong
  As ever any drunkard knew.
And they labored less, and they squandered more,
Chiefly for rum at the village store,
Till called by the sheriff, one bitter day,
To sign the homestead farm away.

> The father, shattered and scented with rum :
>   The mother, sick and pale and thin,
> Under the weight of her sorrows dumb,
>   In debt for the bed she was lying in ;
> I saw the wrecked household around her stand—
> And the justice lifted her trembling hand,
> Helping her, as in her bed she lay,
> To sign the homestead farm away.
>
> Ah, how she wept, and the flood of tears
>   Swept down her temples bare !
> And the father, already bowed with years,
>   Bowed lower with despair.
> Drink ! Drink ! It had ripened into woe
> For them and all they loved below,
> And forced them, poor, and old, and gray,
> To sign the homestead farm away.
>
> Oh, many scenes have I met in my life,
>   And many a call to pray ;
> But the saddest of all was the drunkard's wife,
>   Signing the homestead farm away !
> Home, once richest in all the town,
> Home, in that fatal cup poured down,
> Worse than fire or flood's dismay—
> Drunkards signing the farm away !
>
> — Congregationalist.

I asked a man who has had extensive business dealings as a real estate and produce dealer in an agricultural district, How does intemperance hurt a farmer ? "Well," he answered, "if he goes to the saloon for his drinks, the loss of time is pretty heavy. Perhaps you'll see such a man's horses hitched in front of a saloon from early in the forenoon till along in the afternoon with nothing to eat. Then you may know that man's farm is running down, unless somebody else is doing the work. In any case, there's one man's wages lost, for that man won't do much work after he gets home. Then the money he spends is a good deal, even if he drinks at home. It amounts to more than you could make him believe, generally. But the worst thing is, it *hurts his judgment* about putting in crops, and about trading and dickering; and he always wants to be doing that when he isn't fit for it. Just those times he's always full of confidence, and thinks he knows it all, and anybody can take advantage of him."

"It hurts his judgment." How much that means! I met a stout farmer in town one rainy day with a very cheerful face. On my remarking about the storm, he replied: "I don't mind it a bit. I've got my oats in. Lots of 'em feel bad, though, because they haven't." A difference of a day or two in judgment of the most necessary thing to do made a difference in the result which they might chase in vain all summer.

At another time I myself importuned a Sunday-school superintendent, who was also a good farmer, to come to a Sunday-school picnic. He steadily refused, saying: "I can't do it. I've fifteen acres of clover hay that ought to be cut, and this dry weather has lasted so long that it won't last much longer. I must take care of my crops, if I'm to have anything to give to the church." He resisted all persuasion, went into that hay-field, and the day after the picnic ran his last load of hay onto the barn floor about fifteen minutes before a heavy storm, which was the beginning of three weeks of rainy weather. A little matter of judgment! If you could have got that man to take a little whiskey to distract, a few glasses of beer to stupefy, he would not have had the clear foresight. He would have gone, "like a good fellow," anywhere that promised to be agreeable. I believe my friend hit the nail on the head when he said, "The worst effect of drink on the farmer is that it hurts his judgment." No amount of hard work will make up for blunders of judgment.

We have come across a scrap which well illustrates how the liquor traffic throws the balance of toil and profit against the farmer:

THE COST OF A BUSHEL OF CORN.

There is a statistician about the Palmer House who desires to impress every one with economic facts. Said he recently to a Chicago reporter: "Do you see that man over there? Well, he's a farmer down near Elgin. There he goes with a friend; they are going to get a drink. The farmer will pay for it. Now, let me see. That man will sweat two mortal hours next spring to plough enough ground to raise one bushel of corn. The bushel of corn he will sell for thirty cents. He is going in there now to spend the thirty cents for two drinks. Therefore, the farmer and the corn have parted. Now let me tell you what becomes of the corn. A bushel of corn will make seventeen quarts of whiskey—four and one-quarter gallons. The distillery gets its first profit—forty cents a gallon. There you are—$2 for that bushel of corn. Now the Government comes in, ninety cents a gallon—$3.85 added to the $2 makes $5.85. That brings the product of the bushel of corn down to the jobber and the wholesaler, and finally, by several stages, to the retailer. By the time it reaches the latter the bushel of corn, or its product of four and one-quarter gallons, has been reduced one-half, which means eight and one-half gallons. There are sixty drinks to the gallon; that is the average; eight and one-half gallons mean five hundred and ten drinks, at fifteen cents each; there we have $76.50 as the consumer's price for a bushel of corn which the farmer raises and sells for thirty cents. Who says there is no industry in this country? But the farmer we saw just now spent his whole bushel of corn in the price of two drinks, and the people who did not till the soil get away with $76.15.

It is easy to see that at such a ruinous rate of competition the farmer cannot live. He cannot afford to sell his bushel of corn for thirty cents and buy it back again for $76.50. That is the whole problem.

"Anyway," one man says, "there's a deal of comfort in it, if it does cost dear." Yes, and there are many situations where there is nothing so bad as to feel comfortable. The man who is exposed in a bitter winter night at first suffers keenly. Ears and fingers and feet are stinging with pain. At length he gets all over it. He has no more pain. He has become perfectly comfortable. He will just lie down here out of the wind and rest a little while. Ah, that feeling comfortable means death! If he has a friend who is not so far gone, and who knows what it means, he will rouse him out of that comfort. He will shake him, force him to walk, rub his face and ears with snow till they tingle and burn like fire, beat his numb hands till the pain is almost unendurable. He will make him fearfully uncomfortable —and save him. There's many a farmer out in the pure, open country perfectly comfortable with a foul drain percolating into his well, till he and his family get the typhoid-fever. Pity he had not been worried about it enough to purify and sweeten things. No comfort for me, I thank you, in a freezing night or with a foul well! The comfort of whiskey and beer simply comes from paralysis—the paralyzing of all the finer nerves and sensibilities, till the man is not worried over the old clothes in the broken windows, the neglected crops, the empty pantry, nor the notes coming due which he can't pay. The best investment he could make would be a day of good, downright misery, with enough manhood left to fight the causes of misfortune by square, manly work, sober living, and honorable saving. Wait to be comfortable till the comfort is somewhere outside of your own stomach!

But we are told the liquor traffic is a real financial

benefit to the farmers in buying their grain. Where farmers have been accustomed to selling to brewery and distillery, they actually shiver at the question, "What will you do with your corn?"

A certain amount of grain is, undoubtedly, sold to brewers and distillers, and—what is especially attractive to farmers—sold for cash. Could the farming interest afford to lose the sale of that amount of grain? Let us see.

The following table was given in *The Voice* of May 9th, 1889 :

HOW THE LIQUOR TRAFFIC ROBS THE FARMER.

PROHIBITION WOULD PUT AT LEAST $18 IN HIS POCKET WHERE THE LIQUOR TRAFFIC PUTS IN $1.

Farmers of Pennsylvania, the enemies of Prohibition tell you that to do away with the liquor traffic will ruin the grain market and otherwise depress the interests of agriculture. Let us do a little figuring and see if this is true.

In 1886, according to the report of the Commissioner of Agriculture, the total value of all the products of the farms of the United States for that year, including the live-stock on them, was $6,127,805,932, as follows :

PRODUCTS OF THE FARMS, 1886.

Breadstuffs.

Corn,	1,665,441,000	bushels,	worth	$610,311,000
Wheat,	457,218,000	"	"	314,226,020
Oats,	624,134,000	"	"	186,137,930
Barley,	59,428,000	"	"	31,840,510
Rye,	24,489,000	"	"	13,181,330
Buckwheat,	11,869,000	"	"	6,465,120
Rice............................			"	5,000,000
Meats............................			"	748,000,000
Poultry products..............			"	186,000,000
Hides, hair, etc			"	93,000,000

Dairy products.

Butter			"	192,000,000
Cheese............................			"	32,000,000
Milk............................			"	156,000,000

Textile fibres.

Cotton	worth	$257,295,327
Wool	"	77,000,000
Hemp, flax, etc.	"	9,000,000

Vegetables.

Irish potatoes, 168,051,000 bushels,	"	78,441,940
Sweet potatoes	"	20,000,000
Peas and beans	"	13,800,000
Market-garden productions	"	68,000,000
Fruits	"	175,000,000
Hay, 41,796,499 tons	"	353,437,699
Tobacco, 532,537,000 lbs	"	39,082,118
Hops	"	3,500,000
Sugar, syrup, and honey	"	33,500,000
Clover and grass seed	"	15,000,000

Total.................................$3,717,218,994

The value of farm animals in 1887 was as follows:

Horses	12,496,774	worth	$901,685,755
Mules	2,117,141	"	107,057,538
Milch cows	14,522,083	"	378,769,589
Oxen and other cattle	33,511,750	"	663,137,926
Sheep	44,759,314	"	89,872,389
Swine	44,612,836	"	200,043,291

Total..................................$2,400,586,938

Estimating one-fourth of this $2,400,586,938, or in round numbers, $600,000,000, as the annual increase from the farm animals, the total products of the farms for the year 1886-87 therefore amount in round numbers to $4,317,000,000. What proportion of this value is due to the liquor traffic? Let us see.

FARM PRODUCTS WHICH GO TO MAKE LIQUOR.

During the year ending June 30, 1887, according to the report of the Commissioner of Internal Revenue, the following farm products were used in making distilled liquors:

Malt (from barley)	1,825,627	bushels.
Wheat	45,361	"
Barley	16,110	"
Rye	3,062,947	"
Corn	12,870,255	"
Oats	44,886	"
Mill feed	93,060	"

Other materials.................... 1,319 bushels.
Molasses......................... 2,428,783 gallons.

Total . ...17,959,565 bushels
and 2,428,783 gallons.

The same year 23,121,526 barrels of fermented liquors were made. It takes two bushels of malt, or their equivalents, and two pounds of hops to make a barrel of beer, according to Dr. Francis Wyatt, Director of the National Brewers' Academy. At this rate, about 24,800,000 bushels of barley, corn, etc., and 41,000,000 pounds of hops would be used in the manufacture of malt liquors, which, added to the materials used in making distilled liquors, makes in round numbers the total of the farm products consumed in the liquor business in the years 1886–87:

42,700,000 bushels of grain, worth. $2,300,000
Hops, worth in 1886 to farmers 3,500,000
2,428,782 galls. of molasses, worth to farmers 500,000

Total gain to farmers from liquor traffic...$25,300,000

But this $25,300,000 is *only about five and four-fifths one thousandths* of the annual value of the products of the farm. In other words, if the annual income of the average farmer be $500, about $2.93 of his income, estimating most favorably for the saloon, comes from the liquor traffic.

WHAT THE FARMER LOSES BY THE LIQUOR TRAFFIC.

Leaving out the question of the taxes the farmer pays to support the pauperism, crime, insanity, and other expenses caused by the saloon, Dr. William Hargreaves, the statistician, makes this estimate of the farmers' annual losses from the liquor traffic.

If the $900,000,000 which is every year spent for drink should be spent for the necessaries of life—food, clothing, etc.—as it would be spent under Prohibition, Dr. Hargreaves estimates that the yearly demands for the products of the farms would be increased as follows:

HOW PROHIBITION WOULD INCREASE THE DEMAND FOR FARM PRODUCTS.

Wheat ...83,274,484 more bush.
Corn......20,498,226 "   "
Oats...... 9,802,488 "   "   } worth to farmers $181,157,263
Rye....... 1,110,625 "   "
Buckwheat   444,461   "   "
Milk, butter and cheese from farmers, worth.......... 1,000,000

877,777 more beeves ⎫ 1,116,850 more sheep ⎬ worth to farmers............ 8,049,214 more hogs ⎭	$128,369,452
Cheese made in factories,109,942,175 more lbs. ⎫ to f'rm'rs Butter " " 18,710,892 " ⎬ for mat'ls	9,181,789
Fruit, vegetables, canned goods, etc. (to farmers for materials)	6,025,646
Wool for carpets, 29,800,438 more lbs., worth..........	3,487,564
Cotton, for cotton goods, 375,171,990 more lbs., worth..	43,477,862
Cotton, silk and wool, for mixed textiles, worth........	18,613,870
Wool, for woolen goods, 98,762,477 more lbs., besides washed wool and shoddy and other materials, valued at...	33,690,225
Wool for worsted goods, 33,891,972 more lbs., worth....	7,617,939
Total loss to farmers from liquor traffic..........	$432,621,610

There is no exaggeration in these figures, says Dr. Hargreaves. They are proportionate estimates based on the Census Report of 1880, and they by no means include all the products of the farm, an extra quantity of which the farmer would be called upon to supply should the liquor traffic become a thing of the past, and the tens of thousands of the underfed, under-clothed and ill-sheltered drinkers and their families spend the money for the necessaries of life instead of for liquor.

In the face of this extra $432,000,000 worth of products which the farmer would be called upon to supply under Prohibition, how insignificant appears the paltry $25,000,000 which he now receives from the liquor traffic, and which no one doubts he more than pays out in support of the paupers and criminals produced by the traffic?

Prohibition would put eighteen dollars in the farmer's pocket where the liquor traffic puts in one.

In a country like ours some new use could at any time be found for .58 of 1 per cent. of the total product. The remark of the Illinois farmer never loses its freshness, "We'd raise more hogs and less hell." A few more hogs or young cattle to fatten, a few more cows to milk, or even a good flock of chickens on every farm would dispose of that much.

But the answer is, "We could not get a living price for any of it if that much more was thrown on the general market, for we can't but just live now." The latter is true enough, unfortunately. But, strange to say, you could get a higher price for the whole crop than you can for what is left after selling to the brewers and distillers. We will prove it to you. Will a hungry man buy something to eat if he can get it? Will a poor mother buy food for her hungry children if she can get the money to pay for it? Well, suppose you shut off squarely the $1,000,000,000 which the nation now spends for whiskey and beer, isn't that money going to be spent for something? Won't the families of drinking men— won't the drinking men themselves, when they quit drinking, spend that money for clothes and food and similar articles?

There never should be hard times for the producers when millions of people are hungry for their productions, and there never would be if the hungry people had anything to buy with; and they would have if they did not spend their earnings for liquor. From an economic standpoint it is a monstrous spectacle that in the city there should be children crying for bread, and in the country farmers lamenting that there is no sale for their grain. That is what the liquor traffic does for the farmers.

IT DESTROYS YOUR MARKET.

Here is a city containing thousands of people to be fed. Around it are wide, rich farms, barns full of grain, and a great surplus stacked out in the field. What is the natural relief for the hungry city? To buy the farmers' grain. What is the natural relief for the farmers who so need money? To sell their grain to the hungry city. But now comes along a syndicate and says to the farmers: "We will buy one half of one per cent.

of your grain to carry out a plan we have of robbing that city. It's a brilliant scheme and sure to work. We will take from a large part of the population everything they have and everything they earn. We will share with you to the extent of one half of one per cent. of your total product, if you won't interfere."

The farmer replies, "But what shall I do with the other 99½ per cent. ?" The polite agent of the syndicate shrugs his shoulders and says : " I don't know anything about that. You'll have to sell it for what you can get. Those city people won't have any money after we get through with them." The farmers reply : " Take your half of one per cent. We don't want it ; and now you let those city people alone. Leave them their money and they'll buy our crop, and buy it all. They'll outbuy you a hundred to one." That's exactly the case of the liquor traffic. They buy one half of one per cent. of your grain, and then destroy the natural market for all the rest, depriving the people of their buying power.

The total grist-mill products of the United States, according to the census of 1880, were $505,000,000 in value, almost exactly one-tenth of the total products of all kinds of industries, $5,369,579,191. At the same rate, if our thousand millions of liquor money were spent for useful articles, one-tenth of that amount, or $100,000,000, would be spent for breadstuffs in addition to what is now expended for the same ; that is, instead of $25,000,000, which the farmers now receive for grain used for the destruction of life, health, and happiness, they would receive $100,000,000 for grain used to preserve life, health, and happiness.

Besides this, much of the amount spent for manufactured articles would come to the farmers of the country.

About $100,000,000 would be spent for woollen goods, clothing, bedding, carpets, etc., and to make these our manufacturers would need 118,000,000 pounds of domestic wool. This, at thirty cents a pound, would amount to more than $35,000,000.

The entire amount of foreign wool imported and entered for consumption in 1880, about which a national campaign has been fought, was but 97,231,277 pounds, valued at $14,062,100, on which the duties were $4,730,-000. In whatever way considered, the tariff shrinks into insignificance beside the great problem of the liquor traffic. The simple stoppage of the liquor traffic would create an immediate demand for American wool heavily in excess of the entire foreign importation. There is more money in temperance than there is in tariff.

Then, by spending $96,000,000 for cotton goods, there would be consumed 375,000,000 pounds, costing $43,000,-000. The South, which still feels poor from the great war, what does she say to getting an additional $43,000,-000 for cotton? She can get it by Prohibition.

There is one point in regard to which farmers need to be especially on their guard. The Brewers' Association, at their late meeting, decided to

"WORK THE CIDER RACKET ON THE FARMERS."

You may expect now all manner of encomiums on cider. You will find in your papers, most likely, very pleasant stories, in which the bluff old farmer treats his guests with cider from the big pitcher, and grows genial and mellow in the process; in which shy lovers sip it together; in which little children, in the bright sunshine and sweetness of the autumn fields, bring their tin cups and catch the new cider as it runs from the press; and the "barefoot boy" of Whittier's poem has a delightsome time sucking it through a straw. Wherever you find these things, just know the brewers' trade-mark is on them. However good the paper in which they appear, the sly, stealthy hand of the liquor traffic is behind them. Especially the patent insides are open to this kind of thing, where it only needs to make a contract with one man in Chicago or Cincinnati, and have the matter sent ready printed to thousands of country papers, many of whose editors will never look at what it contains. You may expect casual editorial remarks on the intolerance of Prohibitionists, who would even prohibit the farmer from making a little cider, and the good writer will lament their narrowness and bigotry, which alone keeps him from joining with them. And if you could see the writer, you would see that he is already carrying around about fifty pounds of protuberant beer, and writing this delicate moral squib to get money from the Brewers' Association to buy more. Just say about all those things, "To work the cider racket on the farmers."

Then the question arises, Why do the *brewers* want to boom *cider?* It would seem that they would rather discourage it as competing with beer. They do not sell cider. Why do they wish to promote the cider interest? There is some cat under that meal. What is it? Well, according to their own resolutions they are "unalterably opposed to Prohibition, general and local." The farmers are, however, generally favorable to Prohibition. If they can persuade them that Prohibition would prevent them from ever making another drop of cider they could set a good many against it, and if they can get the farmers to vote against Prohibition in order

to make cider, they will be free to make and sell beer—
that is, the brewers kindly propose to make the farmer
a cat's paw to pull the very hot chestnut of Prohibition
out of the fire. We think our farmers have too much
sense and manliness to be manipulated in that way.

But it may be as well to give, that all may know it,
the words of that eminent jurist, Judge Agnew, to the
farmers of Pennsylvania on this subject. One of the
most valuable of his articles is an appeal to the farmers
not to be misled by the liquor men's claim that the right
to manufacture and sell cider would be interfered with
by the adoption of the Amendment. He says:

"The words of the Amendment are: 'The manufacture, sale, or keeping for sale, of *intoxicating* liquor, to be used as a *beverage*, is hereby prohibited.'

"To make cider is not to manufacture an intoxicating liquor. Cider is the mere juice of the apple, and is not an intoxicant when first made. As well might the eating of apples be forbidden. It requires fermentation to produce alcohol, the intoxicating principle of *hard* cider. Every farmer knows he does not make *hard* cider. It must stand several weeks before it becomes hard, and the next process is the acetous fermentation which makes it vinegar.

"Then look at the absurdity of compelling the constable to visit all the farmers in his township to find out whether the owners have made cider. But if pressing out the juice of apples is manufacturing an intoxicating liquor, the cider-mill is as necessary to be returned as a distillery or a brewery. Such is the absurdity the opponents of a valuable reform are reduced to in order to defame it and carry off votes.

"It is to be hoped no farmer who has an apple orchard will suffer himself to be imposed upon by the silly assertion that cider is within the Amendment until it has undergone fermentation and become *hard*. He can make all the cider he pleases, and sell it before it has reached the point when it becomes intoxicating; or he may keep it until it becomes vinegar, and then sell it.

"Of course, the man who sells or keeps for sale *hard* cider, as a *beverage*, will come within the Amendment. But we presume no farmer wishes or intends to do this. It is not necessary because he makes cider to do it, for then he would voluntarily incur the Prohibition. All farmers have to do is to follow the business of their farms as heretofore, and not to turn themselves into bar-keepers or sellers of intoxicating drinks. The juice of the apple, like the juice of the grape, is harmless when pressed. It is only when fermentation has taken place one becomes *hard* and the other becomes wine."

Many farmers will answer: "Oh, it's easy enough to keep cider from getting hard. Just put in a little salicylic acid."

But do you know the effect of that? Wood's "Therapeutics," one of the foremost medical authorities, speaks as follows, p. 621:

"Salicylic acid has been used to a considerable extent in the preparation of beer and wine. . . . On February 7th, 1881, the French Government interdicted this use, and in 1885 a commission appointed by the Academy of Medicine of Paris, at the suggestion of the Minister of Agriculture, reported (Bull. Acad. Méd., vol. xvi., 1886) that it is proved that the prolonged employment of even very small amounts of salicylic acid is dangerous, and that in susceptible individuals, and especially in aged persons, it is apt to cause disorders of digestion and disease of the kidneys."

"But if we don't use that, the cider will get hard. What shall we do?" Do just what you would with any other alcoholic liquor. Let it alone. Hard cider contains from 4 to 10 per cent. of alcohol. Beer contains 2 to 5 per cent.* The reason for giving up one is a

---

* Cider has a larger per cent. of alcohol than lager beer, strong beer, porter, or ale. The eminent State Assayer of Massachusetts, Dr. Hayes, has furnished us with the following table:

"Lager beer has from $2\frac{1}{4}$ to $3\frac{1}{4}$ per cent. of alcohol.

"Strong beer is variable, but has a larger per cent. of alcohol than lager beer.

"Porter has from 4 to 7 per cent. of alcohol.

"Golden ale has but $5\frac{7}{10}$ per cent. of alcohol.

reason for giving up the other. The alcohol habit is progressive and hereditary. There is a constant demand for a larger and larger amount. Where boys are brought up to drink cider, which, after the first few weeks, contains a considerable quantity of alcohol, where they inherit the taste for it from parents who are in the habit of using it, there will be an alcoholic demand in their systems. When they go to the city, where they cannot get cider readily, they will be pretty sure to substitute beer. Then comes drunkenness with all its woes. Which is worth the most, a hearty, happy, clean, temperate boy, safe anywhere, or a little cider?

But cider is capable of doing the intemperate business very well on its own account. Speaking of it one day in a store, a man who makes no pretence to temperance

"Cider has from 4 to 10 per cent. of alcohol.

"Also, $4\frac{4}{10}$ per cent. of the 'absolute alcohol' in cider is equal to 10 per cent. of rum—that is, ten glasses of cider are equal to one glass of rum."

It appears from this analysis that cider has a larger per cent. of alcohol than either of the other liquors named, and hence must be more intoxicating.

We learn from Brande's celebrated "table, showing the proportion of alcohol in distilled and fermented liquors," that,

       Cider, highest average, is............... 9.37 per cent.
       "   lowest   "   "............... 5.21   "   "

This table was prepared many years ago.

From Johnston's "Chemistry of Common Life" (Appleton's edition, vol. i., p. 262), we extract the following:

"Amid these differences in quality, however, there are certain general chemical characters in which all ciders agree. They contain little extractive or solid nutritious matter. No bitter or narcotic ingredient has been added to them. *They contain, on an average, about nine per cent. of alcohol—thus resembling in strength the common hock, the weaker champagnes, and our strongest English ales.*"—From "Cider in the Pledge," *National Temperance Society.*

came in, and on being appealed to, said : "Well, cider makes the *meanest* drunk of any kind of liquor. I've been drunk on all of 'em, and it's worse than beer or whiskey any day." The wife of an intemperate husband, telling her story, said : "When my husband would get drunk on whiskey he would go to bed and sleep it off, and the worst of it would be over next morning. But when he got drunk on cider, he would be worse the next afternoon than he was at the time."

The general testimony is that cider has a peculiar effect upon the temper, producing a kind of chronic savageness different from the effect of any other kind of liquor. The farmer who drinks such a beverage is doing a damage to himself. Who shall say how many country homes have been made wretched, wives made dreary and sad by constant surliness, boys and girls driven off to the city because home was so hateful, simply by chronic drenching with this "meanest" of intoxicants? It's hardly a thing worth fighting for for one's own use. But to sell it is to do a positive damage to the community. Certainly Judge Agnew is right when he says, "Farmers should not turn themselves into barkeepers or sellers of intoxicating drinks." If the farmer who even likes a little hard cider can, by giving that up, stop the selling of whiskey and beer, with their uncounted damage and woe, in the cities and towns, that will be the best investment he ever made; for it will stop the spoiling of his market by the drinks that make other people too poor to buy his grain and wool. Better buy or raise an extra number of hogs to eat his surplus apples than to keep open the great floodgates of pauperism in ten thousand saloons to make hogs of men—his own sons, perhaps, among them. To the credit and honor of the farmers be it said, they have generally had virtue and intelligence to see this, and in all prohibitory contests they have been the surest and steadiest supporters of Prohibition, as now so grandly in the two Dakotas. There's no money in the liquor traffic, except what the farmer loses and the saloon-keeper gets. Let the sale of liquor be stopped and the drunkard and his family be clothed and fed, and the farmer will get the money—and money that has no curse upon it.

CHAPTER XXIII.

THE HOME.

"The intemperate man, who has no resource but his labor, experiments upon his children to find the minimum of possible subsistence."—*Horace Mann.*

"The child ragged and ill-used is ever the drunkard's child. Education, clothing, food, home care—all are swallowed down with the drink, and the poor child is sent out with curses and threats to force sales on a compassionate public, instead of being folded at home in the arms of parental love."—*The Alliance News.*

INTEMPERANCE is the deadliest enemy of the home. Its first action is to take the man away from his dear ones. If a busy man, he commonly leaves home early in the morning, seeing little of wife and children in the hurry before departure. Perhaps he does not return at noon, or if he does, it is only for a hasty lunch. If he is to have any happy social life with wife and children, it must be in the evening. If that time is given to the saloon he becomes a stranger to his family. He does not know his wife's cares and hopes, nor even the fulness of her love, because she has no opportunity for its free expression. The few brief moments of conversation are almost wholly given to the crowding necessities of life. Then, to a woman who is compelled for the most part to live a secluded home-life, it is disappointing to the last degree—it is even heart-breaking—to have the one to whom she has given her love and her life leave her in the little time they might be together for other society which he prefers to her own. And such society! It is not to be wondered at if she is not cheerful and hopeful, and if she finds it hard to show much tender affection in the face of such neglect. It is not surprising if she finds little encouragement to adorn her home or beautify her person, or give the little touches that make children winsome, for one who will hurry away from it all as soon as he can get through eating.

Still, all this, hard as it is, might be endurable if THE MAN at last came home. But who comes home? Is it the man who walked into her girlish dreams, who was careful in dress, gentle and noble in manner for her dear sake? No, a foul, imbruted being, from whom she would have fled with a shriek if he had suddenly appeared at her father's house. The man from whom every decent man has shrunk away on the street as he came home is the man this wife is to love and cherish.

When we think of the unutterable disgust a sober man —who is only a man—feels for a drunkard; how he loathes the flushed face, the fœtid breath, the incoherent speech, and all the soil and coarseness of intoxication, and then think of putting that being beside a woman with all the delicacy of feeling of her sex, in the privacy of home, the loneliness of night, and the association of marriage, it is a wonder that every wife who has this to bear does not straightway become a maniac.

Then the saloon devours the money on whose wise expenditure much of the happiness of home depends. If the wife has toiled at the wash-tub till every muscle aches and her whole being is weary, it is simply exasperating to have her husband leave her and go to spend in one hour in the saloon the money that would have paid for needed help.

Clothes wear out. No washing and no mending can keep old things forever neat. The rags will come, and when they come those who wear them will look shabby. Not even cleanliness can be fully maintained when there is a lack of changes and a lack of towels, and these cost money. The saloon cuts off the supply. Fuel and light cost money. A smouldering fire and a dim lamp cannot make a cheery room. The saloon puts the fire that should be in the grate into the man's stomach. The rations grow short. The children worry, and the wife is spiritless from exhaustion. The man looks over the bare table and grumbles, "There's no comfort at home." Then he claims that he is *driven* to the saloon because it is so bright and his home so wretched, and authors, moralists, and divines support him in the claim. This is putting effect for cause. The fact is, that if we could put out the saloon lights and fires—every one—empty the barrels, smash the crockery, and make the saloon dark as the traffic is, those homes would soon grow bright. Dickens represents one of his wretched characters showing a cup of foul water to a visitor, and saying: "If you had such water, wouldn't *you* drink gin?" Very touching! *But if that man had been willing to pay for water the price of his gin*, he could have had the clearest ice-water to drink. The saloon becomes bright by making the homes dark. Science tells us that when you light your fire of wood or coal, and the ruddy flame springs up and fills the room with its glow, you are simply basking in the imprisoned sunlight of long ago. So when the saloon throws its light across the highway, a blaze of splendor, you simply see concentrated into one dazzling focus the light that it has stolen from scores of darkened homes. Yet the more of every good it sucks out of a man's life, and the more hopelessly wretched he becomes, the fairer the saloon seems by contrast, till he grows to esteeming his destroyer his only refuge and hope. The lower the saloon casts him down, the more necessary the saloon becomes to him. But his wife and children cannot flee to its glare and oblivion. Our civilization will not yet tolerate that. They must stay in the desolated home. Now if this were honest poverty, forced upon them by hard necessity, which the man was doing all he could to share and brighten, a true wife could rally all "the beauty and truth of woman's devotion" to bear up and sustain her husband amid it all. But when she knows that the husband who brought her to it has deserted her in the midst of it for a selfish and swinish delight which will sink him—and them—lower yet, how does she endure it?

In answer to those who claim that woman might abolish intemperance by making home happy, there is a certain concession to be made. If a girl marries with no skill for the life of home and no heart for its duties, she may have to reap in terrible disaster the fruit of her own criminal incompetency. No man can do a hard day's work on one kind of fancy cake. He must live upon the homely food, and it must be such that he can live upon it. If a man is not fed at his own table, the temptation to drink in the saloon is terribly reinforced. The work must be done. It cannot stop. Others are waiting on his hand or brain. He is faint and weary when he needs to be strong. His companions say: "Take a drink and it will make you feel better." So it does, with its deceptive cheer, enabling him to draw ruinously on the vital forces of the system for the strength which should have been supplied by timely and nutritious food.

Thus the alcohol habit may easily become fixed, the man really thinking it a necessity, and really believing that it helps him till he finds too late that it has destroyed him. *No woman should ever marry till she has learned the trade of home-making.* She should not have to practise all her crude experiments on her husband, lest she ruin the man while she is learning the trade.

But, on the other hand, it must be answered that the majority of drinking men whom we have known have gone down from homes where wise, loving, and devoted wives had done all that womanly skill need do for happiness. This has been clearly proved when the husband has reformed. Always, then, without an exception that we remember, his home has blossomed out in beauty and cheer as soon as he gave his wife the time and money which he had been giving to the saloon.

It is doubtful if the man ever lived who would endure from a drunken wife the half of what thousands of women silently and uncomplainingly endure from drunken husbands, shutting in their own hearts their bitter misery ; teaching their children to pity the father whom they cannot honor ; refusing to testify against the man who has beggared their home and blasted their hopes, when at length he has bruised their bodies and hazarded their lives ; submitting to be robbed over and over again of their hard earnings to minister to his further degradation ; going hungry and thirsty, and seeing their children ragged and starving—all for the young love and early hope that were once so sweet. It passes all that man's heart knows of patience and devotion.

We saw a case once on an ocean steamship where such a man was dragged up to the captain by the boatswain, while the poor wife, whose screams had been echoing from the steerage, followed fast after, white and faint. The captain, a man of many battles, laid a hand on the wretch's collar, with his other hand clenched, and lightning in his eye, when the wife, amid all that crowd of men, threw herself between, one arm around the husband's neck, the other hand on the captain's arm, pleading, "Oh, captain, dear, forgive him this once!" The captain tried to hold the sternness of his face, but his grasp relaxed and he only said: "If this happens again, she sha'n't save you." Then the pitying woman drew the brutal husband off to the steerage, clinging to him all the way, and the men moved away silently, too deeply touched to talk of the scene to each other.

But this contrast will not always last. Woman can inherit the appetite from a drunken father. She can be reduced to a habit of wretchedness where, for her, too, the brilliant, gilded saloon will have irresistible fascination. Then, what language can tell the horror of the curse?

The work is already begun. Our people are tending toward that deepest depth and most hopeless ruin—the drunkenness of woman. The following extract is taken from the Cleveland *Leader*, August 14th, 1889.

FEMALE WINESKINS.

A ROOM FOR THEIR ACCOMMODATION IN EUCLID AVENUE.

MRS. PRATHER'S CHARGE.

She was Horrified at Put-in-Bay to see Drunken Mothers Sleeping in the Grass.

Boys given Wine by the Bottle—Two Girls who made a Show of Themselves.

The regular monthly business meeting of the Non-Partisan Woman's Christian Temperance Union, in their pleasant room at the Nottingham Block yesterday afternoon, was well attended.

* * * * * * * *

Mrs. Prather said that she went to Put-in-Bay a few days ago on a boat which carried twenty-five hundred excursionists. A boat from Detroit brought two thousand, and boats from other places swelled the number. She said that she was horrified, for she never saw so much drinking in her life before. She stated that she saw women who drank wine and then went to sleep on the grass, leaving their young children uncared for. Mrs. Prather said that she was particularly troubled about two young girls who emptied a bottle of wine on the boat. "I also saw young boys," she continued, "carrying bottles of wine down to the boat. These men certainly know that they must not sell to minors. They advertise that the wine is not intoxicating, but I never saw so many drunken people."

Miss Ingersoll said that Mrs. Prather's was the third report of the same kind that she had heard from Put-in-Bay this season.

Mrs. Prather was of the opinion that the Union should protest against drinking at the Bay, and also against the selling of intoxicants to boys. Mrs. Phinney said that the most lamentable fact was that the women drank wine and beer. "Yet," she said, "Kate Field recommended the use of California wine, and if the people cannot get that I presume that they are satisfied with what they can get at Put-in-Bay."

Mrs. Prather said that she had been informed that there was

A WINE-ROOM IN EUCLID AVENUE

which was conducted for the accommodation of women.

Another issue of the same paper gives the following:

"DARKENED STALLS."

THE MAYOR GIVES HIS OPINION ABOUT TWO

BEER GARDENS ON SUMMIT STREET.

He says that they are One of the Worst Iniquities in the City.

At last night's meeting of the Police Board, the Mayor relieved his mind freely of some very pungent ideas concerning two saloon gardens. The subject was brought up by the application of C. H. Kohler for a music permit for Lake View Pavilion, at No. 104 Summit Street.

"I have something to say on this subject," said the Mayor. "I recently visited the Bellevue Garden, at the corner of Erie and Summit Streets, and I have no hesitation in saying that they are 100 per cent. worse than houses of ill-fame. It is one of the worst institutions in the city. I found the stalls poorly lighted, and I was unable to clearly see the men and women who were inside of them. What I saw there was worse than occurs commonly in houses of ill-repute. I saw girls there who were only fourteen, fifteen, and sixteen years old. Perhaps they took their first drinks there, and then they were ruined. It is high time that the police regulated these places if they have the proper authority. And we can do nothing better than close these places completely. And I say to you, sir," turning around to Kohler, who was standing behind him, "that you are doing the greatest possible damage to the citizens of Cleveland."

The home must banish the wine sauces, jellies, etc., which the fashionable cook-books—even some issued by the "Ladies' Aid Societies" of churches—still provide for. Their only possible use can be to minister to the alcoholic appetite. But that appetite is not soothed, but whetted by small doses. The appetite is absolutely insatiable, and when aroused is to be satisfied only by enough to master the nervous system, requiring for that an ever-increasing quantity. Home must not be made a place of temptation. How will you convince a young man at college that there is any harm in the little wine in a tiny crystal glass which holds scarcely more than he would get in a sauce at his mother's table? Of course, those who choose thus to sow the wind cannot be prevented by any warnings; nor if they chance to reap the whirlwind can that be stopped by any consolations. If complete Prohibition should stop the culinary use of alcohol, the loss to taste and fancy would be very slight, while the gain to civilization and home happiness would be incalculable. We do not hear any outcry from the kitchens of Kansas. We do not learn of any defective nutrition among her people, who are exporting the food supply of a nation.

In another point social usages often sin, not only against morality, but against etiquette. The young man, principled against liquor drinking, is coaxed by fascinating women, besieged by brilliant and perhaps venerable men to drink with them, till he feels it utter incivility and rudeness to decline. We need not say how often those who start him are powerless to stop him. We will not speak of the moral side of this, on which all eloquence has been expended, and which is really too plain to need an argument. We wish to say, it is not good manners. If I have a guest who does not like onions, I do not press them upon him, coax him or taunt him until he swallows them against his will to please me and mine. Still more in a matter of principle; if my guest is a Roman Catholic I do not persuade and badger him into eating roast beef on Friday. So far from it, if I know his views, I will not have the objectionable dish on my table when he is present. I will not inflict on him the embarrassment of declining. When Friday comes, my Catholic friend, or even my Catholic servant, shall have fish or other palatable food which shall not raise the question of singularity. This is but true politeness, universally recognized as such among all well-bred people. Why, in Heaven's name, should it not apply when my guest's principle is against the fell destroyer that is cutting through all our homes, high and low, its wide swath of desolation and death? "Society" must come out from the manners of the Dark

Ages, revise its standards of politeness, and reapply to the question of intoxicants what is, in all other things, recognized as the only course becoming the true gentleman or lady. So far from its being an offence for a temperance man not to drink, it is an indecorum for a host or hostess who knows his principles to ask him to do so, or even to seem to observe that he does not.

This also is an economic question, for the temperance reform can never be made complete at the bottom till it is recognized at the top. Those of greatest wealth and influence and of highest culture must set an example of goodness which those of less advantages may wisely follow. " He that is greatest, let him be servant of all."

Alcohol is the destroyer of the home. Home must be the conqueror of alcohol if it would maintain itself or save our civilization.

CHAPTER XXIV.

THE NURSERY.

"It is the same deathless mother's love that has knocked at the doors of the schools through State legislatures, and is to-day knocking at the door of our national capitol, asking that the boys may be taught. We women lay down at the cradle our youth, our beauty, our talents, anything, everything, to the little bit of humanity there. We cannot help it. It is God's providence for the child; and may it not likewise be God's providence for the nation that has roused the heart of women and called the deathless tides of mother love to participate in this great movement? If we save the children to-day we shall have saved the nation to-morrow."—*Mrs. Mary H. Hunt.*

IN strictness this subject might be included in the previous chapter on "The Home," but it is of such special importance as to deserve a place and title for itself. We cannot adequately provide for the prosperity of nations unless we study the economics of the nursery.

By an inscrutable, but most manifest law, everything that vitally affects the constitution and mental and moral character of the parents is transmitted to the child. This is pre-eminently true of the results of alcoholic drinks.

Dr. E. Lancereaux says :*

"The person who inherits alcoholism is generally marked with degeneration particularly manifested in disturbances of the nervous functions. As an infant he dies of convulsions or other nervous disorders ; if he lives he becomes idiotic or imbecile, and in adult life bears these special characteristics : the head is small (tending to

---

* Quoted by Gustafson, "Foundation of Death," p. 175.

microcephalism), his physiognomy vacant, a nervous susceptibility, more or less accentuated, a state of nervousness bordering on hysteria, convulsions, epilepsy, sad ideas, melancholia, hypochondria—such are the effects, and these, with a passion for alcoholic beverages, an inclination to immorality, depravity, and cynicism, are the sorrowful inheritance which, unfortunately, a great number of individuals given to drink bequeath to their children."

Professor Sigismund Jaccoud says :

"A survey of the race leads us to affirm that alcoholism is one of the greatest causes of the depopulation and degeneration of nations."

Dr. Norman Kerr speaks as follows :

"Defective nerve-power and an enfeebled, debilitated *morale* form the fatal legacy of inebriates to their offspring. Some of the circle, generally the daughters, may be nervous and hysterical, are apt to be feeble and eccentric, and to fall into insanity when an unusual emergency takes place. That the impairment of the bodily or mental faculties arises from the intemperance of one or both heads of the family is demonstrated by the healthfulness and intellectual vigor of children born while the parents were temperate contrasted with the sickliness and mental feebleness of their brothers and sisters born after the parent or parents became intemperate. . . . The most distressing aspect of the heredity of alcohol is the transmitted narcotic or insatiable craving for drink—the dipsomania of the physician—which is every day becoming more and more prevalent. Probably the alarming increase of the alcoholic heredity in England is owing in great part to the increase of female intemperance among us. It is well to state that all the evils resulting from hereditary alcoholism may be transmitted by parents who have never been noted for their drunkenness. Long-continued, habitual indulgence in intoxicating drinks to an extent far short of intoxication is not only sufficient to originate and hand down a morbid tendency, but is much more likely to do so than even repeated drunken outbreaks with intervals of perfect sobriety between."

One lingering tradition of the old faith in liquor as a universal remedy still persists in the home. It lingers stubbornly there, because the matters it concerns are by many deemed too delicate for public discussion, and ancient errors are passed from mouth to mouth under the veil of domestic privacy. But we are fast learning that the purest thing is truth, and that where it is thought modest to whisper an error, it cannot be indelicate to speak out the real facts. With what science so clearly teaches now of the intimate connection between the whole life of the mother and the unborn infant, it is manifest that all the harm alcohol can do to adult humanity, it can do most effectually to the delicate organism of the forming being, if the mother uses intoxicants before the birth of her child. Grant, if you please, that it may give a pleasant sense of relief from some distresses, just as a man by getting partially intoxicated will be relieved of a toothache. The tooth is not made sound, however. The relief is simply the paralysis of alcohol. So, nothing in the mother's constitution is improved. She has gained not one atom of nutrition, not one particle of strength, but simply a momentary comfort from the alcohol-paralysis. The influence of it surely and harmfully strikes her child. Dr. E. G. Figg, in his " Physiological Operation of Alcohol," * relates the results of his observation in cases of decided intemperance of mothers before the birth of their children, saying, in conclusion :

"What inference could be drawn from the circumstances, but that when the mother got drunk the child got drunk; when the mother became insensible the child became insensible ; and when the mother was collapsed the child was so also ?"

The same must be true in proportion of more moderate indulgences. Surely no mother is justified, when ample remedies for every really diseased condition can

---

* Gustafson, p. 220.

be obtained which involve no such consequences, in implanting the seeds of alcoholism in the nerves and brain of her child, surely to harm its structure, and perhaps to grow up into an organism that may break her heart and curse society. If, out of the traditions of the past, the dangerous advice is given even by the beloved and honored, the mother of to-day should have the wisdom and independence to walk in our day's clearer light.

But the nursing babe is more especially the victim of the dram. Many pure, high-minded, temperate mothers believe, and are religiously taught, that in order to nurse their children they must take beer, ale, or other liquor. Dr. Edmunds * makes an acute observation here. He says :

"Such mothers fall easy victims to circulars vaunting the nourishing properties of 'Hoare's Stout,' 'Tanqueray's Gin,' or 'Gilbey's Strengthening Port,' circulars which are always backed up by the example and advice of lady friends, who themselves have acquired the habit of using these liquors, *and who view as a reproach to themselves* the practice of any other lady who will not keep them in countenance, as the perfection of all moral and physical propriety."

The writer was once speaking with a wealthy farmer on this subject, who said, with decided emphasis : "My wife always drank ale or beer when she was nursing her children." I asked : "Did you ever feed brewery mash to your cows?" "Yes, sometimes." "What was the effect?" "Well, they gave more milk. But there wasn't any butter in it. You couldn't make a pound of butter from it if you churned all day." Said I : "Would that kind of milk be good for a baby?" "I shouldn't want to try it," he answered. There is a

---

* Gustafson, p. 223.

homely statement of what medical science more exactly teaches.

One of the most striking facts regarding the use of alcohol is the instant and desperate endeavor of the human system to get rid of it. Every excretory organ of the body hastens to throw it out. The familiar instance of this is the breath of the drinker, which is so charged with alcohol as to fill the air around him, the lungs struggling to throw off the destructive agent at every breath. But with the nursing mother the alcohol finds a readier way of escape, as it must escape somewhere or cause the death of the drinker.

The eminent Dr. James Edmunds, in a paper on "Alcoholic Drinks as an Article of Diet for Nursing Mothers," says :*

"It is a matter of common observation that a glass of spirit taken at bedtime by a nursing mother not merely increases the flow of milk during the night, but causes the child to sleep heavily. Under these circumstances the spirit acts, not as a purgative, nor as a diuretic, nor as a diaphoretic, nor does much of it pass off by the lungs, but it acts as a lactogogue, because the breasts are then in a state of great activity, and form the readiest channel through which the mother's system can eliminate the alcohol. In order to effect that elimination, the breasts have to discharge a profuser quantity of milk ; *but the increased quantity of milk is produced by a mere addition of alcohol and water*, or it is produced by impoverishing and straining the system of the mother. In either case the poisonous influence of the alcohol is manifested in narcotizing the child, and it cannot need much reflection to show that children ought not to have alcohol filtered into them as receptacles for matters which the mother's system finds it necessary to eliminate. Probably nothing could be worse than to have the very fabric of the child's tissues laid down from alcoholized blood."

Living at one time where this system was largely prac-

---
* Quoted by Gustafson, pp. 223, 224.

tised by nursing mothers, my observation was that their fat, white babies were always cross, except when they were stupid. That is exactly the condition of a habitual tippler. Take care what you say to him, or how you look at him in the morning before he has had his dram, or when he has gone some time without it. But when he has had a "good drink" you may slap him on the shoulder, and he's "a good fellow." Just such transitions those babies went through. The mother would say: "I don't know what I shall do with him. He is so cross." Then he would be delivered to the nurse or the long-suffering sister to "take him out," to worry through the time till he could get from the maternal fountain another dram.

It is awful to think of a mother running a saloon for her babe in her own breast.

High up in the social scale the danger is often more serious than among the middle class. Fashion and wealth delegate the child's nourishment to the "wet nurse," who probably has not the self-control and high self-respect that the cultured mother would have. She knows how to secure a heavy sleep for herself and the child by night, and uses enough to accomplish the purpose.

Of the effects of this course upon the child, Dr. Edmunds says:

"Infants nursed by mothers who drink much beer become fatter than usual, and to an untrained eye sometimes appear as 'magnificent children.' But the fatness of such children is not a recommendation to the more knowing observer; they are exceedingly prone to die of inflammation of the chest (bronchitis) after a very few days' illness from an ordinary cold. They die very much more frequently than other children of convulsions and diarrhœa while cutting their teeth, and they are very liable to die of scrofulous inflammation of the membranes of the brain, commonly called 'water on the brain,' while their childhood often presents a painful contrast—in the way of crooked legs and stunted or ill-shapen figure—to the 'magnificent and promising appearance of their infancy.'"

There can be no reasonable doubt that a constitutional craving for alcohol is often imbibed by such babes during this impressible forming time through the influence of what Mr. Gustafson calls "lacteal heredity," of which he says: "Virtues, vices, physical characteristics, and the effects of habits indulged in during lactation can be transmitted to the child." This may be one explanation of the sudden fall into intemperate habits of the children of temperate and excellent people. The child was nursed into intemperance in babyhood.

It cannot be too strongly said that the best and the only safe nourishment the mother or nurse can give her babe is that which comes from substantial food well digested by a healthy organism. When that fails, it is by all means safest to resort to the milk of an honest cow, who does not use intoxicants. This is good for the mother, too. A very accomplished physician told us this anecdote. "I was attending," he said, "a young mother with her first child. She said to me: 'I suppose now, doctor, I shall have to drink beer.' 'What for?' I answered. 'Why, to have milk for my baby.' Said I: 'Why don't you drink milk?' She laughed, and asked with surprise: 'Why, would that do it?' 'Of course it would,' I replied, 'and in the surest and quickest way. Good milk contains all the constituents of human life, and while cow's milk would be likely to be too strong for a tender infant, after it has passed through the mother's veins it is mingled in just the right proportions to give the child strength and health.

It will be better for you, too.' She followed my advice, and both herself and her baby prospered."

Of the effects of beer-drinking on the mother, Dr. Edmunds says :*

"I have observed the following facts: The mothers frequently make flesh, and even become corpulent; often, however, at the same time they get pale, and where they are not constitutionally robust in fibre they become inactive, short-breathed, coarse-complexioned, nervous, and irritable, and suffer from weakness of the heart and a long train of symptoms which are more or less severe according to the constitution of the mother and the quantity of alcohol she imbibes. The young mother prematurely loses the bloom and beauty of youth. Often it is quite startling to meet some lady who, during an interval of two years, has been transformed from a sprightly and charming young woman into an uninteresting, coarse-looking matron. She has nursed her first infant for twelve months. With a pure and rational diet she would simply have acquired a more dignified and womanly bearing, with a robuster gentleness of manner; but a liberal supply of 'nourishing' stout, etc., was adopted and imbibed regularly, in order to supply her infant with 'milk.' The presence of a nerveless apathy, or unintelligent irritability, afterward proved that a liberal supply of stimulants was required to support her strength, and although she ceased nursing, her own sensations convinced her of the necessity of continuing them. The outward and visible change is but an exponent of the degenerations and diseases which are taking root within. If there be a predisposition to insanity or consumption, these diseases are developed very rapidly, or they are brought on where proper management might altogether have tided over those periods of life at which the predisposition is prone to become provoked into actual disease."

Another wrong of the nursery is the giving of actual drams to the babe. The child has been left too long, for the mother to "get through her work," or to "see company." The little one has become too faint and chilled to be able to take nourishment or to digest it if taken. Then it is walked with, tossed, trotted, and otherwise

---

* Gustafson, p. 224.

tortured till maternal and paternal endurance is exhausted. Then "hot whiskey and water" is given to intoxicate the little stomach and brain, and the baby goes to sleep on a teaspoonful just as its father would on half a pint. A mother who understands her business will take such an infant—if by accident it ever gets to that stage—put hot flannels over its stomach and feet, give it the hot water with something as innocent as peppermint, and soothe it to a happy sleep, from which it will wake able to take its natural food, with no depressing reaction such as surely follows alcoholic stimulant. Civilization must banish this clinging relic of barbarism, the use of alcohol in the nursery.

Byron said of Greece:

"When riseth Lacedæmon's hardihood,
    When Thebes Epaminondas rears again,
When Athens' children are with hearts endued,
    When Grecian mothers shall give birth to MEN,
Then mayest thou be restored, but not till then."

To have a sound nation we must have wise mothers and healthy babies.

CHAPTER XXV.

POLITICS.

"To preserve the Government we must also preserve a correct and energetic tone of morals. Liberty consists more in the habits of the people than in anything else. There are always men wicked enough to go to any lengths in the pursuit of power, if they can find others wicked enough to support them. Ambitious men must be restrained by the public morality; when they rise up to do evil, they must find themselves standing alone. Morality rests on religion. If you destroy the foundation, the superstructure must fall."—*Daniel Webster, July 4th,* 1802.

"The moral forces of the masses lie in temperance. I have no faith in anything apart from that movement for the elevation of the working class."—*Richard Cobden.*

Dr. Johnson is said to have interpolated the following lines into the "Traveller" of Goldsmith:

"How small, of all that human hearts endure,
That part which laws or kings can cause or cure!"

The doctor called Goldsmith "an inspired idiot," but he would never have thought of that sentence either through his inspiration or his idiocy. Was the tyranny of Nero and Domitian, then, a small matter, when Roman matrons stabbed themselves to death in their own homes to avoid being torn away to the emperor's harem? Was it a small thing when half the population were slaves, and many of the brightest genius liable to be beaten or crucified at the whim of brutal masters? Was it a small thing when prisoners of war were made to fight to the death in the amphitheatre? Was it a small thing when Alexander descended on rich and populous Tyre, and when he captured it after a wasting siege, crucified two thousand of its brave defenders on the sea-shore with their faces turned toward the city they had vainly defended, while the long, weeping train of wives and children was driven away under the lash to be sold into distant slavery? Was the dire oppression of the Bourbon kings a small matter when it drove the French nation into the mad Revolution? Were the Wars of the Roses a small matter when they poured out the best blood of England to decide which of two rival families should furnish England a "king"? Were the wasting wars of Frederick the Great, and of Napoleon, small matters when it might almost be said of Europe, "there was not a house in which there was not one dead"? Has it been a small matter to Mexico, for so many years in the past, not to know who would govern it the next day? Far deeper was the insight, far truer the thought of the New Testament writer, "I exhort, therefore, first of all, that prayers, supplications, and giving of thanks be made . . . for kings and for all that are in authority, that we may lead quiet and peaceable lives in all godliness and honesty." The common sense of mankind has not been in fault when it has led them to forsake home, sacrifice treasure, and lay down life to overthrow bad government and to build up good government—"to establish justice, ensure domestic tranquillity, provide for the common defence, promote the general welfare, and secure the blessings of liberty to themselves and their posterity."

The man who thinks he is too great to attend to questions of good government simply shows that he is too narrow. The man who thinks the business, professional or religious interests he is engaged in are too vast to allow him to consider governmental affairs or help to control them, is simply neglecting one of the greatest factors in the interests for which he lives. Neither home, commerce, literature, art, nor the Church can reach its highest development, or even be itself secure, without the aid of good, pure government.

What shall be said when a paper like the Chicago *Times*, which is by no means a distinctively temperance paper, publishes such an utterance as this (in its issue of June 8th, 1889):

> "The largest brewery in Detroit has been added to a syndicate that threatens to be the most dangerous political power in the United States. The breweries now control the principal distilling interests, and will in future direct every contest in which the people shall endeavor to limit the frightful havoc of the liquor traffic."

That is to say, the worst element in American civilization, the cause of "frightful havoc," is in future to "direct every contest" where the people may strive to shake off the terrible yoke. Is it not time for American manhood to arise and at least make one mighty trial of strength, to see whether this is so or not—whether there is not somewhere in our institutions a power that may preserve all we hold dear against its spoliation?

We are told by leaders of morality and by leaders of religion that "questions of morals must not be brought into politics." In the name of God, in the name of humanity, in the name of freedom, why not?

What is "politics" but a device for securing the good of the people? And what so deeply concerns the good of the people as true morality? Have not all nations that have perished gone down under the weight of their own vices ? It was not the Goths and Vandals who conquered Rome. Rome was conquered long before by the corruption and enervation of its people, which had destroyed truth, honor, purpose, patriotism, home, and even physical manhood. Certainly all that tends to such results is matter for legislation and for politics, which are the foundation of legislation. If politics are not to save a nation from such a doom, what are they for ? Why should we go through the tax and strain, the excitement and expense of elections, if they are not to influence by a feather's weight these matters which most vitally concern the happiness, the welfare, and the very existence of a people ?

There are some very devout and scholarly men who tell us that any political action about morals is a "union of Church and State." How they make it out that in suppressing the saloon the State is interfering with the liberty of the Church, or the Church with the liberty of the State, is beyond all ordinary comprehension. One leading theologian has said : "If I am going to punish a man for sin, I ought to punish him for the greatest of sins, which is not believing in Christ." This is simply trifling with language, and *using the word "sin" in an equivocal sense.* When spoken of liquor selling, it means outward immorality. When spoken of unbelief, it means a state of the secret heart. There is a great fund of common morality which is accepted by all rational and civilized men. It is in substance that contained in the Ten Commandments. Now Ingersoll may not believe them inspired. With that the civil law has nothing to do. But if Ingersoll goes a step further, and because he does not believe them inspired, takes the liberty to steal or commit murder, the law will very promptly punish him without any infringement of religious liberty. We have a concrete case in this very line in American life to-day—the Mormons. They believe polygamy a divine institution. We say the Government has nothing to do with your belief. But if you marry more than one wife we will fine and imprison you for it. Now, if legislation upon morals is an interference with religious liberty, this is a very flagrant case of interference. It comes into the very home circle, into the house which the common law declares the man's "castle," into the most private relations of life, and punishes a man for marrying a woman whom he verily believes he had a divine right to marry, and who verily believes she had a divine right to marry him. In order to make the prohibition of liquor selling a parallel case to this prohibition of polygamy, it will be necessary to show that the saloon-keeper believes it is his divine right and his sacred duty to sell liquor, and that it is taught him by the most sacred teachings of his religion. The danger of interference with religious liberty is not a thousandth part as great in the prohibition of the saloon as in the prohibition of the harem. Let those who are so very anxious lest legislation upon morals shall harm religious liberty awake to the situation in Utah, where the United States Government is enforcing the Seventh Commandment with the strong hand!

But we shall be told "the Government does not legislate against polygamy as wrong, but as injurious to society." Well, if that is the case, what is more fearfully injurious to society than the saloon? Since the liquor selling is doing such manifest damage to society, we may proceed against it for the damage, *even if we also believe it to be wicked.*

But we are ready to go further. We hold that in a case of manifest moral wrong—violation of the great law of common right—we may proceed against the wrong without waiting to prove the injury. For moral wrong *is* the greatest possible injury to society. It is very doubtful if any man can prove that polygamy has been injurious to society in Utah on merely materialistic grounds. The Mormons claim that it has been a benefit. The facts, on the whole, seem to sustain their claim. They are rich, aggressive, prosperous, advancing, colonizing. The strength of our argument against polygamy is that it must do harm, even if we cannot show the harm; that wrong against the marriage relation is itself the greatest harm, corrupting the very springs of public virtue and undermining the foundations of civilized society. We proceed against polygamy because it is wrong, and therefore sure to be injurious. This is the only way we can deal with public wrong, to deal effectively. "Sentence against an evil work is not executed speedily." Often the wrong thing seems the prosperous thing. We cannot wait until it has destroyed a nation. We must deal with it as wrong, and therefore sure to be injurious somewhere and some time. There is a

CASH VALUE IN MORALITY,

though we cannot always show it at the start. Government has no more sacred duty and no higher trust than to conserve the morals of a people. In that it is sure to be providing for their prosperity and security. It is fitting for us to plead against the saloon its vast moral wrong on those common lines of morality which all men recognize.

It was so that we broke down slavery. We did not

find out its economic harm till after we had destroyed it. The South thought it a source of vast prosperity. The slave-holders were not all Haleys or Legrees. Many slaves were so kindly treated that they voluntarily remained with their former masters, even supporting them by their own earnings in the time of poverty and need that followed the war. The great, profoundly moving thought that took hold of the conscience of the North was that "there is no right of property in man." No one will charge Abraham Lincoln with being a foe to religious liberty. There are not many men who would venture to claim that he did not understand the philosophy of government. Abraham Lincoln set himself to oppose slavery after he had come to the conclusion, as expressed in his own terse phrase, "If slavery is not wrong, then nothing is wrong." The key to his whole campaign against Douglas, which roused the hearts of Illinois and of the nation and made him President, was the moral wrong of slavery. He said of it, in the now immortal words:

"He [Douglas] says he 'don't care whether it is voted up or voted down' in the Territories. . . . Any man can say that who does not see anything wrong in slavery, but no man can logically say it who does see a wrong in it; because no man can logically say he don't care whether a wrong is voted up or voted down. He may say he don't care whether an indifferent thing is voted up or down, but he must logically have a choice between a right thing and a wrong thing. He contends that whatever community wants slaves has a right to have them. So they have, if it is not a wrong. But if it is a wrong, he cannot say people have a right to do wrong. . . . And if there be among you anybody who supposes that he, as a Democrat, can consider himself 'as much opposed to slavery as anybody,' I would like to reason with him. You never treat it as a wrong. What other thing that you consider as a wrong do you deal with as you deal with that? Perhaps you say it is a wrong, but your leader never does, and you quarrel with anybody who says it is wrong. . . . You may turn over everything in the Democratic policy from beginning to end, . . . it everywhere carefully excludes the idea that there is anything wrong in it. *That is the real issue.* That is the issue that will continue in this country when these poor tongues of Judge Douglas and myself shall be silent. *It is the eternal struggle between these two principles—right and wrong*—throughout the world. They are the two principles that have stood face to face from the beginning of time, and will ever continue to struggle."

We say of this curse of our day: "If the liquor traffic is not wrong, then nothing is wrong." We claim that, from the economic standpoint, it is proper to urge against the liquor traffic that it is wrong as murder is wrong and as stealing is wrong, for it involves the essence of both; as licentiousness is wrong, for it is the mightiest feeder of that great cancer. In the name of economics we have a right to awaken the public conscience to the liquor crime, as the surest way to abolish the liquor curse. The most sacred trust of politics is the moral well being of a nation. By that we do not mean religion, but rectitude, honesty, truth, and justice from man to man—concrete, tangible right, as against overt wrong with which law can deal. We invoke the power of legislation against the liquor traffic as a mighty, tangible, overt wrong.

Then we invoke it further as against a fearful national loss, waste, and peril, and we claim that by as much as politics may take account of prisons and almshouses and insane asylums—and every legislature and governor has to answer for the record made in these matters in every campaign—by so much politics may take account of the traffic which chiefly fills those institutions of despair. We claim that by as much as politics may take account of the tariff, and rock the country as with an earthquake with that issue, by so much more may politics take ac count of a traffic whose expenses are ten times* more than all the receipts from our tariff, and three times more than the total value of all our imports. The common sense of the people is right. The liquor traffic is in politics, and it is there to stay. It is the most burning question with which our politics have now to deal. The temperance plank—or the want of it—is the first thing the people look for in every State and national platform. It is this in regard to which platform committees are besieged, this with which they wrestle through weary hours, this which decides the fate of elections. It is fitting that it should. It "will never be settled till it is settled right." The only way to get the liquor traffic out of politics is to get the liquor traffic out of the country.

We quote again from Mr. Locke the following striking example of what he calls "the infernal part which it [the liquor traffic] plays in politics":

"In Toledo, with ninety thousand population, there are eight hundred whiskey and beer shops. The vote of the city is fifteen thousand. Now these shops will average two votes each, the proprietor and one assistant, which makes a total of sixteen hundred. This is a tremendous power, especially as it is wielded by one head. All these men belong to the Liquor Dealers' Association, and all act together. These men have no principles. They are not divided upon tariff, currency, and other questions; politics is a part of their business, and their vote is cast as one, that it may be made profitable. They are in a business that everybody looks upon as disreputable; they are in it to make money, and they care not how they make it.

---

* The imports of the United States in 1887 were $679,159,477. The customs receipts (tariff) for the same year were $217,286,893. We have shown that the direct cost of the liquor traffic is more than $1,000,000,000, and the indirect cost as much again. (See Chapter II., page 17.)

"In party contests this power has two points to make. First, to demonstrate that it is a power which is not to be meddled with. No matter whether the candidate aims at the Presidency, a seat in Congress, school directorship, or a park commissionership, the first question the Liquor Dealers' Association asks, is, Is he a temperance man? If he is, the whole power of the organization is turned against him. They want it understood that no one can be elected to any place of honor or profit without their help. The showing of this power insures them against such troublesome interference as the enactment of early-closing laws, Sunday closing, large taxation, and, above all, Prohibition. They aim at control of the law-making power as well as the law-executing power. Secondly, they want their places to be made the centre of political management, the places where committees meet, and from whence money used in the elections is to be dispensed. From this money they take their toll, as a matter of course. The point with the brewer is to make the brewery the one controlling element in politics, and he has succeeded wonderfully. A politician may safely snub the Church, but he grovels in the dust before the wielder of the beer-mallet. He pays no attention to the good classes, but how he bows to the worst! The reason is, the good classes are divided on political and economic questions, while the liquor interest is united solely for one end.

"Once more, as to their strength: add to this vote (which is, of itself, enough to turn the scale as parties are now organized) the collateral branches of trade more or less connected with liquor making and selling. The tobacconists, the coopers, the bottlers, and the different kinds of people who supply the saloon trade, are all under this influence, and half as many more can be added to this sixteen hundred, making it twenty-four hundred.

"But this, large as it is, is the least of it. There is not one of these eight hundred saloons that cannot control four votes besides the two behind the bar, and that comes very close to a full half of all the votes in the city. They control the poor devils who are glad to sell their votes for the beer they can drink a week or two before an election, and one day after.

"Now take this enormous vote, mass the men employed in breweries, the wholesalers and retailers of liquor, the bar-tenders and other assistants directly employed, the collateral branches of trade dependent more or less upon them, and the vast army of hangers-on of the saloons, and it is a power which can and does control the cities of the country. Parties vie with each other in bidding for the saloon vote, nominations are made with sole reference to it, and this unholy power would become the government but for the counteracting influence in the country, which is yet, to some extent, free from its infernal influence.

"Think of a government under control of an organization whose business it is to make criminals and paupers! Think of a government controlled by the worst instead of the best citizens! Think of communities governed by the men whose business it is to make thieves and paupers instead of honest and self-supporting citizens!

"The influence of rum in politics is one of the strongest reasons for Prohibition."

CHAPTER XXVI.

THE PRESS.

"The attitude of the newspapers throughout the Union is greatly to be deprecated. Scores and hundreds of facts prove the efficacy of the law. Atlanta now has peaceful streets and happy homes, with sober husbands, sons, and brothers, with plenty to eat and to wear, where before there were broken hearts, fear of domestic outrage, and sometimes actual want. The great daily press abroad says nothing of the great good that has resulted, but if a hand truck load of jugs is seen (which is no great matter to 60,000 people) this must be magnified into a "jug train" and the whole press of the United States made to ring with it."—*Mayor George Hillyer, of Atlanta.*

THE "daily paper" forms all the thought of the majority of men. There is an educated ignorance which is the most unconquerable and the most fatal of all ignorance. You shall find all over the land clergymen, lawyers, physicians, professors and presidents of colleges, great and learned men, masters in their several departments, who are densely and profoundly ignorant as to the present status of the temperance question, turning over as axioms claims long since disproved, and holding as the latest results of knowledge the crude opinions of twenty-five or fifty years ago. Men who would not think of pronouncing on a new remedy for disease without studying the latest experiments favorable and unfavorable, who would not think of deciding upon a new question of law or a new discovery in science without careful consideration of the last decisions of the courts or the latest scientific authorities, will handle this temperance question any time and anywhere, and show in five minutes that they do not know what has been happening in their own country or their own State in the last five years. Because they are wise and strong in the things they have studied, they deem themselves equally wise and strong in this which they have not studied, and resent any attempt to enlighten them as an insult to their intelligence. Why? Because they have gained all their knowledge on the temperance question from their daily paper, combined supposed facts and inferences ready-made to their hand into fixed opinions, which seem to them as clear as anything else they have ever learned. An eminent lawyer of a Western city said to the writer: "I read nothing but law. I have a large law library at my office and another at my house. At both places I read law. The only exception is that when I start for my office I take my morning paper and read it on the car as I go down. When I return I buy an evening paper and read that on the car as I go home."

Now, in the course of years all that man's mind becomes soaked with the thinking of his favorite journal. He becomes accustomed to its coarseness, so that it does not shock him as it would if he were suddenly to come upon it for the first time. His entire knowledge of governmental matters consists of such "facts" as his one paper chooses to tell him. Its sophistries become his reasoning. Its heartlessness moulds his feelings, controls his emotions. At length he reaches the point where it would be the labor of years to educate him out of the errors he has imbibed. You must go far back to first principles. You must bring evidence to disprove things that never happened. You must conquer deep-seated prejudices that make him blind to evidence. If he is a busy man—as every leading man is sure to be—it becomes true at last that he really "has not time" to unlearn what he has been learning through all his reading years.

In an intensely partisan paper it is impossible to get mere, plain facts—so intermingled are they with comments on the wickedness and meanness of the opposing party. After going through a column to learn the particulars of a five-line incident, you turn the paper in despair, saying: "If I could only be told just what happened, I could form my own opinions."

Our partisan press is educating the nation into a contempt of character and an utter disregard of truth. We need to have it thundered from a new Sinai, "Thou shalt not bear false witness against thy neighbor." No sooner is a man nominated for any office than he is found to be an unmitigated scoundrel. The writer well remembers meeting a merchant of Boston whom he had known as an irreproachable man, superintendent of one Sunday-school for twenty-five years, who had just been nominated for Congress. I congratulated him, saying I was glad to have an opportunity to vote for a good man. He answered: "If you will read the —— ——, you will think I am not a very good man." So it was. The man unchallenged through all his business life was reported as perfidious and dishonorable within a week after his nomination. So far has this gone that no man pretends to believe, or troubles himself to investigate, any charges that are made against political candidates in the papers—of the party he does not belong to. That is, each political division of American voters concludes that all the papers of the country which do not belong to that division are unconscionable liars. The charge that it tells falsehoods is the easiest and safest charge to bring against any political paper in the paper in the United States, because all who do not belong to its own political party will believe it as a matter of course. How is this for "the educational influence of the press"? Is it not time to call loudly for a reform? Is it not time for every man to protect himself; and if he means to be fair and broadminded, to beware of confining himself to the papers of any one party? You believe the tariff is a good thing. Very well. But you cannot be sure you have fathomed the question unless you read what there is to say against it. You believe it is a bad thing. But you cannot claim to know the facts unless you read what there is to be said in its favor. You believe High License is a good thing. But you cannot claim to have an intelligent opinion on the subject unless you read and duly weigh the facts that are alleged against it. You are not competent to instruct your five-year-old boy till you have done so much as that. The quick rejoinder will be, Does not the same rule apply to Prohibitionists? Yes. But as yet Prohibitionists read only too much of what is said against their views. They have no great daily which will give them all the news on other matters. They constantly read—for the news—papers that are in deadly opposition to their principles. If they continue to be Prohibitionists, it is in spite of all that able and hostile papers can say to the contrary. An intelligent Prohibitionist of the present day is likely to be the best-informed man to be found upon the temperance question, because he has read both sides, while the majority of his opponents have read but one. Does this seem to any one a claim of sheer, irrational self-conceit? Then go out to-morrow morning in your own town, and ask the most intelligent and the most learned opponents of Prohibition whom you meet how often they read a Prohibition paper, and see if you are not scornfully told " Never !" or " Very seldom." The ordinary reason given is, " I haven't time"—that is, not time after reading all that a hostile eight-page paper has to say against it.

But it will be said, " This is getting entirely away from the subject of economics." Is it? Has the matter of truth no place in economics? How about the obligation of contracts? What has been the bottom fact in the worst financial crises this country has ever seen? Distrust. Want of confidence of man in man. Great embezzlements and rascalities of trusted men and corporations made every man distrust every other. Capital fled to cover. The business enterprises that were most hopefully represented were looked upon as the most suspicious. The longest tried integrity was at a discount, through fear that the trusted man would be trading on his reputation for honesty, as a means to entrap the unwary. Only slowly has trade revived as confidence returned, and men began to hope that at last, perhaps, most of the rascals were unmasked, and the rest of humanity could be trusted. The press which breaks down faith in human veracity is doing a deadly injury to the finances of a people.

There is perhaps one more fatal thing in this very connection. To create the belief that all men are false is one of the surest ways to make all men so. It is hard enough to be right amid all the world's temptations while looking admiringly to great examples deeply believed to be good and pure. To profoundly distrust all these tends to produce a despair of virtue, which is most perilous to one's own steadfastness. The press cannot be excused for any partisan advantage in bringing down the nation's standard of excellence and the youthful ideal of character. Destroying faith in honesty tends to produce dishonesty, and is full of financial as of moral dangers. We need a reorganized press, taking and holding higher and nobler ground.

The recent Amendment contests in Massachusetts, Pennsylvania, and Rhode Island have shown a condition of things in the partisan press which has been a great surprise to the majority of our people. It was generally believed that in a non-partisan contest the press would tell the substantial facts, or at least tell nothing glaringly false. But when such a man as General Palmer, of Pennsylvania, can say of the press of his State, as he did on June 20th, 1889:

"The liquor men have had a prodigious fund, and have spent not less than $100,000 upon the newspapers of the State. The leading journals have been so debauched that in touching upon the essential points of the Prohibition controversy they have told hardly a word of truth from the beginning. The liquor men's campaign, as made through the press, has been a campaign of lies from the very start.

"The newspapers of the State, with few exceptions, have been nothing but common prostitutes. This language, in view of the truth, is not strong, but calm and gentle. I do not complain because they have opposed Prohibition, but because they have permitted the saloons to use their columns for the most shameful purposes—for systematically deceiving the people. They have printed bogus despatches and unhesitatingly used what they knew was bogus matter in a way to mislead even newspaper men. If their editors deny this charge they deliberately write themselves down liars. They have printed articles manufactured right here in Philadelphia under the guise of honest despatches from Des Moines, Topeka, Atchison, and other places in Prohibition States, giving what pretended to be facts and figures, and asserting the failure of Prohibitory laws and the havoc wrought by them. These 'despatches' have been printed in the ordinary way in the news columns, without any marks to distinguish them as paid matter; yet they have been paid for from the rum funds at so much per line, and this disgraceful work has been going on all over the State right along from the beginning of the campaign,"

then it is surely time to call for a reform. Every citizen can do something to bring it about by procuring independent knowledge of the facts. If business men in every town in Pennsylvania would have written to their correspondents in Iowa and Kansas to know what were the real facts in regard to the working of the Prohibitory laws, they could have gathered a mass of information in every town which would have effectually answered the falsehoods of a mercenary press. The press would have been compelled to change front. They would have seen the disastrous results of continuing to publish what leading business men of their own town knew to be false from documents in their hands, and could any day refute. The people can do much by reading the Prohibition press, even if not agreeing with it in all respects. It is under the argus eye of a host of bitter enemies who have the ear of the people seven days to its one. It is forced to take care that its statements be such as can be proved. Here, too, the people have the verification in their own hands. If it is stated that such a councilman or such a member of the school board keeps a saloon at such and such a place, it is easy to ask, even by postal card, of some trusted correspondent, "Does A. B. keep a saloon at No. —, Blank Street?" If it is stated that your party held a caucus in a saloon at such a corner, that matter is entirely susceptible of proof or disproof by any one who cares to take the trouble. By thus sifting facts the people can largely control the press, and can obtain a sure fund of knowledge on this, the most burning and vital issue before the American people. Let every man be sure that the period of this discussion is one of the historic eras, and not lay up for himself the humiliation of *having to learn from subsequent histories* what happened in a historical crisis in the midst of which he lived. Especially the leaders of opinion should secure, and take great pains to secure, all attainable facts upon a traffic whose cost is measured by the thousand millions, and its victims by the hundred thousand. If the blind lead the blind our glorious nation will fall into the ditch of drunkenness. The facts upon this mighty question must be had from somewhere. If there is now no press which adequately states them, such a press must be created. When two thousand millions of cost and loss are at stake, there can be no better investment of money by patriotic men than to build up a press which shall fully gather the facts and ring out the truth in trumpet tones. For a single illustration of the need : in the late election in the two Dakotas, the writer bought New York dailies, two on one day and four on another, and could find the news of Prohibition in Dakota only by careful search in a few lines in the midst of other matter that almost buried it ; in one instance having to get a friend who knew the paper better to point out to him the item for which he had searched in vain. It may be said, without doubt, that most of the business men of New York, and many of its ministers, have no adequate idea of that struggle and victory, because the sources of information on which they are accustomed to rely did not give them any adequate statement of the facts. But taking up the well-known Prohibition paper of the same city, there was a full page of letters and despatches from the

Dakotas, with names and addresses of the senders, so that any one could verify or refute them by a few minutes' correspondence. Certainly every man who would claim to be intelligent on that subject should read that account, or make sure that he has from somewhere an account as good and complete.

But it is not only by the newspapers that the work of the press is done. Books are a mighty power. The publications of the National Temperance Society and of the Woman's Christian Temperance Union and of many enterprising firms should be scattered far and wide. Every thoughtful man should read them and recommend them to the young people about him. How, for instance, can any intelligent and scholarly man suppose himself well informed on the temperance question who has not read such books as Dorchester's " Liquor Problem in All Ages," and Gustafson's " Foundation of Death," and Richardson's " Medical Use of Alcohol," and Maynard's " Truth about Kansas"? New books must be written. A temperance library must be created. Writers must be found who can do for temperance what Huxley and Tyndall and Joseph Cook have done for science—popularize its results, so as to put them within the reach of those who could not study the facts at first hand ; and to make them attractive and winning in statement, so that the great common people will be glad to read them. The temperance instruction in our public schools must be pushed to greater efficiency and completeness.

The shrewd liquor interest is already taking up this method in their own behalf with an enterprise and efficiency worthy of a better cause. Every patriot and every Christian, every scholar and every capitalist, every minister and teacher and philanthropist should give time, study, and money to the work of disseminating among our people a higher and truer knowledge upon this question which, in the providence of God, has come to our stirring time and to our aggressive people for solution, that our country, yet so prosperous and so fair, may escape a darkly threatening peril, and rise to the sublime possibilities of its future.

CHAPTER XXVII.

THE CHURCH.

"I am speaking for the Church now, and I am free to say that unless she is deliberately ready to make a covenant with death and an agreement with hell, her voice ought to be unanimous for the prohibition of the manufacture and sale of strong drink. If that were her voice, the Government and legislators and Congressmen would not be long in hearing of it and acting accordingly. It should be enough for the Christian that his Bible says : ' Woe unto him that giveth his neighbor drink, that puttest thy bottle to him and makest him drunken,' and when God says ' woe,' no government has a right to say ' weal.' To me it is as clear as day what the voice of the Church ought to be on this question, unless she is ready to be left behind in working righteousness, and to be out-moralled by the moralist and out-humanized by the humanitarians."—*Rev. A. J. Gordon, D.D., before the Evangelical Alliance at Washington, D. C.*

THE scriptural ideal of the Church is broader than the Church itself has ever attained. While the Church is to prepare humanity for another world, it is to prepare the way *to* that world *through* this world. On its earthly side THE CHURCH IS AN ECONOMIC INSTITUTION. It comes to men "as being themselves also in the body."

If we trace Christianity back to its origin we find that the Old Testament was intensely economic. "The mistakes of Moses" were an achievement which the world has not yet caught up with. The law which prohibited idolatry and taught the insufferable majesty of the One living and true God, also taught the people not to eat pork, a law which, if the world had followed it, would doubtless have prevented many diseases. It taught them to wash their clothes and their persons. It quarantined against leprosy. It provided for the homeliest details in policing the camp against all that was impure and insanitary. Even in this current year of the Christian era, the New York papers are publishing statements to show that the "Kosher" meats inspected according to the Mosaic law are the only ones safe from the germs of phthisis or consumption, from which, in consequence, it is affirmed, the Jews as a race do not suffer. That law carefully watched over the rights and needs of the poor and the stranger. Many of its provisions for domestic life are now reaffirmed by the best medical and social science of modern times. We need not attempt to defend the law in all particulars. It was confessedly an imperfect economy for a transition period, to give place "in the fulness of time" to a new and better. But the one fact remains that the Old Testament religion was intensely and minutely economic. It dealt with human beings as those who were to live in domestic, social, and political relations, and whose conduct in those relations would affect their very worship of God. The whole world has learned that its Sabbath rest-day, whatever men's religious creeds may be, is of inestimable value as an economic institution.

Did all this economic element, as lawyers say, "cease and determine," vanish and pass away, on the institution of the New Economy? The very name, long fixed in the literature of Christendom, shows that it did not. The Christian world has felt through the ages that the New Testament is also economic, though how deeply and truly so it has often forgotten.

The very introductory anthem of Christianity was

"peace on earth, good will to men." John the Baptist told the publicans to collect the taxes honestly, and the soldiers to "do violence to no man, and be content with your wages." He directed all the property owners to care for the destitute. "He that hath two coats, let him impart to him that hath none; and he that hath meat, let him do likewise"—a very practical socialism, sharing from above, not plundering from below.

The most striking thing on the surface of Christ's own ministry was His care for the bodies of men—"He went about doing good." He summed up His own work in the memorable words: "The blind receive their sight, and the lame walk, the lepers are cleansed, and the deaf hear, the dead are raised up, and the poor have the Gospel preached to them." He directed His disciples, "When thou makest a feast, call not thy kinsmen, nor thy brethren, nor thy rich neighbors, lest they also bid thee again, and a recompense be made thee"—a death-blow to the customs of "polite society," as still adhered to by the membership of aristocratic churches who visit and receive only "in our set," and keep careful lists of social "indebtedness," and of those to whom they "owe" calls. Then came the positive, "But call the maimed, the poor, the halt, and the blind, for they cannot recompense thee, but thou shalt be recompensed at the resurrection of the just." The Church has long "spiritualized" this as simply a sublime and tender figure of speech, when it becomes not nearly so spiritual as the real doing of the thing in the actual world. That Jesus meant it in the concrete appears from His own action. The converted publican, Levi, "made Him a great feast in his own house: and there was a great company of publicans and of others that sat down with them.

But their scribes and Pharisees murmured against His disciples, saying, Why do ye eat and drink with publicans and sinners?" This was a breaking down of social distinctions, an actual eating and drinking together at the same table. This was the very method of the wise and godly Earl of Shaftesbury in his midnight suppers for the fallen women of London, where he himself and many of the choicest Christian men and matrons of England met at the same table the outcasts of the streets, and made the tract and the prayer follow the supper and the kindly talk, and followed up repentance with the finding of situations for honest work. When Jesus saw a hungry multitude, without waiting for the clamor for food to arise, He fed them with actual bread and fish. We think there are some revivalists of to-day who would never have thought of that, and who, if their attention had been called to it, would have answered: "If these people have not provided for their suppers, I can't help it. My business is to save souls." Jesus seemed to see no incompatibility in doing both.

When the great revival of Pentecost came, one of the very first results was a system of Christian communism. There are no indications that this was meant to be permanent. Certainly it was not compulsory. Ananias was punished, not for keeping back his money, which Peter told him he had a perfect right to do, but for lying about it. But this system of the Pentecostal time is valuable as a clear exhibition of the view of the early Church, led by inspired apostles, that Christianity cared for the bodies of men. Jerusalem was full of strangers unprovided for so long a stay; and doubtless of converts whose business and employment had been interrupted by their profession of Christianity. While anybody in the Church owned anything, these needy ones must not want, was the grand resolve of that exalted day.

In after times we find the Epistles full of directions for the care of "widows" and of "the poor." Paul makes incessant calls upon the wealthy Gentile converts for contributions for "the poor saints at Jerusalem," giving whole chapters to this work in the midst of his expositions of the most sublime themes of the Christian faith, and making journeys to Jerusalem for the express purpose of carrying to its poor the contributions of Corinth and Ephesus. The Apostle James says that if a brother or sister is ragged and hungry, and you give him good wishes and nothing to eat or wear, that is of no use. These are not the exact words, but the thought translated into the English of to-day. He condemns the crowding of the poor man into a poor seat in church as a very worldly minded proceeding.

The New Testament never forgets nor despises the economic idea, though often eclipsing it by the glory of a transcendent spirituality. The Church has not always held the two elements in due proportion.

Christ brings the economic idea into the solemn prophecy of the Judgment Day : "Come, ye blessed of my Father ; . . . I was a hungered, and ye gave me meat : I was thirsty, and ye gave me drink : I was a stranger, and ye took me in : sick and in prison, and ye visited me. . . . . Depart, ye cursed, ... for I was a hungered, and ye gave me no meat : thirsty, and ye gave me no drink : naked, and ye clothed me not : sick and in prison, and ye visited me not."

Who shall dare say this is figurative in view of what Jesus Himself did with His own kingly hands ?

For the Church to apply these ideas to the actual

destitution in the rookeries and slums of our cities, to the apple-woman shivering on the bleak corner, who if she were your mother should have a warm seat by the fire; to the newsboys, some of whom ought to be in the nursery, snatching their precarious living amid the jostling crowd in storm and sun, sleeping in doorways and arches of bridges; to the poor sewing-girls' unutterable woe and heart-breaking battle, would revolutionize our civilization. Ah! if that sewing-girl were your sister or your daughter, my friend, you would leave business and journey across the continent to help her. You would work day and night, and cut down your own living to the barest necessities, if need be, to rescue her from the dire destitution and awful temptation of her life. How will it be when we shall all hear the "I was an hungered"?

There is something wrong in a civilization that allows all this within sight of the homes of wealth, luxury, and splendor.

James Russell Lowell, who has more than once proved himself prophet as well as poet, has given us a "parable" as deeply true as it is exquisitely sad:

> "Said Christ, our Lord, 'I will go and see
> How the men, My brethren, believe in Me.'
> He passed not again through the gate of birth,
> But made Himself known to the children of earth.

> "Then said the chief priests and rulers and kings,
> 'Behold now the Giver of all good things.
> Go to, let us welcome with pomp and state
> Him who alone is mighty and great.'

> "With carpets of gold the ground they spread,
> Wherever the Son of Mary should tread,
> And in palace chambers lofty and rare,
> They lodged Him and served Him with kingly fare.

"Great organs surged through arches dim
　Their jubilant floods in praise of Him ;
And in church and palace and judgment hall,
　He saw His image over all.

"But still, wherever His steps they led,
　The Lord in sorrow bent down His head,
And from under the heavy foundation stones
　The Son of Mary heard bitter groans.

"And in church and palace and judgment hall
　He marked great fissures that rent the wall,
And opened wider and yet more wide
　As the living fountain heaved and sighed.

"'Have ye founded your thrones and altars, then,
　On the bodies and souls of living men?
And think ye that building shall endure
　Which shelters the noble and crushes the poor?

"'With gates of silver and bars of gold
　Ye have fenced My sheep from My Father's fold.
I have heard the droppings of their tears
　In heaven these eighteen hundred years.'

"'O Lord and Master, not ours the guilt,
　We build but as our fathers built ;
Behold Thine images how they stand
　Sovereign and sole through all our land.

"'Our task is hard, with sword and flame
　To hold Thine earth forever the same,
And with sharp crooks of steel to keep
　Still as Thou leftest them Thy sheep.'

"Then Christ sought out an artisan,
　A low-browed, stunted, haggard man,
And a motherless girl, whose fingers thin
　Pushed from her faintly want and sin.

"These set He in the midst of them,
　And, as they drew back their garments' hem
For fear of defilement, 'Lo, here,' said He,
　'The images ye have made of Me.'"

He would be a presumptuous man who should claim to be able to tell all that the Church might do to make things otherwise; but he would be a very shallow thinker who would not admit that it might do vastly more than it is now attempting. One long step toward its possible achievements will be for the Church distinctly to recognize that it has an Economic Mission.

Some conception of this appears in the sending out of medical missionaries to the heathen and in such enterprises as that of Edward Judson, going to the poor where they are, and giving them not only Gospel, but drinking fountains and reading-rooms. The Young Men's Christian Association and the Women's Christian Temperance Union are Christian enterprises in the same direction, though outside of the organized Church. Perhaps the Roman Catholics are here nearest to the true ideal in keeping all their charities in the hand and name of the Church. We have rarely been more touched with the living worth of Christianity than in going, on a recent Sunday, to the Chinese Department of the Baptist Tabernacle in New York, and there finding at little tables all over the room Christian American young ladies, each with a Chinaman beside her, teaching him such things as to spell h-a-d, had, and not to leave the top of an "o" open in writing because that would make a "v." At the head of the room some cultured Chinese gentlemen showed the results of this patient toil. They deeply believed in the Christian Church, which they had found true to the Master's words, "I was a stranger, and ye took me in."

The Church must address itself to this Temperance problem. Many will reply, Are we not doing so? Yes, in a desultory and fragmentary way. But we will ask a return question, Is the Church doing anything comparable to the magnitude of the curse?

We freely admit and highly honor its beneficent work. We see a large proportion of our churches total abstinence societies, in which no liquor-dealer nor liquor drinker can hold membership. We see the ministers and leaders and devout women of the Church the life and soul of temperance societies and at the front of moral and political reform. We are well assured that there is a vast sum of helpful service done which is known only to God. We honor it and rejoice in it all.

Yet we do maintain—and we believe the deep response of the Christian conscience will bear us out in the claim —that if sixty thousand men, or one half that number, were dying yearly in the land from any other single vice; if the innocent women and tender children were doomed in countless homes to agony which the tongue has no power to tell nor the heart to fathom, by any other single curse, the Church would rise in its might and majesty, like the heaving of the sea, till the throne of God in heaven should be reached by her prayers, and the nations on earth be moved as the trees of a wood are moved by a mighty wind. If intemperance is a sin, the Son of man is come to save sinners. If the saloon temptation is a crime, the Son of man is come to destroy the works of the devil. If it is a wide cause of innocent sorrow, the Son of man is anointed to bind up the broken hearted, to preach deliverance to the captives, AND TO LET THE OPPRESSED GO FREE.

When and where should He do all this if not in drink-cursed America now? Here is the Demoniac struggling in the plain whom He would lead His followers down to save from the Mount of Transfiguration, where they fain would dwell.

If there is doubt in any one's mind whether the Church should deal with the liquor curse, let him know that the liquor curse has already come to deal with the Church.

A correspondent from Dayton, O., writes as follows:

"The evils that the saloon is producing were again brought vividly to mind by utterances from the pulpit giving statistics of its effects on young men. It was said that only 5 per cent. of the men between fourteen and thirty-five years of age are in the churches and Christian association. Where are the other 95 per cent.? The same speaker said that a very large part, indeed the majority, spend their evenings, Sundays, and spare time in saloons and gambling dens. Our pastor also said that 90 per cent. of our young men frequent saloons and houses of ill-fame. This is appalling, yet we are assured by Christian ministers that it is true.

"Ministers and laymen of our churches, it is surely time to stop and consider; the Church has been in existence ever since the first settlement of our country; the modern saloon is less than fifty years in our land; yet by carefully collected statistics it is shown that the Church is getting but five young men, while the saloon is getting the majority of the ninety-five who remain outside.

"The speaker said that if the roofs could be lifted from about ten squares of our city, and the fathers and mothers be permitted to look in on what is going on there, they would be filled with horror at the appalling sight. The darling boys who stay out late at night would be found congregated there in dens of iniquity, the companions of thieves and gamblers."

In such a state of things our appeal to the Church is, not to do something, *but to do everything*—to strain to the utmost every human resource, and to bring down all that our compassionate God can give us of the divine. Not till we each can say: "I have done the last and the utmost that I can do," can we rest from the conflict without sin.

In regard to much of the work which the Church may do, such as Gospel temperance meetings, bands of hope, etc., there is no controversy. But one burning question remains beyond, Shall the Church go into politics? Not as a Church. That would work evil in the future greater than all the good it might do in the present. But the Church should lay down the divine line of righteousness straight and clear along the earth. If that line cuts through political camps, it must still be laid down as unfalteringly as the railroad line that cuts the farmer's lands in two. We must simply say, "THIS IS RIGHT. HERE STANDS THE CHURCH." Then, if "the heathen rage," it will not be the first fulfilment of the Master's words, " I came not to bring peace, but a sword." Right does not cease to be the province of the Church because it becomes also the province of politics. In Cincinnati to-day Sabbath observance is a hot political question. The Fourth Commandment is in politics. It is claimed by many that that single question turned the last State election, throwing the dominant party out of power. Must the Church therefore retire from that ground? Must the ministry avoid that part of the decalogue in their Scripture readings, and carefully avoid preaching on Sabbath-keeping till it has been settled whether the saloon-keepers shall ply their trade on Sunday or not? The duty of the Church is plain. The Sabbath does not cease to be her trust because politics has made it its battle-ground. Rather the more must she urge its sacredness because it is endangered. Her ministry must reinforce the sanctions of religion by urging the economics of the Sabbath, that the hesitating and the wavering may see that it is a question of worthy and happy living on earth, as well as of the bliss of heaven.

Then she may leave her members as citizens to apply the divine standards to their political action, as they shall answer for it at the bar of God ; but solemnly teach them that they shall answer for their political action at that solemn and final tribunal.

Her ministers do not cease to be citizens. Outside the church they may—and they should—speak, act, and vote, like any other men, their deep convictions of right. There is in this no "union of Church and State," for they appeal to their fellow-citizens not by any authority they may claim as pastors, but simply by the authority which character, argument, and persuasion may give, just as any other citizens of equal worth and ability might do. If they should be silent, and by their default the Sabbath should be thrown wide open to intemperance, they could not answer for their silence as Christians to their God, nor as citizens to a wronged and degraded community.

The whole giant wrong of the liquor traffic is in politics. If Prohibition were to retire from the political field the liquor traffic would stay there still, holding the balance between the great parties, and sending one up and the other down in the scales, according as either would best fulfil its abominable behest. If the church-member or the minister speaks any political word, writes a political line, or casts any vote whatever, he must take temperance into politics. The only question is, how he may take it there most effectively and victoriously. Intemperance is in the political field. The Christian citizen may not shrink from meeting it there.

We speak of Christ as relying upon moral methods. So, for the most part, He did. But once in His life an evil traffic confronted Him. That He assailed with the strong hand, throwing down the tables of its money-changers, and scourging them out of the temple they had profaned. If ever any money-changers' tables should be overthrown it is these, whose every coin is dripping with blood and tears. If ever there was time and place for the scourge it is against this traffic, which sells not doves, but men,—to drive it out from this fair land, reserved for centuries in the providence of God to be for all nations a house of prayer, which it is fast making a den of thieves.

CHAPTER XXVIII.

CITIES AND IMMIGRANTS.

"Thomas Carlyle predicted that all great modern cities will come finally to the position in which Paris was under the Commune, unless the reputable side of society organizes itself aggressively to counteract the dangers which make universal suffrage a peril. I stood lately among the ruins of the public buildings burned by the mob in Cincinnati. I remember the railway riots of 1877. We are performing an experiment, not only in the face of the whole world, but for the benefit of the entire earth. It is for Americans, who believe in government of the people, for the people, and by the people, to see that such government is made so wise and strong as not to perish from the earth. There is growing up in the liquor traffic a power that already has its clutches on our throats; and a loss of time in organizing national reform may be the loss forever of an opportunity to save our nation from being wrecked by municipal misrule. Therefore, for one, I pray God to send us such a recrystallization of politics as shall throw all the best elements of society into a National Reform Party."—*Joseph Cook.*

"Whiskey is the dynamite of civilization."—*Hon. John D. Long, of Massachusetts, speech against Bonded Whiskey Bill.*

WHAT shall we do with our cities, and what shall we do with our immigrants?

Two tremendous questions, and in them the future of the Republic!

I. With one-fourth of our population in the cities, with the steadily increasing drift toward them, with the field and immunity they give to the vicious classes, and the self-degrading tendencies which so rapidly multiply the number of the vicious already there, thoughtful men are coming to hold their breath at the menace to our civilization. The most startling element in the case is that so many leading men—successful politicians, editors of great dailies and of widely read magazines, distinguished lawyers, eminent clergymen, have practically given up the problem. They take it for granted that the Sunday theatre, the seven-day saloon, the beer garden and the brothel, the ward politician, the bummer, the heeler, and the daily murder "have come to stay"—a cant phrase which, if anything is awkward, unpopular, or dangerous to deal with, is supposed to relieve the soul of all responsibility for letting it go on. If any law is proposed which would effectually restrain any of these things, they answer with the greatest promptness, "You can never enforce it in the cities." That is, it is claimed that THE CITIES HAVE ALREADY PASSED OUT OF THE CONTROL OF THE REPUBLIC, and that the people at large are at their mercy, *to pass only such laws as their worst classes will not object to.* The statement seems a terrible one when put into plain words; but the best thing to do with any idea is to put it into plain words, that we may know whether we believe it, and, if we do, what are we going to do about it.

City domination has been often tried in history, and, in every case, disastrously. When Rome sucked in all the strength and riches of the provinces, so that whoever was master of Rome was master of the empire, the empire became not worth maintaining. Feudalism, though a system of disintegration, was a gain by multiplying centres of influence, and distributing power. When the French kings reversed the process, and drew all the nobility from their estates to reside at court, till it could be said, "Paris is France," they prepared the way for the Revolution. The Revolution was what it was largely because all who determined its destinies could be drawn together by the midnight bells of Paris. Splendid cities and helpless peasantry work ill for any nation. To have the rural districts held by a sturdy, intelligent, honest yeomanry, compelling laws which city as well as country must obey, is the condition of safety and stability. If our cities control us they will destroy us, because their worst elements govern them.

The life of the city is essentially artificial. Its inhabitants have little knowledge of the farmers' needs, and less sympathy for them. But to legislate against the interests of agriculture is to cut the roots of national prosperity. At last we all depend on the farmer. "The king himself is served by the field." Government by cities tends always to prostrate agriculture and to degrade the agricultural classes from a yeomanry into a peasantry. Then the country becomes a hollow shell, with some centres of magnificence rattling around in it.

Within the city the worst elements have exceptional power. A few roughs cannot control a rural village. They are opposed and discounted at every turn. A thing is at once resisted which they are observed to favor. One substantial farmer by a dozen words from his wagon-seat can spoil a month's intrigue of such a clique. The climate does not agree with them. But scrape them out of a thousand villages, and pile them in the city ten stories deep, and the grains which, if separate, might flash harmlessly, combine into a mine of tremendous explosive power. It is very doubtful whether the best elements of the city, unaided, can attain a unity equal to the consolidation of this vicious force, and a steadiness equal to its fury. So far, at least, they are not doing it. The better classes of the cities must be re-enforced by the virtue and intelligence of the rural districts, in order to control their own dangerous classes. Even as we write, one of our religious weeklies comes with an appeal of "Help for Cincinnati"—in view of the general defiance there of Sabbath laws, and most others. It pleads for the virtue and intelligence of the State to aid them through the Legislature in their contest, saying : " Help can only come from the State." The plea is good. The city needs the help of every true heart, hand, and vote in all the rural districts in order to redeem itself.

How can the tendency to dangerous centralization in the cities be checked ? How can the domination of the worst classes in the city over city and country alike be ended ? To answer these questions, we must ask two others :

1. What is the deadliest way in which the city sucks the life-blood of the country ? The answer is, by taking its grain and giving it back intoxicants ; by bringing its brawn and brain to staggering imbecility. Every man so spoiled is a loss to the producing power of the country, and a probable recruit to the dangerous classes in the city—a double weight in the wrong scale. Prohibition of the liquor traffic, while it might not at once stop the sale in the city, could at once blot out the distillery and brewery, and thus keep the city from fattening on the ruin of the country, and breeding there festering sores whose drip must return upon its own vitals. Prohibition has had not quite six years of bitterly disputed control in Iowa, but now the news comes that the great Arensdorf brewery at Sioux City is being fitted up for an oatmeal factory. Spread the consumption of oat-

meal! A rural population without a saloon, a tippler, or a drunkard, will have that ascendency in State and national life which virtue and intelligence always give. They can not only protect themselves, but bring aid to the beleaguered city.

2. What is the great focus of destruction in the city? There is one instant answer—the saloon. If the question is of Anarchy, the saloons are the Anarchists' gathering places; if of crime, the saloons are the criminals' resorts. If a criminal is evading justice, the police watch the saloons for him, and nine times out of ten find him there. The saloon demoralizes by more than the liquor that is drunk. The language that is heard, the stories that are told, the company that is kept, the rehearsal of crime, the familiarity of villainy, the freemasonry of vice, combined with the heating of the brain and the deadening of the finer sensibilities by alcohol, are constantly bringing the better class of young men who frequent them down toward the level of the lower and the lowest. The saloons are constantly recruiting the ranks of the vicious classes from the ranks of the better classes. How can the better classes protect themselves against this steady desertion from their own ranks and this steady re-enforcement of the enemy? They must call in the help of the country. This is no question of the country against the city, but of the country helping the best part of the city against the worst. The better part is the true city; the rest an accretion we endure because we cannot get rid of it. It is as if the worst classes had risen in riot and the troops of the country were called in to suppress it—not to capture the city, but to protect it against an internal foe. The better classes of the city must welcome the aid. When the country is demanding

Prohibition, let no one raise the objection of "It can't be enforced in the city." It can in the country, and that is so much to start with. In the city, too, a part of its enforcement begins from the instant of its enactment, making the manufacture and sale of liquor an outlawed business, driving capital out of it, making insurance companies shy of it, making its debts uncollectible. Then, the weakest enforcement operates as a first-class "restriction," driving the saloon from the open street to alleys and cellars, where self-respecting young men— those best worth saving—will not go after it.

Every year brings Prohibition boys from the country to be rising men in the city, and makes the enforcement of Prohibition constantly easier when once begun. Prohibition is a screw. Once well set, it is only necessary to keep turning the handle, and the pressure grows every moment more irresistible. The longer it is turned on, the more determined the people are not to have it turned back, but to keep twisting the handle further round. Thus, ex-Governor Martin says that, at the recent election in Kansas, "no political party ventured even to offer a resolution in favor of reopening the question." The city can control its foreign population when it can keep them sober; and when the police do not have to watch saloons, they will be in better condition to watch everything else. The country can help the city to do this. The country has a stake in the city as great as the number of its bright boys and girls sure to go there. It has a right to demand a voice in shaping the city's destiny for virtue and temperance. The State must control the city, like every other foot of its territory, in the interest of all the people. When the country can help the city to Prohibition, it can help it to everything else necessary to an honest, clean, safe administration of government, till the city shall cease to be "a menace to civilization."

Nothing so much as Prohibition can enable us to control, purify, and redeem the "slums" of the city. The Cleveland *Press* remarks:

"Perhaps the work of Jack the Ripper may be the cause of some good work which he has not contemplated. The degradation of Whitechapel is only what might be expected in a population which is compelled to live in a condition of brutal degradation. That such dens as those of Whitechapel should exist in a civilized land is a mockery of the very idea of civilization. On this subject the public mind is now thoroughly aroused, and it is to be hoped that the result will be seen in a clean sweep of the whole district. The science of human life has only begun to be a science, and it will continue to be nothing better than impracticable speculation until it is applied to the problem of the life of the poor in the great cities to which population crowds in these times. We know now that the epidemic diseases, the plagues, and the enormous death-rates of former ages were caused by ignorance and carelessness. We have got rid of the ignorance; it is high time that we rose out of the carelessness. It is time, too, that we should realize the fact that epidemics of crime may have their cause in unsound sanitary conditions as well as in other things. It is a fact that cleanliness, if it does not always prove godliness, at least conduces powerfully to decency. Decent living makes decent people; and where decent living is impossible, decent people need not be looked for. *For its own sake society has an interest in the possibility of decent living to all its members.* If one-half, or even one-fifth, of the money expended on converting the heathen were applied to the solution of these pressing home affairs, the face of many great cities, and ultimately of all, would soon begin to wear a different aspect!"

We shall not need, however, to do less for the heathen, and stint the pitiful $5,000,000 which all our American Christendom gives to save the whole heathen world. Only stop using our $1,000,000,000 to make heathen at home, and we can build model lodging-houses, lay out wide, clean, well-lighted streets, care for the women in homes and the children in schools, build churches and chapels and set up mission Sunday-schools, and make these waste places of our civilization blossom like the garden of the Lord.

II. Immigration is denationalizing us, un-Americanizing us. We have to stop and think to know whether we are ourselves, and the rush is so great we haven't the time to stop. We are laying the foundations of empire, and laying them as building materials are dropped out of a cyclone. We want not to stop immigration, but to sift it; to have the wheat of honesty, industry, muscle, intelligence, and religion dropped on our shores, and the chaff of ignorance, degradation, filth, vice, and crime blown back across the sea. For this purpose, national Prohibition will be an unequalled sieve.

Mr. D. W. Gage, of Cleveland, writes in the *New Era:*

> "Coming from Chicago to Cleveland, I met on the train an old Republican friend and ex-senator of the Ohio Legislature. He had been taking a tour to the Rocky Mountains, and had been southwest through Kansas and northwest through Wisconsin. Said he, 'I can tell just as soon as I enter a Chicago depot and look over the crowd of travellers, especially the emigrants, where they are going—whether to Kansas or Wisconsin. You will see the clean, well-dressed, neat, intelligent classes, who use no liquor and little tobacco, going toward Kansas, and the ignorant, poorer clad, unshaved and wooden shod, with breath odorous of beer and whiskey, going toward Wisconsin.' He recognized the cause in Kansas as a Prohibition State and Wisconsin as a license State."

Let Prohibition cover all our territory, and it will be heralded over the sea. Then the criminal, the crook, the tippler who is "never drunk," but if ever sober thinks he is sick, and hurries to take something "as a medicine," the Anarchists and the Lazzaroni, will keep away from a land where they can never again get a square drink. But the sober, the diligent, the saving, the virtuous, even from lands where drinking usages prevail, will recognize the hope that is in our better way. Many a father who drinks in England will be glad of the gain to his boys in bringing them to a land where they will not drink. Many a wife will use woman's quiet influence to get the yet unspoiled husband to a land where he may achieve his best and be saved from sinking to his worst. Prohibition would enable us to pick the best elements from all the nations. Its sifting would shape the coming centuries and mould the very race-type of the future, incorporating with our stock the choicest life-blood of every people. What is called the "one narrow issue" of Prohibition is equal to the solution of some of our gravest problems, and to the widest view of public welfare and national destiny.

What do we wish our immigrants to be? Do we want German provinces, Irish colonies, Scandinavian counties, and Italian wards to make us a polyglot nation, and lay out on the American Continent a new map of Europe, with all the old prejudices, hatreds, and feuds of the ages past? Do we want a Clan-na-Gael running a government inside of our Government, with its own courts, trials, and executions? No. We want Americans, all, speaking one language, all holding our land their country, and centring in it all their loyalty, their sympathies, and their hopes. We want their children to hold this their native country and their fatherland.

There is a good deal in the funny story of the English settler and his American-born boy. The boy proposed to celebrate "the Fourth," and his father asked, "What do you care for the Fourth of July?" "Why, that's the day we whipped you, pa," was the answer. We want every American-born boy and girl to be born into all our American history and institutions. We would make of all these mingled nations one American people, the noblest and most glorious the world ever saw. We would have our immigrants ask, not how they can mould us to the customs of their forefathers in the lands from whose oppression they are fleeing, but how they can mould themselves to the institutions that have made America so free and grand. We would have them not looking back over the sea, but forward to the possible advance of America's future, to a civilization better and richer than they or we have known.

The best way to do this is to take intemperance, with all its waste of money, its disorder, pauperism, and crime out of their path as well as ours, and make the children of all one new people never touched by the curse of the saloon.

CHAPTER XXIX.

THE DEVIL'S FOREIGN MISSION.

"Slavery and alcohol are the twin curses of the Dark Continent. Surely America will not be laggard in seconding the efforts of any Christian power whatever, whether in England or Germany, which will address itself in earnest to the task of their complete suppression. Professor Drummond has appealed for our aid in stemming the encroachments of slave-hunting Arabs in Central Africa. But while the Mohammedan religion permits one form of slavery it does not permit another, and of the two the worse. Turks and Arabs are total abstainers from intoxicants. Shall we, as a Christian nation, have longer any part or lot in the infliction upon Africa of a kind of slavery which ruins both body and soul, and wreaks not merely temporary, but eternity-long disaster?"—*Illustrated Christian Weekly.*

THE tablet on which I am writing has on its cover a picture of Robinson Crusoe under a burning southern sky, dressed from head to foot in thick furs, while he holds over his head a heavy feather umbrella. It seems never to have occurred to the novelist nor to his thousands of boy readers that this costume would be warm. The description is an unconscious testimony to the civilized man's idea that dress is a necessity to human dignity and propriety, even when one civilized man constitutes the entire population of a tropical island. In fact, whatever certain travellers may say of the guileless simplicity of savages, all the people who have ever done anything that history has thought worth recording have been those who wore clothes. The first step of the newly-discovered African up from barbarism will be when he shall cease to be

"The naked Ethiop panting at the line."

In that latitude he will not clothe himself in the skins of beasts, wild or tame, Robinson Crusoe to the contrary notwithstanding. His own rude manufactures will not furnish him much worthy the name of clothing. It is only the products of civilized looms, light enough not to be a burden, bright enough to be attractive, cheap enough to be washed and changed often and replaced when worn out, that can ever bring such a people up the first step from barbarism to civilization.

There are fifty millions of such in the Congo basin alone. All is open to trade as soon as the railroad is built around Livingstone Falls. What a demand for the cotton cloth of the Birminghams, Manchesters, and Lowells is here! By the time this vast population should approximate the civilization of the Hindus, Burmans, and Karens, the demand for cotton cloth alone would be not less than $50,000,000 annually. Missionaries testify that this is one of the first and most striking advances made by the natives who come under the influence of Christianity.

What is the effect of intoxicating liquors upon this demand? What is its effect in civilized lands? Where law, custom, inherited disposition and winters of cruel cold unite to demand abundant clothing, the entire trend of alcohol is toward nakedness. The ragged man, scarcely within the limits of mere decency; the shivering woman with a summer dress on an Arctic day; the children barefooted on the icy streets, are the familiar results of intoxicating drink in civilized lands. Now try it on the

Equatorial savage, where custom, heredity, and climate unite to make costume the most dispensable of all human needs, and what is the result? Rev. James Johnson, the native pastor of the island of Lagos, says:

"As you stand at Lagos you can see fleets of canoes laden with casks of palm-oil, nuts, and other produce. But when they are returning home, what do they carry away with them? *Very few pieces of cloth;* every one of them is laden with rum and gin. We give Europe palm-oil and many other useful things; but what does she give us in return? This vile stuff; this spirit which sends our people drunken and mad.

* * * * * * *

"A friend mentioned to me lately that a member of a Glasgow firm stated to him that he formerly employed a large number of looms weaving cloth for the African market; now he has not one. A trader in the Calabar River wrote recently to his principals *to send no more cloth—drink was the article in demand.* Mr. Joseph Thomson, in his recent journey into the Niger regions, found this evil so abounding therein, that it will render *hopeless the demand, anticipated by some,* by the natives, for *unlimited supplies of calico,* as effectually as will the sterility of the Eastern countries through which he formerly travelled. In all its effects, moral and economical, this traffic is only evil: impeding the work of the Church at home, marring her mission work abroad, and destroying beneficial industry." *

Mr. Johnson himself states :†

"At each port of call the eye becomes bewildered in watching the discharge of thousands of cases of gin, hundreds of demijohns of rum, box upon box of guns, untold kegs of gunpowder, and myriads of clay pipes, while it seems as if only by accident a stray bale of cloth went over the side."

Mr. W. P. Tisdel, special agent of the United States to the Congo, says:

"Unfortunately a few gallons of trade gin will go further in trade

---

* "Africa and the Drink Trade," by Canon Farrar, pp. 24, 25.
† *Ibid.*, p. 31.

with the natives than ten times its value in cloth, and it often happens that traders are compelled to return to the coast without having accomplished a trade because the natives insist upon having gin, while the trader was supplied with cloth alone."

The submission of our makers of cotton goods in allowing the alcoholic trade to close in their faces the market of a continent—the one new door of the world—is supremely astonishing. We should expect that the Parliament of Great Britain and the United States Congress would be flooded with petitions and demands from the great cotton industry against this spoliation. It may be said, without doubt, that if any foreign power had forbidden our cotton manufacturers the ports of Africa, we would go into a new "War of 1812" sooner than allow it. The South would be hot as the North for it, for the shutting out of millions of yards of cloth means the loss of a market for thousands of bales of cotton. It is only the wonderful liquor traffic which can thus sit down on a vast manufacture, and not a voice from the mercantile world be raised against it. Mr. Hornaday, in his "Free Rum on the Congo," says :*

"Why, if there were only *a few millions of money to be made by enforcing temperance* in Africa, there would be ten thousand capitalists clamoring at the doors of Congress to-morrow for the exclusive privilege of performing the task. What is more, every company bidding for the privilege would be ready to deposit $10,000,000 as a guarantee of success, to be forfeited in case of failure. *If the mighty dollar was only there*, there would be no need to raise a temperance army by conscription ; we should be overwhelmed with volunteers."

Well, the mighty dollar *is* there, if our manufacturers could only be got to open their eyes to see it.

The objection will be raised by some that the negroes

---
* P. 116.

would not work without it and would not buy other things anyway if they did not have the liquor. But this objection has had a practical answer. Mr. Hornaday supplies the following interesting facts :

"Notwithstanding the assertions of the traders, of Mr. Tisdel, and even Mr. Stanley himself, that it is utterly impossible to trade with the natives without rum or gin, we have now most positive proof that a large and profitable business can be done without the agency of a single drop of liquor. There is one English trading company, having twelve stations between the coast and the region of the great lakes, which finds it not only possible but profitable to get along without poisoning or debauching the natives. Says the London *Times:*

"'During the eight years in which the company has extended the ramifications of its trade over this immense distance, it has proved that it is possible to trade in india-rubber, wax, oil seeds, and ivory to an enormous amount without defiling the list of their barter goods with a single keg of trade rum, or the all-representative "squareface" of the West Coast trade. It is something to have established proof before us that it is not necessary to carry rum and desolation, headed up in Hamburg casks and Dutch gin bottles, to a new country, before you can hope to see tusks and dividends. The Messrs. Moir, who are entrusted with the concerns of the company, testify that they have already exported 40,815 pounds of ivory, and not imported a glass of spirits.'"*

The destruction of the natives has also its economic side. It is well-nigh impossible for white men to live on the Lower Congo. It is not certain that they can work like the natives anywhere in the country. Certainly they cannot for any such wages. There never was a more short-sighted view of the interests of commerce than that which supposes that the way to make money out of foreign peoples is to strip them, impoverish them, and destroy them off the face of the earth. That is the

---

* "Free Rum on the Congo," p. 73.

old barbarian idea of Cortes and Pizarro. All that Mexico and Peru were good for, in their opinion, was to plunder them of their gold and silver plates, crowns and jewels, then work the natives to death in gangs in mines and on plantations—never mind how fast they died. Even Columbus did not wholly rise above this idea, and one cause of his downfall was that he alienated the gentle Isabella by his persistence in enslaving the natives against her protest. The outcome was almost equal disaster to the conquered and the conquerors. The gorgeous barbarian civilization of the Montezumas and the Incas was destroyed, and nothing given to take its place, while Spain, after a brief blaze of extravagant splendor, became poorer and weaker than before Columbus set sail. In the northern part of North America, on the contrary, the English, French, and Dutch colonists came with no other idea than that of working a subsistence out of the stubborn soil and making money by thrifty trade in furs and other native products that are collected with toil and hardship. The solid prosperity of the Northern States and Canada show the superior excellence of this method on mere economic grounds.

Now the United States are just awaking to the economic possibilities of their American neighbors. But all our hopes of wealth there now are by helping them with capital and inventions and transportation to bring out the full working power of the people and the natural riches which their soil may yield to labor. We have come to see that the simple old expedient of hard work, as in Æsop's fable of the vineyard—work sufficiently encouraged and well directed, may find riches there beyond the Spanish conquerors' dreams. To get those riches we would not destroy the people, nor degrade them, nor rob them, for that would spoil their working and producing and buying power, and so "kill the goose that lays the golden eggs."

The Roman Empire was far from an ideal government, but was, up to its day at least, the most intelligent of conquering powers in its care to preserve the conquered peoples. It would oppress them, it would rob them, but it would not destroy them. It kept up the productive power of the provinces as a means of maintaining the wealth, power, and glory of Rome. Its avowed aim was to awaken among the conquered the tastes and wants of civilization as a means of keeping them in peaceable and willing subjection. Rome would have looked with indignation and horror upon a proposition to introduce among her provinces a traffic which should depress the energies of the conquered people, destroy their hope and ambition, and take away the last desire for any of the advantages of civilization, and at length sweep races and nations out of existence. This all the tyranny of Nero, Caligula, and Domitian, and all the weak misgovernment of the last degenerate Cæsars, never did. In comparison with this the slaughter of a few thousands in her splendid arenas was humane and enlightened. Under her iron rule Britons, Gauls, Spaniards, Greeks, Egyptians, and all the Asiatics were left with national boundaries, languages, and civilizations, with splendid cities, schools of philosophy, eloquence and art, with extensive manufactures, and the great wise system of Roman roads opening profitable avenues of trade to the ends of the earth, while her strong government made the transfer safe wherever her eagles went. Pagan, profligate, heartless, the empire was yet too wise to destroy its producers.

The Saracens, with the sword in one hand and the

Koran in the other, never waged such exterminating war as the Anglo-Saxon, with a shipload of rum in the hold and a missionary on the deck. The superintendent of Lutheran missions in West Africa, writes:

> "On one small vessel on which myself and wife were the only passengers, there were in the hold over one hundred thousand gallons of New England rum."

What we have said of cotton goods applies to every product of civilization up to books and stationery. Let the missionaries try to educate, and what chance have they? Rev. Dr. Sims, of the Baptist mission, says:

> "When I was assisting to conduct a mission at Bamana, the port of the Congo, it was difficult to get the natives to assemble in a sober state on Sabbath morning."

What could a minister do for such a congregation even in America, with no inherited heathenism behind them?

It must be remembered, too, that the gin bottle will travel unaided, like the cholera. It will go—it does go—from hand to hand among the natives hundreds of miles into the interior, where no foot of white man has ever trod; and the most enterprising missionary will find the bodies and souls of the natives pre-empted before his coming by the demon of intoxication. Says Dr. Sims:

> "Rum is now carried into the far interior by natives and retailed at a profit. At my house, three hundred and twenty-five miles in the interior, a bottle of Rotterdam gin has been offered to me at sixteen cents (eight brass rods), and a demijohn at $3. At that place caravans of Bateke and Bakongo continually passed, of which twenty-five men out of every hundred would be loaded with intoxicating drinks. From such sources of supply I have seen many natives and soldiers of the State become drunk immediately upon the arrival of a caravan. It is pretty certain that 50 per cent. of the returned commerce account of the natives who live near the trading houses is given to them in liquor. At Stanley Pool not more than 25 per cent.

of the value of their goods goes back to them in liquor, but that is because of the distance. Were they living near a trader they would be hopelessly drunken. It is a sad thought that where five years ago liquor was unknown and never asked for, the natives now beg for it, and nothing else can better ingratiate one into their favor. As for the kings near the seaside trading houses, intoxication is about their normal condition."*

Not only does the traffic destroy the market for all the products of civilization, but it stops native production. We know how it hinders productive work in civilized lands. Among the Africans, little used at best to continuous labor, it destroys all capacity and purpose for it. Says Mr. Stanley :†

"Gin is used as currency. . . . Gin and rum are also largely consumed as grog by our native workmen. We dilute both largely, but we are compelled to serve it out both morning and evening. A stoppage of this would be followed by a cessation of work. It is ' custom ;' custom is despotic, and we are too weak and too new in the country to rebel against custom. If we resist custom we shall be abandoned. Every visitor to our camp on this part of the Congo [the Lower], if he has a palaver with us, must first receive a small glass of rum or gin. A chief receives a bottleful, which he distributes teaspoonful by teaspoonful among his followers. This is the Lower Congo idea of 'an all-around drink.' I see by the returns of the station chief that we consume one hundred and twenty-five gallons of rum monthly, by distributing grog rations and native demands for it in lieu of a portion of their wages."

Yet in the interior, where Stanley had the African to himself, no leader ever got from any set of men more magnificent and continuous work, and that without the liquor. How they built and fortified their forest camps! How they cut roads and dragged the boats around the endless cataracts! How they marched, almost starving,

---

* "Free Rum on the Congo," p. 76.
† "The Congo," vol. i., p. 193.

faithful unto death! Yet they were almost a pirate crew when they set out from Zanzibar, embroiling the expedition by drunken rows in the villages in their first day's march. When he got them into the interior, where there was no liquor, other motives could move them better—as they can all humanity. It is the old familiar story, the same on every shore: the man who drinks must have it; the man who does not is more capable of every good without it. Commerce has its choice. On one side is a race of lazy, drunken savages, who will work just long enough to get a bottle of gin and "enjoy a fiendish holiday," and who want no other thing that civilized man produces, and have no means to pay for it if they did.

As to the other side, we are told that they are dirty, immoral, etc., which is only to say that they are savages. We are told that they are lazy—a trait which may be observed elsewhere. Stanley did not find much indication of it when they were after him! It took all his energy, enterprise, and indefatigable endurance to get ahead of them. People who can build war canoes seventy and eighty feet long, man them with double ranks of oarsmen and warriors, manœuvre them in fleets, charging and retreating in perfect order and steadiness; who can build villages miles in length, with shady verandas and partitioned rooms; who can keep great cleared spaces in their forests for market-places, which are held as neutral ground, and where tribes from every side assemble to trade on certain specified days; who can take raw iron ore and work it into tools, with nothing better than a clay furnace of their own invention to smelt it in, are capable of civilization. If you doubt it, get down your Cæsar and read what the accomplished and victorious Roman has to say about your own British and Celtic and German ancestors, with their wicker huts and their unclad, tattooed bodies, their aversion to all industries except war, their endless tribal feuds and their human sacrifices, and then consider what very nice people we have come to be, and you will admit that there is a chance even for the African. Keep away the liquor of which he has no knowledge and feels no need till we bring it to him. Offer him the bright garments, the sharp, effective tools ; build some good houses there ; give missionaries a chance to teach a sober people the principles of morality and the elements of knowledge ; and you will have a people rising in the scale of civilization, and a field for a varied, profitable, and enduring commerce, with that steady, healthy increase which is the life of trade.

Mr. Hornaday remarks :*

"Naturally, the Upper Congo country is the garden spot of Africa, and in spite of the present hostility of some of the natives at a few points, the chances are that, if *judiciously* 'developed,' it will eventually produce the finest types of the African race, as well as the greatest commercial riches. If *rum* can be kept from these people, and white thieves, liars, and libertines excluded also ; if they can be shown what a multitude of blessings flow from peace, sobriety, honesty, and industry, their future progress upward is assured.

"*Productions.*—The commercial products of the Congo basin are india-rubber, palm-oil, palm nuts, ground nuts, gum copal, camwood, wax, ivory, orchilla weed, cola nuts, baobab fibre, gum tragacanth, myrrh, nutmeg, ginger, frankincense, coffee, castor-seed, rattan canes, bark cloth, castor-oil nuts, copper, feathers, skins and hides.

"The native food products of the country (the great majority of which must be considered as belonging to the Upper Congo) are ground nuts, bananas, plantains, manioc or cassava, maize, sugarcane, millet, yams, sweet potatoes, beans, brinjalls, cucumbers,

---

* "Free Rum on the Congo," pp. 129, 130.

melons, pumpkins, tomatoes, etc. From Stanley Pool eastward, the officers of the International Association have introduced mangoes, papaws, oranges, limes, coffee, pineapples, guavas, cabbages, Irish potatoes, and onions, all of which appear to thrive."

In view of the threatened destruction of all this trade, well might the Archbishop of Canterbury proclaim in Westminster Abbey of the African liquor traffic:

"It is a dread commerce. But it is rather an *anti-commerce*. *The fear of it and the dread of it will soon be upon commerce itself.* If we have long seen monopolies to be a bar and obstruction to trade—if we have found that to put a whole trade into the hands of one man is to kill trade—what shall we say of a system which, in the name of freedom, *threatens with extinction all trades but one?* What of *bales of goods reshipped because,* in the drunken population, there was *no demand but for drink*—because they would receive nothing else in barter —would take no other wages for the early morning's work, and were incapable when the early morning was past? These, and darker tales than these, are the depositions of eye-witnesses, whom we have no ground to mistrust or even suspect of exaggeration. But these surely must be unexpected results of the foreign diplomacy which insisted, without qualification, on 'the interests of trade' and 'commercial liberty.' It would be treason to our neighbors to suppose that such results were foreseen—such crippling of commerce, such *disabling of industrial energies* as must supervene."

Let us cease boasting of emancipation for awhile till we shall have proved by our deeds that we are of the same race with the men who, against vested interests, against immemorial custom, against the supposed interests of trade, declared the slave should go free. The emancipation of Africa and the isles of the sea from intoxicants is a greater and more needed work. Said Sir Richard Burton: "It is my sincere belief that if the slave trade were revived with all its horrors, and Africa could get rid of the white man, with the gunpowder and rum which he has introduced, Africa would be the gainer by the exchange."

And Rev. James Johnson, the native pastor of the island of Lagos, before referred to, before a meeting of members of the House of Commons in the committee-room on April 1st, 1887, ended his speech by saying:

"The slave trade had been to Africa a great evil, but the evils of the rum trade were far worse. *He would rather his countrymen were in slavery and being worked hard*, and kept away from the drink, than that the drink should be let loose upon them."

We would second Mr. Hornaday's noble proposition that the United States call a new conference of the Powers, and give all its influence for an agreement to absolutely shut out intoxicants from the Congo Free State. Let all the productive industries, all the true arts of peace unite to say to the one destroying trade of ruin and death: "Hands off from the new markets of the world!" Humanity and religion will not plead in vain when commerce shall give its irresistible support to their plea.

It should be remembered that when all the great Powers of Europe proposed to shut out gunpowder and liquor from the Pacific Islands because of the terrible destruction they were working, and invited the United States to join them, our Government blocked the plan by its single veto. Let us hasten to cancel that dark blot by doing, far as the sweep of our commerce and the increasing weight of our national influence can reach, something worthy of the Great Republic.

CHAPTER XXX.

THE GATES OF PARADISE.

"No way so rapid to increase the wealth of nations, and the morality of society, as the utter annihilation of the manufacture of ardent spirits, constituting as they do an infinite waste and an unmixed evil."—*London Times.*

"The evidence is perfectly incontrovertible that the good order, the physical and moral welfare of the community has been promoted by refusing to license the sale of ardent spirits, and that the consumption of spirits has been very greatly diminished in all instances, by refusing to grant licenses; and that, although the laws have been and are violated to some extent in different places, the practice soon becomes disreputable, and hides itself from the public eye by shrinking away into obscure and dark places; that noisy and tumultuous assemblies in the street, and public quarrels cease when licenses are refused; and that pauperism has very rapidly diminished from the same cause."—*Judiciary Committee of the Massachusetts Legislature,* 1837.

"Though we have a population of ten thousand people, for the period of six months no settler or citizen of Vineland has received relief at my hands as overseer of the poor. Within seventy days there has been only one case among what we call our floating population at the expense of $4.00. During the entire year there has only been one indictment, and that a trifling case of battery among our colored population. . . . The police expenses of Vineland amount to $75.00 a year, the sum paid to me, and our poor expenses a mere trifle. I ascribe this remarkable state of things to the industry of our people, and the absence of King Alcohol."—*Report of Mr. Curtis, Overseer of the Poor, and Constable of Vineland, N. J.,* 1883.

SIX million five hundred thousand acres of land open to settlement in Oklahoma, and one hundred thousand men surging like a tide on the borders, only kept back by the military arm! Why? Those six million acres meant new opportunities for industry, new openings for labor. It was not as the early Spaniards went to Mexico and Peru, or the men of '49 to California, to find gold and silver. The men of '89 crowded to Oklahoma simply for a chance to dig and trade. In the common march of life these are the best chances the world has to offer—the chance to do some work the world wants done and to get paid for it. But there is before the Americans of to-day an unoccupied territory compared to which all the acres of Oklahoma and all the square miles the Indians yet hold are insignificant.

All the masters of political economy are saying, as with one voice, that it is not what a man *earns*, but what he *spends*, that determines riches or poverty, independence or pauperism. It is an old, trite truth, but as rich as the aluminium whose strong, bright bars are expected yet to take the place of our clumsy and rugged iron, and which lies all about us in our common clay.

A while ago a daily paper came out with exultant headlines,

SPLENDID SHOWING.

The excess of exports over imports for the year amounts to $165,000,000.

What did that mean? One hundred and sixty-five million dollars more to spend among our own people and pay our own workers, to buy everything our people want to buy, and to pay everybody who has anything to sell. But we are ready to put into the American market $1,000,000,000 to spend among our own people and pay our own laborers, to buy everything our people want to buy, and to pay everybody who has anything to sell. Will not that be something to rejoice over?

Dr. Hargreaves* suggests the following division among other industries of $800,000,000 expenditure for liquors on the basis of the Census of 1880 :†

Food and food preparations	$471,666,612
Boots and shoes	84,025,177
Carpets	15,896,401
Cotton goods	96,045,055
Mixed textiles	33,110,851
Woollen goods	80,303,360
Worsted goods	16,774,971
Total	$797,822,427

But our liquor bill has already run $200,000,000 beyond that amount. So to Dr. Hargreaves's estimates we will add:

Furniture	$45,000,000
Anthracite coal	25,000,000
Bituminous coal	30,000,000

And still we have left $100,000,000 for margin, of which we will treat by and by. But now let us see what the amount already provided for will do. Take the $471,000,000 for food and food preparations.

Dr. Hargreaves divides this amount as follows ("Worse than Wasted," page 69):

Kind of Products.	Value of Products at Factory or Wholesale Price.
Flour and grist mills	$252,592,856
Bread and bakery	32,912,448
Slaughtering and meat packing	151,781,206
Cheese and butter (factory)	12,871,255
Coffee and spices	11,462,447
Food preparations, so called	1,246,612
Fruits and vegetables, canned, etc.	8,799,788
Total	$471,666,612†

Think of all the women and children made hungry by the intemperance of husbands and fathers. Then think of setting before them 16,000,000 barrels of wheat flour,

---

* "Worse than Wasted," p. 66. Cf. *Ibid.*, p. 61.
† See "Compendium Census Report, 1880," pp. 1,130, 1,104, 1,108-9, 1,127, 1,190, 112, 201-4.

200,000 bushels of rye flour, 15,000,000 bushels of corn meal, 20,000,000 pounds of buckwheat flour, 280,000 bushels of hominy! All this to be bought for a small part of the money now spent for liquor—only $250,000,000. Then $150,000,000 of beef, pork, mutton, and veal. No more going without meat in our bitter winters! Then we will allow $42,000,000 for sugar, syrup, and molasses to eat on those 20,000,000 pounds of buckwheat cakes, and we will throw in $11,000,000 worth of tea, coffee, and spices, and $13,000,000 for milk, butter, and cheese, according to Dr. Hargreaves's estimates. He adds still $33,000,000 for bread actually baked, and other bakery products.

We have come upon another table, somewhat differing from the above, which is so refreshing that we must give it for comparison.*

"It is estimated that three millions of homes are affected by the drink curse, and that each home will average four persons. We will now distribute the $900,000,000 among these twelve million persons:

9,000,000 tons coal, $6 a ton	$54,000,000
3,000,000 cook stoves, $15	45,000,000
Total	$99,000,000

NOW BUY FROM THE FARMERS:

3,000,000 cords wood, $4	$12,000,000
6,000,000 bbls. flour, $7	42,000,000
9,000,000 " potatoes, $2	18,000,000
300,000,000 lbs. pork, $15	45,000,000
150,000,000 doz. eggs, 18c	27,000,000
150,000,000 lbs. butter, 20c	30,000,000
75,000,000 " cheese, 10c	7,500,000
6,000,000 bbls. apples, $3	18,000,000
Other fruit, grapes, plums, currants, etc.	9,000,000
Milk	30,000,000
300,000,000 lbs. buckwheat flour, 3c	9,000,000
Beef, valued at	45,000,000
Chickens	18,000,000
Turkeys	18,000,000
Vegetables	9,000,000
Lard	7,500,000
Total to farmers	$345,000,000

* By Mr. Calvin E. Keach in *The Voice* of May 16th, 1889.

THEN BUY FROM THE SHOE TRADE:

Men's boots, 6,000,000 pairs, at $1.50	$9,000,000
Children's shoes, 24,000,000 pairs, at $1	24,000,000
Women's shoes, 6,000,000 pairs, at $2	12,000,000
Total to the shoe trade	$45,000,000

BUY FROM THE WOOLLEN MANUFACTURERS:

3,000,000 suits clothes, men, $10	$30,000,000
3,000,000 woollen dresses, $4	12,000.000
6,000,000 children's dresses, $2	12,000.000
6,000,000 pairs woollen blankets, $2	12,000,000
6,000,000 suits underwear, men's, $2	12,000,000
6,000,000 suits underwear, women's, $2	12,000,000
12,000,000 suits underwear, children's, $1	12,000.000
16,000,000 pairs woollen hose, 15c	2,400,000
Total to woollen manufacturers	$104,400,000

BUY FROM MISCELLANEOUS TRADES:
For each of 3,000,000 families.

Tinware, $3	$9,000,000
1 new table, $5	15,000,000
1 set dishes, $4	12,000,000
2 table-cloths, $4	12,000,000
6 common chairs, $3	9,000,000
1 clock, $2	6,000,000
50 yards cotton cloth, $5	15,000,000
Rent 3,000,000 houses at $76.20	228,600,000
Grand total	$900,000,000

"Here we see that the poor coal-miners of Pennsylvania will have to dig out $54,000,000 worth of extra coal. The iron moulders will have to make three million more stoves, valued at $45,000,000 more. The farmers can dispose of an extra product amounting to $345,000,000 more. And the woollen goods manufacturers will have to supply to a *new* demand in market extra goods of the value of $104,400,000, and the owners of tenement-houses will receive in rents over $228,000,000."

It will be noticed that Mr. Keach allows more for butter, cheese, and milk than Dr. Hargreaves, and less for flour, probably counting at something the flour they must have already. He allows $9,000,000 for fresh vegetables, which Dr. Hargreaves has not provided for.

His "other fruit, grapes, plums, etc.," will just about balance Dr. Hargreaves's "fruits and vegetables canned." The choice would be matter of taste or convenience. It is very good to think of those now poor mothers becoming able to slip a nice red-cheeked apple into the father's lunch-pail and the school-boy's pocket out of two barrels in the cellar. The man will soon find his apple worth more than his glass of beer. There will be more strength, more work, more "staying power" in it. It is very delightful to find "turkeys" among the supplies of these once poor families, and "chickens," too. They can have a nice Thanksgiving and Christmas dinner now, with an occasional treat for a birthday. But isn't $36,000,000 rather a large allowance for something that is rather in the nature of a luxury? We would cut that down considerably. Mr. Keach's allowance for milk, $30,000,000—$10 a year for each family—is an improvement on Dr. Hargreaves's decidedly. We would still increase the amount. It would soon come to pass that the poor would learn the great value of milk for food, especially for children, and, with the $1,000,000,000 of drink money in their pockets, they would have something to pay the milkman with. Many a poor little wan baby, for whom the family "can't afford" to take milk now, will revive and brighten as the mother holds to its lips the brimming, creamy cup. If we could only do it soon enough, before the baby dies! Why, sir, a quart of milk a day for your baby at home is only the price of one glass of beer in the saloon. And the little one can't have it! Let's shut up the places that create such inhumanity as that!

But "man shall not live by bread alone." On the basis of Dr. Hargreaves's estimates we have provided

$471,000,000 for food. We add $42,000,000 for sugar and $30,000,000 for milk, making $543,000,000 for all kinds of food. Returning to his table, we will invest $84,000,000 in boots and shoes. For this he reckons, according to the census reports, 15,000,000 pairs of boots and 47,000,000 pairs of shoes; but this is at wholesale prices, about $1.75 a pair for boots and $1.25 a pair for shoes. We cannot buy at those figures, much as we would like to. We must double them. But one-half the number of pairs—7,500,000 pairs of boots—will furnish our 3,000,000 drinking men with two pairs each on an average, and some extra for those whose occupations wear them out faster than others. Twenty-seven million pairs of shoes will give nine pairs for each of these 3,000,000 families, estimated at three members besides the man, whose boots are already provided for. That will be three pairs a year for each woman and child. No more bare feet on the icy sidewalk!

For wet weather they ought to have rubbers. If we allow one pair each for father and mother, at seventy-five cents, and one pair each to the children, at fifty cents, that will be $2.50 for each family, or $7,500,000 in all. Prohibition will be worth something to the rubber trade.

For woollen goods our $80,000,000 will give us 1,000,000 pairs of blankets, 600,000 woollen coverlets, 36,000,000 yards of "cloths, cassimeres, doeskins, diagonals, and suitings;" also 3,000,000 yards of beavers and overcoatings, besides 9,000,000 yards of satinettes, tweeds, overcoatings, and other goods. Then there would be about 12,000,000 yards of various dress goods, and about 700,000 shawls. Next, the worsted goods at $16,000,000 will pour in their more than 30,000,000 yards of dress goods, 1,500,000 yards of coatings, linings, trimmings, braids, etc., and about 300,000 worsted shawls. Now the poor can go to church.

The $96,000,000 for cotton goods will provide about 1,000,000,000 yards, or 300 yards for each family of the 3,000,000 drinkers. When we consider that this means table-cloths, napkins, towels, sheets, pillow-cases, muslin curtains, calico, and underwear, and that for many families who have been kept very short of all, the amount is not excessive.

We are still able to spend about $15,000,000 for carpets, even including 2,000,000 of Brussels, 4,000,000 yards of tapestry, and about 12,000,000 yards of other varieties, besides 24,000 rugs. How many a dreary room will now be made bright and cheery!

Then we have $45,000,000 worth of furniture, including stoves, to put into all these homes—only $15 into each home, but enough to change its whole aspect as the seasons pass. It is wear without replacement which makes the unspeakable desolation of the drunkard's home. We are going to have articles replaced as they wear out, and new ones added as new needs arise. Now a table, then a few chairs, a bedstead, a set of springs; they come in one after another, and home grows a little more comfortable instead of more dreary all the time.

We will have $25,000,000 worth of anthracite and $30,000,000 of bituminous coal, and we'll stop the shivering over a few embers, we'll break up half the rheumatisms, and head off thousands of cases of consumption. We'll no longer have the woman who has done a hard day's washing over a smouldering fire, going out at four o'clock the next morning in a calico dress, with a little thin shawl and leaky shoes, to pick up enough coal along the railroad track to keep the children from freezing, and call that "practical temperance."

And still we have a good part of our hundred million margin to know what to do with. Let us see how much we have drawn on it. Our $42,000,000 of sugar came out of it; also $30,000,000 for milk, and $7,500,000 for rubbers, making $79,500,000, and leaving a balance of $20,500,000 still to spend.

We will double the salaries of all the ministers of the Gospel, $12,000,000, or—where that is not needed—build or improve chapels. We will nearly double the amount contributed for missions, adding a solid $5,000,000. This will add to the above estimates $17,000,000, making $96,500,000; and as Dr. Hargreaves's estimate was a little more than $2,000,000 short of the $800,000,000, we have in all $5,677,573 from our $1,000,000,000 still to spare. What shall we do with this?

Well, something must be allowed for education, including school and other books, papers and periodicals, popular lectures, etc. Every family where there are children could take the *Youth's Companion*, *Saint Nicholas*, *Wide Awake*, the *Pansy*, or *Babyland*, for instance. That would give the children something to keep them off the street, to talk over with the parents and with each other, and to fill their minds with useful instruction and pleasant images. Some good religious or temperance paper should come in, and occasionally a nice book on a Christmas or a birthday. Something must be allowed for sickness and accident, though both these items would shrink wonderfully among a people with no diseases of intemperance, no drunken harshness or carelessness, and all well fed, well clothed, with plenty of fuel and comfortable homes.

But there is one difficulty here. If we are going into these matters of education, taste, and refinement, that little balance of $5,000,000 won't begin to go around. That is true. But no one need be worried over a small matter like that. We have $1,000,000,000 still in reserve—the indirect expense still untouched. Now let humanity draw its checks for all that makes human existence happy, beautiful, and hopeful, and outside the limits of wasteful luxury we can meet them all.

There will be many differences, according to individual choice. Much of this money will be expended for rents. These drinking men all live somewhere now, but how many of them in wretched habitations! One of the first uses of their saved money will be to rent a better residence. Instead of two miserable rooms, a pretty little house; instead of the filthy alley, a pleasant street; instead of the foul gutter, a patch of grass. New houses will be built by the streetful—new suburbs spring up around all our cities. The real estate business will enter on a new era of prosperity. As the first needs of clothing, furniture, etc., are supplied, many will begin to save up the "drink waste" and pay it in instalments on the purchase of a home which shall be their own. They will have the heart to improve it, to set out vines and flowers, rose-bushes and trees, knowing that all is to be their own or their children's.

What a difference it will make to thousands of women who have now only the wretched rooms with bare floor, whose gaps and splinters are only rendered more manifest by sweeping; mangled furniture, whose dents and scratches are only more hopelessly revealed by dusting; the dingy window, which if cleaned only shows a dingier alley; the faded and ragged calico dress for both morning and evening; little food to cook and less fire to cook it with; children chiefly thought of as creatures with appetites that cannot be satisfied and bodies that cannot be clothed; not a picture, book, or paper to furnish a story to read them or a fresh thought to talk over with them; the husband daily growing coarser, duller, and more purposeless; the certainty that to-morrow shall be as this day and much more disconsolate; that if business improves it will give only so much more to go into the maw of the remorseless saloon!

Then the genial minister tells the poor woman, "Society can do nothing for you. You cannot make men virtuous by law. It is your duty to keep gentle and patient and make home so bright that your husband will want to stay in it." How? God only knows. And *does He know except by changing that state of things*, and giving something to brighten home with? "If a brother or sister be naked and destitute of daily food, and one of you say unto them, Depart in peace, be ye warmed and filled, notwithstanding ye give them not those things needful for the body, what doth it profit? Even so, faith without works is dead, being alone."

But Prohibition crystallizes faith into "the things needful for the body." It puts this oppressed woman into a comfortable home. It puts on the floor a bright carpet, pretty if cheap, curtains at the windows, simple furniture that is neat, trim, and strong, and some of the really beautiful pictures that modern art makes so cheap upon the walls. Now she will find a perfect joy in sweeping the last speck off that carpet, dusting the furniture till it shines, keeping the windows clear as a mountain stream. When she wishes to get dinner, there is a stove that will cook and fuel to put in it. In the pantry there is a sack of flour and her little jar of sugar, and all the spices and sundries that a good housewife needs. In her purse there's the money to make the market stall a promise and not a despair. How she will slave at that cooking because " John is so fond of this," and " those will taste so good to the children !" She will not know that she is hot or tired. When she would sit down to her sewing, she can change the neat working dress of the morning for a pretty home dress for afternoon. She will take some pains to make herself a fair portion of the pretty home scene. When she goes to work on the children's clothes, there's something to make the little garments out of. She will hear songs of hope in the hum of her sewing-machine, and there will be a light in her eyes and a song on her own lips. Good food will bring back the color to her wasted cheek. The children, as they burst in from school, will exclaim, " How pretty you look, mamma !" or, if they don't say it, will have the settled conviction that she is the most beautiful woman in the world ; and the husband will find the charm of long ago drawing him to her side again, now the saloon's fell enchantment is broken forever.

Now there is some use in talking to her of making home bright and attractive, and being gentle and patient amid the worries, of which life will still have enough. How those parents will delight in talking with their children about their school lessons and plays, and in reading with them the books and papers, with their mingled interest and instruction for old and young ! The evenings will be all too short, and the man will wonder that ever he cared to stay in a foul saloon among a herd of rude men, leaving these, his own dear ones, in unpitied misery, and listening to things he would not have them hear for all this world. How the children's eyes will brighten and their faces shine! How strong they will be for play and how ambitious for study! How dear their home will be to them! How the light of love and peace and joy will make their faces beautiful!

Then all around, among the people who were never intemperate, the wave of this prosperity will sweep. The stores and the mills, the railroads and the mines, the ships and farms—all who produce or transport or deal in the goods which these rescued families are now able to buy—will share the blessing. The country will answer back the city's rejoicing. "The trees will clap their hands and the fields be joyful together."

But this is sentiment. So hard is it to keep strictly to dry economics where human hearts are part of the problem. Well, then, let us say this man with the happy home is in no danger of becoming a pauper. The chances that ever he will be a criminal are faint and rare. You'll not need any liquor fund to support his wife and children in your poorhouse, thank you. He is not very likely to go to the insane asylum, nor his wife either. Streets of such homes as his will not breed a pestilence, and will not need half as many policemen to patrol them. The happiness will materialize in cash. With a city, a nation, of such homes, every business will boom, all our nation prospering and exulting through the two thousand million revenue of righteousness! Who would not help to bring the happy, glorious day? What true heart will not bid us God-speed as we toil to hasten its coming?

CHAPTER XXXI.

THE "ORIGINAL PACKAGE" DECISION.

"I HAVE expressed heretofore, and I now repeat, my opposition to the Dred Scott decision, but I should be allowed to state the nature of that opposition, and I ask your indulgence while I do so. What is fairly implied by the term Judge Douglas has used, 'resistance to the decision'? I do not resist it. If I wanted to take Dred Scott from his master, I would be interfering with property, and that terrible difficulty that Judge Douglas speaks of, of interfering with property, would arise. But I am doing no such thing as that, but all that I am doing is refusing to obey it as a political rule. If I were in Congress, and a vote should come up on a question *whether slavery should be prohibited in a new Territory*, in spite of the Dred Scott decision, I WOULD VOTE THAT IT SHOULD.

"That is what I would do. Judge Douglas said last night that before the decision he might advance his opinion, and it might be contrary to the decision when it was made; but after it was made he would abide by it until it was reversed. Just so! We let this property abide by the decision, *but we will try to reverse that decision*. We will try to put it where Judge Douglas would not object, for he says he will obey it until it is reversed. *Somebody has to reverse that decision*, since it is made, AND WE MEAN TO REVERSE IT, and we mean to do it peaceably."—*Abraham Lincoln, in his speech against Douglas at Chicago, July 10th, 1858.*

A SUPREME COURT decision is not a "thus saith the Lord." It is not a finality. It is not above criticism. It is not beyond reversal. It is simply a declaration of the law *de facto*, which is to be obeyed by the citizen until the law shall be changed or otherwise interpreted by competent authority. It does not shut off discussion of the principles of law and of right involved. The people's inalienable right to consider what is desirable as law, and what ought to be law, remains unaffected by any decision the highest court in the land may utter. In fact, as shown by the memorable speech of Abraham Lincoln, it is competent for the people from the moment a decision is uttered which they believe contrary to right and justice, to begin to agitate for a reversal of that decision by the court that uttered it, or for such Congressional action as may destroy or prevent its injurious effects.

Such agitation was begun from the moment the Dred Scott decision was pronounced, by some of the noblest and ablest men our country has ever possessed, with the results known to history. Now we come to another Supreme Court decision whose results are startlingly bad. In its discussion we must consider the principles of right involved. Nothing has ever stood the test of time as enduring law which was contrary to the essential principles of eternal right.

The liquor traffic is just as much a curse as it was before the decision. To debauch and destroy the son of a loving mother, or the husband and father of a happy family, is just as mercenary, cruel and murderous, and just as contrary to the best interests of the Republic, as it was before. To turn those who might be good and industrious citizens into sots, paupers, criminals, maniacs, and incarnate demons is contrary to all the principles and interests for which governments are instituted among men, and menaces the very existence of civilized society.

Now to say that a State which has determined to shut such a traffic out by law is forbidden by its allegiance to the general government to exercise its own police force for its own protection against an evil which is destroying its own dearest interests, is not good ethics, whatever it may be in the technicalities of law. It is not right. If there is a man in my community who, if he drinks whiskey, is likely at any time to burn my house, harm my children, insult my wife or murder me, it is not right nor justice to say that another man may sell him all the whiskey he chooses to sell, because the seller ships the element of destruction in from another State. If anything, *the fact that he is a non-resident is so much the more reason why he should not be allowed* to do mischief where he does not belong, and to injure those whom he does not help to protect, and whose burdens he does not help to bear.

To say that communities which, by shutting out the traffic in intoxicating liquors, are enjoying indescribable peace and happiness, with full schoolhouses and empty jails, with workingmen dwelling in homes of their own and laying up snug little sums in the savings banks, with no tramps, no starvation and no wife beating, shall be compelled by the fiat of the nation to let in that traffic with all these evils again, merely because some heartless citizen of another State is ready to desolate these communities for what he can make out of the desolation, is something more worthy of a despotism than of a republic.

If all America were under Prohibition, and George Kennan were to bring us such a statement as this, "In Russia every province from the Baltic to the Pacific shore and from the Arctic Circle to the wall of China, and every city, town, and village in all that vast domain is compelled to allow the traffic in intoxicating liquors, however great the injury it may do, however many of the people are opposed to it, however earnestly they may plead and pray to be delivered from it. It is forced upon them by the supreme law of the land, and to interfere with it would be a crime," we should hold this to be one of the most terrible indictments of the government of the Czar. Kennan tells of women flogged by brutal officers, and it makes our blood tingle across the sea ; but those women were beaten by strangers with no ties of relationship, no vows of affection, no pledge of protection. In America it is done every day, not in one case, but in hundreds. American women, whom we call free, are beaten, bruised, and murdered by their own husbands in their own homes. We read of it in every morning paper, and our law says this shall go on ; that no State, no county, city or town, no village or hamlet shall be allowed to shut out the one deadly cause of it all.

When the Supreme Court of the United States pronounces such a decision as this, all our American manhood, all our traditions of liberty, all our sense of justice and right rise in vehement and determined protest. This can never be enduring law. It is not in accord with the eternal fitness of things ; it does not establish justice, promote the general welfare, nor secure the blessings of liberty. It is not the will of God.

This decision reflects the increasing dominance of the liquor power since the beginning of the war era. When the New Hampshire Decision of 1847 was rendered, a great tidal wave of temperance was rolling in. Lyman Beecher's thrilling "Six Sermons on Intemperance" had been scattered through the length and breadth of the land. The Washingtonian Movement had seen its pledge signed by 600,000 men. John B. Gough, in the splendor of his early prime, was moving the hearts of thousands by his fiery eloquence. Governors, judges, eminent lawyers, and leading divines were uniting in protest against all license of the liquor traffic as both impolitic and wrong. Local Option had become the law of Massachusetts and other important States, and in Maine that sentiment was rapidly forming which was soon to crystallize in the " Maine Law." Judges are men, and all the opinions rendered on that occasion show that they partook of this strong public sentiment for temperance. This is well exemplified in the clear and forcible words of Justice Grier :*

"The true question presented by these cases, and one which I am not disposed to evade, is *whether the States have a right to prohibit* the sale and consumption of an article of commerce which they believe to be pernicious in its effects, and the cause of disease, pauperism, and crime. I do not consider the question of the exclusiveness of the power of Congress to regulate commerce as necessarily connected with the decision of this point.

"It has been frequently decided by this court that the powers which relate to merely municipal regulations, or which may more properly be called internal police, are not surrendered by the States, or restrained by the Constitution of the United States ; and that, consequently, in relation to these, the authority of a State is complete, unqualified, and exclusive. Without attempting to define what are the peculiar subjects or limits of this power, it may safely be affirmed that *every law for the restraint and punishment of crime, for the preservation of the public peace, health and morals*, must come within this category.

" AS SUBJECTS OF LEGISLATION, THEY ARE FROM THEIR VERY NATURE OF PRIMARY IMPORTANCE ; THEY LIE AT THE FOUNDATION OF SOCIAL EXISTENCE ; THEY ARE FOR THE PROTECTION OF LIFE AND LIBERTY, AND NECESSARILY COMPEL ALL LAWS ON SUBJECTS OF SECONDARY IMPORTANCE, WHICH RELATE ONLY TO PROPERTY, CONVENIENCE OR LUXURY, TO RECEDE, WHEN THEY COME IN CONFLICT OR COLLISION, '*salus populi suprema lex.*'

" If the right to control these subjects be complete, unqualified, and exclusive, in the State legislatures, *no regulations of secondary importance can supersede or restrain their operations, on any ground of prerog-*

---

* Howard's Reports, Vol. V., pp. 631, 632.

alive or supremacy. The exigencies of the social compact require that such laws be executed *before and above all others.*

"It is not necessary, for the sake of justifying the State legislation now under consideration, to array the appalling statistics of misery, pauperism, and crime which have their origin in the use or abuse of ardent spirits. The police power, which is exclusively in the States, is alone competent to the correction of these great evils, AND ALL MEASURES OF RESTRAINT OR PROHIBITION NECESSARY TO EFFECT THE PURPOSE ARE WITHIN THE SCOPE OF THAT AUTHORITY. There is no conflict of power, or of legislation, as between the States and the United States ; each is acting within its sphere, and for the public good ; and if a loss of revenue should accrue to the United States from a diminished consumption of ardent spirits, she will be the gainer a thousand fold in the health, wealth, and happiness of the people."

So when there was a question between State and National jurisdiction, they *gave to Temperance the benefit of the doubt.*

Chief Justice Taney concluded his opinion thus :*

"Upon the whole, therefore, the law of New Hampshire is, in my judgment, a valid one. For although the gin sold was an import from another State, and Congress has clearly the power to regulate such importations under the grant of power to regulate commerce among the several States, yet, *as Congress has made no regulation on the subject,* the traffic in the article may be lawfully regulated by the State as soon as it is landed in its territory, and a tax imposed upon it, or a license required, *or the sale altogether prohibited,* according to the policy which the State may suppose to be its interest or duty to pursue."

This the present Supreme Court has exactly reversed. The same conflict of jurisdictions exists, and the same doubt. Congress has not passed upon the matter during these forty years. But within that time a vast tide of foreign immigration has poured in, bringing the drinking usages and opinions of the Old World. Within that time, too, the United States Government has become the

---

* Howard's Reports, Vol. V., p. 586.

champion liquor-dealer of the world; United States Registered Distilleries and United States Bonded Warehouses fill the country, and the National Government receives close upon a hundred million dollars annually from the traffic which destroys the people. Since President Hayes went out of office, the Presidential mansion has set the example of a profuse hospitality of liquor. The National Liquor Power has become the strongest institution in the United States. Still our Supreme Judges are men. They have felt the effect of the national retrogression. Finding the National and State jurisdiction still in doubt, they have *given the benefit of the doubt to the liquor traffic*, deciding as follows:

"Whenever, however, a particular power of the general Government is one which must necessarily be exercised by it, *and Congress remains silent, this is not only not a concession that the powers reserved by the State may be exerted as if the specific power had not been elsewhere reposed, but, on the contrary, the only legitimate conclusion is that the general Government intended that power should not be affirmatively exercised, and the action of the States cannot be permitted to effect that which would be incompatible with such intention.* Hence, inasmuch as inter State commerce, consisting in the transportation, purchase, sale, and exchange of commodities, is national in its character, and must be governed by a uniform system, *so long as Congress does not pass any law to regulate it, or allowing the States so to do, it thereby indicates its will that such commerce shall be free and untrammelled.*"

Since this decision is thus a reversal of the decision of 1847, and of the policy of the Government for more than a hundred years, it is suspicious from the start.

Its effects have been startlingly bad. The New York *Times* says:

"The brewers and distillers of the neighboring State of Missouri have established a thriving traffic in many Kansas towns by employing as agents men who were formerly saloon-keepers, who have carried on an illicit trade under Prohibition, and sending them beer in 'original packages' *as small as pint bottles,* transported in refrigerator cars, and *whiskey put up in two-ounce vials.* This, in effect, restores all the evils of an unrestricted liquor traffic.

"Original packages are not defined in the Supreme Court decision, and the sale in single bottles, flasks, and vials is an evasion of the probable intent of the decision. Still, it would be a difficult matter to draw the line. That a car-load of such retail packages can be received and peddled out one by one and the operation regarded as part and parcel of inter-State commerce, to be protected against State interference, seems a rank absurdity, but where is the line to be established when sale in original packages through local agents is once authorized?

"The question of *drinking on the premises where the liquor is sold* has not been fully tested, but District Judge Caldwell has decided that the purchaser of a bottle of beer or a vial of whiskey could drink it wherever he pleased. He is not obliged to wait until he goes home, or even until he gets outside the place of sale. If the 'agent' can sell unmolested, anybody may buy without being interfered with, and what he buys he can consume on the spot. That is the law as now applied in Kansas. Another evil that has been re-established is the sale of liquor to minor children. Several 'agents' have been arrested for *selling to minors, including children of ten or twelve years of age,* but they were released on habeas corpus, Circuit Judge Foster holding that the State could in no way interfere with the sale of these imported 'original packages,' as it was a matter of inter-State commerce."

The special correspondence of the New York *Voice* contains the following:

GARNETT, KAN., July 20.

Two original package saloons have been established, and another will be opened soon. It affords the worst phase of whiskey drinking that has ever been in this State. BOYS WHO NEVER SAW A SALOON HAVE BEEN CARRIED HOME DRUNK. The general disorder is worse than it has ever been since Prohibition was established. The first week the saloons were rather orderly, and would not allow drinking near the building. Now they furnish their patrons with a glass and let them drink just outside the door and then return the glass. They override our local laws entirely, and Judge Foster's Court sustains them. The people, *en masse,* tried to persuade them not to open up. Now we are waiting impatiently, of course, to see what Congress will do.

If they fail to give us relief we will carry the hell holes out of town by force. Not since the days of border ruffianism have our people been so greatly agitated as they are about the "Supreme Court saloons."
A. D. McFADDEN, *Mayor*.

Think of the mournful pathos of those two lines we have capitalized—the sorrow, shame, and heartbreak, the possible life-long tragedy—"Boys who never saw a saloon have been carried home drunk!"

Mr. Perkins, of Kansas, said, in the United States House of Representatives:

"Mr. Speaker, as I have suggested, in my judgment no decision rendered in the history of the Supreme Court is more unfortunate than this recent one. In my own State it has sent to us as invaders hundreds of lawless characters from the sister State of Missouri, who have organized in all the towns and hamlets of our State so-called 'United States Supreme Court Saloons.' [Laughter.] They may have left Missouri for the good of Missouri, but they have not come to Kansas for the good of our commonwealth. They come and organize these original-package houses and bring, under the decision of the Supreme Court of the United States, these so-called original packages with them [exhibiting paper box and half-pint flask], and sell them without restraint, without license, without regulation or control, to A, B, or C, and others who will buy them—to minors, to those addicted to habits of using intoxicating liquors, on the Sabbath day, on the 4th day of July, on every other day of the week, and each week in the month, and all restraint and regulation under State legislation is denied and treated with contempt."

The New York *Herald* contains the following item:

KANSAS CITY, Mo., July 6, 1890.

A prominent brewer said to-day:

"The brewers are doing their best to quench the thirst of the Kansans, and are succeeding to a remarkable degree. *Every brewery in the city is running to its fullest capacity,* and still we are not able to supply the demand. *We have established original package houses all over the State, and the sales are simply enormous,* although every sale is attended with great danger. We try to keep our agents within the limits of the law.

"THIS SHOWS PLAINLY TO US THAT IF THE STATE OF KANSAS WAS NOT CLOSED AGAINST OUR BUSINESS WE WOULD HAVE TO DOUBLE THE CAPACITY OF EVERY BREWERY IN THE CITY, AND EVEN THEN WE WOULD NOT BE ABLE TO FILL THE ORDERS. Nor is our business the only one that is benefited. The box factories in the city are now giving employment to 200 more persons than they were before the decision was made."

Much ingenuity is displayed in the manner of putting up "original packages," and each bottle of beer that goes into the State is in a neat little box of its own. If some enterprising man would make packages the size of a drink he would reap a rich harvest.

In the debate in the United States House of Representatives, Mr. Henderson, of Iowa, said:

"I am free to say that no decision that has been rendered by the Supreme Court of the United States since that court decided that a human soul was a proper article of merchandise has so excited the feelings of this nation. . . .

"Since 1882, when my State first took its strongest position touching the regulation of the liquor traffic, we have not had such disgraceful scenes within our borders as this mandate of the Supreme Court has brought to our doors. The letters that have poured in upon me, the resolutions adopted, and mass-meetings held, tell me of a condition of thing for which I must blush, and which I will not describe in the National Capitol. But there is such a condition of things that I would be derelict in my duty as a Representative if I did not seek in some legislative avenue to find a remedy. To this sad condition others have testified also. . . ."

Of the actual working of the decision in Iowa, the following account is given in the *Christian Voice:*

"The 'original package houses' are the latest successors to the old Iowa saloon. A sign before me reads, 'California Wines—Whiskey—Bottles a Specialty,'—a huge board clear across the walk on the main street of Carroll, Iowa, a few steps from the depot. How this last and latest imp from hell posts aloft his wicked invitations to sin! Here in the heart of Iowa, too! Grand old decent, sober, Prohibition Iowa! This foul monster rears aloft his poisonous fangs. You people in license States are so used to it I presume you do not care so much; but here in Iowa the past ten years we have been getting cleaned up, sweet, decent, sober, industrious, and *wonderfully prosper-*

ous, and here, in spite of an overwhelming and strong 'public sentiment,' is the nest of vipers and brood of hell set to hatch and spawn upon the sober, law-abiding Christian people of this grand old State, a brood of loafers, tramps, thugs, and thieves. What a shame is all this! But there is, there must be a remedy. The present Wilson Bill, which has just passed the Senate, must pass the House or there will be woe, trouble, and sorrow in thousands of homes now happy and sober.

"A friend of mine, a deputy sheriff and police officer in one of the largest cities of Iowa, told me last week that this original package business *had produced more drunkenness and arrests in a month than had been seen in the city for years.* The express companies are loaded with beer barrels, and the whole filthy, wicked business seems to be speedily regaining its grip of *death, poverty, and taxes* on the people.

"Let every voter watch and spot every representative that votes against the Wilson Bill in Congress."

We have been told, with utterly wearisome iteration, "Prohibition don't prohibit;" "Prohibition is only another name for free rum," etc., etc. Why, then, this mad rush of "original packages" to the prohibitory States? That deadly enemy of Prohibition, the Omaha *Bee*, inadvertently lets the cat out of the bag in a recent issue as follows:

"A small but enthusiastic bunch of Prohibitionists journeyed to the capital of Kansas last week to proclaim the glories of statutory sobriety, which existed only in their imagination. They trimmed the whiskers of that venerable fiction, 'Prohibition prohibits,' while within a stone's throw of the meeting place was a throng of thirsty residents rushing about with original packages. *For the first time in five years liquor was sold openly in the city,* and *in less than eight hours the supply was exhausted,* without apparently diminishing the demand."

It is manifest to any business man that if that place had been stocked full before with "free rum," it would not have paid to open "original package" establishments there, and they would have met no such rushing demand as to "exhaust the supply in eight hours."

Prohibition had kept liquor from being "sold openly in the city for five years;" and when all is said and done, the illicit sale does not begin to meet the demand of the inebriate portion of any community. Hence the eagerness for "anything to beat Prohibition." Undoubtedly there are horses stolen in Kansas and Iowa now. But it is under difficulties that are very depressing to the business. If only some Supreme Court decision could be secured to make it lawful to steal them "in the original packages," for instance, the farmers would soon discover what a good law they have now. So one effect of the "original package" invasion, and of the exciting meetings and debates on the subject, has been to bring out new evidence of the excellence of Prohibition. The Topeka *Capital* comes out with the following:

TOPEKA DRUNK VS. TOPEKA SOBER.

For a year the most beautiful capital city in the West has been sober. *The peace, the quiet, the good order have become the pride and the glory of the people.* Strangers have commented with wonder and amazement upon the absence of saloons, and the people of the whole State have come to believe the capital of their splendid commonwealth a model city. *The United States Supreme Court's decision has changed all this. The "original packages" are to-day selling $1,000 worth of liquors* under the license of our highest court.

Dozens *of drunken men are to be seen in the alleys, on the streets, at the depot,* and it is with shame and humiliation that we see the work for sobriety and good government crumbling to pieces before our eyes. The old saloon-keepers, driven into Missouri to follow their calling of making drunkards, creating crime and pauperism, are creeping back, and with an insolent leer opening their hell holes in defiance of a public sentiment that finds itself powerless to protect the homes of the people. One benefit of this will be to show the difference between Topeka sober and Topeka drunk.

Every citizen interested in Topeka sober should write our Congressmen and Senators to urge them to give us some legislation. Let Congress give us the relief demanded, and Topeka will crush out every original package house within twenty-four hours. The indignation of the people against these violators of the laws of our State is deep and most determined, and only the respect for the highest courts of the land prevents the original package venders from being summarily driven to Missouri. The *Capital* counsels patience and legal methods until Congress gives the State the right to stop the present sales, and then there should be no mercy upon the mercenary scoundrels who are selling to-day in violation of our constitution and laws.

An enthusiastic convention of 3,000 delegates from all portions of Kansas was held in Topeka July 16th. Meeting in the House of Representatives, they filled that, and overflowed into the Senate Chamber. Filling that, they overflowed upon the steps of the Capitol, and out into the open air. The three meetings were in progress at once. Amid tremendous enthusiasm an address was adopted full of eloquent, heart-stirring, and convincing statements of fact. The address was in part as follows:

"The State of Kansas is the homestead of Prohibition, and Prohibition acquired its right to the soil of our State by permanent occupancy, and by making lasting and valuable improvements. The metes and bounds of its possessions are the exterior lines of the State. Its warranty deed is recorded in the hearts of the people, and its muniments of title can be seen in every church building, schoolhouse and happy home in our prosperous State. It is the fairest inheritance ever given to a contented people, and the rum power has no mortgage on it.

"The following official figures are presented as showing the effects of Prohibition in Kansas and in support of the statement made above.

"The school population of Kansas in 1880 was 340,647; in 1888, a period of eight years, there were 532,010 children of school age on Kansas soil, an increase of 191,363 in eight years.

"In 1880 the assessed valuation of Kansas property was $160,570,-761; in 1889 this aggregate is swelled to $360,815,033, a gain of more than 100 per cent. in nine years of Prohibition.

"As against the argument of financial decay, we offer the additional proof of confidence in the fact that within five years more than five thousand miles of railroad have been constructed within our borders, until Kansas, with her 9,249 miles of main and side track, stands second in point of mileage of all the States in the Union.

"When Prohibition came, Kansas had 917 convicts in her penitentiary and a total population in the State of 996,096; after nine years of Prohibition and an increase in population of 600,000 she has 873 convicts in her penitentiary, an actual decrease of five per cent., notwithstanding the increase in population Our sister State of Nebraska, with a High License system, during the same time has increased her prison population 167 per cent. The prison population of Nebraska has outrun the general growth of population 47 per cent. Kansas, with her 1,600,000 population, has 174 in her reform school for boys. Nebraska, with her estimated population of 1,000,000, has 245 boys in her reform school. Nebraska, with 600,000 less in population, has 71 more boys in prison than Kansas.

"For the purpose of comparison, we will parallel the rates of taxes in Kansas and Nebraska for the same years that we have had Prohibition in Kansas:

		Nebraska.	Kansas.
1880	assessed	95	55
1881	"	85	50
1882	"	96	45
1883	"	81	43
1884	"	76.9	45
1885	"	77.2	39
1886	"	76.2	40
1887	"	80.2	40
1888	"	75	34
1889	"	63.3	40

"The average rate in Kansas under Prohibition has been 43 cents and 5 mills on the $100, while in Nebraska under High License it has been 56 cents and 7 mills; 13 cents and 2 mills lower in Kansas than in Nebraska. The rate has increased in Nebraska and decreased in Kansas, the Nebraska rate for 1889 being nearly 60 per cent higher than in Kansas.

"The material prosperity in Kansas, as shown by the silent records, is more than 100 per cent. better than that of her High License neighbor, Nebraska.

"The revenue paid the general Government on spirituous liquors is a small pittance compared with the total cost of the amount consumed.

"There was paid the Government as revenue in the two States the following sums in the years named:

	Kan. paid.	Neb. paid.
1882	$63,609	$965,149
1883	69,112	1,180,607
1884	64,635	1,354,859
1885	64,344	1,796,031
1886	74,974	1,987,157
1887	57,382	2,142,038
1888	57,382	2,518,742
1889	25,878	2,142,462

"There has been a decrease in Prohibition Kansas of 49 per cent. since 1882, and an increase in High License Nebraska of 122 per cent. Kansas has paid to the Government as revenue on liquors consumed by her people less than one-half million dollars since the days of her Prohibition, while Nebraska, with 600,000 less people, has paid the Government over $14,000,000 in money, or twenty-eight times as much as Kansas."

In a recent letter, written from Ottawa, Kan., by Rev. Dr. J. L. Hurlbut to the *Central New Jersey Times*, he says:

"Some suggestive figures were shown me the other day, supplied by the Secretary of State, for Kansas and Nebraska [quoting the above figures].

"There was also shown me another set of figures, taken from R. G. Dun & Co.'s commercial register, which can hardly be called a temperance text-book. In 1889 there were in Kansas 24,929 business houses, against 20,771 in Nebraska; a difference in favor of Kansas of 4,158, showing that business thrives without liquor stores. But in Nebraska there were in the year 1889, 272 failures in business, against 183 in Kansas, or a difference in favor of Kansas of 89. In other words, Prohibition Kansas had one failure to every one hundred and thirty-six business houses, while High License Nebraska had one failure to every seventy-six business houses. That is, the chance of success in business is nearly twice as great under Prohibition as under license.

"A butcher in a town in Kansas a few weeks ago noticed that *several of his customers, who had for years been paying cash for their meat, were now asking credit and running up accounts.* He found that it was coincident with the opening of an 'original package' store in the town. People were spending their money on bottles of liquor, and hence had *none for the butcher.* This fact was given me by a reputable gentleman, who named the town and named the butcher. Perhaps it will help to explain why there should be less business houses, but more failures in business in a license State than in a Prohibition State."

In the debate, previously referred to, in the United States House of Representatives, Mr. Dingley, of Maine, said in part:

"Our prohibitory laws in Maine have aided materially in making the temperance sentiment which prevails in Maine. . . .

"These general conclusions of our own people as to the benefits of our policy of prohibiting instead of licensing dram-shops are confirmed by an examination of the internal revenue statistics. For revenue purposes, as is well known, the United States imposes a tax on the manufacture and sale of intoxicating liquors. For the year ending May 1st, 1889, the revenue from this source was $98,575,073, or $1.95 per inhabitant on the basis of the population of 1880.

"As these taxes on manufacturers and dealers of intoxicating liquors are collected with substantially uniform thoroughness in every State of the Union, a comparison of the amount collected in the several States gives us some idea of the relative extent of the manufacture and sale of distilled and fermented liquors. In New York the amount of tax collected by the Government from this source was $2.30 per inhabitant; in New Jersey, $2.95; in Pennsylvania, $1.49, and in Maine, 3¾ cents per inhabitant.

"The suggestion has been made that Prohibition mainly interferes with the traffic in malt liquors, but does not seriously restrict the traffic in distilled liquors.

"Inasmuch as the Government imposes a higher tax on retail dealers in distilled liquors than on retail dealers in malt liquors, and keeps the two classes of liquor-dealers separate, we have reliable means of comparing the number of retail dealers of distilled liquors in the several States, as it is well known that nearly all persons who propose to sell such liquors pay the small United States tax of $25 rather than run the risk of incurring the severe penalties of the United States laws.

"According to the official returns of the officers of the internal revenue for the year ending May 1st, 1890, there were 185,868 retail dealers in distilled liquors in the United States, or 1 liquor-dealer to every 275 inhabitants, on the basis of the census of 1880.

"In New York there was 1 retail dealer in distilled liquors to every 150 inhabitants; in New Jersey, 1 to 175; in Ohio, 1 to 230; in Pennsylvania and Massachusetts, 1 to 400; in Indiana, 1 to 325; in Delaware, 1 to 160, and in California, 1 to 75.

"The average in all the States which have general license laws is one dram-shop to 250 inhabitants.

"In Maine there is 1 retail dealer in distilled liquors to every 750 inhabitants; in Vermont, 1 to 820; in Iowa, 1 to 520; and in Kansas, 1 to 800."

When the United States tax on liquors, which elsewhere runs up to $2.95 per inhabitant, is cut down in Maine to 3 cents per inhabitant, it would seem to indicate that Prohibition prohibits. Besides, the Government tax on liquors may be roughly stated at about one-tenth of their actual cost to the consumer. So Maine has spent but thirty cents per inhabitant for liquor, while New York and New Jersey have spent from $23 to $29 per inhabitant. This money which Maine has not spent upon the saloons could be and has been spent upon the homes of the people.

But what of the future? The *Western Broker*, in a despatch from Topeka, Kan., of June 25th, quotes the following from United States District Attorney J. W. Ady:

"The Supreme Court decides that the State laws now in force have no application to the subject of liquors imported and sold in original packages. It is not a crime now to make such sales within the State. Congress has no power to make any act done in Kansas a crime under our State laws, and Congress does not attempt to do so. After the Wilson Bill passes, the sale of liquor in original packages will still continue to be inter-State commerce. The court says inter-State commerce is free, and the presumption that Congress and the States intend that it shall be free will continue until there is a direct act on the subject. *All State laws on that subject now are no laws; they are dead matter. The Wilson Bill will not infuse new life into them."*

This may indicate the future line of battle of the liquor men, and their purpose to challenge the Wilson Bill before the Supreme Court. It is urged that what the court says of "the permission" of Congress is what lawyers call an *obiter dictum*, a passing remark, and by no means equal to a formal decision. The principle of the "original package decision" will still be in question, and to that decision it is to be objected:

1. That it strikes down the police power of the States, which Congress can neither assume nor restore. The general Government cannot exercise police power within a State. That would be the last reach of centralization, and would virtually obliterate all State lines. On this point, Mr. Davis, Counsel for the State of Massachusetts in the License cases of 1847, well said:

"It will appear in the progress of this inquiry that the United States, have no power to regulate the traffic in wines and spirits within the States; and if the State has no such power, then the right is abrogated.

"Is not such a result hostile to the intent of all parties to the Constitution? The framers did not intend it, and the States could not have contemplated it."

The actual effects of the new decision are proving the correctness of this statement. The decision provides for an era of "free rum," such as has never been known on the American continent. Even "in good old colony times" there were some restrictions. Of the present status Senator Edmunds said in the Senate of the United States:

"It is a very curious circumstance, an interesting one, that we have reached a condition of things where, according to the debate here and the judgments of the Supreme Court of the United States, the States, as the Supreme Court say, have no power to deal with this subject ; and now we are told here that Congress has not any power to deal with it. So the result of the performance is that under the Constitution of the United States there must be an inherent, individual civil, personal right in every man in one State to carry whatever another State considers to be injurious to its safety and life and welfare into it and sell it ; that Congress cannot stop it ; the States cannot stop it, say the Supreme Court, unless Congress does something, and we all say Congress cannot do that something. . . . It is enough to state such a proposition to show that somewhere there is a fault in the logic of somebody."

The Supreme Court has abolished the police power of the States, and Congress has and can have no police power to supply its place.

Congress cannot say, for instance, that an "original package" shall not be sold to a minor or a drunkard within a State ; or that it shall not be sold after midnight, or "to be drank on the premises." All those things belong to the police power, which the State alone can wield.

In a previous decision the Supreme Court declared :

"Whatever difference of opinion may exist as to the extent and boundaries of the police power, and however difficult it may be to render a satisfactory definition of it, there seems to be no doubt that it does extend to the PROTECTION OF THE LIVES, HEALTH, AND PROPERTY OF THE CITIZENS, and to the PRESERVATION OF GOOD ORDER AND THE PUBLIC MORALS. THE LEGISLATURE CANNOT, by any contract, DIVEST ITSELF OF THE POWER TO PROVIDE FOR THESE OBJECTS. They belong emphatically to that class of objects which demand the application of the maxim, *salus populi suprema lex;* and they are to be attained and provided for by such appropriate means as the legislative discretion may devise. THAT DISCRETION CAN NO MORE BE BARGAINED AWAY THAN THE POWER ITSELF."

Then it is evident that the States *could not* surrender that power even to the United States Government, and never meant to do so. On this Justice Story said on a former occasion :

"The police power belonging to the States, in virtue of their general sovereignty, extends over all subjects within the territorial limits of the States, and has never been conceded to the United States."

Massachusetts accepted the Constitution of the United States and came into the Union with the Twenty-Eight Gallon Law on her statute-book.

By the Tenth Amendment, "the powers not delegated to the United States by the Constitution, nor prohibited by it to the States, are reserved to the States respectively, or to the people."

The inference is irresistible that the power given to the United States to regulate commerce between the States was never meant to permit the citizens of one State to establish a nuisance in another State—to set up a place for the manufacture of drunkards, or to sell fiery intoxicants to its little children.

If we grant the inter-State commerce power of Congress to be "exclusive" in its sphere as between the States, we must hold the police power of the State *just as exclusive in its sphere* within the State—an older power, and more vital to the existence of civilized society.

2. This decision virtually claims for the United States Government the right to force a sale within a State in the interest of the importer, if buyers can be found. It says:

"The power vested in Congress 'to regulate commerce with foreign nations and among the several States, and with the Indian tribes,' is the power to prescribe the rule by which that commerce is to be governed, and is a power complete in itself, acknowledging no limitations other than those prescribed in the Constitution. It is coextensive with the subject on which it acts, and cannot be stopped at the external boundary of a State, but *must enter its interior and must be capable of authorizing the disposition of those articles which it introduces, so that they may become mingled with the common mass of property within the territory entered.*"

The United States follows the imported package till it is "mingled in the common mass of property" within the State, which will in many cases be only when it is mingled in the stomach of the drinker. Then pauperism, murder, conflagration may follow, and the State be left to bear the consequences and meet the expenses. By this decision a man may lawfully do in another State what he cannot lawfully do in his own. The Cincinnati brewer or distiller cannot sell a drop in a Local Option town in Ohio, but he may sell all he wants to in Local Option towns in New York, where New York brewers and distillers cannot sell. Then the New York brewers and distillers can go right over and sell in all Local Option towns in Ohio, where Ohio brewers and distillers cannot sell. Thus, we have the whole liquor traffic playing at a gigantic game of "Pussy wants a corner." It does not look reasonable.

In the debate in the Senate on the Wilson bill, Senator Edmunds said :

"Now, where is the line? The line is, I think, a line which the Supreme Court of the United States appears to have gone over, that when your act of transportation, your act of commerce among the States or from foreign nations has become complete, and the word 'among' no longer applies, and the commodity is in the State where its transportation is ended, and it is in the hands of its owner there, whether that owner be a citizen of one State or another makes no difference, it is then just like the commodity of the same nature, all the laws being equal, in the hands of the citizen of the State who made it there himself, the subject of the State law ; and that is what the Supreme Court of the United States within the next twenty years will come to."

This would seem to be the only escape from the claim that every man possesses rights in any State where he does not belong, such as no man possesses in the State where he does belong.

This claim, which the Supreme Court maintains, of the right of Congress to follow an imported article in behalf of the importer "till it is broken up and so mingled with the common mass of property within the State," is a doubtful one. True, it has been repeatedly affirmed by the court, but that proves nothing, for, as we now see, decisions that have stood unchallenged for forty years may be swept away in a day. The claim seems to prove too much. For if the prohibition of sale of the original package to the first buyer is a restraint upon inter-State commerce, so is the prohibition of sale to the twentieth buyer. In the license cases of 1847 this was particularly noticed. Justice McLean said:

"This limitation may possibly lessen the sale of the article. *This may be the result of any regulation on the subject.* But it constitutes no objection to the law. *An inn-keeper is forbidden to allow drunkenness in his house*, and if this prohibition be observed, *a less quantity of rum is sold.* Is this unconstitutional because it may reduce the importation of the article? . . . No one could fail to see that the injunction was laid for the maintenance of good order and good morals. To reject this view *would make the excess of the drunkard a constitutional duty*, to encourage the importation of ardent spirits."

In the earlier decision Justice Daniel said even of imports from foreign countries, where it was claimed that the importer purchased the right to sell by paying duty to the Government:

"No such right is purchased by the importer; *he cannot purchase from the Government that which it could not insure him*, a sale independent of the laws and policy of the State."

Chief Justice Taney said:

"Although a State is bound to receive and to permit the sale by the importer of any article of merchandise which Congress authorizes to be imported, *it is not bound to furnish a market for it, nor to abstain from the passage of any law which it may deem necessary or advisable to guard the health or morals of its citizens,* although such law may discourage importation."

More than twenty-five years ago, in the Internal Revenue Act of June 30th, 1864, Section 78, Congress declared that even the payment of a special license fee to the United States should not authorize any person to make sales within a State contrary to the laws of that State. The law still continues in force as a section of the Internal Revenue Laws, as follows :

Section 3243 : " The payment of any tax imposed by the Internal Revenue Laws for carrying on any trade or business shall not be held to exempt any person from any penalty or punishment provided by the laws of any State for carrying on the same within the State, or in any manner to authorize the commencement or continuance of such trade or business contrary to the laws of such State, or in places prohibited by municipal law; nor shall the payment of any such tax be held to prohibit any State from placing a duty or tax on the same trade or business, for State or other purposes."

Commenting on the preparations of the people of Kansas to resist the sales of " original packages," *Bonfort's Wine and Spirit Circular* asks, menacingly :

"Are the people of the State of Kansas ready to rebel against the United States? Whenever they are, they will hear from the Government in a manner not to be misunderstood."

Which is nothing less than a threat to force the saloon at the point of the bayonet upon the people of the pioneer battle State of Freedom ! It has been said that nothing did so much to arouse the North for emancipation as the stretching of chains around Boston Court House, and the marching of slaves back into slavery between files of

United States troops. Then the iron entered into the soul of Northern freemen, and slavery was doomed. We all know that the Liquor Traffic is a hard master. But if a regiment of United States troops should be marched across the border of Kansas to establish the saloon by the bayonet under the dear old flag, the long-suppressed indignation of all the good would rise in a tempest of righteous wrath, and men who never cared for temperance before would suddenly find themselves Prohibitionists.

Yet the logic of the Supreme Court decision leads to just that, to force the saloon by the bayonet—if necessary—upon an unwilling people. If this is not law, it must be shown not to be. If it is law, it must be made not to be.

3. This decision treats intoxicating liquors "like any other commodity." The entire argument is based on this assumption.

The decision says:

"That ardent spirits, distilled liquors, ale and beer are subjects of exchange, barter, and traffic *like any other commodity* in which a right of traffic exists, and are so recognized by the usages of the commercial world, the laws of Congress and the decisions of courts, is not denied. Being thus articles of commerce, can a State, in the absence of legislation on the part of Congress, prohibit their importation from abroad or from a sister State? or when imported, prohibit their sale by the importer? . . . Whatever our individual views may be as to the deleterious or dangerous qualities of particular articles, we cannot hold that *any articles* which Congress recognizes as subjects of inter-State commerce are not such, or that whatever are thus recognized can be controlled by State laws amounting to regulations, while they retain that character."

We are reminded of the strikingly similar language used by the Supreme Court in the old Dred Scott decision:

"*The right of property in a slave is distinctly and expressly affirmed in the Constitution.* The right to traffic in it *like an ordinary article of merchandise and property* was guaranteed, etc. And no word can be found in the Constitution which gives Congress a greater power over slave property, *or which entitles property of that kind to less pro'ection than property of any other description.* The only power conferred is the power coupled with the duty of *guarding and protecting the owner in his rights !*"

Then, as now, the Supreme Court saw only " property," while the nation saw human character and homes, human hearts and lives.

But intoxicating liquors are by almost universal legislation treated as *unlike* " any other commodity." From the foundation of our Government, there have been laws forbidding their sale without a special license, or in less than certain stipulated quantities, 28 gallons, 10 gallons, 5 gallons, etc. Laws forbidding their sale on election days, to minors, to persons in the habit of becoming intoxicated, or forbidding their sale after ten o'clock at night, or other stipulated hour, have been frequently passed. There have been laws giving damages to relatives for any injuries and losses resulting from their sale, and laws prohibiting their sale in thousands of towns, and over the entire area of great States.

What other " commodity " has been treated like this ?

Think of a law forbidding a dry-goods merchant to sell less than twenty-eight yards of calico, or forbidding a grocer to sell sugar to any person under eighteen years of age, or prohibiting the sale of boots and shoes within two miles of an agricultural fair, or of beef and mutton within four miles of a schoolhouse, or of cakes and pies on election day, or of stationery to persons who are in the habit of using it to excess ! Everywhere are laws specially directing against intoxicating liquors, in which they are treated *not* " like any other commodity."

Similar instances might be adduced from almost all civilized nations, showing that intoxicating liquors are looked upon as a class of merchandise separate and distinct, not to be dealt with on indiscriminate rules applying to all "trade" and "commerce." Precedents for such a separation of special articles are readily to be found. We cannot press the laws against diseased meat, infected rags, etc., because those things are not subjects of commerce. But, as the dissenting judges say:

"The police power extends *not only to things intrinsically dangerous* to the public health, such as infected rags or diseased meat, but to things which, *when used in a lawful manner*, are subjects of property and of commerce, and *yet may be used so as to be injurious or dangerous to the life, the health, or the morals of the people.* Gunpowder, for instance, is a subject of commerce and of lawful use, yet because of its explosive and dangerous quality, all admit that the State may regulate its keeping and sale. And there is no article the right of the State to control or prohibit the sale of which within its limits is better established than intoxicating liquors."

Congress has made a special exception, also, in the case of nitro-glycerine and similar explosive substances, providing that, as to them,

"'Any State, Territory, district, city or town within the United States' shall not be prevented by the language used 'from regulating or from prohibiting the traffic in or transportation of those substances between persons or places lying or being within their respective territorial limits, or from *prohibiting the introduction thereof into such limits for sale, use, or consumption therein.*'"

Just such an exception should be made in the case of intoxicating liquors. Give us a good, clean blast of dynamite, blotting out its victim in an instant, with no corruption of character or harm to the immortal soul, rather than the long, lingering degradation and debauchery and the thousand times repeated murder of drunkenness. Permit us to prohibit alcohol, and we will run some chances, if need be, on nitro-glycerine. Any decision of any court, however high, which fails to recognize the exceptional character of intoxicating liquors, is one sided and defective.

A despatch to the New York *World*, dated at Indianapolis, August 9th, quotes Judge Elliott of the Indiana Supreme Court as using the following language at the meeting of the National Bar Association :

"In asserting Federal supremacy in recent decisions, the highest court in the land has moved through a new channel. It has carried the doctrine of central power to the utmost verge of safety. I venture, in the exercise of a citizen's right, to say that in one notable instance, at least, the current of its thought has outrun the lines marked for it by principle and precedent. The decision of the Court in the original package case is a strong, and with profound deference I suggest, a dangerous assertion of central power. *If the police power resides in the State*—and that it does has been time and time again adjudged—THE ONLY FEDERAL QUESTION PRESENTED WAS WHETHER INTOXICATING LIQUOR IS SO FAR DIFFERENT FROM OTHER PROPERTY AS TO BE THE SUBJECT OF POLICE REGULATION. THAT IT IS THERE CAN, IT SEEMS TO ME, BE LITTLE DOUBT.

"It seems to me that the just conclusion is that under our American Constitutions there is neither exclusive central power nor absolute local independence. It is, at all events, quite safe to affirm that it can never be expedient to build up a strong central power at the cost of municipal independence. If there is a right so old and so firmly interlinked with free institutions as to be known of all men, it is the right of local self-government. Of all the rights which found a place on American soil with the coming of Englishmen, it has taken the deepest root and borne the richest fruit."

Hence the conference committee of the two Houses of Congress did well to give the preference to the Wilson bill passed by the Senate, which provides :

" *That all fermented, distilled, or other in'oxicating liquors or liquids* transported into any State or Territory for use, consumption, sale, or storage shall, on arrival in such State or Territory (or remaining therein), be subject to the operation and effect of the laws of such State or Territory *enacted in the exercise of police powers,* to the same extent and in the same manner as though such liquors or liquids had been produced in such State or Territory, and shall not be exempt therefrom by reason of being introduced there in original packages or otherwise."

The exceptional and dangerous character of intoxicating liquors must be recognized in any sound decisions of courts or acts of legislation.

4. This decision never once mentions moral character, or the peace and good order of society, except in quotations. Never once are they considered as matters for legislation or judicial decisions. In summing up what a State may do for its citizens, it is said, "A State may provide for the security of the *lives, limbs, health and comfort of persons* and the *protection of property.*" That is all!

But these higher matters are worth the consideration of legislatures and courts, and most of all things important in all questions of law. The Supreme Court has repeatedly so decided, as, in the previously quoted words of Justice Grier, these "compel all laws on subjects of secondary importance, *which relate only to property, convenience, or luxury,* to recede when they come into conflict or collision." So recently as in 1887, in the Kansas cases, the Supreme Court used the following language:

"For we cannot shut out of view the fact, within the knowledge of all, that *the public health, the public morals and the public safety may be endangered by the general use of intoxicating drinks ;* nor *the fact,* established by statistics accessible to every one, *that the idleness, disorder, pauperism, and crime existing in the country are, in some degree at least, traceable to this evil.* If, therefore, a State deems the absolute prohibition of the manufacture and sale, within her limits, of intoxicating liquors for other than medical, scientific, and manufacturing purposes, to be *necessary to the peace and security of society, the courts cannot, without usurping legislative functions, override the will of the people as thus expressed by their chosen representatives.* . . . And so, if, in the judgment of the Legislature, the manufacture of intoxicating liquors for the maker's own use, as a beverage, would tend to cripple, if it did not defeat the effort to guard the community against the evils attending the excessive use of such liquors, it is not for the courts, *upon their views as to what is best and safest for the community,* to disregard the legislative determination of that question."

Just that which the court in 1887 said "we cannot shut out of view," the court in 1890 does deliberately "shut out of view," and decides simply on the low ground of property—the only ground on which a decision could have been rendered in favor of the liquor power.

This is an inexcusable neglect, and a perversion of the eternal fitness of things. Hearts are more than dollars, character more than trade, virtue more than revenue — more vital to the prosperity and permanence of nations. So the framers of our Constitution thought when they said:

"We, the people of the United States, in order to form a more perfect union, establish justice, insure domestic tranquillity, provide for the common defence, promote the general welfare, and secure the blessings of liberty to ourselves and our posterity, do ordain and establish this Constitution for the United States of America."

Of all these elements, this decision quotes only one— "to form a more perfect union"—and interprets that as union in the liquor trade. This is the fatal wrong of this decision—that when whole communities, towns, villages, counties, and great States were eager to protect the health, the morals, and the homes of the people, to stay the rush of crime and the woes of pauperism, and to save the rising manhood from the ruin of intemperance—that in such a case the Supreme Court saw only the right of the brewer and distiller to coin money out of the desolation, and establish in the fairest and best-guarded portions of the land what the people have aptly termed "Supreme Court saloons!"

Such a state of things cannot endure. A principle of wrong introduced into public administration, whether by decision of a Supreme Court, by act of a Congress, or by fiat of an emperor, becomes like a drop of rattlesnake's venom introduced into the human body, an element of pervading corruption, which, unless counteracted or eliminated, will destroy the whole. Lincoln never secured the reversal by the Supreme Court of the Dred Scott decision, for which he began to agitate. But he was able to sign the Emancipation Proclamation and to see enacted the Constitutional Amendments, which left no slavery to which the Dred Scott decision could apply.

The Wilson bill, which has now become a law, may be contested before the courts on the ground that Congress cannot delegate its power. The claim may be pressed that all Prohibition statutes, including the long-tried "Maine law," are "dead matter" and have always been unconstitutional. Yet, let no friend of the right hesitate or falter. The proved beneficence of Prohibition cannot be abolished from the earth.

The domination of the Liquor Power which would found upon this new decision cannot stand. The stars in their courses will fight against it. All the moral forces of the universe will war upon it to break it down, even, if need should be, through national disaster and downfall; for right and humanity are greater than nations, and mightier factors in the ordering of destiny. If our nation is to endure and realize its high possibilities and its early promise, then either the Supreme Court will come to read the Constitution in harmony with the laws of humanity and of God, or Congress will find a legal way to undo the evil effects of this decision, or the people will lay hold of the primal sources of power, and amend their fundamental law TILL, BEYOND A QUESTION OR A DOUBT, IT SHALL BE CONSTITUTIONAL FOR THEM TO PROTECT THEIR HOMES AND THEIR SONS.

THE END.

INDEX.

Africa, Liquor in, W. T. Hornaday, 443–445; London *Times*, 445; Rum and Missionaries, 449; Honest Trade Destroyed, 452.
Agnew, Judge Daniel, on Cider, 373.
Alcohol, All Animals Have Natural Aversion for, Dr. Felix L. Oswald, 138; in Beer, 146, 374; in Cider, 374.
Alcoholism, 388, 389.
Alliance News, The, The Drunkard's Child, 378.
America's Sacrifice to Drink, Dr. J. G. Holland, 105.
Ames Co., Oliver, Loss of Work through Drink, 107.
Archbishop of Canterbury, Liquor Destroys Heathen Trade, 452.
Argument, Economic, Applicable to all Industries, 15.
Armies, European Standing, Cost of, 27.
Arrests, for Intoxication, 24; in Omaha, 63; so-called, of Prostitutes, 64; in High License and Low License Cities, 66–67; in Pittsburgh and Allegheny, Pa., 76; in Scranton, Pa., 77; in Wilkesbarre, Lancaster and Reading, Pa., 78; by Citizens, Impossible, 161; of Liquor-Dealers in Kansas, 214; Decrease of in Providence, R. I., under Prohibition, 267, 272; in Atlanta, 277, 298; see "Crime;" see also "Statistical Tables," "Letters of Judges," etc., 184–260.
Arthur, P. M., A Strike against Liquor, 338.
Atherton, President J. M., Letter of, Advocating High License and Local Option, 120.
Atlanta, Chapter XVII., 276; *Commonwealth*, High License Injures Business, 292; *Constitution*, Prohibition Does Prohibit, 279; Police Statistics, 298; Business Men Testify, 300.
Avalanche, Memphis, on New Distilleries, 32.

Babes. See "Infants."
Bad Debts a Public Loss, 354; from Liquor Drinking, 312, 353. See "Statistical Tables;" Follow "Original Packages," 482.
Bailey, Joshua L., on High License, 74.

Bangor, Liquor Selling in, 129.
Banks, Savings, Increased Deposits in Maine, 179; in Iowa, 239, 261; Prosperous under Prohibition in R. I, 269.
Barnes, Rev. Albert, Sin of Legalizing Moral Wrong, 148.
Bar, N. Y., Tariff the Friend of the Liquor Traffic, 11.
Barnum, P. T., Offer of, 9.
Bayley, Mrs. Mary, Prosperity a Cause of Intemperance, 85; on Mothers Leaving Home to Earn Wages, 90.
Beecher, Lyman, D.D., The Remedy for Intemperance Must be Universal, 123.
Beer, Gardens, 884; for Nursing Mothers, 391–395.
Bemiss, D., School Superintendent, on Prohibition in Kansas, 226.
Best Customers, The, Chapter XX., 339.
Betton, Labor Commissioner Frank H., on Prohibition in Kansas, 226.
Bible, The, Snares for Priceless Men, 95; Quails and Plague, 98; Building Tombs of Prophets, 104.
Blade, Toledo, on Maine Law, 171.
Blaine, Hon. J. G., Liquor Tax Paid by Consumer, 83; on Prosperity of Maine, 171, 179; Tendency of Liquor Revenues to Increase, 118.
Boies, Gov., on Prohibition, 261.
Bonfort's Wine and Spirit Circular, Iler's Letter in Behalf of High License, 121; High License to Defeat Prohibition, 106.
"Boot-Leggers" Do not Influence Police, 42; Do not Create Demand, 142; Fight Shy of Minors, 159.
Boston *Herald*, High License against Prohibition, 111.
Boys, Cost of Food, Philadelphia *Record*, 100; Made Drunk by "Original Packages" in Kansas, 474; in Reform Schools in Kansas and Nebraska, 480.
Bradford, Attorney-General, on Decreased Crime in Leavenworth, 220.
Brewers, Creating Demand, 137, 144; Starting and Stocking Saloons, 70, 146; a Political Power, Chicago *Times*, 399.
Brooklyn *Eagle* on Brewers Starting and Stocking Saloons, 146.
Brooks Law, The, 36; Receipts from, Compared with Liquor Expenses, 36; *post hoc* and *propter hoc*, 72; Weakened by Decision of Supreme Court of Pennsylvania, 73; Political Prohibitionist for 1889 on the, 74; in Scranton, 77; in Wilkesbarre, 78; in Lancaster, 78; in Reading, 78; Crime under, Philadelphia *Press*, 78.
Burdick, P. A., "Figuring it Out," 824.
Burlington, Iowa, under Prohibition, 250.

INDEX. 501

Census Report on Concentration of Business, 49.
Chautauquan, The, Expending an Income, 328.
Chicago *Freie Presse*, High License Insurance against Prohibition, 110; *Lever*, on Kansas under Prohibition, 221; Prohibition fully Enforced in Oklahoma, 316; *News* on High License, 46; Sunday Liquor Traffic, 17; Reduction of Saloons in, Mr. Onahan on, 48; *Standard* on Failure of High License, 65; on Law Enforcement by Citizens, 160; Saloons and the Cronin Murder, 93; *Times*, Brewers a Political Power, 399; *Tribune*, High License Insurance against Prohibition, 110.
Children, Starving the, Horace Mann, 378.
Cholera, Quarantine by Local Option, 135.
Christian Index, "Have you a Boy to Spare?" 104.
Christian Union Fails to Prove Decreased Consumption through High License, 52.
Church, and State, 400; Duty of the, Rev. A. J. Gordon, D.D., 418; The, an Economic Institution, 418; The, James Russell Lowell, 423; The, What it Must Do, 427.
Cider, Judge Daniel Agnew on, 373; "Racket," Brewers Working the, 371; Salicylic Acid in, 374.
Cincinnati *Journal and Messenger*, High License an Escape from Prohibition, 110; on Kansas under Prohibition, 220.
Cities and Immigration, Chapter XXVIII., 431.
City Domination Dangerous, 432.
Cleveland, Wretched Homes of Drinkers in, 29; *Leader* on the Whiskey Tax, 46; *Leader*, Socialists and Saloons, 329; *Press*, Degradation of Cities, 437; Workhouse Statistics of, 22; Police Expenses of, 38.
Cobden, Richard, Temperance, 397.
Colquitt, Hon. Alfred H., Capital not Driven out by Prohibition, 276.
Comfort from Paralysis, 364.
"Commercialism," President White on, 9.
Competition Crushed by High License, 55.
Concentration of Business, Census Report on, 49.
Confidence, Want of, Destructive to Trade, 412.
Congregationalist, The, "Signing the Farm away," 360.
Congressional Record, Speech of Major Pickler on Oklahoma, 316.
Consumers, Cost of Liquor to, 18; Pay Liquor Tax, J. G. Blaine, 83; *Washington Sentinel*, 83; High License and the, Chapter VI., 83.

Consumption of Liquor in 1889, 18 ; Increase of, 18 ; not Proved to be Diminished by High License, 49–50 ; Increased in Nation while Number of Dealers Reduced, 51 ; Brewers' Congress Uncertain of in Pennsylvania, 52 ; *Christian Union* on, 52 ; not Diminished in Chicago, 62 ; Diminished under Prohibition in Kansas, 184–189, 206–209 ; in Iowa, 240–243, 252 ; in Newport, R. I., 275 ; in Atlanta, Mayor Hillyer's Statement, 277 ; Increased under License, Saloon-Keeper Vaughan's Testimony, 306 ; in Maine, Speech of Congressman Dingley, 482.

Contents, vii.

Cook, Joseph, Dangers of Cities, 431.

Corn, and Liquor, Comparative Labor Cost in each, 351 ; "What Will You Do with It ?" 365.

Cornwall, Professor A. R., on Saloons in Council Bluffs, 151.

Cost, of a Bushel of Corn, The, 363 ; of Feeding Boys, Mimico Industrial School, 100 ; of Intoxicants, Indirect, 20, 30 ; of Liquor Greater than National Debt, 81 ; of Liquor to Consumers, 18, 327 ; of Southern Slave, 102 ; of Liquor in Rhode Island, 275.

Council Bluffs, Saloons in, Professor Cornwall's Testimony, 151.

Country, The, Must Help the City, 434.

Crime, and Intemperance, 17, 21–25, 37 ; Increased in Massachusetts by Repeal of Prohibition, 60 ; in Pennsylvania, 75 ; Decreased in Kansas under Prohibition, 220, 225, 229–230 ; in Iowa, 234, 238 ; in Atlanta, 277 ; Henry W. Grady on, 282, 288 ; Prevented by Prohibition in Oklahoma, 316–318 ; in Whitechapel, London, 437 ; Absence of in Vineland, 452 ; see "Arrests ;" see also "Statistical Tables," "Letters of Judges," etc., 184–260 ; Reduced in Kansas, 480 ; More in Nebraska with Less Population, 480.

Cronin Murder, The, and the Saloons, Chicago *Standard*, 93.

Curtis, County Attorney, on Topeka without Saloons, 231.

Dakota, Paucity of News Concerning Prohibition in, 415 ; Prohibition in, fully Treated, 416.

Dangers of Cities, Joseph Cook, 431.

Davenport, Ia., under Prohibition, 251.

Davis, Supreme Judge, on Good Effects of Maine Law, 177.

Dayton, O., Young Men in Saloons, 427.

Dead Letter Laws, How they Arise, 104.

Deaths from Drink, 20, 104.

Decreased Consumption through High License, *Christian Union* Fails to Prove, 52.

Delinquent Officers Should be Removed, 167, 175.
Depreciation of Property by Saloons, 43.
Derby, Lord, on Swallowing Land, 323.
Devil's Foreign Mission, The, Chapter XXIX., 441.
Dickens, Charles, Self-denial Destroyed by Drinking, 88 ; Water *vs.* Gin, 380.
Dingley, Governor, on Good Effects of Maine Law, 177.
" Dives" the Strongest Temperance Argument, 144.
" Doggery" *versus* " Gilded Saloon," 81.
Dorchester, Daniel, D.D., Average Drink Bill of Each Laboring Man, 321 ; on Results of Maine Law, 179.
Dow Law, Receipts of, Compared with Liquor Expenses, 37.
Drinkers, Buy More Liquor in Larger, Finer Saloons, 80 ; and Pestilence, *New Era*, 95.
Drinking Cheapens Labor, 328; Deepens Misfortune, 331 ; Workmen, in England, How they Live, N. Y. *Tribune*, 85 ; Mrs. Mary Bayley, 85 ; in Fashionable Society, 386.
Druggists in United States, Number of, 86.
Drunkard's Child, The, *Alliance News*, 378.
Drunkenness, in Edinburgh, Rev. Dr. Guthrie, 90 ; from Cider, 376. See " Arrests," " Statistical Tables," " Original Package Decision."
Dubuque, Ia., under Prohibition, 250.
Duke of Alvah's Revenue Scheme, 95.
Dyer, General, on Good Effects of Maine Law, 177.

Economic Argument, The, Chapter I., 9 ; Application of to all Industries, 15.
Edinburgh, Drunkenness and Murder of Infants in, Rev. Thomas Guthrie, D.D., 90.
Edmunds, Dr. James, Beer while Nursing, 391, 392, 393, 395.
Educated Ignorance the Most Unconquerable, 408.
Educational Effect of Law, 154.
Ellis, Secretary Edward, Saloon on Frontier always Ahead of the Gospel, 145.
Ely, Professor, Taxation and Co-operation, 44.
Enforcement of Law, Representative, 166 ; "of Laws we Have," 168 ; see " Law."
European Standing Armies, Cost of, 27.
Eviction, Henry W. Grady, 284.
Executive, Duties of, General Grant, 165 ; Intruding on Legislative Functions, 164 ; Officers the True Law and Order League, 163.

Farmers, Losses from the Liquor Traffic, 367; Market Destroyed by Liquor Traffic, 369; Should Watch City Officers, 176; The, Chapter XXII., 358.
Farmers' Loan and Trust Co. on Prohibition in Kansas, 228.
Finch, John B., Duty of Protecting the Homes in the Cities, 129.
Flour, Sack of, Many Industries Involved in, 348.
France, Recovery of, after Franco-German War, 91.
"Free Rum," Prohibitionists Accused of Wanting, 109.
Frost, Walter B., Prohibition in Rhode Island, 269.
Frye, Hon. William P., on Good Effects of Maine Law, 177.

Gambling Hall Will Develop Passion for Gambling, 138.
Garnisheeing, Henry W. Grady, 287.
Gates of Paradise, The, Chapter XXX., 454.
"Gilded Saloon" *versus* "Doggery," 81.
Gin Palaces Flourish in the Slums, Mr. George R. Sims, 91.
Good Health on Absence of Crime in Kansas, 181.
Gordon, Rev. A. J., D.D., Duty of the Church, 418.
Grady, Hon. H. W., The Home-Owning Wage-Worker, 276; his Speech for Prohibition, 284.
"Gradual Approaches" Do not Approach, 150.
Grain, Table from *The Voice*, 365.
Grant, General, on Duties of the Executive, 165.
Greenhut, President, his Address to Whiskey Trust, 53.
Grosvenor, General Charles H., on the Scott Law, 97.
Guthrie, Rev. Thomas, D.D., on Drunkenness and Murder of Infants in Edinburgh, 90.

Hale, E. E., Expending an Income, 323.
Hargreaves, Dr. William, Better Uses for Liquor Money, 456; Farmers and the Liquor Traffic, 367; Waste of the Drink Traffic, 348.
Harvest of Death, The, Chapter VII., 95.
Harvey, Hon. J. W., on Prohibition in Iowa, 283.
"Have You a Boy to Spare?" *Christian Index*, 104.
High License, Does it Pay? Chapter III., 32; in Omaha, 39; as Monopoly, Chapter IV., 46; Chicago *News* on, 46; Reducing Number of Saloons, 47; Arithmetic, 47; as Affecting Consumption of Liquor, 50; *Christian Union* on, 52; Crushes Competition, 55; Increases Saloon Power in Politics, 55; a Tax upon the Poor, 56; as Restriction, Chapter V., 60; "Dives," St. Louis *Republic* on, 62; Omaha *Bee* on, 63; Failure of, Chicago *Standard*, 65; and

INDEX. 505

Low License Cities, *The Voice*, 66; in St. Paul, *The Voice*, 68; Joshua L. Bailey on, 74; Philadelphia, Arrests under, 75; Pittsburgh, Arrests under, 76; and the Consumer, Chapter VI., 83; not a Step toward Prohibition, Chapter VIII., 106; Insurance against Prohibition, *Bonfort's Wine and Spirit Circular*, 106; Chicago *Freie Presse*, 110; Chicago *Tribune*, 110; Editor Medill, 110; *Journal and Messenger*, Cincinnati, 110; Lowers Public Sentiment, 109; Nebraska Clergymen on, 112; not in Prohibition States before Prohibition, 118; Reduction in Illinois Would Derange Municipal Finances, 118; Distiller J. M. Atherton Favors, 120; Iler & Co. Favor, 121; Gives Saloons Attraction and Power in Omaha Contrasted with Outlawed Saloons of Council Bluffs, 151; Its Appeal to the Taxpayer in Maine, 174; Injures Business, Atlanta *Commonwealth*, 292; in Nebraska Compared with Prohibition in Kansas, 479–482.

Hillyer, Mayor, Prohibition in Atlanta, 277; Unfairness of Newspapers, 408.

Holland, Dr. J. G., America's Sacrifice to Drink, 105.

Home, The, Mothers Compelled by Saloon to Leave for Work, Mrs. Mary Bayley, 90; Chapter XXIII., 378.

Homes, Wretched, of Drinking Men, 29, 380; of Reformed Men, 463.

Hornaday, W. T., Riches of Africa, 451; Temperance in Africa, 444, 445.

Horton, Chief Justice, on Kansas under Prohibition, 220.

Humphrey, Governor, on Prohibition in Kansas, 228.

Hunt, Mrs. Mary H., Mother Love, 388.

Idiocy and Intemperance, 25.
Ignorance, Educated, the Most Unconquerable, 408.
Iler & Co. Favor High License, 60, 121.
Illustrated Christian Weekly, Slavery and Alcohol, 441.
Import Values and Liquor Consumption, 19.
Increase in Retail over Wholesale Price of Liquor, 351; Tendency of Liquor Revenues to, James G. Blaine, 118.
Increased Consumption of Liquor and Reduced Saloons, 18, 51, 61; in 1889, 19.
Indianapolis *Journal*, Prosperity of Iowa, 264.
Indirect Cost of Intoxicants, 20, 30; Taxes not Appreciated, 58.
Infants Murdered by Drunkenness in Edinburgh, Rev. Dr. Guthrie, 90; Unborn, Liquor and, Dr. E. G. Figg, 390; Nursed by Liquor-

Drinking Mothers Unhealthy, 392-393; Giving Liquor to, 395; Milk for, 459.

Ingalls, Senator John J., on Prohibition in Kansas, 181.

Inherited Alcoholism, Dr. E. Lanceraux, 388; Dr. Norman Kerr, 389.

Inquisition, Victims of, Llorente, 104.

Insanity and Intemperance, 25.

Intemperance. See "Arrests," "Crime," "Idiocy," "Insanity," etc.

Internal Revenue, Cleveland *Leader* on, 46; Decrease in Maine, 178; Districts, Maine no Longer among Them, 178; from Liquor, Total in 1888 and 1889, 34; no Test of Consumption of Liquor, 235; in Kansas *vs.* Nebraska, 479; in Maine, 482; Law, Payment of Tax Does Not Give Right to Sell, 489.

Intoxication, Arrests for, 24.

Invention, Valuable, Sold for a Glass of Beer, 88.

Iowa, *State Register* on Taxes, 39; License Fee in before Prohibition, 118; Saloons in Council Bluffs, 151; Chapter XV., 232; District Judges on Prohibition, 252-260; Prosecuting Attorneys on Prohibition, 240-249; Getting Liquor in, 262; under Prohibition, President B. F. Wright on, 232; History of Legislation, 232; Governor Larrabee on, 233; Hon. G. W. Ruddick on, 233; Hon. J. W. Harvey on, 233; Hon. W. P. Wolf on, 234; Effects in Burlington, 250; in Dubuque, 250; in Davenport, 251; Prosperity of, Indianapolis *Journal*, 264; State Debt Paid, 265; See also 476.

Jails Empty, in Kansas, 230; in Iowa, 233, 237, 251.

Johnson, Rev. James, Liquor for the Heathen, 443; Rum Worse than Slavery, 453; Rev. Wayland, on Local Option in Georgia, 131.

Judgment Injured by Drinking, 362.

Kansas, License Fee in before Prohibition, 119; Douglas and Lincoln on Slavery in, 126; Clerk Spotted for One Drink, 152; no Sunday Selling in, 158; Grand Place to Bring up Boys, 159; Effectiveness of Prohibition, 181; *Good Health* on Absence of Crime in, 181; Murray Law, 170, 181; Prohibitory Amendment Adopted in 1880, 181; Senator Ingalls on Prohibition in, 181; Success of Prohibition in, 182; Probate Judges on Prohibition in, 183-203; County Treasurers on Prohibition in, 203-213; Governor Martin on Success of Prohibition in, 214; L. A. Maynard in "Truth about Kansas," 217; Liquor Drinkers in Disrepute, 219; under Prohibition, Chief-Justice Horton on, 220; Chicago *Leter* on, 221; Statement of Prominent Citizens, 153, 223 ; Decrease of Crime at Fort Scott, 225 ; Steel Cell Business Injured by, 225 ; Barrel Manufacturer Complaining, 225 ; Tradesmen Receive Prompter Pay, 225 ; E. B. Purcell on, 225 ; Labor Commissioner Betton on, 226 ; School Superintendent Bemiss on, 226 ; Various Opinions on, 227 ; Governor Humphrey on, 228 ; Farmers' Loan and Trust Co. on, 228 ; *Western Baptist* on, 230 ; Better Class of Immigrants Going to, 438 ; Effects of "Original Packages" in, 474, 475, 478 ; Great Convention at Topeka, 479 ; New Official Statistics of Prohibition, 479–481 ; Rev. Dr. J. L. Hurlbut on, 481 ; Decision of Supreme Court for Prohibition in 1887, 494.

Keach, Calvin E., Better Uses for Liquor Money, 457.
Keosauqua Republican, Governor Larrabee's Letter on Prohibition in Iowa, 233.
Kerr, Dr. Norman, Inherited Alcoholism, 389.

Labor, Loss of through Drink, 21 ; Employed by Liquor Traffic Less than in any Other Business, 351.
Laboring Men, Average Drink Bill of Each, Daniel Dorchester, D.D., 321 ; St. Paul *Pioneer Press*, 321 ; Chapter XIX., 320.
Lager Beer, Increased Per Cent. of Alcohol in, "Nasby," 146.
Lamb, Charles, Intemperance the Death of Determination, 87.
Lancaster, Brooks Law in, 78.
Lanceraux, Dr. E., Inherited Alcoholism, 388.
Larrabee, Governor, on Iowa under Prohibition, 233.
Law, as an Educator, 154 ; Protecting Lands and Crops from Hunters, 155 ; Absence of, a Tacit Sanction, 156 ; as Protection to the Young and Unwary, Hon. Robert C. Pitman, 156 ; Beneficial, Creates Public Sentiment for Itself, 156.
Law Enforcement, Father Taylor on, 160 ; by Citizens, Chicago *Standard*, 160 ; —— Impracticability of, 161 ; —— Incompatible with. Executive Officers, 163 ; —— Opposed to Republican Principle, 165 ; Helped by Strengthening Laws, 169 ; and Counterfeiting, 169 ; Imprisonment Helps in, 175 ; General Grant on, 165.
Lawyer Getting Liquor in Iowa, 262 ; Reading Habits of a, 409.
Leader, Cleveland, Women who Drink, 383.
Leaders of Opinion Should Secure the Facts, 415.
Leavenworth Prosperous under Prohibition, 219.
Legalization Increases Sale, 143.
Lending Umbrella, The, 168.

508   INDEX.

Liberty Dependent upon Morals, Daniel Webster, 397.
License and Taxation in Omaha, 39; Cardinal Manning on, 148; Essential Wrong of, Rev. Albert Barnes, 148; High, see "High License."
Limited Labor Required in Making or Selling Liquor, 351.
Lincoln, Abraham, falsely Represented as Opposing Prohibition, 291; Moral Wrong of Slavery, 403.
Liquor, Literature, 14; Crimes, Judge White on, 17; and Import Values, 19; and Tariff, 19; and Loss of Labor, 21; and Pauperism, 21; Cleveland Workhouse, 22; and Crime, 23; Sickness Caused by, 26; Makers, Lost Labor of, 27; Dealers Non-producers, 27; Indirect Cost of, 20, 30; Bill Compared with National Debt, 31; Dealers in United States, 36; Receipts and Expenses from, in Ohio, 37; More Bought in Finer Saloons, 80; Tax, Paid by Consumer, J. G. Blaine, 83; *Washington Sentinel*, 83; Demand for Increased Dose of, 137; in Case of Cincinnati Merchant, 140; Secret Sale of, 262; How Lawyer Got it in Iowa, 262; Enslaves Labor, R. F. Trevellick, 320; and Corn, Comparative Labor Cost in Each, 351; Traffic Employs Less Labor than Other Business, 351; Traffic Makes more Profit over Cost of Production than any Other Business, 351; Destroys Trade, 443, 452.
Liquor Money, Better Uses for, Dr. William Hargreaves, 456; Calvin E. Keach, 457.
Llorente, Victims of Inquisition, 104.
Local Option Claimed as Peculiarly American, 123; by Towns, Weakness of, 158; in Ohio, 124; Means Option to Permit as well as Option to Prohibit, 124; Contrary to the American Idea, 125; Simply the Douglas Doctrine of "Popular Sovereignty," 126; in Georgia, Number of Inebriates and Ruined Homes Increasing, 127; is Inadequate Protection, 127; Town, the Mother in, 127; Surrenders the Centers of Population, 128; Constantly in Politics, 129; John B. Finch on, 129; Professor H. A. Scomp on, 130; Disintegrates the Temperance Forces, 131; Permits the Liquor Power to Remain Organized, 131; Why not for the Tariff? 134; Applied to Cholera, 135; Successful Instance of, 355.
Locke, D. R. See "Nasby."
London, Dock Laborers' Strike Successful Because under Temperance Influence, 336; *Economist*, Saloons Cut off Market for Goods, 339; *Tid Bits*, a Costly "Beer," 88; *Times*, Prohibition Means Morality and Wealth, 454; *Times*, Temperance in Africa, 445.

Long, Hon. John D., Whiskey is Dynamite, 431.
Loss of Labor through Drink, 21; of Working Power through Drink, Oliver Ames Co., 107.
Lost Labor of Liquor Makers and Dealers, 27.
Lottery Will Develop Demand for Itself, 138.
Lowell, James Russell, A Parable, 423.

Macon *Telegraph* (Anti-Prohibition) favored Local Option in Georgia, 132.
Maine, License Fee in, before Prohibition, 118; Republican State Convention of 1882, 177; Increase of Savings Banks Deposits, 179; Increase of Valuations, 179; Dr. Dorchester on Prohibition in, 179; Vote on Prohibitory Amendment, 1884, 178; Decrease in Internal Revenue since 1863, 178; J. G. Blaine on Prosperity of, 171, 179; Increase of Population, 180.
Maine Law, Toledo *Blade* on, 171; D. R. Locke ("Nasby") on, 171; in Lewiston, N. Y. *World* on, 173; and Politics, 173; Liquor League Desires Repeal of, 173; Governor Dingley on Good Effects of, 177; Governor Perham on Good Effects of, 177; Hon. William P. Frye on Good Effects of, 177; Supreme Judge Davis on Good Effects of, 177; General Dyer on Good Effects of, 177; Latest statistics of, 482.
Man, Cash Value of a, 99, 102.
Manhood, Snares for, Bible, 95.
Mann, Horace, on Starving the Children, 378.
Manning, Cardinal, on Prevention as a Duty, 148.
Martin, Ex-Governor, on Success of Prohibition in Kansas, 214; Repeal not Proposed, 436.
Maynard, L. A., "The Truth about Kansas," 217, 225.
Medill, Editor, High License Insurance against Prohibition, 110.
Metcalf, Hon. Henry B., Repeal of Prohibition in R. I., 273.
Michigan, License Fee in before Prohibition, 118.
Milk for Children *vs.* Liquor for Men, 459.
Minister Influenced by High License Arguments, 108.
Minors Safe in Kansas, 159.
Money used Repeatedly in Trade, 350.
Monopoly, Brewers', St. Louis *Republic*, 70; High License as, Chapter IV., 46; of Sale, Effect on Purchasers, 80.
Mother Love, Mrs. Mary H. Hunt, 388.
Mothers, in Local Option Towns, 127; Using Intoxicants, 389–391; Liquor Injurious to, 395.

Napoleon, "Send me no more Boys," 91.
"Nasby" (D. R. Locke), Brewers Creating a Demand for Beer, 144; on Increased Per Cent. of Alcohol in Lager Beer, 146; on Thirst-Provoking Contrivances in Saloons, 146; on Maine Law, 171; Political Power of the Saloon, 405.
National Baptist on Arrests, 25.
National Labor Tribune, Ambition Destroyed by Drink, 86.
National Temperance Advocate, on Increase of Pauperism in Great Britain, 92.

Nebraska Clergymen on High License, 112.
New Era, Drinkers and Pestilence, 95; Character of Immigration, 438.
New Lands, The, Chapter XVIII., 315.
Newport *Daily News*, Drunkenness Increasing, 275; *Enterprise*, Economic Value of License and Rum, 275.
Newspapers, General, Unfairness of, Mayor Hillyer, 408; In Pennsylvania Amendment Contest, H. W. Palmer, 413; General, Disqualify their Readers to Judge Concerning Temperance, 409; Partisan, Educating into Contempt of Character and Disregard of Truth, 410; Readers Should Test their Assertions, 414.
Nursery, The, Chapter XXIV., 388.
Nursing Mothers, Beer for, 391, 392, 393, 395.

Officers, Delinquent, Should be Removed, 167, 175.
Ohio Receipts and Expenses from Liquor, 37.
Oklahoma Peaceful under Prohibition, Major J. A. Pickler, 316; Prohibition fully Enforced, Chicago *Lever*, 316.
Omaha *World*, on Taxation, 39; *Bee* on High License, "Dives," 63; License and Taxation, 39; Police Reports, 63; License of Prostitution, 64; *Bee* on "Original Packages" in Iowa, 477.
Onahan, Mr., on Reduction of Saloons in Chicago, 48.
"One Liver and Forty Roasts," Bishop J. H. Vincent, 341.
"One Man's Drink Bill," P. A. Burdick, 324.
"Original Package" Decision, The, Chapter XXXI., 467; A Reversal of Decision in New Hampshire Case, 471–473; Justice Grier's Opinion, 471; Chief-Justice Taney's Opinion, 472; Effects of Decision, 473–479; Size of Packages, 474; Drinking on Premises, 474; Sales to Minors, 474; Boys Drunk in Kansas, 474; Representative Perkins on Effects in Kansas, 475; Kansas City's Rushing Business in Beer and Boxes, 475, 476; Representative Henderson on Results in Iowa, 476; *Christian Voice* on Results in

INDEX. 511

Iowa, 476; Omaha *Bee* on Liquor Sales in Topeka "For the First Time in Five Years," 477; Topeka *Capital* on "Topeka Drunk *vs.* Topeka Sober," 478; Great Convention in Topeka, 479; Official Statistics Comparing Kansas Prohibition with Nebraska High License, 479–481; Rev. Dr. Hurlbut on Business Failures in Kansas and Nebraska, 481; Representative Dingley on Prohibitory Law in Maine, 482; U. S. District-Attorney J. W. Ady on Prohibitory Laws "Dead Matter" Now, 483; Destroys Police Power of States, 484; Claims Right to Force a Sale, 487; Senator Edmunds on, 487; Treats Liquor "Like Any Other Commodity," 490; Striking Parallel with Dred Scott Decision, 490; Judge Elliott, at National Bar Association, on, 493; Wilson Law, 493; Morality and Public Order Not Considered, 494; Compared with Decision in Kansas Case, 494; Liquor Domination Cannot Stand, 495–496.

Oswald, Dr. Felix L., on Natural Aversion of Animals for Alcohol, 138.

Paid Labor of Wives and Mothers Injures Home, Mrs. Mary Bayley, 90.
Palmer, General Henry W., Newspaper Deception, 413.
Pauperism and Drink, 21; in London, 92; in Kansas, 230; see "Statistical Tables."
Pawtucket *Gazette and Chronicle*, Non-Enforcement of High License Restrictions, 274; *Record*, Saloons Prosperous under License, 274.
Paying the Piper, Chapter II., 17.
Perham, Governor, on Good Effects of Maine Law, 177.
Philadelphia, Arrests under High License, 75; *Press*, on Crime under the Brooks Law, 78; *Record*, Cost of a Boy's Food, 100.
Pickler, Major J. A., Oklahoma Peaceful under Prohibition, 316.
Piper, Paying the, Chapter II., 17; Will Raise his Price, 94.
Pitman, Judge Robert C., The State the Unit of Sovereignty, 123; on Law as Protection to the Young and Unwary, 156.
Pittsburgh, Arrests under High License, 76; "Speak-easies" in, A. Wisbart, 79.
Poisoners-General, John Wesley on, 95.
Police Efficiency Reduced by Saloons, 41; Statistics, Atlanta, 298; Expenses in Cleveland, 38; Power, Belongs to States, 471; Destroyed by "Original Package" Decision, 484; Never Conceded to the United States, 486.
Political Power, of the Brewers, Chicago *Times*, 399; of the Saloon,

D. R. Locke, 405 ; of Liquor Traffic Increased by High License, 55.
Politics, Chapter XXV., 397.
Polygamy and Law, 401.
Poor, High License a Tax upon the, 56.
Powderly, T. V., Drink the Laborer's Worst Enemy, 336 ; Shut out the Liquor-Dealer, 337 ; Drink Enslaves the Workingman, 338.
Preface, iii.
Press, The, Chapter XXVI., 408.
Prohibition, Effect on Wool, Compared with the Tariff, 12 ; Why Liquor-Dealers Want it Repealed, 142 ; the Best Restriction, 150 ; in Leavenworth, 219 ; Iowa Judges on, 256 ; Governor Larrabee on, 260 ; Governor Boies on, 261 ; in Rhode Island, *Political Prohibitionist* for 1888, 267 ; Walter B. Frost, 269 ; a Good Law, N. Y. *Tribune*, 272 ; Repeal of in Rhode Island, Henry B. Metcalf, 273 ; in Atlanta, Mayor Hillyer, 277 ; Improves Schools, Atlanta *Constitution*, 281 ; Business, Atlanta *Constitution*, 279 ; Does Prohibit, 279 ; Decreases Crime, 282 ; Gives Peace and Order in Oklahoma, Major J. A. Pickler, 316 ; fully Enforced in Oklahoma, Chicago *Lever*, 316 ; Booms Business, 355 ; Press Reliable, 414 ; in Dakota, Paucity of News Concerning, 415 ; News fully Given, 416 ; Will Purify Immigration, 438 ; in Vineland, Constable Curtis, 454.
Prohibitionists Forced to Read all Sides, and Likely to be Best Informed, 411.
Property Depreciated by Saloons, 43.
Public, Morals to be Preserved, 402 ; Sentiment Lowered by High License, 109.
Purcell, E. B., on Prohibition in Kansas, 225.

Reading, Brooks Law in, 78 ; Police Statistics, 78.
Reading of Anti-Prohibition Press not Sufficient, 408 ; of Books and Papers, Influence on Opinion and Life, 409.
Reduction of Saloons and Increased Consumption of Liquor, 51, 61.
Regulation as Applied to Secession, 154.
Remedy for Intemperance Must be Universal, Dr. Lyman Beecher, 123.
Repeal of Prohibition in Rhode Island, H. B. Metcalf, 273.
Republican Convention of 1882 (Maine) on Maine Law, 177.
Restriction, High License as, 60 ; The True, Chapter XI., 148 ; as Hard to Enforce as Prohibition, 149 ; Bitterly Contested by Liquor-

Dealers, 149; Effectual, Reduces Liquor-Dealers' Income, 149; Parallel Propositions Regarding, 149; Prohibition the Best, 150.
Revenues, from License, Total, Mr. E. J. Wheeler, 19; State, 36; Internal, from Liquor, 34; Scheme of Duke of Alvah, 95.
Rhode Island, Chapter XVI., 266; Prohibition in, *Political Prohibitionist* for 1888, 267; Prohibition in, Walter B. Frost, 269; Prosperity of, under Prohibition, 269.
Ruddick, Hon. G. W., on Prohibition in Iowa, 233.
Rum on the Congo, Rev. Dr. Sims, 448; H. W. Stanley, 449; Worse than Slavery, Sir Richard Burton, 452; Rev. James Johnson, 453.

St. Louis *Republic* on Brewers' Monopoly, 70; on High License "Dives," 62.
St. Paul, High License in, *The Voice*, 68; *Pioneer Press*, Average Drink Bill of each Laboring Man, 321.
Saloons, Number and Income in New York City, 13; Total Cost of in New York City, 13; Palatial, Cost of, 29; Reduce Police Efficiency, 41; Depreciate Property, 43; Revenue for Sidewalks, 44; Political Power Increased by High License, 55; Increased Sales in Finer, 80; and the Cronin Murder, Chicago *Standard*, 93; once Started, Make their Own Trade, 140; Splendid, the Most Objectionable, 144; always in Advance of Civilization on Frontier, 145; Cut off Market for Goods, 339; Using Stolen Light, 380; of Dayton, O., Young Men in, 427; Great Focus of Destruction in Cities, 435.
Scomp, Professor H. A., on Local Option in Georgia, 130, 132.
Scott Law, General Charles H. Grosvenor on, 97.
Scranton, Brooks Law in, 77.
Secret Liquor Selling, 262.
Self-denial Destroyed by Drinking, 88.
Selfishness of Drinking, 332.
Sickness Caused by Liquor, 26.
Sidewalks and Saloons, 44.
Sims, George R., on "How the Poor Live," 91; The Depth of the Wound, 345; Rev. Dr., Rum on the Congo, 448.
Slavery, Moral Wrong of, Abraham Lincoln, 403.
Slums, Gin Palaces Flourish in, Mr. George R. Sims. 91.
Socialists and Saloons, Cleveland *Leader*, 329.
Society, Rude Pressure to Drink in, 386.
South, Recovery of after Civil War, 91.
"Speak-Easies" in Pittsburgh, 78, 79.

Stanley, H. W., Rum on the Congo, 449.
Starting a Saloon, 140.
State, The, the Unit of Sovereignty, Judge Robert C. Pitman, 123.
Statistical Tables, XVII,
Sunday, Liquor Traffic, Chicago *News*, 17; Selling, Incident in Drug Store, 154; Closing in Duluth, 157; No Trouble about under Prohibition, 157; Selling, None in Kansas, 158.
Supply of Liquor Creates Demand, Chapter X., 137.
Supreme Court Decisions in New Hampshire Case of 1847, 470; in "Original Package" Case of 1890, 473; in Kansas Case of 1887, 404.
"Swallowing Land," Lord Derby, 828.

Tariff, Main Issue in 1888, 11; the Friend of the Liquor Traffic, N. Y. *Bar*, 11; Effect on Wool Compared with Effect of Prohibition, 12; Import Values Compared with Liquor Consumption, 19; Local Option for, 134.
Taxation, and Co-operation, Professor Ely, 44; and License in Omaha, 39.
Temperance Instruction in Schools Needful, 416; Literature, 416.
Thirst-provoking Contrivances in Saloons, "Nasby," 146.
Thomas, J. L., The Labor Problem the People's Problem, 320.
Tisdel, W. P., Liquor for the Heathen, 443.
Toledo *Blade*, Reply to Letter of Indignant Brewer, 137; on Maine Law, 171.
Topeka without Saloons, County Attorney Curtis on, 231; Drunk *vs.* Topeka Sober, 478.
Tradesman, The, Chapter XXI., 348.
Tradesmen needed, 348; Prospering under Prohibition, 225, 253–257.
Trevellick, R. F., Liquor Enslaves Labor, 320.
Tribune, N. Y., How Drinking Workmen Live, 85.
"Truth about Kansas, The," L. A. Maynard, 225.

Unborn Infants, Liquor and, Dr. E. G. Figg, 390.

Value, Cash, of a Man, 99, 102.
Vincent, Bishop J. H., "One Liver and Forty Roasts," 341.
Voice, The, Table of High License and Low License Cities, 66; High License in St. Paul, 68; Probate Judges on Success of Prohibition in Kansas, 183; County Treasurers on Success of Prohibition in Kansas, 208; Leavenworth under Prohibition, 219; Statement of One Hundred and Fifty-three Prominent Citizens of Kansas, 223; Iowa Judges on Prohibition, 237, 256; Iowa Prosecuting Attorneys' Replies, 239, 249; Prosperity of Iowa, 265; Atlanta's Business Men

Testify, 300, 313; Table Concerning Grain, 365; "Original Package" Saloons in Kansas, 474.

Wage-worker, Home-owning, Hon. H. W. Grady, 276.
Washington Sentinel, Liquor Tax Paid by the Consumer, 83.
Waste of the Drink Traffic, William Hargreaves, M.D., 348.
Wealth-producing Qualities, their Destruction, 84, 92.
Webster, Daniel, Liberty Dependent upon Morals, 397; Dr., United States Consul, How Drinking Workmen Live, 85.
Wesley, John, on Poisoners-General, 95.
Western Baptist on Prohibition in Topeka, 230.
"What Will you do with your Corn ?" 365.
Wheeler, E. J., on Liquor Revenues, 19.
Whiskey, Tax, Cleveland *Leader* on, 46; Trust Policy, President Greenhut's Address, 53; Reducing Number of Establishments, 53.
White, President, "Commercialism," 9; Judge, on Liquor Crimes, 17.
Wife, Leaving Home to Earn Wages, 90; of Drunkard, 378-382; Providing Good Food, 381; Making Home Happy, 464-465; Beating, None in Kansas, 208; Incident at Sea, 383.
Wilkesbarre, Brooks Law in, 78.
Will-Power Destroyed by Drinking, *National Labor Tribune*, 86; Charles Lamb, 87.
Wilson bill on " Original Packages," 493.
Wine Sauce, 385.
Wines, Fred H., on Pauperism and Crime, 21, 23.
Wishart, A., " Speak-Easies" in Pittsburgh, 79.
Wolf, Hon. W. P., on Prohibition in Iowa, 234.
Women, in London Slums, Mr. George R. Sims, 91; who Drink, Cleveland *Leader*, 383.
Women's Starvation Wages, 335.
Wool as Affected by Tariff or Prohibition, 12; Increased Market for, 371.
Workhouse, Cleveland, Intemperance of Inmates, 22.
Workingmen, Injured by Drink, Powderly, 338; Trevellick, 320; the Best Customers, 340. See " Laboring Men."
Wright, President B. F., on Iowa under Prohibition, 232.

Yellowstone Kit in Atlanta, 290.
Young Men and Legalized Saloons in Cities, 128; not Tempted by Outlawed Saloons, 143; not Tempted by Council Bluffs Rookeries, 151 · Reformed by Kansas Prohibition, 152; Visiting Dayton saloons, 427.